Lecture Notes in Computer Science   1358

Edited by G. Goos, J. Hartmanis and J. van Leeuwen

Springer
Berlin
Heidelberg
New York
Barcelona
Budapest
Hong Kong
London
Milan
Paris
Santa Clara
Singapore
Tokyo

Bernhard Thalheim   Leonid Libkin (Eds.)

Semantics
in Databases

 Springer

Series Editors

Gerhard Goos, Karlsruhe University, Germany
Juris Hartmanis, Cornell University, NY, USA
Jan van Leeuwen, Utrecht University, The Netherlands

Volume Editors

Leonid Libkin
Bell Laboratories
600 Mountain Avenue, Murray Hill, NJ 07974, USA
E-mail: libkin@research.bell-labs.com

Bernhard Thalheim
Brandenburg Technical University at Cottbus
Computer Science Department
PO Box 101344, D-03013 Cottbus, Germany
E-mail: thalheim@informatik.tu-cottbus.de

Cataloging-in-Publication data applied for

Die Deutsche Bibliothek - CIP-Einheitsaufnahme

Semantics in databases / Bernhard Thalheim ; Leonid Libkin (ed.). - Berlin ;
Heidelberg ; New York ; Barcelona ; Budapest ; Hong Kong ; London ; Milan ;
Paris ; Santa Clara ; Singapore ; Tokyo : Springer, 1998
 (Lecture notes in computer science ; 1358)
 ISBN 3-540-64199-8

CR Subject Classification (1991): H.2, F3.1, H.3.3

ISSN 0302-9743
ISBN 3-540-64199-8 Springer-Verlag Berlin Heidelberg New York

© Springer-Verlag Berlin Heidelberg 1998
Printed in Germany

Typesetting: Camera-ready by author
SPIN 10661361   06/3142 – 5 4 3 2 1 0   Printed on acid-free paper

FOREWORD

In the early days of database research, issues related to database semantics played a prominent role, and papers discussing database models, conceptual design, integrity constraints and normalization often dominated major database conferences. This began to change more than a decade ago, and nowadays those issues do not appear to be part of the mainstream research. Why is this so? Has the field been exhausted? Or perhaps the focus of research on semantics in databases has shifted to new areas as the field of databases itself matured and began branching out in new directions?

As an attempt to see where the work on databases semantics is now and where it is heading, Bernhard Thalheim organized a workshop on *Semantics in Databases*. It was held in Rez near Prague, in January 1995, following the 5th International Conference on Database Theory. The three-day workshop was informal and did not have published proceedings. It featured more than a dozen one-hour talks, and plenty of time was left for informal discussions. At the conclusion of the workshop, the participants decided to prepare a volume containing full versions of papers presented at the workshop. At that time, Leonid Libkin joined Bernhard Thalheim as a co-editor.

We immediately agreed on the following. First, it was clear that two important areas in database research – spatial databases and database transformations – have not been represented at the workshop. We extended our invitation, to write papers about semantic issues in spatial databases and database transformations, to two groups that were unable to attend the workshop. Second, we decided that all the papers must be reviewed according to a very high standard. Thus, every paper was assigned to two reviewers who were asked to consider it to be closer to journal-style reviewing. At the end, several submissions were rejected. We also asked the authors to write papers that present at least a partial survey of a respective area. We hope that all the papers in this volume are self-contained and require only some basic knowledge of database fundamentals.

Most submissions arrived during the second half of 1995. All papers were reviewed by the end of 1996, and at that time all acceptance and rejection decisions were made. By this time, we collected all the revised versions. Each of them went through the second round of refereeing.

This volume contains nine papers dealing with various aspects of semantics in databases. We hope that these papers will demonstrate that there are new and interesting developments in the field – both in a more traditional branch, dealing with integrity constraints and conceptual modeling, and in new areas of database theory, such as constraint and spatial databases. Several papers show how formal semantics helps understand some of the classical issues – object-orientation, incomplete information, and database transformations.

The first group consists of four papers dealing with traditional aspects of database semantics. The paper *Achievements of Relational Database Schema Design Theory Revisited* by Joachim Biskup surveys some of the best known achievements of design theory from the point of view of four main heuristics that typically guide the design process. When certain aspects of an application are enumerated, they are represented by the formats which are statically declared in the schema. The Separation of Aspects heuristic postulates that each declared format enumerates exactly one aspect, and the Separation of Specializations heuristic postulates that each declared format conforms to exactly one specialization of an aspect. The schema must be complete in the sense that every meaningful aspect that is not enumerated by a declared format must be inferable (typically in a given query language); this is called Inferential Completeness. Finally, the Unique Flavor heuristic is used to express the requirement that all meaningful aspects be understood by expressing their basic attributes. The paper argues that normal forms assure the first requirement, Separation of Aspects, while Inferential Completeness is formalized as view support (which in turn can be formalized in a variety of ways). The Unique Flavor heuristic is formalized by considering the hypergraph structure of a database schema, and corresponds to the familiar notions of acyclicity. The paper surveys some of the major results related to those concepts.

Another paper dealing with design theory is *Redundancy Elimination and a New Normal Form for Relational Database Design* by Millist W. Vincent. This paper contributes to understanding and justifying the use of normal forms from a semantic perspective. It gives a formal definition of redundancy and redundancy-free normal form, and connects this definition with the known normal forms in the case when constraints contain functional and join dependencies. It is first shown that the redundancy-free normal form implies the fourth normal form. Then the paper introduces a new normal form, called key-complete, and shows that it is equivalent to redundancy-free normal form when constraints include functional and join dependencies. This new normal form turns out to be weaker than the projection-join normal form, which is a normal form proposed for join dependencies almost 20 years ago.

The third paper in this group is *An Informal and Efficient Approach for Obtaining Semantic Constraints Using Sample Data and Natural Language Processing* by Meike Albrecht, Edith Buchholz, Antje Düsterhöft, and Bernhard Thalheim. The efficiency of a database depends crucially on the correctness of the design, and hence on the knowledge of database semantics. Thus, acquisition of semantics constraints is critical for the database performance; at the same time, it is a very difficult task because many database designers may have difficulty with the formal definitions of database constraints. The paper describes the system called RADD (Rapid Application and Database Development) that is designed to overcome these problems. The system conducts a natural language dialog with the designer, in an attempt to produce a conceptual design and acquire semantic constraints. The acquisition stage is followed by validation, and finally by the selection of candidates for constraints.

The last paper in the group is *The Additivity Problem for Data Dependencies in*

Incomplete Relational Databases by Mark Levene and George Loizou. If a relational database does not contain null values, then satisfying a set of constraints Φ is the same as satisfying every single constraint $\varphi \in \Phi$ – this is called the additivity property. When null values are present, the definition of satisfaction is usually replaced by satisfaction in a possible world for an incomplete database. The paper shows that when constraints include functional and/or inclusion dependencies, the additivity property fails if null values are present. The paper characterizes additivity for databases with incomplete information in three scenarios: when constraints include only functional dependencies, when constraints include only unary inclusion dependencies, and when both functional and unary inclusion dependencies are allowed. Furthermore, properties of constraints that ensure additivity in these cases are tractable.

The second group consists of three papers whose major theme is understanding the semantics in well established database areas: object-oriented databases, partial information, and database transformations.

The paper *The Evolving Algebra Semantics of Class and Role Hierarchies* by Georg Gottlob, Gerti Kappel, and Michael Schrefl explains that several features of the object-oriented model, such as methods and inheritance, cannot be handled in first-order logic. It suggests using evolving algebras to provide semantics of object-oriented data models. Evolving algebras were introduced by Y. Gurevich as a framework for defining operational semantics of programming languages. The paper introduces an object-oriented data definition and manipulation language called EasyOBL. It provides support for many object-oriented features, including encapsulation and message passing, dynamic object creation, inheritance and dynamic binding; it can also be statically typechecked. The paper presents an evolving algebra semantics of the main EasyOBL features.

The paper *A Semantics-Based Approach to Design of Query Languages for Partial Information* by Leonid Libkin argues that while most of work on partial information in databases asks which operations of standard languages can be performed correctly in the presence of nulls, it is perhaps worthwhile to understand the semantics of partiality and use it as a guide to design languages specifically tailored to deal with partial information. The paper identifies several sources of partiality, such as missing or disjunctive information and conflicts. It develops a common semantic framework for them, that is based on ideas used in the semantics of programming languages, and represents partiality via orderings on the domains of types. The paper describes the basic principles of an approach that turns operations naturally associated with the datatypes into programming syntax. This approach is applied to partial information: the analysis of semantic domains of types reveals what the main programming primitives should be. The paper shows how resulting languages subsume some of those known in the literature. It also discusses constraints within the ordered semantics framework and extensions to recursive types.

The paper *Semantics of Database Transformations* by Peter Buneman, Susan Davidson, and Anthony Kosky starts by surveying a number of approaches to transforming instances of one or more source schema into instance of some target schema. By assessing their strengths and weaknesses, the paper develops formal requirements for specifying database transformation. In particular, it concentrates on ensuring correctness of transformations. In order to be able to reason about both transformation and constraints, one needs a unifying framework for them. The paper presents such a framework. It describes the language called WOL that specifies both transformations and constraints. Its data model supports object identities, classes, and complex objects. A formal semantics of database schema, instances and keys is presented. The language itself is based on Horn clause expressions, and has a small number of primitives; at the same time, it is powerful enough to express most constraints typically found in established data models. The language is also capable of expressing constraints that span multiple databases, and can be used to specify transformations and ensure their correctness. The approach of WOL differs from a large body of research on transforming schemas, as it deals with transforming both schemas and the underlying data.

The other two papers deal with constraint databases and spatial databases. The constraint model, introduced by Kanellakis, Kuper, and Revesz in 1990, is designed to deal with finite representations of potentially infinite sets. A typical example is in spatial databases, where a region can be represented by constraints defining it; for example, $x^2 + y^2 \leq 1$ is a finite representation of the infinite set of points on the real plane that satisfy this constraint.

The paper *Constraint Databases: A Survey* by Peter Revesz gives a comprehensive survey of the area. It shows how to extend standard relational languages – relational calculus, datalog, and stratified datalog – to the constraint setting, where databases are finite sets of constraints. The paper explains how queries are evaluated, and gives a survey of complexity results for a variety of constraints, including dense order constraints, linear and polynomial (in)equality constraints, and integer gap-order constraints. It also briefly discusses optimizations, surveys results on expressive power of constraint query languages, and gives pointers to several prototype systems.

The paper *Semantics in Spatial Databases* by Bart Kuijpers, Jan Paredaens, and Luc Vandeurzen discusses two models for spatial applications – the linear model and the topological model – and languages to query databases in both models. The linear model is essentially the constraint model with linear inequality constraints, such as $2x + 5y \leq 3$. This model is well suited for geographical and CAD/CAM applications. While often polynomial constraints give a better representation, spatial operations on curved data are hard to implement efficiently, and approximation with linear functions is often sufficient and easy to understand. As the language for this model, the authors propose the linear spatial calculus, which is essentially relational calculus with linear constraints. The second model is topological; a typical application is finding a route on a railway or highway map. The exact geographical information is not important, but the information about connections (e.g., there is a link from city A to city B) is. The paper defines a model for representing this kind of information and a first-order language for querying spatial databases in the topological data model.

We would like to thank all the attendees at the workshop for very productive discussions that led to this volume. We thank the referees, Catriel Beeri, Joachim Biskup, Francois Bry, Wolfram Clauss, Michael Doherty, Antje Düsterhöft, Stacy Finkelstein, Georg Gottlob, Tim Griffin, Rick Hull, Achim Jung, Gyula Katona, Anthony Kosky, Mark Levene, Rainer Manthey, Rona Machlin, Heikki Mannila, Doron Peled, Peter Revesz, Klaus-Dieter Schewe, Dan Suciu, Ramesh Viswanathan, and Limsoon Wong for their efforts.

November 1997

Leonid Libkin
Bell Labs
Bernhard Thalheim
Cottbus University

Contents

An Informal and Efficient Approach for Obtaining Semantic Constraints Using Sample Data and Natural Language Processing[*]

Meike Albrecht, Edith Buchholz, Antje Düsterhöft,
Bernhard Thalheim

University of Rostock, Department of Computer Science
e-mail: {meike/buch/duest}@informatik.uni-rostock.de

Cottbus Technical University, Department of Computer Science
e-mail: thalheim@informatik.tu-cottbus.de

Abstract

The main objective of database modelling is the design of a database that is correct and can be processed efficiently by a database management system. The efficiency and correctness of a database depends among other things on knowledge about database semantics because semantic constraints are the prerequisite for normalization and restructuring operations. Acquisition of semantic constraints remains one of the bottlenecks in database design because for most database designers formal definition of semantic constraints is a very difficult task.

Within the framework of the project RADD (*Rapid Application and Database Development*) experience was gathered with the informal modelling of database structures.

In this paper we show an approach for the acquisition of semantic constraints which is informal, easy to understand and efficient. This method uses natural language input, sample data and a discussion of sample relations to find out semantic constraints of a database.

1 Introduction

The performance of a database (especially efficiency and consistency) heavily depends on design decisions. In order to achieve an effective behaviour of the database, database designers are requested to find the best structure and the simplest basic database operations.

The efficiency and correctness of a database depends among other things on

---

[*]This work is supported by DFG Th465/2.

knowledge about database semantics because semantic constraints are the prerequisite for normalization and restructuring operations.

1.1 Problems in the Acquisition of Semantic Constraints

Formal determining of semantic constraints is one of the most difficult tasks in database design. We concentrate in our tool on the most commonly used constraints (functional dependencies, keys, inclusion dependencies, exclusion dependencies, cardinality constraints).

The the acquisition problems of these constraints are caused by the following reasons:

- For the correct utilization of the semantic information a deep understanding of logic's is required. This task not only demands high abstraction abilities but it is also very complex in general, especially for relations with many attributes and for large databases.

- Nearly all design methods need complete semantic information to get the right results (for instance in the normalization of relational databases). Incomplete information causes wrong or inefficient databases.
  But even if a designer is able to determine formal semantic constraints he/she may forget some constraints because they are either too obvious or too difficult.

- Designers often misunderstand semantic constraints and consequently they interpret them wrong. In another case it could happen if different designers work together that they interpret the same semantic constraints in different ways. For that reason the meaning of the semantic constraints must be determined.

Consider these problems a support for the acquisition of semantic constraints is desirable which suggests semantic constraints to the database designer. Using this idea we have to deal with the following questions:

- Some constraints are complicate to decide for a database designer. Especially, if they are defined over many attributes.

- Not all semantic constraints can be visualized in a graphical notation.

- The number of semantic constraints which has to be checked is exponential in the number of attributes.

In this paper we want to show an approach which overcomes these problems.

1.2 Characteristic of our Approach

We focus on an *informal* and *efficient* approach which enables the designer to determine semantic constraints correctly. The search for semantic constraints has to be minimized considering the number of possible constraints that has to be checked. Achieving this aim *heuristic rules* can be taken. In general we try to *combine the structural design and the determination of semantic constraints.* The main parts of our approach are implemented as a tool within the RADD database design project. The basis of this project and of our tool is an extended entity-relationship model. (You can find an detailed representation in [BOT90].) In the tool we concentrate on the acquisition of the following semantic are defined in [MaR92] and *exclusion dependencies.* We also want to acquire *cardinality constraints.* These are defined in the following way: If R_1 is a relationship type, R_2 an entity or relationship type then card$(R_1, R_2) = (min, max)$ specifies that in each consistent state of the database an item from R_2 appears in R_1 at least *min* and at most *max* times.

1.3 Objectives and Related Research

Starting from [Che83] several work (e.g. [FPR85] or [TjB93]) exist for mapping the natural language utterances onto entity relationship models. The project ANNAPURA ([Eic84]) implements a dialogue tool for designing a binary relational model and for supporting the translation into a logical schema. Natural language sentences are the input to the system. [CGS83] shows an approach for the acquisition of semantics and behaviour of the database using natural language. [Ort93] studies the technical language (German) which is used in working situations in order to develop a standardized enterprise language for the software development. The idea of our work is the development of a complex dialogue tool for getting information about structure, semantic and behaviour of the prospective database from natural language utterances.

Informal acquisition of semantics is not often treated in the relevant literature. A method for the derivation of keys and functional dependencies from data is described by [CaS93] and [MaR92]. In this method a closed-world assumption is taken for granted, or the derived constraints are simply confirmed (pseudo natural language acquisition in [BGM85] and Armstrong relationships in [MaR92]). Simple heuristics for the search for keys [StG88] and foreign key [CBS94] are offered. The approach presented here is an expansion of them and offers heuristics for the search for further constraints. In addition, methods for the efficient acquisition of constraints are used. We take also in consideration not valid constraints. For the validation of constraints we are using queries by means of examples representing these semantic constraints.

2 General Approach

2.1 Treatment of Semantic Constraints

In database design we want to know which semantic constraints must be valid in every consistent state of the database. We are not interested in the semantic constraints which are valid in one relation or database. Therefore, in this paper we do not handle only the set of valid semantic constraints but also the set of not valid constraints. Information about not valid constraints can be often found easier than information about valid semantic constraints. They restrict search space. Consequently, it is useful to collect and exploit them too. Both information are derivable from the input information of our approach. These two sets are collected as:

- valid semantic constraints and

- not valid semantic constraints.

The collection and storing of not valid constraints as well as valid constraints enables the derivation of unknown semantic constraints. All unknown semantic constraints could be valid. Therefore, it must be checked if they are fulfilled. The number of these unknown semantic constraints can be $O(2^n)$. So it is not possible to check all unknown semantic constraints one after the other. We will show methods which determine which of the still unknown semantic constraints seem probable be fulfilled and which of them seem to be not valid. We use heuristic rules which exploit vague information about semantic constraints in the database. This information enters in the candidate sets for semantic constraints:

- candidates for valid semantic constraints and

- candidates for not valid semantic constraints.

In the tool candidates are validated in a dialogue with the designer. From the set of candidates valid or not valid semantic constraints are derived in that way. We can determine if all semantic constraints are known. So we can ensure that no semantic constraints are forgotten.

2.2 Overview on the Approach

Databases can be designed using a a natural language description of an application. Information about the structure of a database and candidates for semantic constraints can be captured from natural language sentences (section 3). But utterances in natural language in general are vague and ambiguous. For that reason also the derived database structure and the semantic constraints are vague. In section 4 we declare how the structural information can be validated.

As a next step we collect further information about the database to validate the semantics. The designer is asked to enter sample data. From these data some not valid semantic constraints are derivable (section 5).

An explicit determining of semantic constraints is also supported in the tool (section 6).

From descriptions in natural language, sample data and explicit entered semantic constraints not all semantic constraints are derivable. Therefore, it is necessary to search for further candidates for semantic constraints. In section 7 different heuristics are shown for this task.

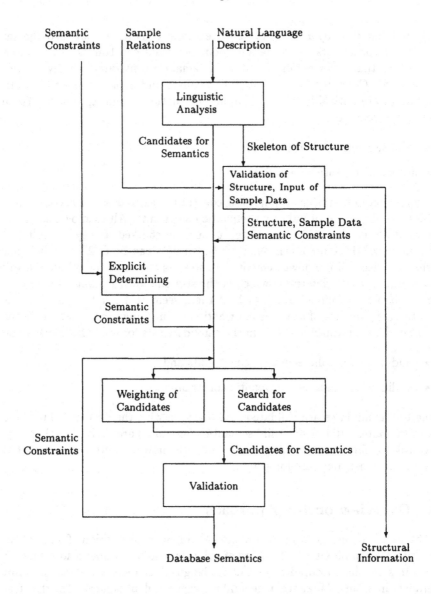

Semantic Constraints | Sample Relations | Natural Language Description

Linguistic Analysis

Candidates for Semantics | Skeleton of Structure

Validation of Structure, Input of Sample Data

Structure, Sample Data Semantic Constraints

Explicit Determining

Semantic Constraints

Weighting of Candidates | Search for Candidates

Semantic Constraints | Candidates for Semantics

Validation

Database Semantics | Structural Information

All candidates for semantic constraints which are derived from the natural language input and the heuristic rules are vague. For that reason they must be validated. An informal approach based on an example discussion is used for this task (section 8). Further, we show in this section how the inquire of candidates can be made efficiently.

Section 9 gives a conclusion.

The advantage of our approach is that especially unskilled database designers are able to use natural language. Otherwise, the validation of structure is supported by an comfortable graphical editor. Also the informal validation of constraints with examples is easy to understand.

3 The Linguistic Approach

3.1 Aims of the Linguistic Approach

The aim of the natural language component is to offer the designer the possibility to present his informal knowledge in natural language. Basic prerequisite for the adequate modelling of an application concerning the database design is the presentation of it. We believe that an application expressed in natural language will offer more information on its structure, its semantics as well as its behaviour than any other mode of expression.

The natural language approach does not fit all users. But the RADD-system allows the user to decide which design tool he/she likes best. The natural language interface is especially designed for the following user groups:

- users which have no experience with database design and are not familiar with formal constructions
- users which have to confirm the correctness of modelling the application
- users which will work with specific parts of the database; they have view-oriented requests

In database design a rough structure of the application is obtained first. In doing so, a special language is used in which words have no longer a wide scope of meaning. In a special context ambiguities are mostly soluble. In this respect the German language because of its variable sentences structure offers even more means of expression than the English language.

Recently computational linguistics has produced a series of outstanding contributions to automatic processing of natural language (e.g. in the field of semantics [Pin93]). In order to use these new findings in design tools further linguistic analysis and restrictions to special domains of language are needed.

It has become evident that a 'general-purpose-system' for complex applications is not feasible. Complex applications are marked by an variety of semantic constructs as well as by a frequent use of formal parts. Database design is an example of such a complex application. On the one hand it requires a formalized description, on the other hand it requires a language which has certain standardized forms. Thus database design is well suited to use approaches of computational linguistics and to demonstrate how a natural language interface can help to make the design more effective.

3.2 General Analysis of Natural Language Input

The natural language interface will be developed as a dialogue component working interactively together with the other components of the RADD system. It consists of a dialogue tool, a syntax tool, a semantics tool and a pragmatics tool. For a more detailed description of these tools see [BuD94] and [BCDMT95].

For the acquisition of designer knowledge we decided to develop a dialogue tool as a question-answer system. This tool reacts appropriately to every input, and it asks for additional input if this is needed for the acquisition of database design information. The questions are frames which are constantly being updated as the dialogue proceeds. The designer inputs his answers in natural language sentences or parts of sentences.

The designer input into the dialogue tool is first submitted to a syntax analyser. In order to check the syntax an ID/LP parser was implemented. The parser works on the basis of a lexicon of German words and phrases and was built for a restricted area of German sentences (descriptions and definitions).

The semantic tool is used to obtain an interpretation of the semantics of the designer input. The interpretation consists of two stages: firstly the semantics of the individual words and secondly the semantics of complete utterances and sentences will be defined. For the identification of the meaning of sentences we have used the model of semantic roles: the units of an utterance or a sentences are seen to fulfil certain functional roles.

The aim of the pragmatic interpretation is the mapping of the natural input, i.e. the results of the syntactic and semantic analyses, onto the entity-relationship model. This transformation is handled like a compiler process using an attribute grammar. The results of this process are a skeleton design, a list of possible semantic constraints and information on the behaviour of the prospective database. Interface procedures are used to transform these results into the Data Dictionary structure.

The NLI has been designed for a specific domain: the library processes. It can easily be adopted for closely related domains - in our case all lending processes (e.g. 'rent-a-car'-processes or lending processes of videos). Some new entities (nouns) and relationships (verbs mainly) will have to be entered into a specific domain lexicon. Even loosely related processes, e.g. all selling and vending processes, or the processes of storing objects, can make use of the same interface after establishing at the outset that the entities which will form the stock of the database will normally not be returned. A specific domain library will have to be updated and specified prior to the design dialogue.

3.3 The Linguistic and Pragmatic Basis for extracting Semantic Information

3.3.1 The Transformation Process

The acquisition of database semantics, e.g. the acquisition of keys or cardinalities from natural language sentences is part of the process of the pragmatic interpretation of the natural language input. Special functions within the attribute grammar are used for the transformation of the natural language semantics into a database semantics. In a natural language description the designer uses semantic nuances intuitively. New findings in the field of computational linguistics are integrated in order to capture these nuances (e.g. [Pin93]).

3.3.2 Linguistic principles

For the acquisition of the database semantics we use linguistic methods which define rules for the assignment of meaning.

Principle of compositionality. [GaM89, 280] describe Frege's principle: 'The meaning of the whole sentence is a function of the meaning of the parts.' In other words, the meaning of a sentences is composed of the meanings of its parts. The meanings of the parts are then described as the meaning of the subphrases and so on. In the end we have to examine the meaning of the words. For this reason the basis of the semantics of a sentence is the semantics of words and phrases defined in the lexicon.

Let us consider this principle for our database design application. First we have to define which parts of a sentence will play an important part during the acquisition of database semantics and which words form the basis of these parts (cf. also [Pin86]).

Meaning as a reference. If we accept the principle of compositionality then we have to answer the question which relation exists between the parts or words of a sentence. In order to handle this problem we have developed a classification of words. This classification is integrated into the knowledge base (e.g. the verb 'eat' belongs to the verb class of activity verbs and correlates with the noun class 'food'). The classifications and relations are only partially domain independent. Special knowledge or information about the domain is necessary for all applications. In this way the description of meaning can also be seen as a 'feature instantiation'.

3.3.3 Pragmatic approach

Certain parts of the technical language are characterized by pragmatic properties which can be found in all applications. These pragmatic properties are discovered and confirmed by statistic observations. So the word 'several' implies a set greater than two. A designer using the word 'several' rarely wants it to refer to a set of two elements.

The acquisition of the semantic information needed for the design of a database is based on a set of heuristic assumptions which are linguistically motivated. These assumptions some of which are illustrated in the following section are integrated into the knowledge base.

3.4 Selected Examples of the Acquisition of Semantics

Key candidates. Assumptions for the acquisition of key candidates are:

1. the first named attribute of an entity is defined as a key candidate
2. attributes which have the character of numbers are defined as key candidates
3. identifying nouns which are marked in the lexicon

The key candidates thus extracted are described as keycand(entity- or relationship-name, key attribute). For readability reasons we show the examples in German (the implementation language) and in English. The results of the analysis are given in English only.

The first assumption is based on the observation that a designer names the most important attribute first. We assume that the user identifies the entity with this attribute and for that reason it can be a key candidate.

> Example: 'Ein Gewässer hat einen Namen und einen Standort.'
> (Waters have a name and a site.)
> Key: keycand(water,name)

Assumption 2 goes along with the fact that the named attribute reflects a number. We define the 'character of numbers' according to specific German nouns like 'Hausnummer' (house number), 'Kartennummer' (card number), 'Datum' (date), 'Zeit' (time). The same applies to nouns which have these nouns as substrings. All these *domain independent* nouns are integrated into the knowledge base and marked as prospective key candiadates.

> Example: 'Eine Messung ist gekennzeichnet durch ein Datum, eine Uhrzeit und eine Konzentration.'
> (A measurement is characterized by a date, a time and a concentration.)
> Key: keycand(measurement,date)
> keycand(measurement,time)

The third assumption is based on the character of certain *domain independent* nouns which idicate identifiers. This group comprises words such as 'Kennzeichnung' (label), 'Bezeichnung' (term), 'Benennung' (naming) or 'Identifikator' (identifier). The nouns are also defined within the knowledge base.

> Example: 'Eine Ionenkonzentration hat eine Bezeichnung und einen Typ.'
> (A concentration of ions has a term and a type.)
> Key: keycand(concentration of ions, term)

According to the assumptions 2 and 3 the user can also define nouns which have the character of numbers or nouns which are identifiers *only whithin a certain domain*; e.g. whithin the field of library the words 'ISBN' (isbn) or 'Signatur'(signature). These nouns can be additionaly and explicitly integrated into the knowledge base. They will be handled like the other nouns which refer to key candidates.

For the identification of words reflect key assumptions synonym and frequency dictionaries are used.

Cardinalities. Linguistic studies of special determiners (e.e. 'ein' (a), 'der' (the), 'jeder' (every) or 'mehrere' (several)) are used for the acquisition of cardinalities in natural language utterances. A designer uses these determiners consciously or subconsciously defines certain cardinalities of an application and has his personal interpretation of the determiners. We try to extract *the most plausible interpretations*.

At first we define a list of possible interpretation for every determiner. Each interpretation has a specific number which goes from '1' (the most plausible interpretation) to 'n' (another possible interpretation). The designer input is checked whether a determiner is occured. The interpretations of this determiner are mapped onto the input structure. The resulting cardinalities are defined as cardcand(number,relationship-name,entity-name,mincard,maxard).

The assumptions of semantic constraints are validated (shown in *section7*). The number of a cardinality candidate is used to find the most plausible candidate first and then the other candidates (from number '1' to 'n') in order to find the right semantic constraints quickly.

The German word 'ein' (a) has the following meanings:

1. mindestens ein (at least one) - 1:n - or

2. genau ein (exactly one) - 1:1-.

Any other variants of the interpretation of 'ein'(a) are not relevant.

If a designer uses the word 'ein'(a) explicitly we assume that is more likely that he/she wants to describe a 1:1 cardinality.

Example: 'Ein Gewässer weist eine Ionenkonzentration auf.'
(A water has a concentration of ions.)
Cardinality constraint: cardcand(1,has,water,1,1)
cardcand(2,has,water,1,n)
cardcand(1,has,water,1,1)
cardcand(2,has,water,1,n)

The zero article (non-occupance of an article) mainly appears in connection with plural words. These words suggest the repeated occurance of objects or executers. We assume that the developer when using zero articles does not want to describe exact and concrete objects or executers but prefers a 1:n cardinality.

Example: 'Gewässer werden durch Faunen besiedelt.'
(Waters are populated by faunae.)
Cardinality constraint: cardcand(1,populate,waters,1,n)
cardcand(2,populate,waters,1,1)
cardcand(1,populate,faunae,1,n)
cardcand(2,populate,faunae,1,1)

The German word 'mehrere' (several) reflects a 1:n relation. An interpretation of 'exactly one' is improbable.

Example: 'Für ein Gewässer werden mehrere Eintrittspunkte definiert.'
(Several points of entry are defined for waters.)
Cardinality constraint: cardcand(1,define,water,1,1)
cardcand(2,define,waters,1,n)
cardcand(1,define,points of entry,1,n)

Determiners have to be analysed for potential cardinalities. Then they are labelled before integration into the knowledge base. In many languages including German determiners are a manageable number of words. Labels on the cardinality potential describe internal characteristics of determiners and are for that reason domain independent.

Inclusion and Exclusion Dependencies. Inclusion or exclusion dependencies are assumed in natural language sentences when entities are enumerated for which a hyperonym (a superordinate concept) exists. Enumeration exists when nouns are connected by connectors such as 'und' (and), 'oder' (or), 'sowohl als auch' (as well as) or by a comma.

Detected inclusion and exclusion dependencies are presented in the form inclcand(entity/ relationship, entity included/ relationship) and exclcand(list of entities/ relationship).

> Example: 'Seen, Flüsse und Teiche sind Gewässer.'
> (Lakes, rivers and ponds are waters.)
> exclusion dependency: exclcand([lake,river,pond])
> inclusion dependency: inclcand(water,lake)
> inclcand(water,river)
> inclcand(water,pond)

Inclusion and exclusion dependencies have direct pendants in the natural language quantifiers: 'alle' (all), the negation 'nicht alle' (not all) and 'kein' (no/not a/not any).

> Example: 'Ein Fluß ist kein See.'
> (A river is not a lake.)
> exclusion dependency: exclcand([river,lake])

Negated excklusion dependecies are assumed if the designer describes exceptions. So, we consider that e.g. the quantifier 'nicht alle' (not all) is equivalent to the quantifier 'fast alle' (nearly all) and means that the number of exceptions is small in comparison with the number of the elements of the whole set. neg-exclcand([Entity-Name1,...,Entity-NameN]) describes a list of entities EName1 to ENameN which have not an empty average.

> Example: 'Nicht alle Studenten sind Bibliotheksbenutzer'
> (Not all students are borrowers.)
> Negated exclusion dependency: neg-exclcand([student, borrower])

The following table ilustrates the quantifiers and their interpretation in the design process.

	Q	¬ Q	Q ¬	Q ~
quantifier	'alle' (all)	'nicht alle' (not all)	'kein' (no/not a/not any)	e.g.'einige' (some)
dependency	inclusion	negated inclusion	exclusion	negated exclusion

Synonyms. For a further definition of inclusion and exclusion dependencies by examples the tool searches the lexicon for synonyms of all identifiers appearing in the natural language input (entity-names, relationship-names, attribute-names). If these synonyms appear in the skeleton design as well, they are made available in the form of a fact synonym(identifier,list-of-synonyms).

3.5   Example of a dialogue

The following example of a dialogue shows the basic course of the dialogue. In this dialogue the developer makes so-called content utterances, e.g. 'Several points of entry are defined for a body of water.' when given so- called content prompts or questions. Such prompts are hidden in questions such as 'Are there any more details?'. The system can put additional questions for the clarification of linguistic or pragmatic ambiguities or defects. A linguistic clarification is aimed at by the following question: How is the act of 'defining' done? A pragmatic clarification question by the system could be: 'How is point of entry characterized?'. This questions aim at a completion of the design.

When looking at the general acquisition of knowledge through natural language input, this seems to be best achieved by putting such pragmatic questions to the developer that will yield an exact definition of the cardinalities. This will, however, make the dialogue very long and tedious. Furthermore, developers are mostly not able to answers these questions correctly. Therefore we will limit the elucidation process to the acquisition of cardinality candidates only. They are verified by means of examples at a later point (see chapter 4).

```
>: ...
- Ein Gewässer weist Ionen auf.
(A water has a concentration of iones.)
>: Wodurch ist - Gewässer - gekennzeichnet?
(How is -water- characterized?)
- Ein Gewässer hat einen Namen und einen Standort.
(A water has a name and a site.)
>: Wodurch ist - Ion - gekennzeichnet?
(How is -concentration of ions- characterized?)
- Durch den Typ, die Art und eine Bezeichnung.
(The type, the kind and the term.)
>: Gibt es weitere Details?
(Are there any more details?)
- Seen, Flüsse und Teiche sind Gewässer.
(Lakes, rivers and ponds are waters.)
```

>: Muß man -See- außer mit
-Name- -Standort-
noch weiter kennzeichnen? Wenn ja, wie?
(Does -lake- have to characterized any more? If yes, how?)
- Ein See hat eine Größe und eine Tiefe.
(A lake has a size and a depth.)
>: Muß man -Fluß- außer mit
-Name- -Standort-
noch weiter kennzeichnen? Wenn ja, wie?
(Does -river- have to characterized any more? If yes, how?)
- Ein Fluß hat eine Länge.
(A river has a length.)
>: Gibt es weitere Details?
(Are there any more details?)
- Für ein Gewässer werden mehrere Eintrittspunkte definiert.
(Several points of entry are defined for waters.)
>: Auf welche Art und Weise wird die Aktion - definieren - durchgeführt?
(In what way is the action -define- carried out?)
- Mit einer Datenblattnummer.
(With a number of a data paper.)
>: Wodurch ist - Eintrittspunkt - gekennzeichnet?
(How is point of entry characterized?)
- Ort, Tiefe, Fließvektor.
(Place, depth, vector of flowing.)
>: Gibt es weitere Details?
(Are there any more details?)
- An jedem Eintrittspunkt werden Ionen gemessen.
(Ions are measured on every point of entry.)
>: Auf welche Art und Weise wird die Aktion - messen - durchgeführt?
(In what way is the action -measure- carried out?)
- Es wird eine Konzentration an einem bestimmten Tag und in einer
bestimmten Tiefe gemessen.
(A concentration is measured on a particular day and a particular depth.)
>: Gibt es weitere Details?
(Are there any more details?)
- Gewässer werden durch Faunen besiedelt.
(Waters are populated by faunae.)
...

The following suggestion of a skeleton design is derived from the example of a
dialogue:

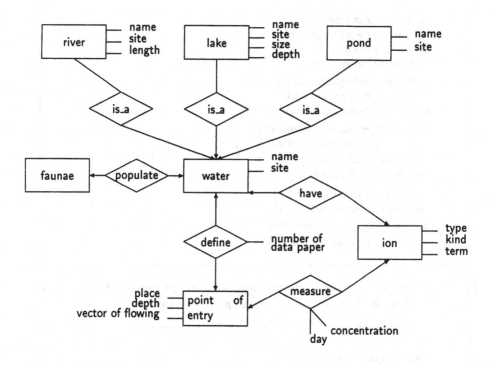

The following key candidates are derived from the example:

```
keycand(water,name).
keycand(ion,term).
keycand(lake,name).
keycand(river,name).
keycand(pond,name).
keycand(lake,size).
keycand(lake,depth).
keycand(river,length).
keycand(define,number of data paper).
keycand(point of entry,depth).
keycand(measure,day).
keycand(measure,depth).
```

The following candidates of cardinalities are acquired from the example:

```
cardcand(1,has,gewässer,1,1).
cardcand(2,has,gewässer,1,n).
cardcand(1,has,ion,1,n).
cardcand(2,has,ion,1,1).

cardcand(1,define,water,1,1).
cardcand(2,define,water,1,n).
cardcand(1,define,point of entry,1,n).

cardcand(1,measure,point of entry,1,1).
cardcand(2,measure,point of entry,1,n).
cardcand(1,measure,ion,1,n).
cardcand(2,measure,ion,1,1).

cardcand(1,populate,water,1,n).
cardcand(2,populate,water,1,1).
cardcand(1,populate,faunae,1,n).
cardcand(2,populate,faunae,1,1).
```

The following inclusion and exclusion dependencies are extracted from the example as well as the following synonyms using the lexicon:

```
exklcand([lake,river,pond]).
inklcand(water,lake).
inklcand(water,river).
inklcand(water,pond).
synonym(name,[term]).
synonym(size,[place]).
```

All derived information are vague therefore, they must be checked in a dialogue with the designer.

4 Validation of Structure

From the natural language description a skeleton of the database was derived. This skeleton can only be a first proposal for the database structure.

Derived database structure must be confirmed or corrected and extended by the designer, therefore a graphical representation in entity-relationship diagrams which was already shown in the last section for the example is useful. For this task a graphical editor was developed [TAA94, Alt94]. The editor is not only a tool that supports development of entity-relationship models but it also declares design decisions and suggests further design steps. In that way it comfortably supports changes and extensions in entity-relationship diagrams.

The derived database structure also must be completed by attribute types and lengths. These are technical details therefore asking for them already in the natural language design dialogue is not useful.

Incomplete or wrong designed parts of the database can be found if the database designer enters real world data. That is why we support input of sample data in the tool.

5 Sample Relation Exploitation

Sample data entered by the designer are very useful to search for semantic constraints because background knowledge of the designer is implicitly contained in the data.

We can derive from the sample data which semantic constraints are not valid. If we found candidates for semantic constraints that are not fulfilled in the examples than we know that these candidates cannot be valid.

From sample relations the following not valid semantic constraints are derivable:

- **not valid keys**
  If in the sample relations there are two tuples which have the same values in some attributes then these attributes cannot be keys because they do not identify all tuples of the sample relation.

- **not valid functional dependencies**
  A not valid functional dependency $X \not\rightarrow Y$ exists if there are two tuples t, t' in the sample relation and $t[X] = t'[X]$ and $t[Y] \neq t'[Y]$. If we find those tuples then we can conclude that no functional dependency between X and Y exists.

- **not valid exclusion dependencies**
  If there are two attributes or attribute sequences which contain the same values in the sample databases then an exclusion dependency between these attribute sequences is not valid.

- **not valid cardinality constraints**
  From sample data it is derivable that cardinalities $\mathsf{cand}(R_1, R_2) = (\_, 1)$ are not valid if in R_1 the same value in the foreign key from R_2 occurs twice or more times.

Sample data entered by the designer normally contain only a few tuples. Therefore, only some not valid semantic constraints are derivable.

We try to get more information about the database from the designer. Therefore, he/she is asked whether he/she can determine how many tuples will occur in every relation of the database and how many distinct values every attribute will have. From this information further not valid semantic constraints are derivable:

- **not valid keys**
  If there exist attributes or attribute sets which have less different values then the number of tuples in the relation then these attributes cannot identify all tuples and therefore they are no keys.
  Example: In a relation Students=(Stud_nr,Course,Department) shall be 5000 tuples. In such a relation there are 5000 different values in Stud_nr, 20 different values in Department because the university has only 20 different departments and 12 different values in Course. Then we know that Course and Department and Course,Department cannot be key.

- **not valid functional dependencies**
  A not valid functional dependency exists between two attributes (X and Y) if there is an attribute or attribute set (X) which has less different values than another attribute (Y).
  For the example: Course,Department $\nrightarrow$ Stud_nr and Course $\nrightarrow$ Department are derivable from the distinct values.

- **not valid inclusion dependencies**
  If there is an attribute which has more different values than another attribute then an inclusion dependency between these attributes cannot be valid. This information is only sensible if the attributes coincide in attribute types and lengths.

- **not valid cardinality constraints**
  Also from the number of tuples of the relations not valid cardinalities can be derived. If R_1 contains more tuples than R_2 then we can derive that cand(R_1,R_2)=(_,1) is not valid.

The information about the number of tuples and the number of distinct values is not necessary in the tool but it is very useful for derivation of not valid constraints and as we will show also in the heuristic rules.

6   Explicit Determining of Semantic Constraints

Our system supports informal acquisition of semantic constraints. Sometimes, designers can determine some constraints, for instance a key of a relation. In that case a long search for these semantic constraints is not sensible, therefore in the tool it is also possible to enter formal semantic constraints. It is checked whether the semantic constraints are not in contradiction to the already known semantic constraints and the sample relation.
By that, it is possible to support users with different abilities. A designer can determine all formal semantic constraints which he/she knows and in addition further constraints that he/she forgot are discussed in the tool.

7 Heuristics to Derive Candidates for Constraints

Now, some valid and not valid semantic constraints are known from the exploitation of sample data, distinct values and the explicit determining of semantic constraints. Further, we have some candidates for semantic constraints derived from the natural language input. In general, these candidates are not complete. Therefore, in the tool a search for further candidates for semantic constraints takes place.

Heuristic rules are used to find further candidates. Structural information, already known semantic information, sample relations and sample transactions (if known) are utilised in the heuristic rules. These heuristics are shown in this section.

The number of unknown keys and functional dependencies of a relation is $O(2^n)$ where n is the number of attributes of the relation. A tool cannot be able to check all semantic constraints but with the heuristics it can estimate how probable the constraints are fulfilled and can check the constraints that probable seem to be valid.

By using many different heuristic rules which try to exploit the background knowledge contained in the database we can find nearly all valid semantic constraints.

Some of the heuristic rules were used in the natural language interface, too. That is why both tools are part of a complete design system and it also shall be possible to use the tool to acquire semantic constraints without the NLI tool.

7.1 Heuristics to Find Keys

Candidates for keys can be derived from structural information of the database, sample data, already known semantic constraints and transactions. The following heuristic rules can be used to find keys:

Exploitation of Structural Characteristics

1. Often artificial keys are defined in relational databases. Most of them are numbers. If there is an attribute which is defined as an integer with a long length then this attribute can be such an artificial key.

2. Sometimes an attribute name indicate keys. If the substring -name-, -key-, -identifier-, -number-, -#- is part of the attribute name, it points to an artificial key. These two methods are also suggested in [StG 88] and in [ChV 92] for forms.

Indications in the Sample Relations

3. A running number in an example of the relation is a very strong indication of the existence of an artificial key. This method is suggested in [ChV 92] for forms, it can also be used for relations.

4. Also the distinct values (if known) can be used to derive candidates for keys. Attributes which have more distinct values than other attributes in a relation are more probably key or part of a key.

Semantic Constraints

5. Conclusions about keys are derivable from the set of already known valid and not valid functional dependencies.

   For each attribute A the following dependencies point to the possibility that A is a key attribute:

nontrivial valid functional dependency	$X \longrightarrow Y, A \subseteq X$
not valid functional dependency	$Y \nrightarrow A$

   These dependencies point to the possibility that the attribute A is no key:

nontrivial valid functional dependency	$Y \longrightarrow A,$
not valid functional dependency	$X \nrightarrow Y, A \subseteq X$

   In this way, further candidates for keys are derivable from the already known semantic constraints.

6. If there are attributes in a relation which are already determined as keys of another relation then these attributes are checked for being key of this relation, too.

   The two heuristic rules which exploit semantic constraints are especially useful because the results of these heuristics improves during the acquisition of semantic constraints.

Transactions

7. Attributes which are rarely or seldom updated are more probably keys than attributes which are often changed.

8. Attributes which are used in update or delete operations to identify tuples can be keys of the relation.

These eight heuristic rules are utilized and weighted. Therefore a simple estimation is used:

$$Plausibility(A \text{ is part of a key}) := \sum_{i=1}^{8} (w_i r_i(A))$$

r_i is the result of heuristic rule i between $0..1$ and
w_i are weights between $0..100$,
$$w_1 + w_2 + w_3 + w_4 + w_5 + w_6 + w_7 + w_8 = 100.$$

This estimation cannot be correct because the heuristic rules are not independent. But for finding candidates for keys this estimation will do, because the established heuristic values get higher if more heuristic rules indicate a key.

The *weights* can be *adapted to the database designer* and the *field of application* in a simple way: in the beginning they are determined, rules which have been successful several times are weighted higher in the next search for key candidates. Every user develops his special style in creating databases. For instance, if a designer uses artificial keys then we often can derive key information from the attribute types and names. With the adaptation of the heuristic rules onto the designer and the database we can find valid semantic constraints of the database more efficient.

With this estimation we determine the plausibility that every attribute is part of a key. The plausibility of being key for an attribute set with more than one attribute is estimated as the mean value of the probabilities of all attributes of the set:

$$Plausibility(X = \langle X_1..X_n \rangle \text{ is key}) := (\frac{1}{n} \sum_{i=1}^{n} Plausibility(X_i \text{ is part of a key})$$

Not valid keys are the negation of a valid key. Therefore, the same heuristic rules can be used for the estimation how probable a key is not valid:

$$Plausibility(X \text{ is no key}) := 100 - (\frac{1}{n} \sum_{i=1}^{n} Plausibility(X_i \text{ is part of a key})$$

In that way we can find candidates for valid and not valid keys and how probably they seem to be fulfilled.

7.2 Heuristic Rules to Find Functional Dependencies

There are some heuristic rules that can derive candidates for functional dependencies from the database structure, already known semantic constraints, sample data, and transactions.

Derivation of Candidates for Functional Dependencies from Sample Relations:

1. From sample relations we cannot derive valid functional dependencies. But we can try to find candidates for valid functional dependencies in the sample data. For all attribute sequences with more than one attribute we find out how many tuples of the sample relations coincide in the attributes of the attribute sequence.

Example:

Person_no	Surname	First_name	City	ZIP	Street	Number
39283	Schmidt	Peter	Berlin	12555	Mollstrasse	20
48934	Meier	Paul	Berlin	12555	Mozartstr	13
23299	Schulz	Paul	Rostock	18055	Gerberbruch	12
12983	Lehmann	Karl	Rostock	18055	Grubenstr	6

In this small sample relation we have twice the same values in City and ZIP. The following candidates for functional dependencies are derived:

$$\text{City} \xrightarrow{?} \text{ZIP and ZIP} \xrightarrow{?} \text{City}$$

If there are many tuples having the same value in the attribute sequence, then a functional dependency between the attributes is more probable than between attributes which always have different values.

Especially, for larger sample relations we can derive detailed information about valid semantic constraints in that way.

Exploitation of Structural Characteristics and Sample Data

2. If there is an integer attribute (X) in a relation having values which are always the sum or product of two other integer attributes (YZ), then the functional dependency ($YZ \longrightarrow X$) can be expected. Therefore, for all integer attributes of a relation all tuples have to be checked. If this characteristic is not fulfilled it can be seen in one tuple, only. Test data normally contain only a few tuples, therefore, it is possible to carry out this check.

   In the same way it can be checked if the values of an integer attribute (X) are always a constant percentage of another integer attribute (Y) then the functional dependency ($Y \longrightarrow X$) is expected.

   Relations with such functional dependencies often occur in economic and technical applications.

Semantic Constraints

3. Further, vague conclusions about functional dependencies are derivable from the set of already known valid and not valid functional dependencies.

   For each attribute A the following dependencies point to the possibility that A is left side of further functional dependencies:

nontrivial valid functional dependency	$X \longrightarrow Y, A \subseteq X$
not valid functional dependency	$Y \not\longrightarrow A$

   These dependencies point to the possibility that the attribute A is on the right side of a functional dependency:

nontrivial valid functional dependency	$Y \longrightarrow A,$
not valid functional dependency	$X \not\longrightarrow Y, A \subseteq X$

In this way, further candidates for keys are derivable from the already known semantic constraints.

Analysis of Transactions

4. From update transactions we can derive that the attributes (X) which identify the tuples are the left side of a functional dependencies, the attributes (Y) which are changed in the operation are the right side. This dependency $(X \longrightarrow Y)$ must has been fulfilled in the instance on which the transaction has been run.

These heuristic rules are also weighted against each other in a simple way. All derived candidates for functional dependencies has to be validated.

7.3 Heuristic Rules to Search for Analogue Attributes

Synonyms are attributes which have the same meaning but different names. Homonyms are attributes having the same name and different meaning. Prerequisite for detecting inclusion dependencies, exclusion dependencies and cardinality constraints is finding attributes which have the same meaning. We call these attributes *analoga*.

Some analoga are derivable from the structure of entity-relationship diagrams. To enter data in entity-relationship diagrams these diagrams must be translated into relational models. Thereby, foreign keys are assigned to the relationships. These foreign keys of relationships and the belonging keys of entities are analoga. Cardinality constraints must be determined, here.

But it is possible that users forget pathes in the design. Therefore, we also search for further attributes in the database seeming to be analoga. If we find those, we can find forgotten paths in the diagrams and also inclusion and exclusion dependencies which are not represented in the structure.

In the analoga synonyms shall be contained, but homonyms not. That is why we concentrate in the determining of analoga not only on the attribute names but also on further characteristics of the database.

All attributes of a database having the same type and similar length are checked for being analoga. The following information are exploited:

Derivation from Structural Characteristics

1. Same or similar attribute names point to analoga.

2. Similar relation names are an indication for analoga between these relations.

3. Path information in the entity-relationship diagrams determine which nodes of a database belong closely together. Therefore we can find more probably analoga between nodes which are directly connected by a path than between attributes which do not have a closed connection.

Exploitation of Sample Relations

4. If there exist attributes in the database having the same values in the sample data then these attributes can be analoga.

5. If we know that attributes in the database have the same or similar number of distinct values then these attributes can be analoga.

Transactions

6. From sample transactions vague information about analoga are derivable. If in a transaction there are update or insert operations in two relations where the same value is updated or inserted in two or more attributes it is possible that these attributes are analoga.

Semantic Constraints

7. If we have found analoga (or inclusion/ exclusion dependencies or foreign keys) between two relations then even more analoga between these relations can occur because there can exist attribute sequences which are contained in both relations.

The different heuristics are also weighted against each other. We get candidates for analogue attributes which are used to derive candidates for inclusion and exclusion dependencies and cardinality constraints. We show in the next sections how it can be done.

7.4 Derivation of Candidates for Inclusion and Exclusion Dependencies

The analoga are prerequisite to derive candidates for inclusion and exclusion dependencies. We exploit the *sample data* entered by the designer to follow candidates for inclusion and exclusion dependencies from analoga.

If there are no dependencies known between two relations R, S and we found analoga $R.X \approx S.Y$, then the following dependencies are checked:

- If the values of $R.X$ are completely contained in the values of $S.Y$ then we obtain a candidate for an inclusion dependency $(R.X \subseteq S.Y)$.
  If the values of $S.Y$ are subset of the values of $R.X$ then we obtain a candidate for inclusion dependency $(S.Y \subseteq R.X)$.

- If identical values in $R.X$ and $S.Y$ occur but the values are no subsets then it is also possible that there exists an inclusion dependency $(R.X \subseteq S.Y)$ or $(S.Y \subseteq R.X)$. These constraints have to be validated.

- Candidates for exclusion dependencies can be obtained if we found analoga $(R.X \approx S.Y)$ which do not have the same values in sample relations $(R.X \parallel S.Y)$.

In that way we can find candidates for inclusion and exclusion dependencies in the databases. These candidates for inclusion and exclusion dependencies do not only base on structural characteristics.

7.5 Cardinality Constraints

From the structure of entity-relationship models we can derive which cardinality constraints have to be determined. These are specified with path information.

The entity-relationship diagrams are derived from the natural language input. It is possible that the user did not specify some relationships. We can find these additional relationships by using the information about analoga and the key information. If we find attributes seeming to be analoga $(R.X, S.Y)$ and Y is key in S then the additional relationship between R and S is necessary and the cardinality card(R, S) must be determined.

For example: In a database we have the following entities Student(Name, First_name, Subject) and Person(Name, First_name, Address) without a connection in the diagram. The analoga Person.Name, Person.First_name and Student.Name, Student.First_name can be found because of the same attribute names. If Name and First_name are key of the entity Person then a relationship between Person and Student has to be added and the cardinality has to be determined.

Especially, if there are parts of the designed entity-relationship diagram which have no connection to others then we try to find further cardinality constraints in that way.

The values of these candidates for cardinality constraints are derived from the natural language input or the sample data. The validation of these candidates is shown in section 8.

8 Informal and Efficient Validation

In the previous section we showed how candidates for semantic constraints are derivable. All these candidates are vague. Therefore, a validation by the database designer is necessary. We want to chose an approach which is easy to understand even for unskilled designers and therefore ensures correct results.

We use an informal approach for validation in the tool. We will show that this approach is efficient, too.

8.1 Informal Validation

For validation of candidates for semantic constraints we use an approach based on examples. Only one candidate for a semantic constraint is shown in a sample relation at a time and is inquired. We want to show this method for exclusion dependencies and cardinality constraints.

A candidate for an exclusion dependency or a not valid exclusion dependency can be inquired in the following way:

Lake:	Name	Cite	Area	Depth
	Pel			

River:	Name	Cite	Length
	Pel		

Is it possible that the same values are in — Lake.Name — and — River.Name — (yes/no/unknown)?

From the decision of the designer the following constraints can be obtained. If this sample relation can occur then we concluded that the exclusion dependency is not valid (Lake.Name ∦ River.Name). Otherwise, if the example cannot occur, then this exclusion dependency (Lake.Name ∥ River.Name) is valid.

We also want to demonstrate validation of candidates for semantic constraints for cardinality constraints:

have:	Water.Name	Ion.Destignation
		Fe^{3+}
		Fe^{3+}

Can same values in — Ion.Destingnation — occur twice or more times (yes/no/unknown) ?

If the example can occur we know that the cand(have,Ion,_,1) is not correct otherwise cardcand(have,Ion,_,1) is valid. The minimum value of the cardinality can be determined with an example discussion, too.

These two examples show that formal semantic constraints can be inquired with a sample data discussion. For the other semantic constraints (functional dependencies, keys, inclusion dependencies) acquisition can be achieved in the same way [Alb94b].

8.2 Sequence of Validation

It is not possible to check all unknown and inderivable constraints in an ordered way, because the number of independent functional dependencies of a relation is $O(2^n)$ where n is the number of attributes of a relation. The number of unary inclusion and exclusion dependencies is $O(n^2)$ where n is the number of attributes of the database as a whole. Therefore, also the number of derived candidates for semantic constraints can be very large.

From a set of semantic constraints further constraints are derivable. We use this property to make the dialogue for validation more effective.

Therefore, it is determined how many unknown semantic constraints are derivable from every candidate for a semantic constraint or how many information one semantic constraints will bring. The following formula can be used for that task:

$$Information(X) := (\frac{P(X)}{100} * N(X)) + (\frac{P(\neg X)}{100} * N(\neg X))$$

X is a still unknown semantic constraint,
N the number of unknown semantic constraints derivable from X and
P the probablity that X is valid

In the tool inquiring of semantic constraints with examples starts with those semantic constraints from which most other unknown constraints are derivable. In that way the number of dialogue steps for validation can be decreased.

8.3 Incomplete Acquisition of Semantic Constraints

For large relations or databases it is not possible to inquire all semantic constraints because the dialogue for validation of all unknown semantic constraints would be too long. But because of the many different heuristic rules we derive candidates for semantic constraints which seem to be probably valid. We can inquire these candidates in the tool. Often in that way all or the most important valid semantic constraints can be found because of the lot of heuristic rules.

9 Conclusions

We have introduced an informal approach for especially unskilled database designers. The designer can describe an application using natural language and sample data.

We derive the structure of the prospective database and semantic constraints from natural language utterances. The results of this interpretation have to be evaluated in reasons of ambiguity and fuzzieness of the natural language.

The structural design can be validated using the graphical editor.

The semantic constraints resulting from the natural language interpretation and from the sample data are discussed with sample relations. We have shown methods for minimizing the search for possible semantic constraints using heuristic rules.

Main parts of the appproach are currently implemented as a part of our database design system RADD (Rapid Application and Database Development).

The derivation of semantic constraints from sample databases, the heuristic rules for the determination of semantic constraints and the informal validation are also usable in the field of reverse engineering. These methods can be taken to find out the valid semantic constraints of databases. These semantic constraints are prerequisite for translating existing databases into other data models.

References

[Alb93]   M. Albrecht, Akquisition von Datenbankabhängigkeiten unter Verwendung von Beispielen, GI-Workshop, Grundlagen von Informationssystemen Graal-Müritz, 1993, Universität Rostock, Informatik-Berichte 3/93, S. 5-9

[Alb94a]   M. Albrecht: Ansätze zur Akquisition von Inklusions- und Exklusionsabhängigkeiten in Datenbanken, GI-Workshop, Tutzing, 1994, Informatik-Berichte, Universität Hannover, S.162-169

[Alb94b]   M. Albrecht: Semantikakquisition im Reverse-Engineering, Technische Universität Cottbus, Reihe Informatik I-4/1994

[Alb97]   M. Albrecht: Akquisition von Integrit"atsbedingungen in Datenbanken, Dissertation, Universit"at Rostock, 1997

[Alt94]   M.Altus: A User-Centered Database Design Environment. In: The Next Generation of Case Tools, Proceedings of the fifth Workshop on NGCT, Utrecht, The Netherlands. 1994.

[BCN92]   C. Batini, S. Ceri, S. B. Navathe: Conceptual Database Design, The Benjamin/ Cummings Publishing Company, Inc., 1992

[BGM85]   M. Bouzeghoub, G. Gardarin, E. Metais: An Expert System Approach, Proceedings Very Large Databases, 1985, pp. 82-94

[BOT90]   P. Bachmann, W. Oberschelp, B. Thalheim, G. Vossen: The Design of RAD: Towards to an Interactive Toolbox for Database Design, RWTH Aachen, FG Informatik, Aachener Informatikberichte 90-28

[Buc93]   B. G. Buchanan: Readings in knowledge acquisition and learning, San Mateo: Morgan Kaufmann Publishers, 1993

[BuD94]   E. Buchholz, A. Düsterhöft: Using natural language for database design. In: Proceedings Deutsche Jahrestagung für Künstliche Intelligenz 1994 - Workshop 'Reasoning about Structured Objects: Knowledge Representation meets Databases'. 18-23. September 1994, Saarbrücken

[BCDMT95]   E. Buchholz, H. Cyriaks, A. Düsterhöft, H. Mehlan, B. Thalheim: Applying a Natural Language Dialogue Tool for Designing Databases. In: Proceedings of the First International Workshop on Applications of Natural Language to Databases, 28-29th June 1995, Versailles, France

[CaS93]   M. Castellonos, F. Saltor: Extraction of Data Dependencies, Universitat Politecnica de Catalunya, Barcelona, Spain, Report LSI-93-2-R

[Che83]   P.P. Chen: English Sentence Structure and Entity Relationship Diagrams. In: Information Science 29(2), 1983, S.127-149

[CBS94]   R. H. L. Chiang, T. M. Barron, V. C. Storey: Reverse engineering of relational databases: Extraction of an EER model from a relational database, Data & Knowledge Engineering 12 (1994), 107-142

[CGS83]   M. Colombetti, G. Guida, M. Somalvico: NLDA: A Natural Language
          Reasoning System for the Analysis of Data Base Requirements. In: Ceri,
          S. (ed.): Methodology and Tools for Data Base Design. North-Holland,
          1983

[D"us97] A. Düsterhöft: Zur natürlichsprachigen interaktiven Unterstützung im
          Datenbank-Entwurf. Dissertation, Technische Universit"at Cottbus, 1997

[Eic84]   Ch. F. Eick: From Natural Language Requirements to Good Data Base
          Definitions - A Data Base Design Methodology. In: Proc. of the Interna-
          tional Conference on Data Engineering, pp.324-331, Los Angeles, USA,
          24.-27.4.1984

[FPR85]   B. Flores, C. Proix, C. Rolland: An Intelligent Tool for Information De-
          sign. Proc. of the Fourth Scandinavian Research Seminar of Information
          Modeling and Data Base Management. Ellivuori, Finnland, 1985

[GaM89]   G. Gazdar, C. Mellish: Natural language processing in PROLOG: an
          introduction to computational linguistics. Addison-Wesley Wokingham,
          England,1989

[MaR92]   H. Mannila, K.-J. Räihä: The Design of Relational Databases, Addison
          Wesley, 1992

[Ort93]   E. Ortner: KASPER - Konstanzer Sprachkritik-Programm für das
          Software-Engineering. Universität Konstanz, Informationswissenschaft,
          Bericht 36-93, September 1993

[Pin86]   M. Pinkal: Definite noun phrases and the semantics of discourse.
          COLING-86, S.368-373

[Pin93]   M. Pinkal: Semantikformalismen für die Sprachverarbeitung. Universität
          des Saarlandes, CLAUS-Report Nr.26, Januar 1993

[StG88]   V. C. Storey, R. C. Goldstein: Methodology for Creating User Views in
          Database Design, ACM Transactions on Database Systems, Sept. 1988,
          pp 305-338

[TAA94]   B. Thalheim, M. Albrecht, E. Buchholz, A. Düsterhöft, K.-D. Schewe: Die
          Intelligente Tool Box zum Datenbankentwurf RAD, GI-Tagung, Kassel,
          1994, Datenbankrundbrief, Ausgabe 13, Mai, S. 28-30

[Tha93]   B. Thalheim: Fundamentals of Entity-Relationship Modelling, Annals of
          Mathematics and Artificial Intelligence, J. C. Baltzer AG, Vol. 7 (1993),
          No 1-4, S. 197-256

[TjB93]   A M. Tjoa, L. Berger: Transformation of Requirements Specifications
          Expressed in Natural Language into an EER Model. Proceeding of the
          12th International Conference on ER-Approach, Airlington, Texas USA,
          Dec. 15-17th, 1993

Achievements of Relational Database Schema Design Theory Revisited

Joachim Biskup

Fachbereich Informatik,
Universität Dortmund,
D-44221 Dortmund,
Germany,
biskup@ls6.informatik.uni-dortmund.de

Abstract. Database schema design is seen as to decide on formats for time-varying instances, on rules for supporting inferences and on semantic constraints. Schema design aims at both faithful formalization of the application and optimization at design time. It is guided by four heuristics: Separation of Aspects, Separation of Specializations, Inferential Completeness and Unique Flavor. A theory of schema design is to investigate these heuristics and to provide insight into how syntactic properties of schemas are related to worthwhile semantic properties, how desirable syntactic properties can be decided or achieved algorithmically, and how the syntactic properties determine costs of storage, queries and updates. Some well-known achievements of design theory for relational databases are reviewed: normal forms, view support, deciding implications of semantic constraints, acyclicity, design algorithms removing forbidden substructures.

1 Introduction

Due to its great importance for database applications, database schema design has attracted a lot of researchers, and, accordingly, a lot of insight into good schemas has been obtained. On the one side, practical experience suggests to follow some basic design heuristics, which have been ramified into considerable detail. On the other side, theoretical investigations have accumulated many formal notions and theorems on database schema design. Unfortunately, however, theory apparently does not have much impact on practice yet.

The purpose of this paper is to improve on this mismatch of theory and practice by presenting well-known theoretical results on schema design within a fresh and unifying framework. In a companion paper [Bis95a] we also discuss the present shortcomings of database schema design theory and suggest some directions for its future elaboration. This paper does not aim at providing a complete survey on well-established and current contributions but at highlighting important examples. Accordingly, all references to the literature are to be understood just as hints for further reading.

2 Problem of Schema Design

The purpose of a database system can be roughly summarized as follows: a database system aims at persistently and dependably storing a large amount of *structured* data, shared by *many and various* users, and at *efficiently* managing this data with respect to update execution and query evaluation. The database itself, i.e. the structured data, is organized in a self-describing way: it consists of a time independent part, its *schema*, and a time-varying part, its *instance*, where the schema describes the structure and the formal semantics of the possible instances. At design time, the database administrator (representing the group of people involved), basically, has to perform two steps: first abstracting and modeling the application, then formalizing and formatting the model.

In the first step, the administrator *models* the application at hand by employing some well-disciplined linguistic framework for descriptions of reality, let's say the framework of the widely accepted entity-relationship approach [Che76]. In the second step, the administrator *formalizes* the model and declares a database schema, using a data definition language, which is an implemented fragment of a first order logic, esssentially.

This two-step procedure is based on the fundamental paradigm of the semantic triade: reality – space of concepts (ideas) and laws of logic – language. Fig.1 sketches the basic assumptions of this paradigm, which is not at all obvious or indisputable, but rather a tried attempt helpful for restricted tasks.

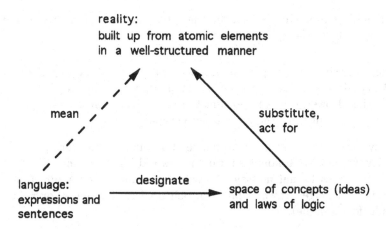

Fig.1. Fundamental paradigm of the semantic triade

Fig.2 indicates some correspondences between the framework of the entity-relationship approach, an approved heuristic tool for detecting and reconstructing the pertinent concepts, and the syntax of first order logic and its set theory based semantics, a well-studied formal language for declarative programming.

ER-approach	logic and set theory	
	syntax	semantics
entity $\begin{cases} \text{simple} \\ \text{composed} \end{cases}$	constant symbol ground term (with function symbol)	element of a universe
relationship	ground fact	tuple of a relation
property (attribute)	$\begin{cases} \text{(binary) ground fact} \\ \text{ground term} \end{cases}$	tuple of a (binary) relation value of a function
role	place of a predicate symbol	component of a relation
abstraction		
universe of discourse	set of constant symbols	universe
separation/specialization	formula Φ	comprehension[1], power set
generalization	$\vee$	union
aggregation	$\wedge$, $=$	intersection, Cartesian product
constraint	(implicational) statement	model class
key constraint	with equality-conclusion	
isa constraint		
partition constraint		
many-one constraint	with equality-conclusion	
existence constraint		
referential constraint		
view rule	set of formulas	relation
action		
message	statement	
(positive) information	conjunctively added statement	reduction of model class

Fig.2. Some correspondences between the entity-relationship approach and first order logic with set theory based semantics

Both steps of the design require taking decisions. In the first step the administrator has to decide on the relevance of certain aspects of the "miniworld" under consideration. However, it is important to realize that a database system can be seen under three different though related viewpoints:

- the system constitutes a formal image of an outside miniworld;
- or it manages an autonomous formal miniworld (of documents, for example);
- or it mediates formal messages between communicating actors (one actor inserts a message, which is later on delivered to another actor as a query result, for example).

---

[1] If M is a structure with universe d and Φ is a formula with free occurances of the variables $x_1, \ldots, x_n$, then the *comprehension* is defined by

$$d_{M,\Phi} := \left\{ \big(\beta(x_1), \ldots, \beta(x_n) \big) \mid \beta \text{ is variable assignment into universe } d, \text{ and } \Phi \text{ is true} \right.$$
$$\left. \text{in structure } M \text{ under assignment } \beta \right\} \subset \underset{i=1,\ldots,n}{\times} d.$$

In fact, the last viewpoint appears to be most comprehensive:

- human individuals act communicatively within the (outside) miniworld (of the application),
- the basic facts and events of which are reflected by formal documents
- that in turn are mediated over time and space by the database system.

Thereby the database becomes part of the already overwhelming "formalism reality" [Bis94] surrounding its users.

Once the decisions about the relevant aspects are available from the first step of the design, in the second step the administrator has to decide on the structure of their formalization. More specifically, he has to decide on the following problems, essentially:

- Which aspects of the application should be *enumerated*, i.e. represented by a time-varying enumeration of ground facts the *formats* of which are statically declared in the schema?
- Which aspects of the application should be *inferrable*, i.e. derivable from the time-varying enumerations, possibly complemented by additional input, by *rules* which are declared in the schema?
- Which aspects should *constrain* the enumerations under updates, i.e. which format-conforming enumerations of ground facts should be considered meaningful in the sense that they satisfy *semantic constraints*, which are declared in the schema.

The decisions result in a *schema* that comprises

- the *formats* for enumerations (the time-varying extensional instances produced over the life time of the database),
- the *rules* (for intensional views supporting queries),
- and the *semantic constraints*.

Being fixed over the time, the schema statically determines the future dynamic behaviour of the database and, in particular, its usefulness for its end users. Fig.3 illustrates the design and the usage of a database, and it summarizes the terminology introduced so far.

The quality of a schema can be evaluated along two lines of reasoning:

- The schema should *formalize* the application as *faithful* as achievable.
- The schema should allow to execute queries and updates, as far as these operations can be foreseen, as efficiently as possible. From this point of view, schema design can be understood as *optimization at design time*.

Whether a *faithful formalization* has been achieved or not, cannot be evaluated solely based on formal mathematical reasoning. Rather we have to investigate whether the database will successfully provide technical support for communications among those persons that employ the database as end users. Presumably, successful support is based on a common agreement on the following questions:

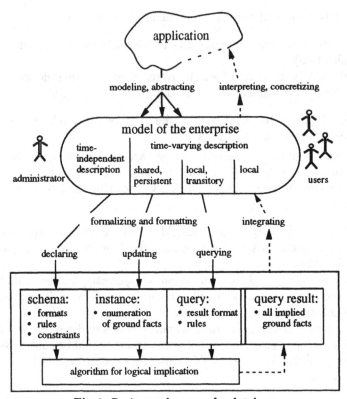

Fig.3. Design and usage of a database

- Which *entities* are to be considered basic?
- Which *relationships* are to be considered basic and
- how to select from the basic ones those for actual redundancy-free enumerations, such that all relationships can be completely inferred?
- Which actions are to be considered basic?

Optimization at design time, however, can be evaluated in formal mathematical terms by considering

- storage costs (basically determined by the size of the enumerated instances),
- query costs (basically the time complexity of anticipated queries, in particular those that are declared as rules in the schema),
- update costs (basically the time complexity of anticipated insertions and deletions, including maintenance of the semantic constraints that are declared in the schema).

3 Design Heuristics

Most guidelines for schema design can be summarized by the following four heuristics:

Separation of Aspects: A declared format should be appropriate to enumerate *exactly one aspect.*

Separation of Specializations: A declared format should be appropriate to conform to *exactly one specialization* of an aspect.

Inferential Completeness: All meaningful aspects that are not enumerated according to a declared format should be inferrable by using the query language.

Unique Flavor: Meaningful aspects should be identified and understood by expressing their basic attributes only (and omitting additional context information).

Clearly, an administrator will tentatively apply a separation heuristic by using an agreement that the entities or relationships of some class are considered basic. But afterwards he has to justify that property mathematically with respect to the formally declared schema and the inferential power of the formal query language. Similarly, an administrator will tentatively apply the Inferential Completeness heuristic by using an agreement on the selection of basic relationships for enumerations, and afterwards he has to justify the claimed completeness property mathematically with respect to the selected formalization. In the same spirit, an application of the Unique Flavor heuristic is, firstly, based on some intuitive agreements, which, afterwards, are subject to mathematical verification with respect to the selected formalization.

Having in mind the achievements of design theory presented in the rest of this paper, we will somehow artificially distinguish desirable syntactic properties of schemas from worthwhile semantic requirements: the former properties only refer to the purely syntactically given schema, whereas the latter requirements are explicitly related to the semantics of the query language. Accordingly, the separation heuristics will primarily suggest desirable syntactic properties, and the completeness and uniqueness heuristics worthwhile semantic requirements. It should be understood, however, that, on the one side, syntax and semantics are always closely related, and, on the other side, in computing we aim at eventually finding appropriate syntactic expressions for any kind of notion.

4 Tasks of Design Theory

In order to be helpful in achieving faithful formalizations and in pursuing the design heuristics, the following tasks of design *theory* are due:

- **Task 1:** Formalize the worthwhile semantic requirements and the desirable syntactic properties of schemas!

- **Task 2:** State and prove relationships between the formalized versions of worthwhile semantic requirements and desirable syntactic properties!
- **Task 3:** Find algorithms for deciding on or even achieving syntactic properties of schemas, and prove their correctness and efficiency!

In order to be helpful for optimization at design time, additionally, design *theory* should tackle a fourth task:

- **Task 4:** Prove that desirable syntactic properties actually ensure low costs!

Being supplied with appropriate solutions for these tasks, an administrator can effectively benefit from design theory. For, at design time,

- the administrator, essentially, has to deal with syntactic material only (supported by Task 3)
- which must be evaluated with respect to its semantic properties (as stated by Task 1 and Task 2) on the one side
- and the future operational cost (as stated by Task 4) on the other side.

5 Achievements for Relational Databases

5.1 Notations

For the sake of readability and conciseness we will employ (more or less) standard notations in a somehow sloppy, and sometimes also imprecise, way. In order to study carefully elaborated versions of the notations and of the results, the reader should consult the references, in particular the textbooks [Mai83, Ull88, Ull89, PDGvG89, Vos91, MR92, AD93, AHV95, Bis95b].

$(R_i, X_i, SC_i)^1$	denotes a relation scheme where
R_i	is a relation symbol,
X_i	is a set of attributes (possibly with a range for its values), i.e. a format, and
SC_i	are the local semantic constraints.

A (database) schema comprises relation schemes, rules, and global semantic constraints:

$\langle (R_1, X_1, SC_1), \ldots, (R_n, X_n, SC_n)\|$	relation schemes for extensional enumerations,
$Q_1, \ldots, Q_m\|$	rules (queries) for intensional views,
$SC_{global} \rangle^1$	global semantic constraints.

Semantic constraints are denoted as follows where X, Y, Y_i, Z are sets of attributes and R_i, R_j are relation symbols:

---

[1] Later on we will sometimes omit those components which are not relevant for the current discussion. For instance, using the notation $(\,, U, SC)$, we indicate that only the set of attributes U and the semantic constraints SC are important, but not the omitted relation symbol.

$X \to Y$	functional dependency,
$X \twoheadrightarrow Y|Z$ or $\bowtie [X \cup Y, X \cup Z]$	multivalued dependency,
$\bowtie [Y_1, \ldots, Y_k]$	join dependency,
$\Pi_X(R_i) \subset \Pi_Y(R_j)$	inclusion dependency,
SC^+	implicational closure of a set of semantic constraints SC.

5.2 Normal Forms: Separation of Aspects Formalized as Desirable Syntactic Property

The first design heuristic, Separation of Aspects, can be rephrased by considering formats and semantic constraints as some kind of structure and by requiring that any nontrivial substructure should correspond to, refer to or identify exactly one aspect of the application. Depending on the class of semantic constraints involved, we can define different notations of "nontrivial substructure"; but in all cases the notion of "exactly one aspect" is related to the concept of identification of unit pieces of information. In order to formalize the heuristic as desirable syntactic property, normally referred to as "normal form", see Task 1, we favor expressing the separation requirement in a negative form: the structure should *not* contain any *forbidden substructures* that might be harmful with respect to the quality measures. Then most algorithms to achieve high quality schemas can be conveniently described as iterated *schema transformations* that stepwise detect and remove forbidden substructures.

The most popular normal forms are listed in Fig.4, giving their names and forbidden substructures [Cod70, Cod72, Fag77, Del78, Zan76, BBG78, Fag81, Ken83, MR86, BDLM91, DF92]:

name	forbidden substructures
3 NF, third normal form	$Z \to A \in SC^+$, $A \notin Z$, A nonkey-attribute, (but) $Z \to X_i \notin SC^+$.
BCNF, Boyce/Codd normal form	$Z \to A \in SC^+$, $A \notin Z$, (but) $Z \to X_i \notin SC^+$.
4 NF, fourth normal form	$X \twoheadrightarrow Y \in SC^+$, $Y \not\subset X$, $X \cup Y \subsetneqq X_i$, (but) $X \to X_i \notin SC^+$.
5 NF, fifth normal form	$\bowtie [Y_1 \ldots Y_k] \in SC^+$, $\bowtie [Y_1 \ldots Y_{i-1}, Y_{i+1}, \ldots, Y_k] \notin SC^+$ for $i = 1, \ldots, k$, (but) there exists j : $Y_j \to X_i \notin SC^+$.
referential normal form	$\Pi_X(R_i) \subset \Pi_Y(R_j) \in SC^+$, $i \neq j$, (but) $Y \to X_j \notin SC^+$.
unique key normal form	$X \to X_i \in SC^+$, X minimal, $Y \to X_i \in SC^+$, Y minimal, (but) $X \neq Y$.

Fig.4. Normal forms and their forbidden substructures

5.3 View Support: Inferential Completeness Formalized as Worthwhile Semantic Requirements

The third design heuristic, Inferential Completeness, can be rephrased by considering those aspects of the application that are not explicitly represented by enumerations and by requiring that these aspects are completely supported as intensional views by appropriate rules. There are, essentially, three versions of support: *view instance support, view query support, view update support.*

Restricting our discussion to one-relation views or even so-called universal relation views, we suppose that a database schema of the form
$$DS = \langle \text{schemes for extensional enumerations} | \quad | \text{global semantic constraints} \rangle$$
is given, and that some candidate view (or external schema)
$$ES = (\ , U, SC)$$
with set of attributes U and semantic constraints SC should be supported.
Then we state the following formal versions of the heuristic as worthwhile semantic property, see Task 1.

- Schema DS provides *view instance support* for ES
  :iff there exists a query Q on DS such that
  $\{instances\ of\ ES\} \subset Q[\{instances\ of\ DS\}]$.

If we have even equality, the view instance support is called *faithful*. In that case, if, additionally, the supporting query Q is injective on $\{instances\ of\ DS\}$, the view instance support is called *unique*.

- Schema DS provides *view query support* for ES
  :iff for each query P on ES there exists a query P' on DS such that:
  for all instances u of ES there exists an instance $(r_i)_{i=1,...,n}$ of DS such that
  $P(u) = P'((r_i)_{i=1,...,n})$.

Under some rather weak assumptions on the query language we have a fundamental equivalence [AABM82, Hul86, BR88]:

Theorem 1. *DS provides view instance support for ES iff DS provides view query support for ES.*

If DS provides view query support for ES, then the query P' corresponding to the identity query on ES supports the instances of ES. On the other hand, if DS provides view instance support for ES by some query Q, then Q can be composed with queries on ES. Such compositions yield a query translation from queries on the view to queries on the full schema.

For the support of *updates* on views, however, we essentially need that the view instance support is *unique*. For otherwise, well-known as the *view update problem* [BS81, DB82, FC85, Kel86, GHLM93], there is no information available to resolve the ambiguity caused by non-injectivity.

5.4   Syntactic Characterization of View Support

According to Task 2, the worthwhile semantic requirements of view support should be related to desirable syntactic properties of a schema. The main results available concern universal relation views, the supporting query of which is the natural join. For instance we have the following theorems [Ris77, Ris82, BBG78].

Theorem 2. *A schema DS with formats $X_1, \ldots, X_n$ for the extensional enumerations (ignoring local and global semantic constaints of DS) supports a universal relation view (, U, SC) by the natural join iff $\bowtie [X_1, \ldots X_n] \in SC^+$.*

Theorem 3. *A schema DS with formats $X_1, \ldots, X_n$ for the extensional enumerations and functional dependencies $F_1, \ldots, F_n$ as local semantic constraints faithfully supports a universal relation view (, U, F), where F is a set of functional dependencies, by the natural join if $\bowtie [X_1, \ldots X_n] \in F^+$ and $(\bigcup_{i=1,\ldots,n} F_i)^+ \supset F$.*

The proof of Theorem 2 is straightforward just by confirming that the formal semantics of join dependencies is appropriately defined. The faithfulness of the natural join results from the inclusion $r_j \supset \pi_{X_j}(\bowtie_{i=1,\ldots,n} r_i)$, showing that functional dependencies that are valid in some component r_j are also valid in the join $\bowtie_{i=1,\ldots,n} r_i$. More refined results appear for example in [Var82, CM87].

In [Heg94] a rather general theory of schema decomposition is presented. This theory explores an algebraic framework, in which the class of instances of a database schema is partially ordered and possesses a least element and the inverses of supporting queries (which are the projections in case of a natural join) are isotonic and preserve least elements. It turns out that, within this framework, the components of a schema DS faithfully supporting a universal relation view uniquely "complement" each other. Besides treating many further topics, the theory also deals with the union as supporting query (with the selection as inverse) and thus with the so-called horizontal decomposition [DP84, PDGvG89], and it clarifies the role of null values in schema decomposition.

5.5   Deciding Desirable Syntactic Properties for Normal Forms and View Support

Both heuristics treated so far finally lead to syntactic properties that are basically expressed in terms of implications of semantic constraints. In Section 5.2 normal forms, formalizing the Separation of Aspects heuristic, are just defined in these terms, and in Section 5.4 view support, formalizing the Inferential Completeness heuristic, has been reduced to these terms. According to Task 3, then, we have to design algorithms to decide implications among semantic constraints and, additionally, to explore all relevant implications systematically .

Here are some prominent examples for results [Arm74, Men79, Bis80, BV84a,

BV84b, Var84, Mit83, KCV83, CFP84, CV85, FV84, Var88a, Tha91, BC91, Her95]:

Theorem 4. *The implication problem of "$\Phi \in SC^+$" is decidable for "many important classes" of semantic constraints.*

Theorem 5. *The implication problem "$\Phi \in SC^+$" is undecidable for the class of "functional and inclusion dependencies".*

The important semantic constraints can be expressed as implicational first order logic formulae. Then the various proof procedures, called chase procedures, are based on specialized versions of the more general proof techniques of (hyper-) resolution and paramodulation. Roughly described, hyperresolution, applied to an implicational formula with a nonequality-conclusion and its previously generated premises, yields the conclusion as additional statement, and paramodulation, applied to an implicational formula with an equality-conclusion and its previously generated premises, equates the terms in the equality-conclusion, i.e. one side is substituted by the other side. Chase procedures are designed to apply such rules, starting with the premises of the constraint to be decided, until no further change can be produced. If the procedure terminates, the constraint is implied iff its conclusion is among the finally produced statements.

In general, the implication problem for semantic constraints is fairly well understood in the relational case:

- As long as the constraints are "full", i.e., basically, in their implicational formulae no existentially quantified variable occurs positively, we have decidability.
- Otherwise, for "embedded" constraints, we have undecidability due to positively occuring existentially quantified variables. Such variables can cause the generation of an unlimited number of terms in executing proof procedures that do not terminate in this case.

Actually, even for the restricted case of embedded multivalued dependencies the implication problem has been proved to be undecidable [Her95]. The sophisticated proof employs a reduction of the word problem for finite semigroups, known to be undecidable, to the implication problem for embedded multivalued dependencies.

As already mentioned above, null values are important for the theory of schema decompositions [CM87, Heg94] and also for so-called "representative instances" of fragmented database schemas [Hon82, Sag83, GMV86]. Accordingly, the meaning of semantic constraints in the presence of relations with null values and the corresponding variant of the implication problem have been studied [Lie79, Vos79, Gra84, AM86, Tha91, LL94].

Theorem 6. *For the class of relation schemes (, U, F), where F is a set of functional dependencies, the problem "(, U, F) is in third normal form" is NP-complete.*

The deep reason for the negative result is that, in this situation, the problem "attribute A appears in a key of relation scheme $(\ ,U,F)$" is already NP-complete; this result in turn is related to the fact that a relation scheme $(\ ,U,F)$ can possibly have exponentially many keys [LO78, JF82, MR83, Kat92, VS93a, DKMST95].

Theorem 7. *For the class of relation schemes $(\ ,U,F)$, where F is a set of functional dependencies, the problem "$(\ ,U,F)$ is in Boyce/Codd normal form" is decidable in polynomial time.*

Indeed, a decision procedure can be based on the following equivalence [Osb78]: Boyce/Codd normal form iff for all $X \to Y \in F$ with $Y \not\subseteq X : X \to U \in F^+$. It should be noted, however, that also for Boyce/Codd normal form some important decision problems are of high computational complexity. In particular, deciding Boyce/Codd normal form for a *projection* of a scheme is coNP–complete [BB79]. This result on intractability as well as Theorem 6 contrast to the fact that the corresponding decision problems for relations, rather than schemes, are decidable in polynomial time (in the number of attributes and tuples of the relation under consideration) [DLM92].

Theorem 8. *For the class of relation schemes $(\ ,U,F)$, where F is a set of functional dependencies, the problem "$(\ ,U,F)$ is in unique key normal form" is decidable in polynomial time.*

Again, a decision procedure can be based on an equivalence statement [BDLM91]: unique key normal form iff $\{A \mid A \in U \text{ and } U \backslash A \to A \notin F^+ \} \to U \in F^+$.

5.6 Achieving Normal Forms and View Support Simultaneously

So far, the Separation of Aspects and the Inferential Completeness heuristics have been treated separately, although, as we have seen in Section 5.5, both heuristics lead to related implication problems. According to Task 2, we have to explore the relationship between their formalizations in more detail, in particular, whether their formal versions are compatible. As far as we can actually achieve the desirable syntactic properties simultaneously, according to Task 3, we have to design algorithms to obtain them.

The following two theorems are the most well-known examples of results on compatibility.

Theorem 9. *For every (universal relation) scheme $ES = (\ ,U,F)$, where F is a set of functional dependencies, there exists a database schema DS with relation schemes $(\ ,X_1,F_1),\ldots,(\ ,X_n,F_n)$ for extensional enumerations such that:*
i) Schema DS supports ES by the natural join.
ii) Each scheme $(\ ,X_i,F_i)$ of DS is in Boyce/Codd normal form.

Theorem 10. *For every (universal relation) scheme $ES = (\ ,U,F)$, where F is a set of functional dependencies, there exists a database schema DS with relation schemes $(\ ,X_1,F_1),\ldots,(\ ,X_n,F_n)$ for extensional enumerations such that:*

i) Schema DS faithfully supports ES by the natural join.
ii) Each scheme (, X_i, F_i) of DS is in third normal form.

The proofs of these and related theorems are constructive, yielding outlines of design methods of decomposition and synthesis, respectively [Cod72, Fag77, Fag81, Ber76, BB79, BDB79, KM80, LTK81, BK86, SR88, BM87, TLJ90, YÖ92a, YÖ92b]. Such methods will be discussed in a more general framework in Section 5.11.

5.7 Normal Forms Ensure Low Storage and Update Costs

We have introduced normal forms as desirable syntactic properties, formalizing the Separation of Aspects heuristics. According to Task 4, we now justify these normal forms in terms of cost, thus providing formal counterparts to informal motivations of the Separation of Aspects heuristic to avoid so-called "update anomalies".

The benefits of all purely decompositional normal forms in terms of *storage costs* are summarized as follows:

Theorem 11. *A relation scheme (, U, SC) is in decompositional normal form (i.e. BCNF, 4 NF, 5 NF), relative to the class of semantic constraints considered in SC (i.e. functional dependencies, multivalued dependencies, join dependencies)*
iff for each decomposed database schema DS that supports (, U, SC) by the natural join, for each instance of (, U, SC):
size (instance of (, U, SC)) $\leq$ size (decomposed instance).

Here size means the number of occurences of constant symbols in the instances. This "folklore theorem" is closely related to a theorem of [VS93b] that characterizes normal forms in terms of data redundancy. The intuitive reasoning of the proof is the following. Assume that (, U, SC) is already in decompositional normal form. Then any further decomposition would result in duplicating the key components of tuples (and thus would increase the size) without getting any compensating size benefit. If on the other hand (, U, SC) is not in decompositional normal form, then the forbidden substructure can cause a redundant representation of facts, and the size benefit of removing this redundancy by decomposition can exceed the disadvantage of duplicating tuple components, necessary for support by the natural join.

Decompositional normal forms are also helpful to ensure low *update costs* [BG80, Vos88, Bis89, Cha89, HC91, BD93]. As an example, we present a theorem that takes care of functional and inclusion dependencies [BD93]. The theorem characterizes those database schemas that allow maintenance of all semantic constraints by simply checking whether a newly inserted tuple does not violate a key condition.

Theorem 12. *A database scheme DS with relation schemes* $(R_1, X_1, F_1), \ldots,$ (R_n, X_n, F_n) *with functional dependencies as local semantic constraints and inclusion dependencies I as global semantic constraints allows* $X \subset X_i$, *for some i, as* update object, *i.e.*

i) $X \to X_i \in (I \cup \bigcup_{i=1,\ldots,n} F_i)^+$ *and*

ii) *for each instance* $(r_1, \ldots, r_i \ldots, r_n)$ *of DS, for each tuple* μ *with*
$\mu \lceil X \notin \pi_X(r_i):$
$(r_1, \ldots, r_i \cup \{\mu\}, \ldots, r_n)$ *is instance of DS*

iff the following properties hold:

iii) R_i *is "not referencing" by inclusion dependencies of I.*

iv) R_i *is in unique key normal form.*

v) R_i *is in Boyce/Codd normal form.*

The proof is based on a careful analysis and equivalent reformulations of the fundamental notions, as well as, on separation conditions that restrict the interaction of functional dependencies and inclusion dependencies (which may be very complex in general, according to Theorem 5).

5.8 Unique Essences: Unique Flavor Formalized as Worthwhile "Semantic" Requirement

The fourth design heuristic, Unique Flavor, can be formalized in the framework of designing a so-called universal relation interface for a database schema [MUV84, KKFVU84, Var88b, BB83, BBSK86, BV88, Lev92]. Such an interface should translate queries, which are expressed in terms of attributes only (omitting the information about relation schemes), into join paths within the hypergraph structure of the schema. If there are several candidate join paths, then, according to the Unique Flavor heuristic, all these candidates should provide essentially the same query answer [BBSK86].

Given a database schema DS, a formalized version of this requirement is defined as follows:
$U := \bigcup_{i=1,\ldots,n} X_i$ and $H := \{X_1, \ldots, X_n\}$ describes the *hypergraph* of DS.
$jp : \wp U \to \wp \wp H$, $jp(Y) := \{E \mid E \subset H, \ E \ connected, \ Y \subset \bigcup E, \ E \ minimal\}$
defines the translation from a set of attributes into *join paths.*
$essence(E, Y) := \{X_i \cap (Y \cup \bigcup_{X_j \in E, X_j \neq X_i} X_j) \mid X_i \in E\}$ is the *essence* of a join
path E over a set of attributes Y.

- Finally, Unique Flavor motivates that essences should be unique:
  For all $Y \subset U$, for all $E, F \in jp(Y) : essence(E, Y) = essence(F, Y)$.

Of course, here the property of unique essences is already defined in purely syntactic terms although it is "semantically" motivated.

5.9 Acyclicity: Unique Flavor Formalized as Desirable Syntactic Property

The fourth design heuristic, Unique Flavor, can also be rephrased by considering the hypergraph *structure* of a database schema, as defined by the formats, and by requiring that the hypergraph is to some degree acyclic [Fag83, BFMY83, BBSK86]. The two most important degrees are listed below by their names and their *forbidden substructures*:

– γ-acyclic:

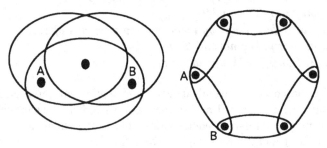

– α-acyclic: a nontrivial hypergraph as produced by the GYO-reduction applied to the schema [Gra79, YÖ79].

As a contribution to Task 2, it turns out that γ-acyclicity syntactically characterizes the "semantic" property of Section 5.8 [BBSK86]:

Theorem 13. *DS is γ-acyclic iff DS has unique essences.*

We can easily construct join paths over some set of attributes Y with different essences from the cyclic substructures forbidden for γ-acyclic database schemas: in each case, $Y := \{A, B\}$ is contained in a single relation scheme, which constitutes a trivial covering join path, and Y is covered by an essentially different join path containing two or more relation schemes (namely those connecting A with B running the "long way"). The converse claim of the theorem is proved by a tedious and subtle examination of the so-called *intersection hypergraph* of DS, which is generated from the hypergraph by adding all nonempty intersections of its hyperedges.

As a contribution to Task 3, the desirable syntactic property of acyclicity can be efficiently decided [YÖ79, Gra79, Fag83, TY84, DM86]:

Theorem 14. *The problems "DS is γ-acyclic" and "DS is α-acyclic" are decidable in polynomial time.*

For each degree of acyclicity a recursive decision procedure can be based on a "pruning" predicate on hyperedges. At each stage the procedure can delete a hyperedge that satisfies the predicate. The initial schema is acyclic iff the procedure succeeds in reducing the schema to nothing. The pruning predicate for γ-acyclicity can be paraphrased by "either there exists another hyperedge that has the same set of intersections with the remaining hyperedges or all nonempty intersections with the remaining hyperedges are identical". The pruning predicate for α-acyclicity can be paraphrased as "there exists a remaining hyperedge that contains all the intersections with the remaining hyperedges". These decision procedures are elaborated variants of the well-known acyclicity test for ordinary graphs: the test recursively deletes a leaf and its corresponding edge and recognizes acyclic graphs, i.e. trees, as those graphs that can be reduced to nothing.

5.10 Acyclicity Ensures Low Query Costs

According to Task 4, the impact of acyclicity as desirable syntactic property on costs should be examined. As suggested by the corresponding worthwhile semantic requirement, the evaluation of view queries that are join paths should be efficient. Indeed, we have the following assertions which have subtle and tedious proofs [Fag83, BFMY83]:

Theorem 15. *DS is γ-acyclic*
iff all *noncartesian join trees are* monotone
    (i.e. for pairwise consistent relations $r_1, \ldots r_n$ all partial results are consistent)
iff projections $\pi_Y(u)$ with $u := \underset{i=1,\ldots,n}{\bowtie} r_i$, $r_i := \pi_{X_i}(u)$,
    can be computed by determining a covering join path and evaluating it
    (i.e. $\pi_Y(u) = \pi_Y(\underset{X_i \in E}{\bowtie} r_i)$ for some $E \in jp(Y)$).

Theorem 16. *DS is α-acyclic*
iff there exists a monotone join tree
    (which, essentially, is determined by the GYO-reduction).

5.11 Design Algorithms Remove Forbidden Substructures

Fig.5 summarizes the presented achievements with respect to Tasks 1, 2 and 4. Finally, according to Task 3, a lot of design methods for *achieving* desirable syntactic properties have been proposed. Apparently, any concrete refinement of such a method will, necessarily, result into a highly interactive design procedure. The general skeleton of such procedures and the division of labour between the insightful administrator and the automatic algorithm [Bis95, BC86, BC89, Bis95b] can be outlined as shown in Fig.6.

formalize heuristics		
separation	**unique flavour**	**inference**
Task 1. syntactic properties no forbidden substructure: – 3 NF – BCNF – 4 NF – 5 NF – referential NF – unique key NF	*Task 1. "semantic" requirements* – join paths are essentially unique *Task 1. syntactic properties* no forbidden substructure: – γ-acyclic – α-acyclic	*Task 1. semantic requirements* – (faithful) view instance support – view query support *Task 2. syntactic characterization* for FDs, join support: – $\bowtie [X_1, \ldots, X_n] \in SC^+$ – $(\bigcup_i F_i)^+ \supset F$

Task 2. relationships between syntactic properties and semantic requirements

– BCNF and join support are compatible (decomposition)
– 3 NF and faithful join support are compatible (synthesis)
– γ-acyclic iff join paths are essentially unique

optimize at design time		
Task 4. syntactic properties ensure low costs		
storage	**query**	**update**

– normal forms	– γ-acyclic:
	  • join trees are monotone
	  • projection by covering joins
	– α-acyclic: existence of monotone join trees
		$-\begin{cases} \text{not referencing} \\ \text{one key} \\ \text{BCNF} \end{cases}$

Fig.5. A short summary of presented achievements with respect to Tasks 1, 2 and 4.

```
[modeling by administrator]
 model the application;
 document the model;
[parametrization by administrator]
 identify the desirable syntactic properties Ω of particular
 interest;
 define the appropriate worthwhile semantic requirements Γ
 related to Inferential Completeness;
[initialization by administrator and algorithm]
 initialize the current database schema DS as formalization of
 the model such that DS satisfies the semantic requirements Γ;
[achieve_properties]
LOOP {DS satifies Γ}
 [check_of_properties by algorithm]
 determine the set of all Ω-forbidden substructures of the
 current database schema DS;
 IF this set is empty THEN EXIT
 ELSE
    [investigate_forbidden_substructure by administrator]
    select an Ω-forbidden substructure forb;
    IF forb appears to be inherent in the application
    THEN mark forb as unavoidable and adjust Ω accordingly
    ELSIF forb stems from faulty modeling
    THEN improve the model and adjust Ω and Γ if necessary
    ELSIF forb arises from bad formalization of an agreed model
    THEN
      [remove_forbidden_substructure by algorithm]
      DS:=Transform(DS, forb)
      [where Transform is a schema transformation that removes the
      forbidden substructure forb from the current schema DS while
      it leaves the semantic requirements Γ invariant, i.e. the
      transformed schema satisfies Γ again]
    ENDIF;
 ENDIF;
ENDLOOP {DS satisfies Γ and Ω};
```

Fig.6. Outline of interactive design procedures.
[ ] embraces comments indicating a module together
    with its active entity or semantics, respectively;
{ } embraces state conditions, i.e. the invariant
    and the post condition of the main loop.

We shortly discuss some examples that fit the skeleton of Fig.6 by indicating Ω, Γ and $Transform$:

- Classical *decomposition*, based on Theorem 9 and related statements, identifies Ω as Boyce/Codd or higher normal form and selects Γ as view support of an initial universal relation scheme by the natural join. $Transform$ splits a current relation scheme with attribute set X_i into fragments that are determined by the components of the forbidden join dependency; $Transform$ is Γ-invariant by the semantics of join dependencies (and because any functional dependency implies a corresponding multivalued dependency).

- Classical *synthesis*, based on Theorem 10 and related statements, has two phases. The first phase achieves faithfulness, and the second phase adds view support of an initial universal relation scheme by the natural join. In the first phase Ω is identified as third normal form, and Γ is selected as faithfulness (syntactically characterized as the preservation of the given set of functional dependencies). $Transform$ removes all kinds of redundancy (which can lead to Ω-forbidden substructures) from the functional dependencies. An early version of synthesis [Ber76] achieves this goal by computing a minimal cover of the functional dependencies, leaving Γ invariant. A later version [BM87] achieves this goal by removing so-called "abnormal nonprime" attributes from relation schemes following some sophisticated strategy, whereby a somewhat stronger invariant Γ (namely faithfulness and "object-faithfulness" and "strong normativity") is preserved. In the second phase view support of an initial universal relation scheme by the natural join is guaranteed by ensuring the existence of a relation scheme that contains a global key [BDB79]. If necessary, such a key component is added (in this case as a previously "missing substructure").

- In *view integration*, as formalized in [BC86], Ω is identified as absence of so-called "integration constraints", which indicate a redundant overlap of views and, thus, are interpreted as forbidden substructures in the wanted integrated schema, and Γ is selected as view support of all given view database schemas. $Transform$ removes an integration constraint by appropriately merging the relation schemes involved, leaving Γ invariant.

Examining the general skeleton of design procedures, we can further comment on the tasks of design theory. The parametrization step is based on Task 1 and Task 2. The check_of_properties step and the remove_forbidden_substructure step are based on Task 3. Finally, after getting the final output schema, the administrator can evaluate the quality of the design based on results of Task 4, and, if necessary, he can iteratively process the design procedure using a different parametrization.

The skeleton also shows the impact of the administrator's interaction: he is responsible for modeling, parametrization, selection and investigation of forbidden substructure. While modeling and investigation of forbidden substructures is principally outside the scope of automatic algorithms, parametrization and selection of forbidden substructures could possibly be better supported by algorithms as known today.

6 Final Remarks

Since the first pioneering work of E.F. Codd [Cod70, 72] and W.W. Armstrong [Arm74], a substantial body of results on database schema design theory has been published. This paper summarizes only a small part of the highly detailed work. It emphasizes the tasks of design theory in producing and using interactive design tools. In a companion paper [Bis95a] three main topics for further enhancement of the design theory are outlined: all current achievements still have to be carried out within one unifying framework; the current achievements have to be embedded in the full design process and to be extended to deal more deeply with advanced database features like incomplete information, recursive query languages, complex objects or object identifiers; all achievements have to be reconsidered from the viewpoint of distributed computing, abandoning the classical centralized approach to databases.

Acknowledgement: I would like to thank Ralf Menzel and Torsten Polle for valuable discussions. I am also grateful to an anonymous reviewer for helpful remarks and hints.

References

[AABM82] P. Atzeni, G. Ausiello, C. Batini, and M. Moscarini. Inclusion and equivalence between relational database schemata. *Theoretical Computer Science*, 19:267–285, 1982.

[ADA93] P. Atzeni and V. De Antonellis. *Relational Database Theory*. Benjamin/Cummings, Redwood City, CA, 1993.

[AHV95] S. Abiteboul, R. Hull, and V. Vianu. *Foundations of Databases*. Addison-Wesley, Reading, MA, 1995.

[AM86] P. Atzeni and N. M. Morfuni. Functional dependencies and constraints on null values in database relations. *Information and Control*, 70(1):1–31, 1986.

[Arm74] W. W. Armstrong. Dependency structures of data base relationships. In J. L. Rosenfeld, editor, *Proceedings of IFIP Congress 1974*, pages 580–583. North-Holland, Amsterdam, 1974.

[BB79] C. Beeri and P.A. Bernstein. Computational problems related to the design of normal form relational schemas. *ACM Transactions on Database Systems*, 4(1):30–59, 1979.

[BB83] J. Biskup and H. H. Brüggemann. Universal relation views: A pragmatic approach. In *Proceedings of the 9th International Conference on Very Large Data Bases*, pages 172–185, 1983.

[BBG78] C. Beeri, P. A. Bernstein, and N. Goodman. A sophisticated introduction to database normalization theory. In *Proceedings of the 4th International Conference on Very Large Data Bases, Berlin*, pages 113–124, September 1978.

[BBG78] C. Beeri, P. A. Bernstein, and N. Goodman. A sophisticated introduction to database normalization theory. In *Proceedings of the 4th International Conference on Very Large Data Bases, Berlin*, pages 113–124, September 1978.

[BBSK86]   J. Biskup, H. H. Brüggemann, L. Schnetgöke, and M. Kramer. One flavor assumption and γ-acyclicity for universal relation views. In *Proceedings of the Fifth ACM SIGACT-SIGMOD Symposium on Principles of Database Systems*, pages 148–159, 1986.

[BC86]   J. Biskup and B. Convent. A formal view integration method. In *Proceedings of the ACM SIGMOD International Conference on Management of Data, Washington*, pages 398–407, 1986.

[BC89]   J. Biskup and B. Convent. Towards a schema design methodology for deductive databases. In J. Demetrovics and B. Thalheim, editors, *Proceedings of the Symposium on Mathematical Fundamentals of Database Systems (MFDBS '89)*, number 364 in Lecture Notes in Computer Science, pages 37–52. Springer, 1989.

[BC91]   J. Biskup and B. Convent. Relational chase procedures interpreted as resolution with paramodulation. *Fundamenta Informaticae*, XV(2):123–138, 1991.

[BD93]   J. Biskup and P. Dublish. Objects in relational database schemes with functional, inclusion and exclusion dependencies. *Informatique théorique et Applications / Theoretical Informatics and Applications*, 27(3):183–219, 1993.

[BDB79]   J. Biskup, U. Dayal, and P. A. Bernstein. Synthesizing independent database schemas. In P. A. Bernstein, editor, *Proceedings of the ACM SIGMOD International Conference on Management of Data (SIGMOD '79)*, Boston, pages 143–151, New York, NY, 1979. ACM.

[BDLM91]   J. Biskup, J. Demetrovics, L. O. Libkin, and I. B. Muchnik. On relational database schemes having unique minimal key. *Journal of Information Processing and Cybernetics EIK*, 27(4):217–225, 1991.

[Ber76]   P. A. Bernstein. Synthesizing third normal form relations from functional dependencies. *ACM Transactions on Database Systems*, 1(4):272–298, December 1976.

[BFMY83]   C. Beeri, R. Fagin, D. Maier, and M. Yannakakis. On the desirability of acyclic database schemes. *Journal of the ACM*, 30:479–513, 1983.

[BG80]   P. A. Bernstein and N. Goodman. What does Boyce-Codd normal form do? In *Proceedings of the 6th International Conference on Very Large Data Bases*, pages 245–259, 1980.

[Bis80]   J. Biskup. Inferences of multivalued dependencies in fixed and undetermined universes. *Theoretical Computer Science*, 10:93–105, 1980.

[Bis85]   J. Biskup. Entwurf von Datenbankschemas durch schrittweises Umwandeln verbotener Teilstrukturen. In *Tagungsband GI-EMISA-Fachgespräch Entwurf von Informationssystemen — Methoden und Modelle, Tutzing*, pages 130–148, 1985.

[Bis89]   J. Biskup. Boyce-Codd normal form and object normal forms. *Information Processing Letters*, 32(1):29–33, 1989.

[Bis94]   J. Biskup. Impacts of creating, implementing and using formal languages. In K. Duncan and K. Krueger, editors, *Proceedings of the 13th World Comupter Congress 94*, volume 3, pages 402–407. Elsevier (North-Holland), Amsterdam etc., 1994.

[Bis95a]   J. Biskup. Database schema design theory: achievements and challenges. In *Proceedings of the 6th International Conference on Information Systems and Management of Data (CISMOD '95)*, number 1006 in Lecture Notes in Computer Science, pages 14–44, Bombay, 1995. Springer, Berlin etc.

[Bis95b]   J. Biskup. *Grundlagen von Informationssystemen.* Vieweg, Braunschweig-Wiesbaden, 1995.

[BK86]   C. Beeri and M. Kifer. An integrated approach to logical design of relational database schemes. *ACM Transactions on Database Systems,* 11(2):134–158, 1986.

[BM87]   J. Biskup and R. Meyer. Design of relational database schemes by deleting attributes in the canonical decomposition. *Journal of Computer and System Sciences,* 35(1):1–22, 1987.

[BR88]   J. Biskup and U. Räsch. The equivalence problem for relational database schemes. In *Proceedings of the 1st Symposium on Mathematical Fundamentals of Database Systems,* number 305 in Lecture Notes in Computer Science, pages 42–70. Springer-Verlag, Berlin etc., 1988.

[BS81]   F. Bancilhon and N. Spyratos. Update semantics of relational views. *ACM Transactions on Database Systems,* 6(4):557–575, 1981.

[BV84a]   C. Beeri and M. Y. Vardi. Formal systems for tuple and equality generating dependencies. *SIAM Journal on Computing,* 13(1):76–98, 1984.

[BV84b]   C. Beeri and M. Y. Vardi. A proof procedure for data dependencies. *Journal of the ACM,* 31(4):718–741, October 1984.

[BV88]   V. Brosda and G. Vossen. Update and retrieval in a relational database through a universal schema interface. *ACM Transactions on Database Systems,* 13(1988):449–485, 1988.

[CFP84]   M. A. Casanova, R. Fagin, and C. H. Papadimitriou. Inclusion dependencies and their interaction with functional dependencies. *Journal of Computer and System Sciences,* 28(1):29–59, 1984.

[Cha89]   E. P. F. Chan. A design theory for solving the anomalies problem. *SIAM Journal on Computing,* 18(3):429–448, June 1989.

[Che76]   P. P.-S. Chen. The entity-relationship-model — towards a unified view of data. *ACM Transactions on Database Systems,* 1(1):9–36, March 1976.

[CM87]   E. P. F. Chan and A. O. Mendelzon. Independent and separable database schemes. *SIAM Journal on Computing,* 16(5):841–851, 1987.

[Cod70]   E. F. Codd. A relational model of data for large shared data banks. *Communications of the ACM,* 13(6):377–387, June 1970.

[Cod72]   E. F. Codd. Further normalization of the database relational model. In R. Rustin, editor, *Database Systems,* number 6 in Courant Institute Computer Science Symposia Series, pages 33–64. Prentice Hall, Englewood Cliffs, NJ, 1972.

[CV85]   A. K. Chandra and M. Y. Vardi. The implication problem for functional and inclusion dependencies is undecidable. *SIAM Journal on Computing,* 14(3):671–677, 1985.

[DB82]   U. Dayal and P. A. Bernstein. On the correct translation of update operations on relational views. *ACM Transactions on Database Systems,* 8(3):381–416, 1982.

[Del78]   C. Delobel. Normalization and hierarchical dependencies in the relational data model. *ACM Transactions on Database Systems,* 3:201–222, 1978.

[DF92]   C. J. Date and R. Fagin. Simple conditions for guaranteeing higher normal forms in relational databases. *ACM Transactions on Database Systems,* 17:465–476, 1992.

[DKM+95]   J. Demetrovics, G. O. H. Katona, D. Miklos, O. Seleznjew, and B. Thalheim. The average length of key and functional dependencies in (random) databases. In G. Gottlob and M. Y. Vardi, editors, *Database Theory—ICDT '95*, pages 266-279. Springer-Verlag, Berlin etc., 1995.

[DLM92] J. Demetrovics, L. Libkin, and I.B. Muchnik. Functional dependencies in relational databases: a lattice point of view. *Discrete Applied Mathematics*, 40:155-185, 1992.

[DM86] A. D'Atri and M. Moscarini. Recognition algorithms and design methodologies for acyclic database. In P. C. Kanellakis and F. Preparata, editors, *Advances in Computing Research*, volume 3, pages 164-185. JAI Press, Inc., Greenwich, CT, 1986.

[DP84] P. DeBra and J. Paredaens. Horizontal decompositions for handling exceptions to functional dependencies. In H. Gallaire, J. Minker, and J. M. Nicolas, editors, *Advances in Database Theory*, volume 2. Plenum, New York - London, 1984.

[Fag77] R. Fagin. Multivalued dependencies and a new normal form for relational databases. *ACM Transactions on Database Systems*, 2(3):262-278, September 1977.

[Fag81] R. Fagin. A normal form for relational databases that is based on domains and keys. *ACM Transactions on Database Systems*, 6(3):387-415, 1981.

[Fag83] R. Fagin. Degrees of acyclicity for hypergraphs and relational database schemes. *Journal of the ACM*, 30(3):514-550, July 1983.

[FC85] A. L. Furtado and M. A. Casanova. Updating relational views. In W. Kim, D. S. Reiner, and D. S. Batory, editors, *Query Processing in Database Systems*. Springer-Verlag, Berlin, 1985.

[FV84] R. Fagin and M. Y. Vardi. The theory of data dependencies - an overview. In *Proceedings of the 11th International Colloquium on Automata, Languages and Programming*, number 172 in Lecture Notes in Computer Science, pages 1-22. Springer-Verlag, Berlin etc., 1984.

[GHLM93] J. Grant, J. Horty, J. Lobo, and J. Minker. View Updates in Stratified Disjunctive Databases. *Journal of Automated Reasoning*, 11:249-267, 1993.

[GMV86] M. H. Graham, A. O. Mendelzon, and M. Y. Vardi. Notions of dependency satisfaction. *Journal of the ACM*, 33(1):105-129, 1986.

[Gra79] M. H. Graham. On the universal relation. Systems research group report, University of Toronto, 1979.

[Gra84] G. Grahne. Dependency satisfaction in databases with incomplete information. In U. Dayal, editor, *Proceedings of the 10th International Conference on Very Large Data Bases*, pages 37-45, Singapore, 1984.

[HC91] H. J. Hernández and E. P. F. Chan. Constant-time-maintainable BCNF database schemes. *ACM Transactions on Database Systems*, 16(4):571-599, December 1991.

[Heg94] S. J. Hegner. Unique complements and decompositions of database schemata. *Journal of Computer and System Sciences*, 48:9-57, 1994.

[Her95] C. Herrmann. On the undecidability of implications between embedded multivalued dependencies. *Information and Computation*, 122:221-235, 1995.

[Hon82] P. Honeyman. Testing satisfaction of functional dependencies. *Journal of the ACM*, 29(3):668-677, 1982.

[Hul86] R. Hull. Relative information capacity of simple relational database schemata. *SIAM Journal on Computing*, 15(3):856-886, 1986.

[JF82]   J. H. Jou and P. C. Fischer. The complexity of recognizing 3NF relation schemes. *Information Processing Letters*, 14(4):187–190, 1982.

[Kat92]   G. O. H. Katona. Combinatorial and algebraic results for database relations. In *Database Theory—ICDT '92*, number 646 in Lectures Notes in Computer Science, pages 1–20. Springer-Verlag, Berlin etc., 1992.

[KCV83]   P. C. Kanellakis, S. S. Cosmadakis, and M. Y. Vardi. Unary inclusion dependencies have polynomial time inference problems. In *Proceedings of the 15th Symposium on Theory of Computing, Boston*, pages 246–277, 1983.

[Kel86]   A. M. Keller. The role of semantics in translating view updates. *IEEE Computer*, 19(1):63–73, January 1986.

[Ken83]   W. Kent. A simple guide to five normal forms in relational databases. *Communications of the ACM*, 26(2):120–125, 1983.

[KKF+84]   H. F. Korth, G. M. Kuper, J. Feigenbaum, A. VanGeldern, and J. D. Ullman. A database system based on the universal relation assumption. *ACM Transactions on Database Systems*, 9(1984):331–347, 1984.

[KM80]   P. Kandzia and M. Mangelmann. On covering Boyce-Codd normal forms. *Information Processing Letters*, 11:218–223, 1980.

[Lev92]   M. Levene. *The Nested Universal Relation Database Model*. Lecture Notes in Computer Science 595. Springer, Berlin etc., 1992.

[Lie79]   Y. E. Lien. Multivalued dependencies with nulls in relational databases. In *Proceedings of the 5th International Conference on Very Large Data Bases*, pages 61–66, 1979.

[LL94]   M. Levene and G. Loizou. The nested universal relation model. *Journal of Computer and System Sciences*, 49:683–717, 1994.

[LO78]   C. L. Lucchesi and S. L. Osborn. Candidate keys for relations. *Journal of Computer and System Sciences*, 17(2):270–279, 1978.

[LTK81]   T.-W. Ling, F. W. Tompa, and T. Kameda. An improved third normal form for relational databases. *ACM Transactions on Database Systems*, 6(2):329–346, 1981.

[Mai83]   D. Maier. *The Theory of Relational Databases*. Computer Science Press, Rockville, MD, 1983.

[Men79]   A. O. Mendelzon. On axiomatizing multivalued dependencies in relational databases. *Journal of the ACM*, 26(1):37–44, 1979.

[Mit83]   J. C. Mitchell. The implication problem for functional and inclusion dependencies. *Information and Control*, 56(3):154–173, 1983.

[MR83]   H. Mannila and K.-J. Räihä. On the relationship of minimum and optimum covers for a set of functional dependencies. *Acta Informatica*, 20:143–158, 1983.

[MR86]   H. Mannila and K.-J. Räihä. Inclusion dependencies in database design. In *Proceedings of the Second International Conference on Data Engineering*, pages 713–718, Washington, DC, 1986. IEEE Computer Society Press.

[MR92]   H. Mannila and K.-J. Räihä. *The Design of Relational Databases*. Addison-Wesley, Wokingham, England, 1992.

[MUV84]   D. Maier, J. D. Ullman, and M. Y. Vardi. On the foundations of the universal relation model. *ACM Transactions on Database Systems*, 9(2):283–308, June 1984.

[Osb78]   S. L. Osborn. *Normal Forms for Relational Data Bases*. PhD thesis, Department of Computer Science, University of Waterloo, 1978.

[PDGvG89] J. Paredaens, P. DeBra, M. Gyssens, and D. van Gucht. *The Structure of the Relational Database Model.* Number 17 in EATCS Monographs on Theoretical Computer Science. Springer-Verlag, Berlin, 1989.

[Ris77] J. Rissanen. Independent components of relations. *ACM Transactions on Database Systems,* 2(4):317–325, 1977.

[Ris82] J. Rissanen. On equivalence of database schemes. In *Proceedings of the 1st ACM SIGACT-SIGMOD Symposium on Principles of Database Systems,* pages 23–26, 1982.

[Sag83] Y. Sagiv. A characterization of globally consistent databases and their correct access paths. *ACM Transactions on Database Systems,* 8(2):266–286, 1983.

[SR88] D. Seipel and D. Ruland. Designing gamma-acyclic database schemes using decomposition and augmentation techniques. In *Proc. 1st Symposium on Mathematical Fundamentals of Database Systems,* number 305 in Lecture Notes in Computer Science, pages 197–209. Springer-Verlag, Berlin etc., 1988.

[Tha91] B. Thalheim. *Dependencies in relational databases.* Teubner, Stuttgart - Leipzig, 1991.

[TLJ90] P. Thanisch, G. Loizou, and G. Jones. Succint database schemes. *International Journal of Computer Mathematics,* 33:55–69, 1990.

[TY84] R. E. Tarjan and M. Yannakakis. Simple linear-time algorithms to test chordality of graphs, test acyclicity of hypergraphs, and selectivity reduce acyclic hypergraphs. *SIAM Journal on Computing,* 13:566–579, 1984.

[Ull88] J. D. Ullman. *Principles of Database and Knowledge-Base Systems (Volume I).* Computer Science Press, Rockville, MD, 1988.

[Ull89] J. D. Ullman. *Principles of Database and Knowledge-Base Systems (Volume II: The New Technologies).* Computer Science Press, Rockville, MD, 1989.

[Var82] M. Y. Vardi. On decomposition of relational databases. In *Proc. 23rd Symposium on Foundations of Computer Science,* pages 176–185, 1982.

[Var84] M. Y. Vardi. The implication and finite implication problem for typed template dependencies. *Journal of Computer and System Sciences,* 28:3–28, 1984.

[Var88a] M. Y. Vardi. Fundamentals of dependency theory. In E. Börger, editor, *Trends in Theoretical Computer Science,* pages 171–224. Computer Science Press, Rockville, 1988.

[Var88b] M. Y. Vardi. The universal-relation data model for logical independence. *IEEE Software,* 5(1988):80–85, 1988.

[Vas79] Y. Vassiliou. Null values in database management, a denotational semantics approach. In *Proc. ACM SIGMOD Symp. on the Management of Data,* pages 162–169, 1979.

[Vos88] G. Vossen. A new characterization of FD implication with an application to update anomalies. *Information Processing Letters,* 29(3):131–135, 1988.

[Vos91] G. Vossen. *Data Models, Database Languages and Database Management Systems.* Addison-Wesley, Wokingham, England, 1991.

[VS93a] M. W. Vincent and B. Srinivasan. A note on relation schemes which are in 3NF but not in BCNF. *Information Processing Letters,* 48:281–283, 1993.

[VS93b] M. W. Vincent and B. Srinivasan. Redundancy and the justification for fourth normal form in relational databases. *International Journal of Foundations of Computer Science,* 4:355–365, 1993.

[YÖ79]   C. T. Yu and Z. M. Özsoyoğlu. An algorithm for tree-query membership of a distributed query. In *Proceedings of the 3rd IEEE COMPSAC, Chicago*, pages 306–312, 1979.

[YÖ92a]   L.-Y. Yuan and Z. M. Özsoyoğlu. Design of desirable relational database schemes. *Journal of Computer and System Sciences*, 45:435–470, 1992.

[YÖ92b]   L.-Y. Yuan and Z. M. Özsoyoğlu. Unifying functional and multivalued dependencies for relational database design. *Information Science*, 59:185–211, 1992.

[Zan76]   C. Zaniolo. *Analysis and design of relational schemata for database systems*. PhD thesis, University of California Los Angeles, Computer Science Department, 1976. Technical Report UCLA-ENG-7669, July 1976.

Semantics of Database Transformations*

Susan Davidson[1], Peter Buneman[1], and Anthony Kosky[2]

[1] Dept. of Computer and Information Science, University of Pennsylvania,
Philadelphia, PA 19104
[2] Lawrence Berkeley National Laboratory, Berkeley, CA 94705.

Abstract. Database transformations arise in many different settings including database integration, evolution of database systems, and implementing user views and data-entry tools. This paper surveys approaches that have been taken to problems in these settings, assesses their strengths and weaknesses, and develops requirements on a formal model for specifying and implementing database transformations.

We also consider the problem of insuring the correctness of database transformations. In particular, we demonstrate that the usefulness of correctness conditions such as information preservation is hindered by the interactions of transformations and database constraints, and the limited expressive power of established database constraint languages. We conclude that more general notions of correctness are required, and that there is a need for a uniform formalism for expressing both database transformations and constraints, and reasoning about their interactions.

Finally we introduce *WOL*, a declarative language for specifying and implementing database transformations and constraints. We briefly describe the *WOL* language and its semantics, and argue that it addresses many of the requirements on a formalism for dealing with general database transformations.

1   Introduction

The need to implement transformations between distinct, heterogeneous databases has become a major factor in information management in recent years. Problems of reimplementing legacy systems, adapting application programs and user interfaces to schema evolution, integrating heterogeneous databases, and merging user views or mapping between data-entry screens and the underlying database all involve some form of transformation. The wide variety of data models in use, including those supporting complex data structures and object-identities, further complicate these problems.

A *database transformation* is a set of mappings from the instances of one or more *source* database schemas to the instances of some *target* schema. The schemas involved may be expressed in a variety of different data-models, and

* This research was supported in part by DOE DE-FG02-94-ER-61923 Sub 1, NSF BIR94-02292 PRIME, ARO AASERT DAAH04-93-G0129, ARPA N00014-94-1-1086 and DOE DE-AC03-76SF00098.

implemented using different DBMSs. Incompatibilities between the sources and target exist at all levels – the choice of data-model, the representation of data within a model, the data of an instance – and must be explicitly resolved within the transformation.

Much of the existing work on transformations concentrates on the restructuring of source database schemas into a target schema, either by means of a series of simple manipulations or by a description in some abstract language, and the mappings of the underlying instances are determined by the restructurings of schemas. In some cases this emphasis is at the expense of a formal treatment of the effect of transformations on instances, which is stated informally or left to the intuition. However there are, in general, many possible interpretations of a particular schema manipulation. For example, in a data model supporting classes of objects and optional attributes of classes, suppose we changed an attribute of an existing class from being optional to being required. There are a number of ways that such a schema manipulation can be reflected on the underlying data: we could insert a default value for the attribute where ever it is omitted, or we could simply delete any objects from the class for which the attribute is missing.

It is clear that there may be many transformations, with differing semantics, corresponding to the same schema manipulation, and that it is necessary to be able to distinguish between them. In contrast to existing work, our focus in this paper is therefore on how transformations effect the underlying data itself. We will use the term *"database transformations"*, as opposed to the more common "schema transformations", in order to emphasize this distinction.

Implementations of database transformations fall into two camps: those in which the data is actually transformed into a format compatible with the target schema and then stored in a target database, and those in which the data remains stored in the source databases and queries against the target schema are translated into queries against the source databases. The first of these approaches can be thought of as performing a *one-time bulk transformation*, while the second approach evaluates transformations in a *call-by-need* manner.

For example, the most common approach adopted within federated database systems [14] is call-by-need [25,10,22]. This approach has the advantage that the source databases retain their autonomy, and updates to the various source databases are automatically reflected in the target database. However, in cases where accessing the component databases is costly and the databases are not frequently updated, actually merging the data into a local unified database may be more efficient. Furthermore, maintaining integrity constraints over a federated database system is a much more difficult task than checking data integrity for a single merged database [30,39]. As a result, the approach of performing a one-time bulk transformation is taken in [38].

Some work on schema evolution also advocates implementing transformations in a call-by-need manner [5,33,35]. In this case multiple versions of a schema are maintained, and data is stored using the version for which it was originally entered. The advantage of the approach is that major database reorganizations can be avoided, and applications implemented for an earlier version of a schema can still be used. However, for applications built on old versions of a schema to be applied to new data, reverse transformations must also be implemented. Furthermore the cost of maintaining multiple views and computing compounded transformations may be prohibitively expensive. These problems are especially significant when schema evolutions are frequent, and it is not possible a priori to tell when old views or data cease to be relevant. Consequently some practical work on implementing schema evolutions has been based on performing bulk transformations of data [27].

It is clear that the implementation method appropriate for a particular transformation will depend on the application and on the databases involved. However, the semantics of a transformation should be independent of the implementation method chosen as well as of the application area itself. Unfortunately, for much of the work in the area of database transformations this is not the case, primarily due to the fact that there is no independent semantics for the transformation. A focus of this paper is therefore to develop a semantics of database transformations, and examine various metrics for the "goodness" or "correctness" of such transformations.

We start in the next section by giving an informal example of a database transformation as it might arise within heterogeneous database integration, and surveying approaches that have been taken within this domain. The example is used to illustrate that while many of the ideas in these approaches are useful, none of them capture all necessary structural manipulations and that there is therefore a need for a more general and flexible formalism for expressing such transformations.

Section 3 formalizes the example by presenting a data model which gives a precise semantics to a database schema, instances and keys. The model is used in section 4 to examine the notion of information capacity preserving transformations. We argue that while this is an appealing "correctness" metric for database transformations, it is not always useful because it does not capture intuitively meaningful transformations, and fails to take into account implicit constraints on the databases being transformed. We conclude that there is a need to express and test more general correctness conditions, and to derive constraints on the databases being transformed from such conditions.

Section 5 presents a declarative language for expressing database transformations and constraints called *WOL* (Well-founded Object Language). We show that *WOL* is not only sufficient for expressing the transformations occuring in existing work, but that it is more expressive than existing transformation languages for the data-models being considered. *WOL* can also be used to

express the constraints on individual databases and *between* databases necessary to ensure correctness of transformations, hence filling a significant need
in the field of database transformations.

2 Transformations in Database Integration

In this section we will look at some examples of database transformations,
particularly in the context of database integration, and show how some parts
of these examples are addressed by existing work, while others require more
general transformation techniques. The context of database integration is
particularly appropriate since much of the most significant work in database
transformations stems from this field. In contrast, transformations proposed
in say the area of schema evolution are comparatively simple [28,35,27,5,33],
normally being based on a single model and a small set of basic schema
modifications, such as introducing specialization and generalization classes,
adding or removing attributes, and so on. It is not clear whether the reason
for this is historical, since database integration became a significant problem
earlier in terms of the need for formal tools and techniques, or because the
transformations involved in database integration are inherently more difficult
than those arising in other areas.

2.1 Database Integration: An Example

The objective of database integration is to make data distributed over a
number of distinct, heterogeneous databases accessible via a single database
interface, either by constructing a (virtual) view of the component databases
to give them the appearance of a single database, or by actually mapping
data from the component databases into a single unified database. In either
case, the problem from the perspective of database transformations is how
to transform data from the various formats and structures in which it is
represented in the component databases into a form compatible with the
integrated database schema.

Example 1. **Figure 1** shows the schemas of two databases representing US
Cities and States, and European Cities and Countries respectively. The graphical notation used here is inspired by [3]: the boxes represent *classes* which are
finite sets of objects; the arrows represent *attributes*, or functions on classes;
and *str* and *Bool* represent sets of *base values*. An instance of such a schema
consists of an assignment of finite sets of objects to each class, and of functions on these sets to each attribute. The details of this model will be made
precise in section 3.

The first schema has two classes: *City* and *State*. The City class has two
attributes: *name*, representing the name of a city, and *state*, which points to

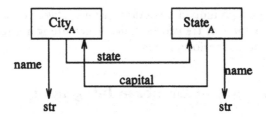

Schema of US Cities and States

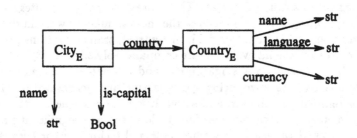

Schema of European Cities and Countries

Fig. 1. Schemas for US Cities and European Cities databases

the state to which a city belongs. The *State* class also has two attributes, representing its name and its capital city.

The second schema also has two classes, this time *City* and *Country*. The *City* class has attributes representing its name and its country, but in addition has a Boolean-valued attribute *capital* which represents whether or not it is the capital city of a country. The *Country* class has attributes representing its name, currency and the language spoken.

Suppose we wanted to combine these two databases into a single database containing information about both US and European cities. A suitable schema is shown in figure 2, where the "plus" node indicates a variant. Here the *City* classes from both the source databases are mapped to a single class *City* in the target database. The *state* and *country* attributes of the *City* classes are mapped to a single attribute *place* which take a value that is either a *State* or a *Country*, depending on whether the *City* is a US or a European city. A more difficult mapping is between the representations of capital cities of European countries. Instead of representing whether a city is a capital or not by means of a Boolean attribute, the *Country* class in our target database has an attribute *capital* which points to the capital city of a country. To resolve this difference in representation a straightforward embedding of data will not be sufficient; we will need to do some more sophisticated structural transformations on the data. Further constraints on the source database, ensuring that each *Country* has exactly one *City* for which the *is_capital* attribute is true, are necessary in order for the transformation to be well defined. (The interaction between constraints and transformations will be explored in section 4.2).

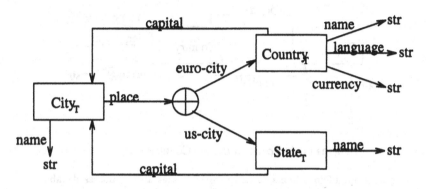

Fig. 2. An integrated schema of European and US Cities

The problem of database integration may therefore be seen as forming an *integrated schema*, which represents the relevant information in the component source databases, together with transformations from the source databases to this integrated schema.

2.2 Resolving Structural Conflicts in Database Integration

In [7] Batini et al. noted that schema integration techniques generally have two phases: conflict resolution and merging or unioning of schemas. Although schema merging has received a great deal of attention, it is only a small (and usually the last) step in the process of database integration. The more significant part of the process is manipulating the component databases so that they represent data in a compatible way. In order to do this it is necessary to resolve naming conflicts between the schemas (both homonyms and synonyms), and also to perform structural manipulations on data to resolve conflicts in the way data is represented. The structural manipulations required are usually computationally simple, and do not normally involve any unbounded computation (iteration or recursion). An example of such a structural manipulation was given by how the capital attribute was represented in the European Cities schema.

The order in which the conflict resolution and schema merging phases are carried out varies between different database integration methods. For example, in Motro[25] component schemas are first unioned to form disjoint components of a "superview" schema, and the superview is then manipulated in order to combine concepts and resolve conflicts between the component schemas. In contrast, [26,8,32] assume that conflicts between schemas are resolved prior to the schema merging process, and [6] interleaves the two parts of this process.

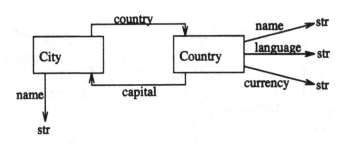

Schema of European Cities and Countries

Fig. 3. A modified schema for a European cities and countries database

Example 2. Returning to example 1, it is necessary to perform a structural modification on the database of European Cities and Countries to replace the Boolean *is_capital* attribute of the *City* class with a *capital* attribute of class *Country* going to the class *City*. This yields an intermediate database with the schema shown in figure 3. It is then necessary to associate the classes and attributes of the two source databases, so that the *City* classes and *name* attributes, and also the *state* and *country* attributes, are associated, and the remainder of the transformation could be implemented by means of an automated schema-merging tool.

There are two basic approaches to systems for implementing transformations to resolve such structural conflicts: using a small set of simple transformations or heuristics that can be applied in series [25,5,24,32], or using some high-level language to describe the transformation [1,10]. Examples of such approaches will be given in section 2.3.

The advantage of using a small set of pre-defined atomic transformations is that they are simple to reason about and prove correctness for. For instance, one could prove that each transformation was information preserving [29,24], or if necessary associate constraints with each transformation in order for it to be information capacity preserving, and deduce that a series of applications of the transformations was information preserving. The disadvantage of this approach is that the expressivity of such a family of transformations is inherently limited. For example the family of transformations proposed in [25] are insufficient to describe the transformation between an attribute of a class and a binary relation between classes: that is, one cannot transform from a class *Person* with an attribute *spouse* of class *Person* to a binary relation *Marriage* on the *Person* class. Although it might be easy to extend the family of atomic transformations to allow this case, which is a common source of incompatibility between databases, there would still be other important transformations that could not be expressed. The restructuring described in example 2 also can not be expressed using any of the families of transformations mentioned above.

A potentially much more flexible approach is to use some high-level language for expressing structural transformations on data. However programming and checking a transformation in such a language is a more laborious task. Further, if it is necessary to ensure that a transformation is information preserving then additional constraints may be needed on the source databases, and in general these constraints will not be expressible in any standard constraint language. This will be taken up again in more detail in section 4. We therefore believe that there is a need for a declarative language for expressing such transformations and constraints, which allows one to formally reason about the interaction between transformations and constraints and which is sufficiently simple to allow transformations to be programmed easily. Such a language will be presented in section 5.

2.3 Schema Integration Techniques

In [7] Batini et al. survey existing work on *schema integration*. They observe that schema integration arises from two tasks: *database integration*, which we have already discussed, and *integration of user views*, which occurs during the design phase of a database when constructing a schema that satisfies the individual needs of each of a set of user groups. However they fail to note that these two kinds of schema integration are fundamentally different. The reason for this can be seen by considering the direction in which data is transformed in each case. For database integration, instances of each of the source databases are transformed into instances of the merged schema. On the other hand, when integrating multiple user views instances of the merged schema must be transformed back into instances of the user views (see figure 4). The intuition is that when integrating user views *all* of the underlying information must be represented; no objects or attributes can be missing since some user may want the information. However, when integrating pre-existing databases the best that can be hoped for is that attributes of objects that are present in every underlying database will definitely be present in the integration; attributes that are present in some but not all of the underlying databases may be absent in the integration. In [8] it was observed that integrating user views corresponds to the "least upper bound" of the component schemas in some information ordering on schemas, while in database integration what is required is the "greatest lower bound" of the component schemas in some information ordering on schemas. A good schema-integration method should therefore take account of its intended purpose and include a semantics for the underlying transformations of instances.

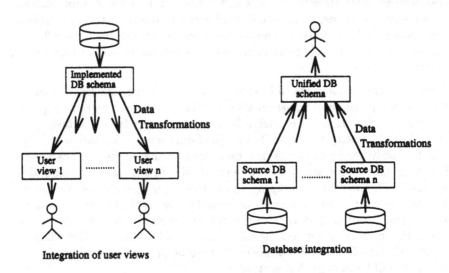

Fig. 4. Data transformations in applications of schema integration

In this section we will concentrate on methodologies intended for database-integration, and look at some representative examples of the various approaches to this problem.

Example 3. Continuing with our example of database integration, we can use the technique of Motro[25] to integrate the *Cities* and *States* database of figure 1 with the restructured *Cities* and *Countries* database of figure 3.[1] The process is illustrated in figure 5. First, a disjoint union of the two schemas is formed (a), and then a series of "macro" transformations are applied to form the desired integrated schema.[2] The transformations applied include introducing generalizations (b), deriving new attributes as compositions or combinations of existing attributes (c), and combining classes (d).

In this particular integration method, the semantics of the transformations are strongly linked to the implementation method. The intention is that the integrated database be implemented as a *view* of the component databases,

---

[1] Recall that this methodology is not expressive enough to express the transformation from the *Cities* and *Countries* database of figure 1 to that of figure 3.

[2] In the model of [25] generalizations are represented by classes with *isa* edges, though for consistency we present this example using variants instead.

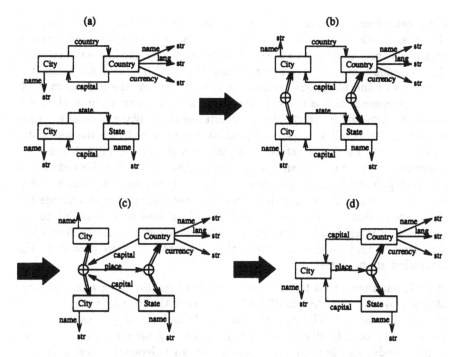

Fig. 5. A schema integration using the methodology of Motro

and that queries against the integrated database be executed by translating them into queries against the component databases and then combining the results. The semantics of the individual transformations are given by their effects on queries. However the lack of any independent characterization of their semantics makes it difficult to reason about or prove properties of the transformations, or to use any alternative implementation of the methodology.

A more expressive and flexible way of specifying transformations is to use some sort of high-level transformation language. An example of such an approach is the system of rewrite rules for nested relational structures proposed by Abiteboul and Hull in [1]. The model of [1] is purely *value-based*: there is no concept of object identity. Consequently it is necessary to use some notion of *keys* in order to represent recursive structures such as those of figure 1, and to reference values in one table or class from values in another (see section 3)

A number of other approaches to schema merging [26,8,32] take component schemas – such as those of figures 1 and 3 – together with constraints relating the elements of the schemas – for example saying that the *City* classes of the two schemas and the *state* and *country* attributes correspond – and apply an algorithm which returns a unified schema. In these approaches the transformations are generally simple embeddings of data and type coercions.

For most schema integration methodologies the outcome is dependent on the order in which schemas are integrated: that is, they are not associative. Intuitively this should not be the case, since the integration of a set of schemas should depend only on the schemas and the relations between them; the semantics of the integration should be independent of the algorithm used. As a consequence of this non-associativity, a schema integration method will specify an ordering in which schema integrations take place, such as a binary tree or ladder, or all at once, and possibly a way of ordering the particular schemas. For example [6] states that schemas should be ranked and then integrated in order of relevance, although no justification for this ordering is given: why shouldn't it be appropriate to integrate the most relevant schemas last, or in the middle, rather than first? Further enforcing such an ordering is not acceptable in a system in which new databases may be added to the system at a later date: if a database is added to an established federation the result should be the same as if the database had been present in the federation at the outset.

In [8] it was shown that the non-associativity of schema integration methodologies is due to new "implicit" nodes or classes that are introduced during the merging process. The variant of the *State* and *Country* classes in example 1 is an example of such an implicit node. By taking account of these implicit nodes and how they are introduced, an independent semantics can be given to the merge of a set of schemas and the relations between them, and an associative schema merging algorithm defined [8].

2.4 Merging Data

Once transformed into a suitable form, data from the component databases must be merged. In a value based model without additional constraints, this is simply a matter of taking the union of the relevant data. However, when more complex data models are used, such as those supporting object identity or inter-database constraints, this task becomes more difficult since it necessary to resolve conflicts and equate objects arising from different databases [34,17].

This problem is not apparent in our running example because the databases of *Cities* and *States* and *Cities* and *Countries* represent disjoint sets of objects. However suppose we were also interested in integrating a third database including international information about Cities and Countries with the schema shown in figure 6. This schema has three classes: *City*, *Country* and *Region*. Each *City* is in a *Region*, and each *Country* has a set (indicated by a "star" node) of *Regions*. The exact meaning of *Region* depends on the country to which it belongs. For example, in the United States, Regions would correspond to States (or Districts), while in Great Britain Regions might be counties. This database might contain data which overlaps with the other two databases. For example there might be objects representing the city

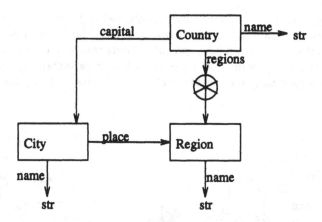

Fig. 6. A schema for a international database of Cities and Countries

Philadelphia in both the International Cities and Countries database and in the Cities and States database, in which case it would be necessary to map both objects to the same object in the integrated database. Equally there might be objects representing the same City or Country in both the International and the European Cities databases, which would need to be combined in the target database.

An important point to note here is that transformations from the various source databases to an integrated database are not independent: it is not sufficient to merely write a transformation from each individual database to the target database. Instead, we must write a transformation that takes a *set* of database instances, one for each source schema, and transforms them into a target instance.

The problem of resolving object identity over multiple databases with constraints is examined in [17,12,37]. [19] gives an analysis of the more general problem of how to compare and equate object identities, and concludes by recommending a system of *external keys* for identifying object identities.

3   Data Models for Database Transformations

Works on transformations between heterogeneous databases are usually based around some sufficiently expressive data-model, or *meta*-data-model, which naturally subsumes the models used for the component databases. Various data models have been used, ranging from relational and extended entity-relationship models to semantic and object-oriented models. The main requirements on such a meta-data-model are that the models of component databases being considered should be embeddable in it in a natural way, and that it be sufficiently simple and expressive to allow data to be represented in multiple ways, so that conflicts between alternative representations of data can be resolved. In [31] the requirements on a model for transforming heterogeneous databases are examined, and the authors conclude that a model supporting complex data-structures (sets, records and variants), object-identity and specialization and generalization relations between object classes is desirable.

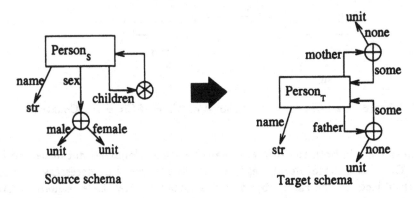

Fig. 7. A transformation between recursive data structures

Some notion of referencing, such as *object-identities* or *keys* is essential in order to represent recursive data-structures such as those of figures 1 and 2. However, in order to transform databases involving such recursive structures, it is also necessary to have a notion of *extents* or *classes* in which all objects of a database must occur. To see this, let us look at another example, namely the transformation between the two schemas shown in figure 7. Suppose we considered the first schema merely to define a recursive type $Person_S$. A value of type $Person_S$ would be a record with attributes *name*, *sex* and *children*, such that the *children* attribute would be a set of records of type $Person_S$. In order to transform a source database consisting of a set of values of type $Person_S$, we would have to recursively apply a restructuring transformation to each set of children of each person in the database. This recursion could be arbitrarily deeply nested, and, in the case of cyclic data, non-terminating.

Fortunately the source schema of figure 7 conveys some important information in addition to describing a recursive type: namely it tells us that our database consists of a *finite extent* or *class* $Person_S$, and that all the people represented in the database are reachable as members of this extent. In particular it tells us that, if X is an object in the class $Person_S$ and $Y \in X.children$ (Y is a child of X), then Y is also in the class $Person_S$. Consequently, when transforming the database, we can iterate our transformation over the elements of the class $Person_S$, and do not have to worry about recursively applying the transformation to the children of a person.

Note that in performing a transformation, it may be necessary to create and reference an object-identity before it has a value associated with it. In this example, if we perform the transformation by iterating over the class *Persons*, it may be necessary to create an object in the target class *Person_T*, with *father* and *mother* attributes both set to *some* person, before the objects corresponding to the parents of the person being transformed have been encountered in the class *Persons*. In this case it is necessary to create and reference object identities for the two parents, even though the corresponding values have not yet been formed. Keys provide a mechanism for such early creation and referencing of object identities.

Keeping these requirements in mind, we now present the data-model for *WOL* so that it can be used for examples throughout the remainder of this paper. It is presented in three stages: First we present schemas, then instances, and then keyed-schemas and instances.

3.1   The *WOL* Data-Model

The data-model for *WOL* supports object-identities, classes and complex data-structures. However we prefer to view specialization and generalization relations as particular examples of constraints which can be expressed separately using a general constraint language. The model is basically the same as that of [2] and is equivalent to the models implemented in various object-oriented databases [4], except for the omission of direct support for inheritance. It is also necessary to have some mechanism to create and reference object-identities. Since object identities themselves are generally considered to be abstract values, which are not directly visible, some value-based handle on them is desirable. We follow [18] in using surrogate keys for this purpose.

We assume a fixed set of *base types*, $\mathcal{B}$, ranged over by $\underline{b}, \underline{b}', \ldots$, and a countable set of *attribute labels*, $\mathcal{A}$, ranged over by $a, a', \ldots$, together with some fixed arbitrary ordering on $\mathcal{A}$. Our definition of types will be relative to a particular finite set of *classes*.

Assume a finite set $\mathcal{C}$ of *classes* ranged over by $C, C', \ldots$. The **types** over $\mathcal{C}$, ranged over by $\tau, \tau', \ldots$, consist of *base types*, $\underline{b}$, *class types* C, where $C \in \mathcal{C}$, *set types* $\{\underline{b}\}$ and $\{C\}$ for each base type $\underline{b}$ and class type C, *record types* $(a_1 : \tau_1, \ldots, a_k : \tau_k)$, where $a_1, \ldots, a_k$ are arranged according to the ordering on $\mathcal{A}$, and *variant types* $(a_1 : \tau_1, \ldots, a_k : \tau_k)$. We write *Types*$^{\mathcal{C}}$ for the set of types over $\mathcal{C}$. The restriction on set types, that they be either sets of base or class type, can be relaxed and replaced by some more general but complicated constraints on set types and on expressions dealing with sets, as in [20]. A restriction of this nature is necessary in order to be able to navigate and identify elements in nested sets. We need to avoid types such as sets of sets $(\{\{\tau\}\})$, particularly in the target database of a transformation, where sets may only be partially instantiated as the transformation progresses, and therefore cannot be compared or equated.

A **schema**, S, consists of a finite set of classes, C, and for each class $C \in C$ a corresponding type $\tau^C \in Types^C$ where τ^C is not a class type.

For each base type $\underline{b}$ we assume a countable set $\mathbf{D}^{\underline{b}}$ corresponding to the *domain* of $\underline{b}$. Suppose we have a schema S with classes C, and for each $C \in C$ we have a disjoint set σ^C of object identities of class C. The set of values associated with a particular type are dependent on the object identities present in an instance. For each type $\tau \in Types^C$ we define a set $[\tau]\sigma^C$ as in figure 8.

$$[\underline{b}]\sigma^C \equiv \mathbf{D}^{\underline{b}}$$
$$[C]\sigma^C \equiv \sigma^C$$
$$[\{\underline{b}\}]\sigma^C \equiv \mathcal{P}_{fin}(\mathbf{D}^{\underline{b}})$$
$$[\{C\}]\sigma^C \equiv \mathcal{P}_{fin}(\sigma^C)$$
$$[(a_1 : \tau_1 \ldots, a_k : \tau_k)]\sigma^C \equiv [\tau_1]\sigma^C \times \ldots \times [\tau_k]\sigma^C$$
$$[\langle a_1 : \tau_1, \ldots, a_k : \tau_k \rangle]\sigma^C \equiv (\{a_1\} \times [\tau_1]\sigma^C) \cup \ldots \cup (\{a_k\} \times [\tau_k]\sigma^C)$$

Fig. 8. The semantic operator on types

An **instance**, $\mathcal{I}$, of a database schema S consists of a family of sets of object identities, σ^C, and for each class $C \in C$, a mapping $\mathcal{V}^C : \sigma^C \to [\tau^C]\sigma^C$. We write *Inst*($S$) for the set of instances of schema S.

Example 4. The first schema illustrated in example 1 has two classes representing *Cities* and *States*, with each city having a *name* and a *state*, and each state having a *name* and a *capital city*. The set of classes for the schema is therefore $C_A \equiv \{City_A, State_A\}$ and the associated types are

$$\tau_A^{City_A} \equiv (name : str, state : State_A)$$
$$\tau_A^{State_A} \equiv (name : str, capital : City_A)$$

The second schema has classes $C_E \equiv \{City_E, Country_E\}$ and associated types

$$\tau_E^{City_E} \equiv (name : str, is\_capital : Bool, country : Country_E)$$
$$\tau_E^{Country_E} \equiv (name : str, language : str, currency : str)$$

An instance of the second schema would consist of two sets of object identities, such as

$$\sigma^{City_E} \equiv \{London, Manchester, Paris, Berlin, Bonn\}$$
$$\sigma^{Country_E} \equiv \{UK, FR, GM\}$$

and functions $\mathcal{V}^{City}$ on σ^{City} and $\mathcal{V}^{State}$ on σ^{State}, such as

$$\mathcal{V}^{City_E}(London) \equiv (name \mapsto \text{``London''}, country \mapsto UK, is\_capital \mapsto tt)$$

$$\mathcal{V}^{City_E}(Manchester) \equiv (name \mapsto \text{``Manchester''}, country \mapsto UK,$$
$$is\_capital \mapsto ff)$$

$$\mathcal{V}^{City_E}(Paris) \equiv (name \mapsto \text{``Paris''}, country \mapsto FR, is\_capital \mapsto tt)$$

$$\mathcal{V}^{Country_E}(UK) \equiv (name \mapsto \text{``United Kingdom''}, language \mapsto \text{``English''},$$
$$currency \mapsto \text{``sterling''})$$

$$\mathcal{V}^{Country_E}(FR) \equiv (name \mapsto \text{``France''}, language \mapsto \text{``French''},$$
$$currency \mapsto \text{``franc''})$$

and so on.

A **key specification**, $\mathcal{K}$, for a schema $\mathcal{S}$ with classes $\mathcal{C}$ consists of a type κ^C for each $C \in \mathcal{C}$, where κ^C contains no class types, and for any instance $\mathcal{I} \in Inst(\mathcal{S})$, a family of functions $\mathcal{K}_{\mathcal{I}}^C : \sigma^C \to [\kappa^C]$ for each $C \in \mathcal{C}$.[3]

An instance $\mathcal{I}$ of schema $\mathcal{S}$ is said to *satisfy* a key specification $\mathcal{K}$ on $\mathcal{S}$ iff for each class $C \in \mathcal{C}$ and any $o, o' \in \sigma^C$, if $\mathcal{K}_{\mathcal{I}}^C(o) = \mathcal{K}_{\mathcal{I}}^C(o')$ then $o = o'$.

A **keyed schema** consists of a schema $\mathcal{S}$, and a key specification $\mathcal{K}$ on $\mathcal{S}$. An instance of a keyed schema $(\mathcal{S}, \mathcal{K})$ is an instance $\mathcal{I}$ of $\mathcal{S}$ such that $\mathcal{I}$ satisfies $\mathcal{K}$. We write $Inst(\mathcal{S}, \mathcal{K})$ for the instances of $(\mathcal{S}, \mathcal{K})$.

In general we will use $\mathcal{S}, \mathcal{T}, \ldots$ to range over both keyed and un-keyed schemas, and will specify either a keyed or un-keyed schema when we are interested exclusively in one or the other.

Example 5. For the European Cities and Countries schema defined in example 4 we might expect each *Country* to be uniquely determined by its name, and each *City* to be uniquely determined by its name and the name of its country (two Countries might both contain Cities with the same name). The key specification for this schema might have types

$$\kappa^{Country_E} \equiv str$$
$$\kappa^{City_E} \equiv (name : str, country\_name : str)$$

and functions defined by

$$\mathcal{K}_{\mathcal{I}}^{Country_E} \equiv \lambda x \cdot x.name$$
$$\mathcal{K}_{\mathcal{I}}^{City_E} \equiv \lambda x \cdot (name = x.name, country\_name = x.name.name)$$

where the notation $x.a$ means if $x \in \sigma^C$ then take the value $\mathcal{V}^C(x)$, which must be of record type, and project out the attribute a.

---

[3] If τ is a type which does not involve any class types, then the value of $[\tau]\sigma^C$ is independent of the choice of object identities, σ^C. In this case we write $[\tau]$ for the set $[\tau]\sigma^C$ for an arbitrary choice of σ^C.

3.2 Well-defined Key-Specifications

As we remarked earlier, object-identities are generally taken to be abstract entities that are not directly visible in a database. In practice they are frequently generated as they are needed by a DBMS. Consequently we would like the meaning of a database instance to be independent of the choice of object-identities in the instance, or the order in which they were generated, and to depend only on the data represented by the instance. In particular, if two instances differ only in their choice of object identities, we would like to consider them to be the same, and to ensure that any queries or operations on those two instances give equivalent results. We define the notion of *isomorphism* to represent when two instances differ only in their choice of object-identities.

Given two instances of an unkeyed schema S, say $\mathcal{I}$ and $\mathcal{I}'$, with families of object identities σ^C and σ'^C respectively, and a family of functions $f^C : \sigma^C \rightarrow \sigma'^C$, for $C \in \mathcal{C}$, we can extend f^C to functions on general types $f^\tau : [\tau]\sigma^C \rightarrow [\tau]\sigma'^C$, so that $f^{\underline{b}}$ is the identity on $\mathbf{D}^{\underline{b}}$ for each base type $\underline{b}$, and f^τ is defined in the obvious manner for each higher type τ.

An *isomorphism* from instance $\mathcal{I}$ to instance $\mathcal{I}'$, consists of a family of *bijective* functions $f^C : \sigma^C \rightarrow \sigma'^C$ such that for each class $C \in \mathcal{C}$ and each $o \in \sigma^C$, $\mathcal{V}'^C(f^C(o)) = f^{\tau^C}(\mathcal{V}^C(o))$. We say instances $\mathcal{I}$ and $\mathcal{I}'$ are **isomorphic** and write $\mathcal{I} \cong \mathcal{I}'$ iff there is an isomorphism f^C from $\mathcal{I}$ to $\mathcal{I}'$.

A key specification $\mathcal{K}$ on schema S is said to be **well-defined** if for any two instances $\mathcal{I}$ and $\mathcal{I}'$ of S and isomorphism f^C from $\mathcal{I}$ to $\mathcal{I}'$, if $\mathcal{I}$ satisfies $\mathcal{K}$ then so does $\mathcal{I}'$, and further, for any class $C \in \mathcal{C}$ and $o \in \sigma^C$, $\mathcal{K}_{\mathcal{I}}^C(o) = \mathcal{K}_{\mathcal{I}'}^C(f^C(o))$. Intuitively a key-specification is well-defined if it is not dependent on the particular choice of object identifiers in an instance.

For the remainder we will assume that any key specifications are well-defined.

4 Information Dominance in Transformations

One of the important questions of database systems is that of *data-relativism*, or when one schema or data-structure can represent the same data as another. From the perspective of database transformations this can be thought of as asking when there is a transformation from instances of one schema to another such that all the information in the source database is preserved by the transformation. Such a transformation would be said to be *information preserving*.

There are a number of situations when dealing with database transformations where we might want to ensure that a transformation is information preserving. For example when performing a schema evolution, we might want to ensure that none the information stored in the initial database is lost in the evolved database, or when integrating databases, we might wish to ensure that all the information stored in one of the component databases is reflected in the integrated database.

Example 6. For the schema integration described in example 1 the transformation from the database of US Cities and States to the schema of figure 2 is information preserving, in that all the information stored in an instance of the first schema will be reflected in the transformed instance. Equally the transformation from the restructured European Cities and Countries schema of figure 3 to the schema of figure 2 is information preserving.

However the transformation from the first European Cities and Countries schema in figure 1 to the restructured schema of figure 3, and hence to the schema of figure 2, is not information preserving. This is because the transformation to the restructured schema assumes that, for each *Country* in the original schema, there is exactly one *City* of that *Country* with its *is_capital* attribute set to *True*. However the original schema allows a country to have multiple capitals: there may be many *Cities* with their *is_capital* attribute set to *True*, in which case the transformation would not be defined. If we were able to associate an additional constraint with European Cities and Countries schema of figure 1 stating that each there can be at most one capital City in each Country, then the transformation would be information preserving, and we could say that the schema of figure 2 *dominates* both of the schemas of figure 1.

In section 4.1 we will briefly describe the notions of *information dominance* defined in [15], and see how they can be related to transformations using the data model of section 3. In section 4.2 we consider the recent work of Miller in [23,24] which studies various applications of database transformations, and the need for transformations to be information preserving in these situations.

4.1 Hull's hierarchy of information dominance measures

In [15] Hull defined four progressively more restrictive notions of information dominance between schemas, each determined by some reversible transformation between the schemas subject to various restrictions. Although [15] dealt only with simply keyed flat-relational schemas, the definitions and some of the results can be easily generalized to the more general model used here.

Given two schemas, S and T, a transformation from S to T is a partial map σ from instances of S to instances of T, $\sigma : Inst(S) \rightarrow Inst(T)$. Intuitively the transformation is information preserving iff there is a second transformation from T back to S, say ρ such that ρ recovers the instance of S. That is, for any $\mathcal{I} \in Inst(S)$, $\mathcal{I} \cong (\rho \circ \sigma)(\mathcal{I})$. (Note that we are concerned here with transformations which preserve instances up to isomorphism, since the particular choice of object identities is immaterial.) In such a situation we say that T **dominates** S **via** (σ, ρ).

A problem with this notion is that the transformations σ and ρ may be arbitrary mathematical functions, and will not necessarily provide a semantically meaningful interpretation of the instances of S in terms of the instances of T. In [15] a series of progressively more restrictive notions of **information dominance** are defined by imposing various restrictions on the transformations σ and ρ that may be used to implement a dominance relation. This series ends with the notion of *calculus dominance*: T is said to **dominate** S **calculously** iff there are expressions in some fixed calculus representing transformations σ and ρ such that T dominates S via (σ, ρ).

An important conclusion of [15], however, is that none of these criteria capture an adequate notion of semantic dominance, that is, whether there is a semantically meaningful interpretation of instances of one schema as instances of another. Consequently the various concepts of information dominance can be used in order to test whether semantic dominance between schemas is plausible, or to verify that a proposed transformation is information preserving, but the task of finding a semantically meaningful transformation still requires a knowledge and understanding of the databases involved.

Another significant problem with this analysis is that it assumes that all possible instances of a source schema should be reflected by distinct corresponding instances of a target schema. However, in practice only a small number of instances of a source schema may actually correspond to real world data sets. That is, there may be implicit constraints on the source database which are not included in the source schema, either because they are not expressible in the data-model being used or simply because they were forgotten or not anticipated at the time of initial schema design. An alternative approach, pursued in [11], is to attempt to define information preserving transformations and valid schemas with respect to some underlying *"universe of discourse"*. However such characterizations are impossible or impractical to represent and verify in practice.

4.2 Information Capacity and Constraints

In [23,24] Miller et al. analyse the information requirements that need to be imposed on transformations in various applications. The restrictions on transformations that they consider are somewhat simpler than those of [15] in that they examine only whether transformations are injective (one-to-one) or surjective (onto) mappings on the underlying sets of instances. For example they claim that if a transformation is to be used to view and query an entire source database then it must be a total injective function, while if a database is to be updated via a view then the transformation to the view must also be surjective. Having derived necessary conditions for various applications of transformations, they then go on to evaluate existing work on database integration and translations in the light of these conditions.

An important observation in [23] is that database transformations can fail to be information capacity preserving, not because there is anything wrong with the definition of the transformations themselves, but because certain constraints which hold on the source database are not expressed in the source database schema. However the full significance of this observation is not properly appreciated: in fact it is frequently the case that the constraints that must be taken into account in order to validate a transformation have not merely been omitted from the source schema, but are not expressible in any standard constraint language.

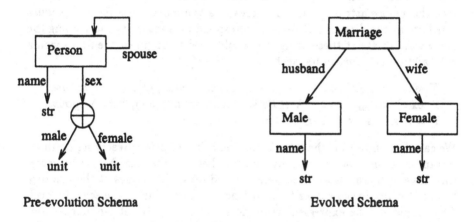

Pre-evolution Schema   Evolved Schema

Fig. 9. An example schema evolution

Example 7. Consider the schema evolution illustrated in figure 9. The first schema has only one class, *Person*, with attributes representing a person's *name*, *sex* (a variant of *male* and *female*) and *spouse*. In our second (evolved) schema the *Person* class has been split into two distinct classes, *Male* and *Female*, perhaps because we wished to start storing some different information for men and women. Further the *spouse* attribute is replaced by a new class, *Marriage*, perhaps because we wished to start recording additional information such as dates of marriages, or allow un-married people to be represented in the database.

It seems clear that there is a meaningful transformation from instances of the first database to instances of the second. The transformation can be described by the following *WOL* program:

$X \in Male, X.name = N \Longleftarrow Y \in Person, Y.name = N, Y.sex = ins_{male}();$
$X \in Female, X.name = N$
$\qquad \Longleftarrow Y \in Person, Y.name = N, Y.sex = ins_{female}();$
$M \in Marriage, M.husband = X, M.wife = Y$
$\qquad \Longleftarrow X \in Male, Y \in Female, Z \in Person, W \in Person,$
$\qquad\qquad X.name = Z.name, Y.name = W.name, W = Z.spouse;$

where "$Y.sex = ins_{male}()$" indicates that the sex is a male variant; details of *WOL* will be given in the next section. Although this transformation intuitively appears to preserve the information of the first database, in practice it is not information preserving. The reason is that there are instances of the *spouse* attribute that are allowed by the first schema that will not be reflected by the second schema. In particular the first schema does not require that the *spouse* attribute of a man goes to a woman, or that for each *spouse* attribute in one direction there is a corresponding *spouse* attribute going the other way. To assert these things we would need to augment the first schema with additional constraints, such as:

$X.sex = ins_{male}() \Longleftarrow Y \in Person, Y.sex = ins_{female}(), X = Y.spouse;$
$Y.sex = ins_{female}() \Longleftarrow X \in Person, X.sex = ins_{male}(), Y = X.spouse;$
$Y = X.spouse \Longleftarrow Y \in Person, X = Y.spouse;$

We can then show that the transformation is information preserving on those instances of the first schema that satisfy these constraints. Notice however, that these constraints are very general, and deal with values at the instance level of the database, rather than just being expressible at the schema level. They could not be expressed with the standard constraint languages associated with most data-models (functional dependencies, inclusion dependencies, cardinality constraints and so on).

This highlights one of the basic problems with information capacity analysis of transformations: Such an analysis assumes that schemas give a complete description of the set of possible instances of a database. In practice schemas are seldom complete, either because certain constraints were forgotten or were not known at the time of schema design, or because the data-model being used simply isn't sufficiently expressive. When dealing with schema evolutions, where information capacity preserving transformations are normally required, it is frequently the case that the transformation implementing a schema evolution appears to discard information, while in fact this is because the new schema is a better fit for the data, expressing and taking advantage of various constraints that have become apparent since the initial schema design.

Further, when dealing with transformations involving multiple source databases, even if the transformations from individual source databases to a target database are information preserving, it is unlikely that the transformations will be jointly information preserving. This is in part due to the fact that the source databases may represent overlapping information, and inter-database constraints are necessary to ensure that the individual databases do not contain conflicting information. It may also be due to the fact that information describing the source of a particular item of data may be lost.

An additional limitation of the information capacity analysis of transformations is that it is very much an all-or-nothing property, and does not help us to establish other less restrictive correctness criteria on transformations. When dealing with database integration, we might only be interested in a small part of the information stored in one of the source databases, but wish to ensure that the information in this subpart of the database is preserved by the transformation. For example, we might be integrating our database of US cities and states with a database of European cities or towns and countries, and only be interested in those cities or towns with a population greater than a hundred thousand. However we would still like to ensure that our transformation does not lose any information about European cities and towns with population greater than one hundred thousand.

It therefore seems that a more general and problem specific correctness criteria for transformations is needed, such as relative information capacity. In addition, a formalism in which transformations and constraints can be jointly be expressed is needed in which to test these more general correctness criteria. As a first step in this direction we present the the language *WOL*, which provides a uniform framework for specifying transformations as well as constraints.

5 The *WOL* Language

WOL is a declarative language for specifying and implementing database transformations and constraints. It is based on the data-model of section 3, and can therefore deal with databases involving object-identity and recursive data-structures as well as complex and arbitrarily nested data-structures. Due to space limitations, we will omit or simplify certain details in the definitions and semantics of *WOL*. Full details can be found in [20].

The previous sections have shown that there are important interactions between transformations and the constraints imposed on databases: constraints can play a part in determining a transformation, and also transformations can imply constraints on their source and target databases. Although most data-models support some specific kinds of constraints, in general it is a rather ad hoc collection, included because of their utility in the particular examples that the designer of the system had in mind rather than on any sound theoretical basis. For example, relational databases will often support keys and sometimes functional and inclusion dependencies [36], while semantic models might incorporate various kinds of cardinality constraints and inheritance [13,16]. The constraints that occur when dealing with transformations often fall outside such predetermined classes; further it is difficult to anticipate the kinds of constraints that will arise. We therefore propose augmenting a simple data-model with a general formalism for expressing constraints, such that the formalism makes it easy to reason about the interaction between transformations and constraints.

Example 8. For example, in our Cities and States database of example 4, we would want to impose a constraint that the capital City of a State is in the State of which it is the capital. We can express this as

$$X.state = Y \Longleftarrow Y \in State_A, X = Y.capital$$

This can be read as "if Y is in class *State* and X is the *capital* of Y, then Y is the *state* of X". Suppose also that our States and Cities each had an attribute *population* and we wanted to impose a constraint that the population of a City was less than the population of the State in which it resides. We could express this as

$$X.population < Y.population \Longleftarrow X \in City_A, Y = X.state;$$

Such a constraint cannot be expressed in the constraint languages associated with most data models.

We can also use constraints to express how the keys of a schema are derived:

$$X = Mk^{City_A}(name = N, state\_name = S)$$
$$\Longleftarrow X \in City_A, N = X.name, S = X.state.name.$$

This constraint says that the key of an object of class *City* is a tuple built out of the *name* of the city, and the *name* of its *state*. Such constraints are important in allowing us to identify objects in transformations.

WOL is based on Horn clause logic expressions, using a small number of simple predicates and primitive constructors. However it is sufficient to express a large family of constraints including those commonly found in established data-models. In fact the only kinds of constraints which occur in established data-models but can not easily be expressed in *WOL* are finite cardinality constraints: these are constraints that might state, for example, that a certain set-valued attribute has cardinality between 2 and 3. Though it would be possible to extend *WOL* with operators to express such constraints, we have omitted them since they are of little theoretical interest and it is not clear that they are of any great practical significance.

The language *WOL* can also be used to express constraints that span multiple databases, and, in particular, can be used to specify transformations. A *transformation specification* may viewed as a collection of constraints stating how data in a target database arises from data stored in a number of source databases. In general however there may be any number of target database instances satisfying a particular set of constraints for a particular collection of source instances. It is therefore necessary to restrict our attention to *complete* transformation specifications, such that for any collection of source database instances if there is a target instance satisfying the transformation specification then there is a *unique smallest* such target instance.

Possibly the closest existing work to *WOL* are the structural manipulations of Abiteboul and Hull [1] described in section 2. The rewrite rules in [1] have a similar feel to the Horn clauses of *WOL* but are based on pattern matching against complex data-structures, allowing for arbitrarily nested set, record and variant type constructors. *WOL* gains some expressivity over the language of [1] by the inclusion of more general and varied predicates (such as not-equal and not-in), though we have not included tests for cardinality of sets in *WOL*. The main contributions of *WOL* however lie in its ability to deal with object-identity and hence recursive data-structures, and in the uniform treatment of transformation rules and constraints.

The language of [1] allows nested rewrite rules which can generate more general types of nested sets, whereas in *WOL* we require that any set occuring in an instance is identifiable by some means external to the elements of the set itself. Recall that in the data-model presented here, a set occurs either as a class or as part of the value associated with some object identity. Comparing the expressive power of the two formalisms is difficult because of the difference between the underlying models, and because the expressive power of each language depends on the predicates incorporated in the language. However if the rewrite rules of [1] are extended to deal with the data-model presented here, and both languages are adjusted to support equivalent predicates (for example adding inequality and not-in tests to [1] and cardinality tests to *WOL*) then *WOL* can be shown to be at least as expressive as the rules of [1]. In particular, given the restrictions on types considered here, nested rewrite rules do not give any increase in expressive power.

5.1 Syntax and semantics of *WOL*

We will assume some fixed, keyed schema, (S, K) with classes C, and define a version of *WOL* relative to this schema. We will write WOL^{SK} when we wish to be explicit that the language is parameterized on a particular schema.

Terms and Atoms For each base type $\underline{b}$ we will assume a countable set of constant symbols ranged over by $c^{\underline{b}}, \ldots$, and for each type τ we will assume a countably infinite set of variables ranged over by $X^{\tau}, Y^{\tau}, \ldots$. The **terms**

of WOL^{SK}, ranged over by $P, Q, \ldots$, are given by the abstract syntax:

$$
\begin{array}{lll}
P ::= & C & \text{— class} \\
| & c^{\underline{b}} & \text{— constant symbol} \\
| & X & \text{— variable} \\
| & \pi_a P & \text{— record projection} \\
| & ins_a P & \text{— variant insertion} \\
| & !P & \text{— dereferencing} \\
| & Mk^C P & \text{— object identity referencing}
\end{array}
$$

A term C represents the set of all object identities of class C. A term $\pi_a P$ represents the a component of the term P, where P should be a term of record type with a as one of its attributes. $ins_a P$ represents a term of variant type built out of the term P and the choice a. $!P$ represents the value associated with the term P, where P is a term representing an object identity. The term $Mk^C P$ represents the object identity of class C with key P.

We define the typing relation $\vdash$: on terms and types to be the smallest relation satisfying the rules:

$$
\overline{\vdash C : \{C\}}
\qquad\qquad
\overline{\vdash c^{\underline{b}} : \underline{b}}
$$

$$
\overline{\vdash X^\tau : \tau}
\qquad\qquad
\frac{\vdash P : (a_1 : \tau_1, \ldots, a_k : \tau_k)}{\vdash \pi_{a_i} P : \tau_i}
$$

$$
\frac{\vdash P : \tau_i}{\vdash ins_{a_i} P : \langle\!\langle a_1 : \tau_1, \ldots, a_k : \tau_k \rangle\!\rangle}
\qquad\qquad
\frac{\vdash P : C}{\vdash !P : \tau^C}
$$

$$
\frac{\vdash P : \kappa^C}{\vdash Mk^C P : C}
$$

A term P is said to be **well-typed** iff there is a type τ such that $\vdash P : \tau$.

Atomic formulae or *atoms* are the basic building blocks of formulae in our language. An atom represents one simple statement about some values.

The **atoms** of WOL^{SF}, ranged over by $\phi, \psi, \ldots$, are defined by the abstract syntax:

$$
\begin{array}{ll}
\phi ::= & P \doteq Q \\
| & P \dotne Q \\
| & P \doteq_\in Q \\
| & P \dotnotin Q \\
| & \textbf{False}
\end{array}
$$

The atoms $P\doteq Q$, $P\dotne Q$, $P\dot\in Q$ and $P\dot\notin Q$ represent the obvious comparisons between terms. **False** is an atom which is never satisfied, and is used to represent inconsistent database states.

An atom ϕ is said to be **well-typed** iff

1. $\phi \equiv P \dot{=} Q$ or $\phi \equiv P \dot{\neq} Q$ and $\Gamma \vdash P : \tau$, $\Gamma \vdash Q : \tau$ for some τ; or
2. $\phi \equiv P \dot{\in} Q$ or $\phi \equiv P \dot{\notin} Q$ and $\Gamma \vdash P : \tau$, $\Gamma \vdash Q : \{\tau\}$ for some τ; or
3. $\phi \equiv$ **False**.

Intuitively an atom is well-typed iff that atom *makes sense* with respect to the types of the terms occuring in the atom. For example, for an atom $P \dot{=} Q$, it wouldn't make sense to reason about the terms P and Q being equal unless they were potentially of the same type.

Range restriction The concept of *range-restriction* is used to ensure that every term in a collection of atoms is bound to some constant or value occurring in a database instance. This is necessary to ensure that the truth of a statement of our logic depends only on the instance and not the underlying domains of the various types.

Suppose Φ is a set of atoms, and P is an *occurrence* of a term in Φ. Then P is said to be **range-restricted** in Φ iff one of the following holds:

1. $P \equiv C$ where $C \in \mathcal{C}$ is a class;
2. $P \equiv c^{\flat}$ where $c^{\flat}$ is a constant symbol;
3. $P \equiv \pi_a Q$ where Q is a range restricted occurrence of a term in Φ;
4. P occurs in a term $Q \equiv ins_a P$, where Q is a range-restricted occurrence of a term in Φ;
5. $P \equiv !Q$ where Q is a range-restricted occurrence of a term in Φ;
6. P occurs in an atom $P \dot{=} Q$ or $Q \dot{=} P$ or $P \dot{\in} Q$ in Φ, where Q is a range-restricted occurrence of a term in Φ;
7. $P \equiv X$, a variable, and there is a range-restricted occurrence of X in Φ.

Clauses A **clause** consists of two finite sets of atoms: the **head** and the **body** of the clause. Suppose $\Phi = \{\phi_1, \ldots, \phi_k\}$ and $\Psi = \{\psi_1, \ldots, \psi_l\}$. We write

$$\psi_1, \ldots, \psi_l \Longleftarrow \phi_1, \ldots, \phi_k$$

or

$$\Psi \Longleftarrow \Phi$$

for the clause with head Ψ and body Φ. Intuitively the meaning of a clause is that if the conjunction of the atoms in the body holds then the conjunction of the atoms in the head also holds.

For example, the clause

$$Y.state \dot{=} X \Longleftarrow X \dot{\in} State, Y \dot{=} X.capital$$

means that, for every object identity X in the class *State*, if Y is the capital of X then X is the state of Y.

A set of atoms Φ is said to be **well-formed** iff each atom in Φ is well-typed and every term occurrence in Φ is range restricted in Φ.

A clause $\Psi \Longleftarrow \Phi$ is said to be **well-formed** iff Φ is well-formed and $\Phi \cup \Psi$ is well-formed.

Intuitively a clause is well-formed iff it makes sense, in that all the terms in the clause range over values in a database instance, and all the types of terms are compatible with the various predicates that are applied to them. All the clauses we deal with in the remainder of this paper will be well-formed.

Semantics of *WOL* clauses An *environment* binds values to the variables occuring in a *WOL* term, atom or clause. Suppose $\mathcal{I}$ is an instance, with object-identifiers σ^C. An $\mathcal{I}$-**environment**, ρ, is a partial function with finite domain on the set of variables such that $\rho(X^\tau) \in [\tau]\sigma^C$ for each variable $X^\tau \in dom(\rho)$.

If $\mathcal{I}$ is an instance, ρ an $\mathcal{I}$-environment and P a term of type τ with variables taken from $dom(\rho)$, then we define a value $[P]\mathcal{I}\rho \in [\tau]\sigma^C$ by structural induction on P. We present some sample steps in the definition below. For full details see [20].

$$[X]\mathcal{I}\rho \equiv \begin{cases} \rho(X) & \text{if } X \in dom(\rho) \\ \text{undefined otherwise} \end{cases}$$

$$[ins^a P]\mathcal{I}\rho \equiv (a, [P]\mathcal{I}\rho)$$

$$[!P]\mathcal{I}\rho \equiv \begin{cases} \mathcal{V}^C([P]\mathcal{I}\rho) \text{ if } [P]\mathcal{I}\rho \in \sigma^C \text{ for some } C \in \mathcal{C} \\ \text{undefined} \quad \text{otherwise} \end{cases}$$

$$[Mk^C(P)]\mathcal{I}\rho \equiv \begin{cases} o & \text{if } [P]\mathcal{I}\rho \in [\kappa^C]\mathcal{I} \text{ and } o \in \sigma^C \\ & \text{such that } \mathcal{K}^C(o) = [P]\mathcal{I}\rho \\ \text{undefined otherwise} \end{cases}$$

For any well-typed atom ϕ with variables taken from $dom(\rho)$ we define a boolean value $[\phi]\rho$. For example $[P\dot{=}Q]\rho = \mathbf{T}$ iff $[P]\rho = [Q]\rho$; $[P\dot{\in}Q]\rho = \mathbf{T}$ iff $[P]\rho \in [Q]\rho$; $[\mathsf{False}]\rho = \mathbf{F}$ and so on.

The variables in the body of a clause are taken to be universally quantified, while any variables which occur only in the head of a clause are existentially quantified. Consequently a clause is said to be satisfied by an instance iff for any binding of the variables in the body of the clause which makes all the atoms in the body true, there is an instantiation of any remaining variables which makes all the atoms in the head true too.

Given a set of atoms Φ, we write $Var(\Phi)$ for the set of variables occuring in Φ.

Suppose $\Psi \Longleftarrow \Phi$ is a well-formed clause. An instance $\mathcal{I}$ is said to **satisfy** $\Psi \Longleftarrow \Phi$ iff for any $\mathcal{I}$-environment ρ such that $dom(\rho) = Var(\Phi)$ and $[\phi]\rho = \mathbf{T}$ for each $\phi \in \Phi$, there is an extension ρ' of ρ (that is, $\rho'(X) = \rho(X)$ for each $X \in dom(\rho)$), such that $\rho'(\psi) = \mathbf{T}$ for each $\psi \in \Psi$.

Example 9. For the instance of the European Cities and States database described in example 4, suppose the environment ρ is given by:

$$\rho \equiv (X \mapsto UK, Y \mapsto London)$$

Then

$$[X \dot{\in} Country_E]\rho = \mathbf{T}$$
$$[Y \dot{\in} City_E]\rho = \mathbf{T}$$
$$[Y.country \dot{=} X]\rho = \mathbf{T}$$
$$[Y.is\_capital \dot{=} tt]\rho = \mathbf{T}$$

Further we can check that, for any other binding of X to an element of $\sigma^{Country_E}$ which makes the first atom true, there is a binding of Y to an element of σ^{City_E} which makes the remaining three atoms true. Hence the instance satisfies the clause

$$Y \dot{\in} City_E, \; Y.country \dot{=} X, \; Y.is\_capital \dot{=} tt \; \Longleftarrow \; X \dot{\in} Country_E$$

5.2 Expressing database transformations using *WOL*

So far we have defined the language *WOL* to deal with a single database schema and instance. However in order to express transformations we need to be able to write *WOL* clauses concerning multiple databases. In particular we will need to write clauses involving one or more *source* databases and a distinguished *target* database.

Partitioning schemas and instances If $\mathcal{S}_1, \ldots, \mathcal{S}_n$ are schemas with disjoint sets of classes then we can define $\mathcal{S} \equiv \mathcal{S}_1 \cup \ldots \cup \mathcal{S}_n$ by taking the classes of $\mathcal{S}$ to be the union of the classes of $\mathcal{S}_1, \ldots, \mathcal{S}_n$, and the type corresponding to each class in $\mathcal{S}$ to be the same as the type corresponding to that class in the relevant $\mathcal{S}_i$. $\mathcal{S}_1, \ldots, \mathcal{S}_n$ are said to be a **partition** of $\mathcal{S}$.

Given instances $\mathcal{I}_1, \ldots, \mathcal{I}_n$ of disjoint schemas $\mathcal{S}_1, \ldots, \mathcal{S}_n$, we can form an instance $\mathcal{I} \equiv \mathcal{I}_1 \cup \ldots \cup \mathcal{I}_n$ of $\mathcal{S}_1 \cup \ldots \cup \mathcal{S}_n$ by taking the unions of the components of $\mathcal{I}_1, \ldots, \mathcal{I}_n$. Further given an instance $\mathcal{I}$ of $\mathcal{S}$ and a partition $\mathcal{S}_1, \ldots, \mathcal{S}_n$ of $\mathcal{S}$, we can find unique instances $\mathcal{I}/\mathcal{S}_1, \ldots, \mathcal{I}/\mathcal{S}_n$ of $\mathcal{S}_1, \ldots, \mathcal{S}_n$ respectively, such that $\mathcal{I} = \mathcal{I}/\mathcal{S}_1 \cup \ldots \cup \mathcal{I}/\mathcal{S}_n$.

Given disjoint keyed-schemas, $(\mathcal{S}_1, \mathcal{K}_1), \ldots, (\mathcal{S}_n, \mathcal{K}_n)$, we can form a keyed schema $(\mathcal{S}, \mathcal{K}) \equiv (\mathcal{S}_1, \mathcal{K}_1) \cup \ldots \cup (\mathcal{S}_n, \mathcal{K}_n)$ in a similar manner (details may be found in [20]).

Transformation rules and constraints In looking at transformations we will concentrate on the case where we have a schema $(\mathcal{S}, \mathcal{K})$ with partition $(\mathcal{S}_{Src}, \mathcal{K}_{Src}), (\mathcal{S}_{Tgt}, \mathcal{K}_{Tgt})$, and use the language WOL^{SK} in order to define transformations from $(\mathcal{S}_{Src}, \mathcal{K}_{Src})$ to $(\mathcal{S}_{Tgt}, \mathcal{K}_{Tgt})$.

A term occuring in a set of atoms Φ is classified as a **source term** or a **target term** depending on whether it refers to a value in the source database or the target database. Note that it is possible for a term to be classified as both a source term and a target term.

For example, if $Country_E$ is a class in our source schema, $Country_T$ is a class in our target schema, and Φ is the set of atoms

$$\Phi \equiv \{X \dot{\in} Country_E,\ X.name \dot{=} N,\ Y \dot{\in} Country_T,\ Y.name \dot{=} N\}$$

then the terms X and $X.name$ are source terms, the terms Y and $Y.name$ are target terms, and the term N is both a source and a target term.

There are three kinds of clauses that are relevant in determining transformations:

target constraints — containing no source terms;
source constraints — containing no target terms; and
transformation clauses — clauses of the form $\Psi \Longleftarrow \Phi$ where each term occuring in Ψ is a target term, and $\Psi \cup \Phi$ contains no negative atoms involving target terms ($P \dot{\not\in} Q$ or $P \dot{\neq} Q$), and no comparisons of set-valued target terms.

So a transformation clause is one which does not imply any constraints on the source database, and which only implies the existence of certain objects in the target database.

The restrictions against "negative" target atoms or comparisons of target sets are necessary to allow us to apply transformation clauses while the target database is only partially instantiated, and to ensure that any tests which become true at some point during the implementation of a transformation will remain true even if additional elements are added to the target database. For example, suppose we allowed the following transformation clause

$$1 \in X.a \Longleftarrow X \in C,\ Y \in C,\ X.a = Y.a$$

where C is a class with corresponding type $\tau^C \equiv (a : \{int\})$. Then suppose, at some point during the transformation, we were to find an instantiation of X and Y to two objects, say o_1 and o_2, of class C, such that the body of the clause was true at that point in the transformation. Then the clause would cause the constant 1 to be added to the set $X.a$, thus potentially making the body of the clause no longer true.

Transformation programs A transformation program, **Tr** from a schema $(\mathcal{S}_{Src}, \mathcal{K}_{Src})$ to a schema $(\mathcal{S}_{Tgt}, \mathcal{K}_{Tgt})$ consists of a set of source and target constraints and transformation clauses in the language WOL^{SK}, where $(\mathcal{S}, \mathcal{K}) = (\mathcal{S}_{Src}, \mathcal{K}_{Src}) \cup (\mathcal{S}_{Tgt}, \mathcal{K}_{Tgt})$.

Example 10. Let us consider the transformation from the schema of European Cities and Countries from example 4 to the schema illustrated in figure 2. We will assume that the key for the class $Country_T$ is its *name* attribute, and the key for the class $City_T$ is a record of type (*name* : *str*, *place_name* : *str*), where the first attribute is the name of a City, and the second is the name of the Country or State pointed to by its *place* attribute.

Then we have the following source constraints:

$$Y \dot{\in} City_E, \ Y.country \dot{=} X, \ Y.is\_capital \dot{=} tt \ \Longleftarrow \ X \dot{\in} Country_E$$

$$X \dot{=} Y \ \Longleftarrow \ X \dot{\in} City_E, \ Y \dot{\in} City_E, \ X.country \dot{=} Y.country,$$
$$X.is\_capital \dot{=} tt, \ .is\_capital \dot{=} tt$$

which state that every Country has a capital City, and that the capital City of a Country is unique.

We also need target constraints describing how the keys for our classes are generated:

$$Y \dot{=} Mk^{Country_T}(Y.name) \ \Longleftarrow \ Y \dot{\in} Country_E$$

$$Y \dot{=} Mk^{State_T}(Y.name) \ \Longleftarrow \ Y \dot{\in} State_E$$

$$X \dot{=} Mk^{City_T}(Z), \ Z.name \dot{=} X.name, \ Z.place\_name \dot{=} Y.name$$
$$\Longleftarrow \ X \dot{\in} City_T, \ Y \dot{\in} Country_T, \ X.place \dot{=} ins_{euro\text{-}city}(Y)$$

$$X \dot{=} Mk^{City_T}(Z), \ Z.name \dot{=} X.name, \ Z.place\_name \dot{=} Y.name$$
$$\Longleftarrow \ X \dot{\in} City_T, \ Y \dot{\in} State_T, \ X.place \dot{=} ins_{us\text{-}city}(Y)$$

Our transformation clauses are:

$$Y \dot{\in} City_T, \; Y.name \dot{=} X.name, \; Y.place \dot{=} ins_{euro\text{-}city}(Z)$$
$$\Longleftarrow \; X \dot{\in} City_E, \; Z \dot{\in} Country_T, \; Z.name \dot{=} X.country.name$$

$$Y \dot{\in} Country_T, \; Y.name \dot{=} Z.name, \; Y.currency \dot{=} Z.currency,$$
$$Y.language \dot{=} Z.language$$
$$\Longleftarrow \; Z \dot{\in} Country_E$$

$$Y.capital \dot{=} Z \; \Longleftarrow \; Y \dot{\in} Country_T, \; Z \dot{\in} City_T, \; Z.place \dot{=} ins_{euro\text{-}city}(Y),$$
$$X \dot{\in} City_T, \; X.name \dot{=} Z.name, \; X.country.name \dot{=} Y.name,$$
$$X.is\_capital \dot{=} tt$$

The first of the transformation clauses says that, for every object in the source class $City_E$ there is a corresponding object in the target class $City_T$ with the same value on its name attribute, and with its place attribute set to an object in class $Country_T$ with the same name as the name of the country of the city in class $City_E$. The second clause says that, for every country in the source class $Country_E$, there is a corresponding country with the same name, currency and language, in the target class $Country_T$, and the third clause tells us how to derive the capital attribute of an object in the class $Country_T$.

Note that, in the above example, a complete description of an object in the target database may be spread over several transformation rules, and that transformation rules may define one target object in terms of other target object. This highlights one of the strengths of WOL: it allows us to split transformations over large and complicated data-structures with many interdependencies into a number of small relatively simple rules.

The clauses of the transformation program above may however be unfolded in order to give an equivalent program in which all the clauses give complete descriptions of the target database in terms of the source database only, and which can then be implemented in a simple manner [21].

Semantics of transformation programs Suppose **Tr** is a transformation program, and $\mathcal{I}_{Src}$ an instance of $(\mathcal{S}_{Src}, \mathcal{K}_{Src})$. An instance $\mathcal{I}_{Tgt}$ of $(\mathcal{S}_{Tgt}, \mathcal{K}_{Tgt})$ is said to be an **Tr-transformation** of $\mathcal{I}_{Src}$ iff for every clause $\Psi \Longleftarrow \Phi$ in **Tr**, $\mathcal{I}$ satisfies $\Psi \Longleftarrow \Phi$, where $\mathcal{I} = \mathcal{I}_{Src} \cup \mathcal{I}_{Tgt}$.

Unfortunately the **Tr**-transformation of a particular instance will not in general be unique: a transformation program will imply that certain things must be included in the target database instance, but will not exclude other additional things from being included. Consequently there may be infinitely many **Tr**-transformations of a particular instance, representing the inclusion of arbitrary additional data. It is therefore necessary to characterize the *unique* *smallest* Tr-transformation of an instance, when it exists. To do this, we construct a size ordering on instances, taking into account the fact that instances may have different sets of object identifiers. We refer the reader to [20] for details.

A transformation program, **Tr** is then said to be **complete** iff for any instance $\mathcal{I}_{Src}$ of $(\mathcal{S}_{Src}, \mathcal{K}_{Src})$, if there is a **Tr**-transformation of $\mathcal{I}_{Src}$, then there is a unique (up to isomorphism) smallest such **Tr**-transformation $\mathcal{I}_{Tgt}$.

Intuitively a complete transformation program is one in which the target database instance is determined unambiguously by the source instance. In particular, a transformation program is complete if, whenever it implies the existence of some object in the target database, it provides a "complete" description of that object. For example if the second transformation clause of example 10 was replaced by the clause

$$Y \dot{\in} Country_T,\ Y.name \dot{=} Z.name \ \Longleftarrow\ Z \dot{\in} Country_E$$

(and no additional clauses were added) then the program would no longer be complete. This is because, for a suitable source instance, the above clause would imply the inclusion of an object identity in the target $Country_T$ class with some specific value for the *name* attribute of the associated record, but none of the clauses of the transformation program would assert what the *language* and *currency* attributes of the associated record should be. Consequently there would be many possible minimal instances of the target database satisfying the program, all including objects of class $Country_T$ with the appropriate *name* attribute but with arbitrary values assigned to their *language* and *currency* attributes.

Given a complete transformation program, the "unique smallest" transformation of an instance represents precisely the data whose presence in the target database is implied by the transformation program, and is therefore the transformation we are interested in.

Example 11. Consider transforming the instance described in example 4 taking **Tr** to be the transformation program of example 10. The choice of object identities in our target database is arbitrary. We will take them to be:

$$\sigma^{City_T} \equiv \{London', Manchester', Paris', Berlin', Bonn'\}$$
$$\sigma^{Country_E} \equiv \{UK', FR', GM'\}$$

The mappings are then given by

$$\mathcal{V}^{City_T}(London') \equiv (name \mapsto \text{``London''}, place \mapsto (euro\_city, UK'))$$
$$\mathcal{V}^{City_E}(Manchester') \equiv (name \mapsto \text{``Manchester''}, place \mapsto (euro\_city, UK'))$$
$$\mathcal{V}^{City_E}(Paris') \equiv (name \mapsto \text{``Paris''}, country \mapsto (euro\_city, FR'))$$

$$\mathcal{V}^{Country_B}(UK') \equiv (name \mapsto \text{"United Kingdom"}, language \mapsto \text{"English"},$$
$$currency \mapsto \text{"sterling"}, capital \mapsto London')$$
$$\mathcal{V}^{Country_B}(FR') \equiv (name \mapsto \text{"France"}, language \mapsto \text{"French"},$$
$$currency \mapsto \text{"franc"}, capital \mapsto Paris')$$

and so on.

This is the smallest instance which is a Tr-transformation of the instance of example 4: there are many other Tr-transformations which can be formed by including additional objects to the instance. However any other *minimal* Tr-transformation will be isomorphic to this one. Since we can always find such a smallest Tr-transformation of an instance, if we can find a Tr-transformation at all, it follows that the transformation program is complete.

We therefore have a precise semantics for complete transformation programs. Unfortunately it is not in general decidable whether a transformation program is complete. However it is possible to construct fairly general syntactic conditions which ensure that a transformation program is complete. For programs which meet these syntactic conditions, it is also possible to efficiently compute the unique smallest transformation of a set of source instances (see [20] for details). We have prototyped such a system for a subset of *WOL* and are currently testing it on a number of sample biological database transformations [9].

6 Conclusions

There is a considerable need for database transformations in the areas of reimplementing legacy systems, reacting to schema evolutions, merging user views and integrating existing heterogeneous databases, amongst others. Though work exists to address certain aspects of these problems, a general formal approach to specifying and implementing such complex structural transformations has not yet been completely developed. Many existing approaches lack formal semantics, while others are limited in the types of transformations that can be expressed, or in the data model being considered. In addition it is frequently necessary to ensure the "correctness" of such database transformations. Notions of correctness or information preservation of transformations should therefore be tied to database transformation techniques.

In this paper we surveyed various approaches to database transformations and notions of information preservation, and reached a number of conclusions. Firstly, approaches which allow a fixed set of well-defined transformations to be applied in series are inherently limited in the class of transformations that can be expressed. As an example we demonstrated a complex structural manipulation which could not be expressed in one such methodology, but which commonly arises in practice. Using a high-level language for expressing transformations can provide greater expressive power, but makes it more difficult to reason about and prove properties of transformations. We concluded that a high-level language is necessary in order to express general transformations, but that such a language should be *declarative* and should have a well-defined formal semantics, in order to minimize the problems of reasoning about transformations.

Secondly, the choice of an underlying data model impacts the types of transformations that can be expressed. The main requirement of the model underlying a transformation language is that it subsume the various models which might be used in the databases being transformed. In particular, it should include support for complex data-structures (sets, records and variants), object-identity and recursive structures. To reason about transforming recursive structures, it is also necessary to have a notion of extents or classes in which all the objects in a database must occur.

Thirdly, to reason that a transformation is correct, constraints should be expressed in the same formalism as the transformation. Constraints on the source and target databases are crucial to notions of information preservation, but typically are not – or cannot – be expressed in the models of the underlying databases. Furthermore, when integrating multiple heterogeneous databases it is necessary to reason about inter-database constraints. Since such constraints are crucial to the correctness of transformations they should be expressed as part of the transformation program.

These conclusions have driven the design of the transformation language *WOL*. As a declarative language built on Horn clause logic expressions, it allows a general class of transformations to be expressed and unifies the treatment of transformations and constraints. The class of constraints that can be expressed in *WOL* encompasses those found in most data models, such as keys, functional dependencies and inclusion dependences. Furthermore, our experience in using *WOL* to specify database transformations within biological databases [9] indicates that it is intuitive and easy to use since transformations over large and complicated data structures can be split into a number of relatively small and simple rules. However, while the mechanics for checking information preservation appear to be in place for *WOL* we feel that more general, problem specific notions of correctness need to be developed as well as sound techniques for proving these properties.

References

1. S. Abiteboul and R. Hull. Restructuring hierarchical database objects. *Theoretical Computer Science*, 62:3–38, 1988.

2. S. Abiteboul and P. Kanellakis. Object identity as a query language primitive. In *Proceedings of ACM SIGMOD Conference on Management of Data*, pages 159–173, Portland, Oregon, 1989.

3. Serge Abiteboul and Richard Hull. IFO: A formal semantic database model. *ACM Transactions on Database Systems*, 12(4):525–565, December 1987.

4. F. Bancilhon. Object-oriented database systems. In *Proceedings of 7th ACM Symposium on Principles of Database Systems*, pages 152–162, Los Angeles, California, 1988.

5. J. Banerjee, W. Kim, H. Kim, and H. Korth. Semantics and implementation of schema evolution in object-oriented databases. *SIGMOD Record*, 16(3):311–322, 1987.

6. C. Batini and M. Lenzerini. A methodology for data schema integration in the entity-relationship model. *IEEE Transactions on Software Engineering*, SE-10(6):650–663, November 1984.

7. C. Batini, M. Lenzerini, and S. Navathe. A comparative analysis of methodologies for database schema integration. *ACM Computing Surveys*, 18(4):323–364, December 1986.

8. P. Buneman, S. Davidson, and A. Kosky. Theoretical aspects of schema merging. In *LNCS 580: Advances in Database Technology — EDBT '92*, pages 152–167. Springer-Verlag, 1992.

9. S. B. Davidson, A. S. Kosky, and B. Eckman. Facilitating transformations in a human genome project database. In *Proc. Third International Conference on Information and Knowledge Management (CIKM)*, pages 423–432, December 1994.

10. U. Dayal and H. Hwang. View definition and generalisation for database integration in Multibase: A system for heterogeneous distributed databases. *IEEE Transactions on Software Engineering*, SE-10(6):628–644, November 1984.

11. C. Eick. A methodology for the design and transformation of conceptual schemas. In *Proceedings of the 17th International Conference on Very Large Databases, Barcelona, Spain*, pages 25–34, September 1991.

12. F. Eliassen and R. Karlsen. Interoperability and object identity. *SIGMOD Record*, 20(4):25–29, December 1991.

13. N. Hammer and D. McLeod. Database description with SDM: A semantic database model. *ACM Transactions on Database Systems*, 6(3):351–386, September 1981.

14. Dennis Heimbigner and Dennis McLeod. A federated architecture for information management. *ACM Transactions on Office Information Systems*, 3(3), July 1985.

15. R. Hull. Relative information capacity of simple relational database schemata. *SIAM Journal of Computing*, 15(3):865–886, August 1986.

16. Richard Hull and Roger King. Semantic database modeling: Survey, applications, and research issues. *ACM Computing Surveys*, 19(3):201–260, September 1987.

17. W. Kent. The breakdown of the information model in multi-database systems. *SIGMOD Record*, 20(4):10–15, December 1991.

18. Setrag N. Khoshafian and George P. Copeland. Object identity. In Stanley B. Zdonik and David Maier, editors, *Readings in Object Oriented Database Systems*, pages 37–46. Morgan Kaufmann Publishers, San Mateo, California, 1990.

19. Anthony Kosky. Observational properties of databases with object identity. Technical Report MS-CIS-95-20, Dept. of Computer and Information Science, University of Pennsylvania, 1995.

20. Anthony Kosky. *Transforming Databases with Recursive Data Structures*. PhD thesis, Department of Computer and Information Science, University of Pennsylvania, Philadelphia, PA 19104, November 1995.

21. Anthony Kosky. Types with extents: On transforming and querying self-referential data-structures. PhD Thesis Proposal, Technical Report MS-CIS-95-21, University of Pennsylvania, May 1995.

22. W. Litwin, L. Mark, and N. Roussopoulos. Interoperability of multiple autonomous databases. *ACM Computing Surveys*, 22(3):267–293, September 1990.

23. R. J. Miller, Y. E. Ioannidis, and R Ramakrishnan. The use of information capacity in schema integration and translation. In *Proc. 19th International VLDB Conference*, pages 120–133, August 1993.

24. R. J. Miller, Y. E. Ioannidis, and R Ramakrishnan. Schema equivalence in heterogeneous systems: Bridging theory and practice. *Information Systems*, 19, 1994.

25. A. Motro. Superviews: Virtual integration of multiple databases. *IEEE Transactions on Software Engineering*, SE-13(7):785–798, July 1987.

26. S. Navathe, R. Elmasri, and J. Larson. Integrating user views in database design. *IEEE Computer*, 19(1):50–62, January 1986.

27. D. Penney and J. Stein. Class modification in the gemstone object-oriented dbms. *SIGPLAN Notices (Proc. OOOPSLA '87)*, 22(12):111–117, October 1987.

28. John F. Roddick. Schema evolution in database systems — An annotated bibliography. *SIGMOD Record*, 21(4):35–40, December 1992.

29. A. Rosenthal and D. Reiner. Theoretically sound transformations for practical database design. In S. T. March, editor, *Entity-Relationship Approach*, pages 115–131, 1988.

30. M. Rusinkiewicz, A. Sheth, and G. Karabatis. Specifying interdatabase dependencies in a multidatabase environment. *IEEE Computer*, December 1991.

31. F. Saltor, M. Castellanos, and M. Garcia-Solaco. Suitability of data models as canonical models for federated databases. *SIGMOD Record*, 20(4):44–48, December 1991.

32. P. Shoval and S. Zohn. Binary-relationship integration methodology. *Data and Knowledge Engineering*, 6:225–249, 1991.

33. Andrea H. Skarra and Stanley B. Zdonik. Type evolution in an object oriented database. In Bruce Shriver and Peter Wegner, editors, *Research Directions in Object Oriented Programming*, pages 392–415. MIT Press, Cambridge, Massachusetts, 1987.

34. S. Spaccapietra and C. Parent. Conflicts and correspondence assertions in interoperable dbs. *SIGMOD Record*, 20(4):49–54, December 1991.

35. M. Tresch and M. Scholl. Schema transformation without database reorganization. *SIGMOD Record*, 22(1):21–27, March 1993.

36. Jeffrey D. Ullman. *Principles of Database and Knowledgebase Systems I*. Computer Science Press, Rockville, MD 20850, 1989.

37. S. Widjojo, R. Hull, and D. S. Wile. A specificational approach to merging persistent object bases. In Al Dearle, Gail Shaw, and Stanley Zdonik, editors, *Implementing Persistent Object Bases*. Morgan Kaufmann, December 1990.

38. S. Widjojo, D. S. Wile, and R. Hull. Worldbase: A new approach to sharing distributed information. Technical report, USC/Information Sciences Institute, February 1990.
39. G. Wiederhold and X. Qian. Modeling asynchrony in distributed databases. *Proc. 1987 International Conference on Data Engineering*, pages 246–250, 1987.

The Evolving Algebra Semantics of Class and Role Hierarchies

Georg Gottlob[1] and Michael Schrefl[2]

[1] Institut für Informationssysteme
Technische Universität Wien
[2] Institut für Wirtschaftsinformatik
Universität Linz

Keywords: evolving algebra, operational semantics, object-oriented data models, inheritance, roles

Abstract. The formal description of the semantics of object-oriented data models is still a heavily debated research problem. This paper shows how evolving algebras provide an elegant way to specify the operational semantics of object-oriented data models. In particular, we define the formal semantics of a novice feature of object-oriented data models proposed recently by different authors: role hierarchies. As opposed to traditional class hierarchies, role hierarchies allow objects to dynamically acquire multiple independent types.

1 Introduction

The favorite approach of database theoreticians to define semantics in terms of first-order logic can not be applied straightforwardly to object-oriented data models. Defining characteristic features of object-oriented data models, such as methods and inheritance, involves investigating data and schema. As pointed out by Beeri [Bee90], it is burdensome to describe these with first order logic, whereas higher order logic is not axiomatizable in general.

We propose to specify the operational semantics based on evolving algebras as an alternative. Evolving algebras have been introduced recently by Yuri Gurevich as a framework to define the operational semantics of programming languages [Gur88b]. A major advantage of the operational approach is that language constructs involving data and schema can be handled rather easily. Evolving algebras support another main characteristic of object-oriented systems, the dynamic creation and deletion of objects. Objects are represented as elements of universes which are expanded and shrunk dynamically.

In this paper we show how evolving algebras can be employed to specify the semantics of role hierarchies and their interaction with class hierarchies. Recently, several research groups [ABGO93, Pap91, Per90, RS91, WdJS94, GSR96] have suggested to extend traditional class hierarchies with roles. The concept of roles overcomes the deficiencies of class hierarchies to model objects taking on different roles over time, e.g., a person being a student and an employee. Many class-based object-oriented systems have serious difficulties in representing objects taking on different roles over time, as they require the association between an instance and a class to be exclusive and permanent. This is not the case with role hierarchies. A real world object may be represented as several, yet different instances of several role types in a role hierarchy, where each instance represents the real world object in a specific context. The employee record and the student record of one person are a good analogy for two role instances of one real world entity.

This paper combines and extends two of our previous research contributions. In [GKS90] we have shown how the semantics of object-oriented data models can be specified using the evolving algebra approach. In [GSR96] we have shown how a class-based object-oriented system can be extended with role hierarchies. In this paper we build on the framework introduced in [GKS90] and define the formal semantics of the full set of operators introduced in [GSR96] to create and manipulate roles. Intentionally, we use a very simple language EasyRoles rather than our extension of Smalltalk with roles in [GSR96]. As the aim of this paper is to show how evolving algebras can be used to specify the semantics of novice object-oriented concepts, we believe the reader will benefit if we use a restricted language.

The paper is outlined as follows. To make the paper self-contained, we explain the evolving algebra approach in section 2 and review the concepts of classes and roles in section 3. In section 4, we introduce EasyRoles, an object-oriented language that supports all methods for creating and manipulating roles introduced in [GSR96] but that has been kept simple in all other aspects. Section 5 gives the evolving algebra of EasyRoles. We conclude with a short discussion in section 6.

2 Evolving Algebras

The idea of using evolving algebras to describe the operational semantics of programming languages has been first presented by Yuri Gurevich in [Gur88b]. In general, the *operational semantics* of a language L is defined by an *abstract machine* which interprets the constructs of L and changes its state accordingly. Yuri Gurevich proposes to use an *evolving algebra* to define the abstract machine.

Definition: An *evolving algebra* for a language L is a pair (A_L, T_L) with A_L being a many-sorted, partial algebra of some signature describing the initial state of the abstract machine, and T_L being a set of transition rules of the same signature describing the state changes of the abstract machine.

An evolving algebra (A_L, T_L) reflects the operational semantics of a given program written in L as follows. The algebra A_L is used to define program code and data. In A_L, the program is represented in terms of its parse tree. The set T_L of transition rules is used to define the execution of operations (or methods). The transition rules are applied repeatedly on the parse tree starting with the root node until all nodes have been evaluated and the execution of the program terminates. Each state of the abstract machine defined by an evolving algebra (A_L, T_L) is described by a many-sorted, partial algebra. The result of applying some transition rule to a state described by an algebra A'_L is another algebra A''_L. The initial state is described by A_L.

The algebra A_L comprises static and dynamic universes (carrier sets of the elements of the algebra), and static and dynamic functions on Cartesian products of universes. The functions may be total or partial. Static universes have a fixed set of elements, whereas dynamic universes may grow and shrink as transformation rules are applied. Similarly, static functions do not change in time, whereas dynamic functions do. The domain as well as the values of a dynamic function may change. In general, A_L consists of universes and functions which are applicable for different programs written in L and of those which are specific to a particular program in L.

The transition rules T_L describe the execution of a program by specifying how dynamic functions evolve. The set T_L is the same for all programs written in L. A transition rule has the form **if** b **then** r_1, ..., r_n **endif**, where b is a closed boolean expression over the signature of the evolving algebra, and r_1, ..., r_n are of one of the following two kinds:

1. *function updates:* let f be a dynamic function in A_L with domain $U_1 \times ... \times U_k$ and range U_0, where each U_i is a universe. Let $e_0, ..., e_k$ be closed (i.e., without free variables) expressions over $U_0, ..., U_k$. Then $f(e_1, ..., e_k) := e_0$ is a function update, i.e., if $e_0, ..., e_k$ are evaluated to $a_0, ..., a_k$, then a_0 is assigned to $f(a_1, ..., a_k)$.

2. *extensions of universes:* let U be a universe, and $f_1, ..., f_m$ a list of function updates. Then **let** $temp = New(U)$ **in** $f_1, ..., f_m$ **endlet** is a universe extension, where $temp$ is a temporary variable used in some $f_1, ..., f_m$. The meaning of this transition rule is the following. First, a new element of U is created and $temp$ names it temporarily. Second, the function updates $f_1, ..., f_m$ are performed in turn. The scope of $temp$ is bounded by **let** and **endlet**.[3]

The semantics of transition rules is the following. The body of a transition rule is performed if and only if its precondition is true. A transition rule is performed by executing its function updates and universe extensions in sequence. We require that the preconditions of all transition rules are mutually exclusive.

Transition rules may be nested for notational convenience. For example, the transition rule **if** b **then if** b_1 **then** r_1 **endif**, **if** b_2 **then** r_2 **endif endif** is a shorthand for the two rules (1) **if** $b \wedge b_1$ **then** r_1 **endif**, and (2) **if** $b \wedge b_2$ **then** r_2 **endif**.

Evolving algebras give the operational semantics of a language by defining the semantics of a program in terms of its input-output behavior. Two programs are called equivalent, i.e., have the same semantics, if they exhibit the same input-output behavior. It is shown in [Gur88b] that evolving algebras can be used to

---

[3] Another characteristic feature of evolving algebras is that the sizes of universes may have an upper bound [Gur88a], which allows to model limited resources, such as memory. In this paper, however, we assume unbounded universes and neglect universe contractions.

reason about the equivalence of programs, although this can be cumbersome.

So far, to our knowledge, evolving algebras have been employed to define the operational semantics of Modula-2 [GM88, Mor88], Occam [GM90], Prolog [B90a, B90b, B90c], Concurrent Prolog [RB92], Smalltalk [Bla92], and C [Gur92].

3 Class and Role Hierarchies

Class hierarchies a' la Smalltalk support sharing of structure and behavior among several classes due to inheritance. Instance variables and instance methods defined in some class are inherited by its subclasses. Consider the nodes depicted by rectangles in Figure 1. They form a class hierarchy in which subclass relationships are depicted by solid arrows pointing from the subclass to the superclass. For simplicity, only instance variables of classes are depicted. Instance methods are not shown. The class hierarchy expresses that companies and persons are legal entities. The class **LegalEntity** defines the instance variables **idNo** and **name**. These are inherited by the subclass **Person**, which defines the two additional instance variables **birthDate** and **phoneNo**.

In a class hierarchy, every real-world entity is represented as an instance of the most specific class for which it qualifies. An instance stores a value for each instance variable defined in or inherited by its class. Figure 2 shows three instances of the class hierarchy of Figure 1. For example, Mr. Miller is a person. He is represented as an instance of class **Person** with instance variables **idNo** and **name**, which are inherited by the class **Person** from its superclass **LegalEntity**, and with instance **birthDate** and **phoneNo** defined at class **Person**.

Class hierarchies have serious difficulties in modeling evolving objects because they apply specialization at the class level (see [GSR96] for several examples). When objects change their type dynamically, it is more appropriate to apply specialization and inheritance at the instance level. This is the case with role hierarchies. A role hierarchy consists of a tree of role types and defines how some kind of entity may evolve. At the schema level, a role hierarchy looks like a class hierarchy. Every role type defines a set of instance variables and a set of instance methods. The difference with respect to class hierarchies is that a subtype in a role hierarchy does not inherit the definitions of instance variables and instance methods from the supertype. As we will see later, inheritance is defined at the instance level rather than at the class level. Consider the nodes depicted by circles in Figure 1. They form a role hierarchy: **Student** and **Employee** are role types of **Person**, and **Department Manger** is a role type of **Employee**. Every role type is connected by a shaded arrow to the class or role type whose objects may take on that role. Double circles represent qualified roles, which are discussed later.

At the instance level, a real-world entity is represented as an instance of the root type and as an instance of every role type for which it currently qualifies. As definitions of instance variables are not inherited between role types, every instance of a role type possesses only values for instance variables directly defined for that role type. An instance of a role type and an instance of the role type's ancestor that represent the same real-world entity are related by a roleOf-relationship. Although a role type in a role hierarchy does not inherit definitions of instance variables or instance methods from its ancestor, every instance of a role type inherits from its corresponding instance of the role type's ancestor. Every message not understood by the former is delegated to the later. Figure 2 shows an extension of the role hierarchy with root Person. Mr. Miller is a person, but neither a student nor an employee. Mrs. Smith is an employee and a student, but neither a department manager nor a project manager. She is represented by an instance of Person with instance variables idNo, name, birthDate and phoneNo, by an instance of Employee with instance variables salary and phoneNo and by an instance of Student with instance variables university, major, minor, and phoneNo. The employee instance as well as the student instance is linked by a roleOf relationship to the corresponding person instance.

A role type defines a *qualified role* if a real-world entity may have several occurrences of that role. Occurrences of the same entity are distinguished by the value of a special instance variable named *qualifier*. A role type which does not define a qualified role is called a *simple role type*. In our example, ProjectManager is a qualified role type. The qualifier takes on the Project supervised.

Figure 2 depicts an extension of the qualified role ProjectManager. Mr. De Campo, who manages two projects, "CAD/CAM" and "ooDB", is represented by two instances of ProjectManager. Mr. De Campo has different responsibilities in the two projects. He is responsible for "reuse management" in the former, and for "quality assurance" in the latter.

Classes and roles can be combined orthogonally. Classes may have subclasses and may function as the root of role hierarchies, e.g., the class LegalEntity has subclasses Person and Company, and is role supertype of role type Customer. Roles may have subroles and subclasses. We have seen an example of the former. Role type Employee has subroles DepartmentManager and ProjectManager. We get an example of the latter by subclassing role type Student to ForeignStudent (cf. Figure 1). This means that the student role of a person is classified into either Student or ForeignStudent. For foreign students, the country is recorded next to the university, major, minor and phoneNo (cf. Figure 2). The latter instance variables are inherited by role type ForeignStudent at the class level from role type Student.

To distinguish subclasses of role types from ordinary object classes, they are depicted by ovals (cf. ForeignStudent in Figure 1).

4   EasyRoles, a Class and Role Language

In this section we describe EasyRoles, a very simplified version of our extension of Smalltalk with roles [GSR96]. EasyRoles supports the class and role hierarchies as explained in the previous Section.

EasyRoles is a database language. It has a schema definition part and a data manipulation part. The database schema consists of a set of object classes and role types, which are defined in a syntax similarly to Smalltalk. But, which is different to Smalltalk, we do not assume a meta class level. All EasyRoles language constructs are predefined and can be compiled.

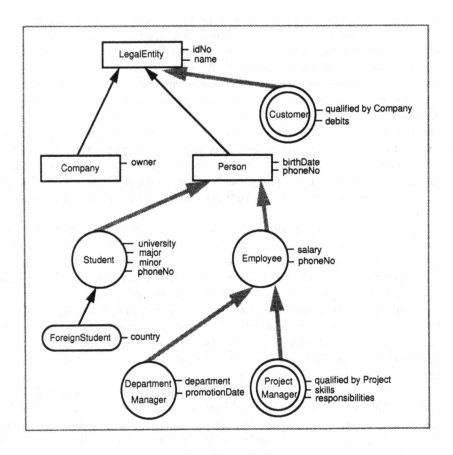

Fig. 1. A class and role hierarchy

In the following, we give the statements for defining object classes and role types, and the predefined methods for manipulating roles. We use Backus-Naur Form (BNF) to define the syntax of EasyRoles statements. The full syntax of EasyRoles is given in the Appendix.

4.1 Defining Object Classes and Role Types

The schema of an EasyRoles database and a database for this schema is defined by the statement **EasyRoles define** ⟨dbName⟩ { ⟨typeDef⟩ } { ⟨varDecl⟩ } **end schema**, where ⟨typeDef⟩ is the definition of an object class or a role type, and ⟨varDecl⟩ is the definition of a set of persistent global variables.

An object class is defined by the statement

```
⟨typeName⟩
      subclass: #⟨className⟩
      variables: ' { ⟨varName⟩ } '
      [ methods: ' { ⟨methDef⟩ } ' ].
```

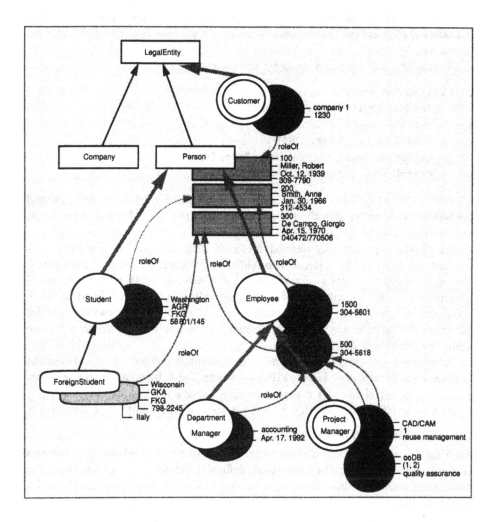

Fig. 2. An extension of a class and role hierarchy

where ⟨**className**⟩ is the name of the defined object class, ⟨**varName**⟩ the name of an instance variable, and ⟨**methDef**⟩ the definition of an instance method; ⟨**typeName**⟩ is the predefined object class **ObjectWithRoles**, or the unique name of some other previously defined object class or role type.

A simple role type is defined by the statement

```
RoleType
     defRoleType: #⟨roleTypeName⟩
     variables: ' { ⟨varName⟩ } '
     [ methods: ' { ⟨methDef⟩ } ' ]
     roleSuperType: #⟨nameOfRoleSuperType⟩.
```

where ⟨roleTypeName⟩ is the name of the defined role type and ⟨nameOfRoleSuperType⟩ is the unique name of a previously defined object class or role type.

A qualified role type is defined by the statement

```
QualifiedRoleType
    defRoleType: #⟨roleTypeName⟩
    variables: ' { ⟨varName⟩ } '
    [ methods: ' { ⟨methDef⟩ } ' ]
    roleSuperType: #⟨nameOfRoleSuperType⟩.
    classOfQualifyingObj: #⟨className⟩
```

where ⟨roleTypeName⟩ is the name of the defined qualified role type and ⟨nameOfRoleSuperType⟩ is the unique name of a previously defined object class or role type.

EasyRoles supports user-defined methods with none or one parameter. A method is defined by the statement ⟨methName⟩ [⟨formalParName⟩] ⟨methBody⟩. The method body consists of a sequence of messages, being either a message referring to a user-defined method, a message referring to a predefined method, a variable assignment, or a return statement. For simplicity, we assume that for any instance variable x a method x to read the variable and a method x:v to write the variable is implicitly defined.

A message referring to a user-defined method is defined by the statement ⟨addressee⟩ ⟨methName⟩ [⟨actualPar⟩], where the actual parameter is either given by a string or number constant or by a variable.

Figure 3 defines the schema depicted graphically in Figure 1 in EasyRoles.

4.2   Manipulation of Roles

An EasyRoles data manipulation program refers to a database and consists of a set of messages, which refer to predefined methods or to methods in the database schema. In this subsection, we introduce the predefined methods for manipulating roles:

- *Creating role instances:* An instance of a simple role type can be created using a message of type ⟨simpRoleTypeName⟩ newRoleOf: ⟨superObject⟩ qualifiedBy: ⟨qualObj⟩ where ⟨superObject⟩ becomes the ancestor of the new instance of role type ⟨simpRoleTypeName⟩. Figure 4 illustrates how the employee and student roles of Mr. De Campo can be defined. The method ⟨qualRoleTypeName⟩ newRoleOf: ⟨superObject⟩ qualifiedBy: ⟨qualObj⟩ is predefined for creating new qualified role instances. Figure 4 illustrates the use of this message. Employee De Campo is made manager of two projects.
- *Abandoning a role:* Message ⟨receiver⟩ abandon invalidates the addressed role object.[4]

---

[4] Like Smalltalk, EasyRoles has no explicit function to remove an object no longer being used. An object is reclaimed automatically when there are no references to it from other objects. The purpose of the message abandon is to indicate that some role is no longer played by a real-world entity.

- *Checking on role existence:*
  Message ⟨receiver⟩ existsAs: ⟨simpleRoleTypeName⟩ checks whether an instance of ⟨simpleRoleTypeName⟩ exists that represents the same real-world entity as the ⟨receiver⟩. E.g., message emp1 existsAs: Employee can be used for checking in our database whether student De Campo is also an employee. Message ⟨receiver⟩ existsAs: ⟨qualRoleTypeName⟩ of: ⟨qualObj⟩. checks whether the ⟨receiver⟩ exists as instance of ⟨qualRoleTypeName⟩ that is qualified by ⟨qualObj⟩.

- *Switching roles:* Several message signatures are provided for switching the behavioral context of an entity: Message ⟨receiver⟩ roleOf returns the ancestor of the receiver in the role hierarchy. E.g., message student1 roleOf retrieves in our database Mr. De Campo as an instance of Person. Message ⟨receiver⟩ root returns the root of the receiver's role hierarchy. E.g., message oodbProjMg1 root retrieves in our database Mr. Campo as Person. Message ⟨receiver⟩ as: ⟨simpRoleTypeName⟩ retrieves that instance of ⟨simpRoleTypeName⟩ that represents the same real-world entity as the ⟨receiver⟩. An error is raised if no such instance exists. E.g., message student1 as: Employee retrieves in our database that instance of Employee representing Mr. Campo.

- *Entity equivalence:* Two instances are *entity equivalent* if they correspond to the same real-world entity. This is the case if they have a common root instance. Message ⟨receiver⟩ entityEquiv: ⟨anotherObj⟩ can be used for checking whether ⟨receiver⟩ and ⟨anotherObject⟩ represent the same real-world entity. E.g., message emp1 entityEquiv: projMg1 checks whether the objects referenced by emp1 and projMg1 represent the same person.

5 Evolving Algebra for EasyRoles

In this section we define the evolving algebra $(A_{EasyRoles}, T_{EasyRoles})$ for an EasyRoles data manipulation program. The static universes and static functions of $A_{EasyRoles}$ represent the parse tree of the EasyRoles data manipulation program and the parse tree of the schema of the used EasyRoles database. The dynamic universes and dynamic functions represent during program execution the current program state and the current database state. The evolving algebra for EasyRoles is based on the evolving algebra of Modula-2 [GM88, Mor88] as far as non object-oriented features are concerned. We use those universes and functions from [Mor88] which are equally applicable to EasyRoles and we adapt some transformation rules of [Mor88] to fit our needs. As in [GM88], we assume that a correct and statically type checked EasyRoles program is represented by its parse tree.

To concentrate on the semantics of class and role hierarchies, we do not include universes and functions needed to define the semantics of standard concepts such as parameter passing or maintaining a stack of active methods. The reader interested in these concepts is referred to the papers by Yuri Gurevich [GM88, GM90].

```
EasyRoles define PersonellDB

ObjectWithRoles
    subclass: #LegalEntity
    variables: 'idNo name'.

LegalEntity
    subclass: #Person
    variables: 'birthDate phoneNo'.

LegalEntity
    subclass: #Company
    variables: 'owner'.

RoleType
    defRoleType: #Student
    variables: 'university major minor phoneNo'
    methods: 'country: ^"Austria".'
    roleSuperType: #Person.

RoleType
    defRoleType: #Employee
    variables: 'salary phoneNo'
    roleSuperType: #Person.

RoleType
    defRoleType: #DepartmentManager
    variables: 'department promotionDate'
    roleSuperType: #Employee.

Student
    subclass: #ForeignStudent
    variables: 'country'.

QualifiedRoleType
    defQualifiedRoleType: #ProjectManager
    variables: 'skills responsibilities'
    roleSuperType: #Employee
    classOfQualifyingObj: #Project.

ObjectWithRoles
    subclass: #Project
    variables: 'projNo name budget'.

| person1 emp1 student1 proj1 proj2 projMg1 projMg2 |

end.
```

Fig. 3. Sample Schema Definition in EasyRoles

5.1 Universes

Static universes represent parse tree elements, such as parse tree nodes and grammar symbols, and program elements, such as object types. Dynamic universes represent objects, which are created dynamically as instances of object types. (Note: Dynamic universes are also needed to represent stacks of nested method invocations during program execution. But as already mentioned, we will not treat this aspect here.)

Static Universes The elements of the universe *nodes* represent parse tree nodes of an EasyRoles program. The universe *grammarsymbol* holds labels for the non-

```
EasyRoles use PersonellDB

person1 <- Person new.
person1 idNo: 300.
person1 name: 'De Campo, Giogio'.
person1 birthDate: 'Apr. 15, 1970'
person1 phoneNo: '040472/770506'.

emp1 <- Employee newRoleOf: personDeCampo.
emp1 salary: 500.
emp1 phoneNo: '304-5618'.

student1 <- ForeignStudent newRoleOf: personCampo.

proj1 <- Project new.
proj1 name: 'ooDB'.
projMg1 <- ProjectManager newRoleOf: empDeCampo qualifiedBy: proj1.
proj2 <- Project new.
proj2 name: 'CAD/CAM'.
projMg2 <- ProjectManager newRoleOf: empDeCampo qualifiedBy: proj2.

end.
```

Fig. 4. Sample Data Manipulation Program in EasyRoles

leaf nodes, which are non-terminal grammar symbols. Such a grammar symbol denotes the production rule used to expand the labeled node.

The universes *typeNames*, *classNames*, *simpRoleNames*, and *qualRoleNames* hold the names of object types, class names, simple role types and qualified role types, respectively (*typeNames* = *classNames* ∪ *simpRoleNames* ∪ *qualRoleNames*; *classNames* includes the predefined class name **ObjectWithRoles**). Names of direct or indirect subclasses of simple roles types (qualified role types) are elements of the universes *classNames* and *simpRoleNames* (*qualRoleNames*, rsp.). The universes *instVarNames*, *globalVarNames* and *parNames* represent the unique identifiers of instance variables, global variables and formal parameters; the universe *varNames* represents their union. The elements of the universe *methNames* represent the names of instance methods.

Dynamic Universes The universe *objects* holds all instances of predefined types (like **Number**, **String**, and **Bool**) and instances of object types created during program execution.

5.2 Functions

Static functions are used to represent the parse tree of a program, the class hierarchy and the role type hierarchy. Dynamic functions represent state information during program execution and the role hierarchy. All functions are total, unless stated otherwise. A partial function evaluates to "undefined" for all elements of its domain, unless the function is set explicitly.

5.3 Static Functions

Several functions assist in navigating through the parse tree. The partial function *Parent: node → node* maps a node in the parse tree to its parent node and the partial function ⟨*child*⟩*: node → node* maps a node in the parse tree to one of its child nodes, where ⟨*child*⟩ stands for the label of the actual child node.[5]

The function *MethImpl: typeNames × methNames → node ∪ { "notImpl"}* can be used in the search for the implementation of a method. It maps a pair (o, m) to the method m, if it has been implemented at the object type o, or to the string constant *"notImpl"*, otherwise.

The partial function *HasSuperclass: classNames → typeNames* represents the class hierarchy. The functions *simpRoleTypeOf: SimpRoleTypeNames → typeNames* and *QualRoleTypeOf: QualRoleTypeNames → typeNames* represent the role hierarchy. The function *ClassOfQualObj: QualRoleTypeNames → typeNames* represents the required type of the qualifier of a qualified role. Note: If n' is the name of a direct or indirect subclass of a role type n, then *SimpRoleTypeOf (n') = SimpRoleTypeOf (n)*; and if n' is the name of a direct or indirect subclass of a qualified role type n, then *QualRoleTypeOf (n') = QualRoleTypeOf (n)* and *ClassOfQualObj (n') = ClassOfQualObj (n)*.

We use some auxiliary functions to simplify transition rules. The partial function *Id: node → varNames ∪ typeNames ∪ methNames* maps a node labeled ⟨*varName*⟩, ⟨*typeName*⟩ *(or* ⟨*className*⟩, *or* ⟨*simpleRoleTypeName*⟩, *or* ⟨*qualRoleTypeName*⟩*)* ⟨*methName*⟩ to the name of a variable, to the name of an object type, or to the name of a method, respectively. The partial function *Label: node → grammarsymbol* maps a node to the non-terminal grammar symbol used in the left-hand side of the production rule expanding the node. The function *RootClass:objectType → objectType* maps an object type to the root of the class hierarchy in which it resides. The total function *HasSuperclass* :typeNames × typeNames → { "true", "false"}* represents the transitive and reflexive closure of the function *HasSuperclass*; it evaluates to *"true"* for a pair *(c, c')*, if c=c' or if c' is a direct or indirect ancestor of c in the class hierarchy.

5.4 Dynamic Functions

The dynamic functions can be differentiated in functions needed for reflecting the current program state and in functions reflecting the current database state.

Dynamic functions reflecting the program state The function *NV: node → node ∪ objects ∪ typeNames ∪ { "ok", "uneval", "error"}* maps each node of the parse tree to the result of executing its subtree. Initially, all nodes are mapped to *"uneval"*.

Several 0-ary functions represent distinguished elements of universes: *AN* points to the active node in the parse tree where control currently resides. *Receiver* holds the object on which a method is performed, and *TypeOfReceiver* the object type of the receiver.

---

[5] As a notational convention, we start function names pointing to a child node with a lower case letter, and all other function names with an upper case letter.

Dynamic functions reflecting the database state The function *HasType:*
objects → typeNames maps each object to its object type. The internal state of an
object is represented by the partial function *InstVarVal: objects × instVarNames*
→ objects, which maps a pair (o, v) to the value of variable v of object o. The
state of a global variable is represented by the function *VarVal: globalVarNames*
→ objects. The partial function *RoleOf: objects → objects* represents the role
hierarchy. The partial function *Root: objects → objects* maps an instance of a
role type to the root instance of the role hierarchy. The partial function *Qualifier:*
objects → objects maps each instance of a qualified role to the qualifying object.

Navigation in the role hierarchy of objects is facilitated by three auxiliary
functions: The function *Root: objects → objects* maps an instance of a role type to
the root of the role hierarchy defined by the function *roleOf*. The partial function
HasSimpleRole: objects × roleTypeNames → objects, maps a pair (o, r) to that
instance o' of role type r such that o and o' have the same root, providing such
an instance exists and r is a simple role type. The partial function *HasQualRole:*
objects × qualRoleTypeNames × objects → objects maps a triple (o, r, q) to that
instance o' of role type r such that o and o' have the same root and o' is qualified
by q, again, providing such an instance exists and r is a qualified role type.

5.5 Transition Rules

The transition rules $T_{EasyRoles}$ of the evolving algebra $(A_{EasyRoles}, T_{EasyRoles})$
define transitions between consecutive execution states of an EasyRoles data
manipulation program. The execution state is described by dynamic universes
and dynamic functions of $A_{EasyRoles}$. The application of a transition rule changes
the dynamic universes and functions.

The initial execution state of an EasyRoles data manipulation program is
reflected by the algebra $A_{EasyRoles}$ as follows:

1. All static universes and static functions are set.
2. All nodes in the parse tree are unevaluated, i.e., the value of the function
   NV is "uneval" for each node in the parse tree.
3. AN points to the **use** statement of the data manipulation program. (The
   use-statement identifies the database to be accessed.)
4. The universe *objects* is initialized with the number and string constants used
   in the program, with the two values of **Bool**, *true* and *false*.
5. All dynamic functions but NV and AN are initialized with "undefined" for
   all elements in their domains.

We assume a single-user mode of the data base and employ a shadowing
approach to ensure atomicity of data manipulation programs.

When a data manipulation program is started, the dynamic universe *objects*
is unioned with the objects in the used database, and the dynamic functions
reflecting the database state (see: above) are initialized with the corresponding
functions representing the state of the used database. The execution of an Easy-
Roles data manipulation program terminates if the program has been evaluated,
i.e., $NV(\langle EasyRolesDM \rangle) \neq$ "uneval". If $NV(\langle EasyRolesDM \rangle) \neq$ "error", then

the dynamic universe *objects* and the dynamic functions reflecting the current database state are copied into the persistent database.

5.6 Some General Transition Rules

In this subsection we give an example of a transition rule which is not specific to object-oriented systems and we give the transition rules for dynamic binding of a method name in a user-defined message to the method body to be executed.

The general strategy how a program is interpreted is the following: The function AN identifies the node in the parse tree where control currently resides. If the active node is not yet evaluated its children are evaluated from left to right, before the active node itself is evaluated. If the active node has been evaluated, control goes back to its parent node. The latter is expressed by the transition rule given in Figure 5.

if $NV(AN) \neq$ *"uneval"* **then**
   $AN := Parent(AN)$
endif

Fig. 5. Transition rule for navigating up the parse tree

The operational semantics of handling a message can be described informally as follows:

1. The *addressee* of the message is determined. Note: The addressee of a message is not necessarily the object on which the method is actually performed. To distinguish the former from the latter, we call the latter the *receiver* of the message.
2. The receiver is determined and the method name is bound to an method implementation. This step is explained in more detail below.
3. The actual parameters are determined and assigned to the formal parameters of the method.
4. The method is performed on the receiver. Its result constitutes the answer of the message.

Steps 1, 3 and 4 are rather straightforward and very much similar to non object-oriented languages. Step 2 needs some further explanation. The receiver and the method implementation are determined as follows: Initially, the addressee becomes the receiver of the message. An implementation of the method (methName) is searched for at the object type of the receiver. If it is not found there the search continues in this object type's class hierarchy. If the root has been reached and no implementation has been found, inheritance at the instance level comes in. If the receiver is a role of some other object, this object becomes the new receiver and the search continues in the class hierarchy of the receiver as explained above. If the receiver is not a role of some other object and no implementation has been found, the message is not understood by the addressee and an error is raised.

As an example, consider the message **student1 name()**. In the following paragraphs we explain how such a message is interpreted by our abstract machine.

The message is represented by a parse tree whose root labeled ⟨*userDefMsg*⟩ has three child nodes, ⟨*addressee*⟩, ⟨*methName*⟩, and ⟨*actualPar*⟩. The message is evaluated by evaluating its children nodes first. Let us assume, that the child ⟨*addressee*⟩ has been evaluated already. Then the node value of the node ⟨*addressee*⟩ is the object addressee by the message, and the 0-ary functions *Receiver* and *ActualType* are defined as follows: *Receiver* maps to the addressee, and *ActualType* to the object type of the addressee.

After the addressee of a message has been determined, the method name is bound to an implementation. For this, the object type which implements the method needs to be searched. If the search has been successful, *ActualType* maps to the object type implementing the method and *Receiver* maps to the object on which the method is to be performed.

Figure 6 gives the transition rule for binding a method name to a valid implementation. The precondition of the rule states that the active node labeled ⟨*methName*⟩ has not yet been evaluated. Furthermore, it states that the actual type does not implement the method. The nested transition rules of the body describe the search, which alternates between the class hierarchy and the role hierarchy.

```
if Label(AN) = ⟨methName⟩ and NV(AN) = "uneval" and
MethImpl(ActualType,Id(MethName(AN))) = "notImpl" then
    if HasSuperClass(ActualType) ≠ "undefined" then
        ActualType := HasSuperclass(ActualType)
    endif,
    if HasSuperclass(ActualType) = "undefined" then
        if RoleOf(Receiver) ≠ "undefined" then
            Receiver := RoleOf(Receiver),
            ActualType := HasType(Receiver)
        endif,
        if RoleOf(Receiver) = "undefined" then
            AN := ⟨ EasyRolesDM ⟩, NV(AN) := "error"
        endif
    endif
endif
```

Fig. 6. Transition rule for dynamic binding

Consider our example. Initially, *ActualType* maps to **ForeignStudent**. As this object type does not implement the method **name**, the function *ActualType* is redefined to map to its superclass **Student**. Again, this object class does not implement the method **name**. The object class **Student** has no superclass. Thus, inheritance at the instance level comes in. The function *Receiver*, which currently maps to an instance of **ForeignStudent**, is redefined to map to the more general instance of **Person** of which the instance of **ForeignStudent** represents a role. The function *ActualType* is redefined to map to object type **Person**. The search succeeds at this type's superclass, **LegalEntity**.

5.7 Transition Rules for Manipulating Roles

In the following, we give the transition rules for the different predefined messages for manipulating roles introduced in Section 3.

Figure 7 illustrates the transition rule of creating a new simple role of an object. The precondition of the rule states that the active node, i.e., the node where control currently resides, is a node labeled ⟨*newSimpRoleMsg*⟩ which has not yet been evaluated. Furthermore, it states that its child node ⟨*superObject*⟩ has been evaluated already.

The first nested rule raises an error if a second instance of a simple role type[6] with the same root object should be created or if the superobject is not of the expected type.

The second nested rule applies otherwise. The body of this rule describes how the evolving algebra is changed such that it reflects the execution of the *newRoleOf:*-message.

1. A new element *temp* of the universe *objects* is created. It represents the unique object identifier of a new object.
2. The function *HasType* is defined to map the new element to the identifier of the child ⟨*simpRoleTypeName*⟩ of the active node. It is recorded that the new object is an instance of the object type given in the message.
3. The function *RoleOf* is defined to map the new element to the node value of the child ⟨*superObject*⟩ of the active node. It is recorded that the new object represents a role of the object held by the variable given in the message. Also, the functions *Root* and *HasSimpleRole* are set accordingly.
4. The node value of the child ⟨*superObject*⟩ of the active node is set to "uneval". The parse tree is cleaned up such that the message can be executed later again.
5. The node value of the active node is set to *temp*. The message has been successfully executed and the new object is returned.

Figure 8 gives the transition rule for creating a new qualified role. The transition rule is similar to that for a simple role, except that the qualifying object and its type has to be considered.

Figure 9 gives the transition rule for abandoning a role. If the role to be abandoned has no subrole the dynamic functions reflecting the role hierarchy are reset, otherwise an error is raised. Alternatively, the subtree beyond the role to be abandoned could be abandoned, too. The transition rule for the corresponding

---

[6] or any of its subclasses

let o = $NV(superObject(AN))$, r = $Id(simpleRoleTypeName(AN))$ in
if $Label(AN)$ = $\langle newSimpRoleMsg \rangle$ and $NV(AN)$ = "uneval" and
$o \neq$ "uneval" then
   if $HasSimpleRole(Root(o),RootClass(r)) \neq$ "undef" or
   $HasSuperClass^*(HasType(o), SimpleRoleTypeOf(r)) \neq$ "true" then
     AN := $\langle EasyRolesDM \rangle$, $NV(AN)$:= "error"
   endif
   if $HasSimpleRole(Root(o),RootClass(r))$ = "undef" and
   $HasSuperClass^*(HasType(o), SimpleRoleTypeOf(r))$ = "true" then
    let temp = New(objects) in
      $HasType(temp)$:= r,
      $RoleOf(temp)$:= o,
      $Root(temp)$:= $Root(o)$,
      $HasSimpleRole(Root(o),RootClass(r))$:= temp,
      $NV(superObject(AN))$:= "uneval",
      $NV(AN)$:= temp
    endlet
endif
endlet

Fig. 7. Transition Rule for "newRoleOf:"-message

message for qualified roles, which must also consider the qualifier, is very similar and is not shown.

Figure 10 shows the transition rule for the **existsAs**-message used for checking whether an object exists in a particular simple role. Note: The condition check "RootClass (t) = t" reflects the current restriction of the implementation presented in [GSR96] that no subclass of a role type may be used in the "existsAs:"-message. The transition rule for the corresponding message for qualified roles is not shown. This rule is very much similar to the **as:Of**-message given in Figure 11.

Figure 11 shows the transition rule for the **as:Of:**-message used for switching to a particular qualified role. The transition rule for the corresponding message for simple roles is not shown. This rule is very much similar to the **existsAs:**-message given in Figure 10.

Figure 12 shows the transition rule for the **entityEquiv:**-message used for checking whether two objects represent the same real world entity.

6 Conclusion

We have presented the operational semantics of class and role hierarchies. Using evolving algebras, we have defined how traditional inheritance at the class level interacts with inheritance in role hierarchies at the instance level. Further, we have specified the semantics of predefined messages to create and to query role hierarchies.

let $o = NV(superObject(AN))$, $r = Id(qualRoleTypeName(AN))$, $q=NV(qualObj(AN))$ in
if $Label(AN) = \langle newQualRoleMsg \rangle$ and $NV(AN) = $ "uneval" and
$o \neq$ "uneval" and $q \neq$ "uneval" then
  if $HasQualRole(Root(o),RootClass(r),q) \neq$ "undef" or
  $HasSuperClass^*(HasType(o),\ qualRoleTypeOf(r)) \neq$ "true" or
  $HasSuperClass^*(HasType(q),\ ClassOfQualObj(r)) \neq$ "true" then
    $AN := \langle\ EasyRoleDM\ \rangle$, $NV(AN) :=$ "error"
  endif
  if $HasQualRole(Root(o),RootClass(r),q) = $ "undef" and
  $HasSuperClass^*(HasType(o),\ qualRoleTypeOf(r)) = $ "true" and
  $HasSuperClass^*(HasType(q),\ ClassOfQualObj\ (r)) = $ "true" then
    let temp $=$ New(objects) in
      $HasType(temp):= r$,
      $RoleOf(temp):= o$,
      $Qualifier(temp):= q$,
      $Root(temp):= Root(o)$,
      $HasQualRole(Root(o),RootClass(r),q) := temp$,
      $NV(superObject(AN)) := $ "uneval"
      $NV(qualObject(AN)) := $ "uneval"
      $NV(AN) := temp$,
    endlet
endif
endlet

Fig. 8. Transition Rule for "newRoleOf:QualifiedBy:"-message

let $o = NV(receiver(AN))$ in
if $Label(AN) = \langle abandonMsg \rangle$ and $NV(AN) = $ "uneval" and
$o \neq$ "uneval" then
  if $\exists\ o' \in$ objects: $roleOf(o') = o$ then
    $AN := \langle\ EasyRoleDM\ \rangle$, $NV(AN) :=$ "error"
  if $\not\exists\ o' \in$ objects: $roleOf(0') = o$ and
  $TypeOf(o) \in SimpRoleTypeNames$ then
    $HasSimpleRoles(root(o),\ RootClass(TypeOf(o))) := $ "undef",
    $RoleOf(o) := $ "undef",
    $Root(o) := $ "undef",
    $NV(receiver(AN)) := $ "uneval",
    $Label(AN) := $ "eval",
  endif
endif
endlet

Fig. 9. Transition Rule for "abandon"-message

let $o = NV(receiver(AN))$, $t = Id(simpleRoleTypeName(AN))$ in
if $Label(AN) = \langle existsAsMsg \rangle$ and $NV(AN) = $ "uneval" and
$o \neq$ "uneval" then
   if $RootClass(t) \neq t$ then
     $AN := \langle\ EasyRolesDM\ \rangle$, $NV(AN) := $ "error"
   if $hasSimpleRole(o,t) = $ "undef" and $RootClass(t) = t$ then
     $Label(AN) := $ "false"
   endif
   if $hasSimpleRole(o,t) \neq$ "undef" and $RootClass(t) = t$ then
     $Label(AN) := $ "true"
   endif
endif
endlet

Fig. 10. Transition Rules for "existsAs:"-message

let $o = NV(receiver(AN))$, $t = Id(qualRoleTypeName(AN))$, $q = NV(qualObject(AN))$ in
if $Label(AN) = \langle existsAsMsg \rangle$ and $NV(AN) = $ "uneval" and
$o \neq$ "uneval" and $q \neq$ "uneval" then
   if $hasQualRole(o,t,q) = $ "undef" or $RootClass(t) \neq t$ then
     $AN := \langle\ EasyRolesDM\ \rangle$, $HV(AN) := $ "error"
   endif
   if $hasQualRole(o,t,q) \neq$ "undef" and $RootClass(t) = t$ then
     $Label(AN) := hasQualRole(o,t,q)$
   endif
endif
endlet

Fig. 11. Transition Rule for "as:Of:"-message

let $r = NV(receiver(AN))$, $o = NV(anotherObject(AN))$ in
if $Label(AN) = \langle entityEquiv: \rangle$ and $NV(AN) = $ "uneval"
   and $r \neq$ "uneval" and $o \neq$ "uneval" then
   if $root(r)=root(o)$ and $root(o) \neq$ "undef" then
     $Label(AN) := $ "true"
   endif
   if $root(r) \neq root(o)$ or $root(o) = $ "undef" then
     $Label(AN) := $ "false"
   endif
endif
endlet

Fig. 12. Transition Rule for "entityEquiv"-message

The operational semantics given by an evolving algebra is equally good understood by language designers, compiler constructors, and programers. Transition rules, although not prescribing a particular implementation, can easily be mapped into an interpreter for a language. For example, the implementation of the predefined methods to manipulate roles provided by our extension of Smalltalk [GSR96] often closely match the logical structure - but not the syntax - of the transition rules given in this paper. Transition rules, however, abstracting from implementation details provide a more concise and a more easy to read representation. They express precisely the meaning and limits of particular language constructs. For example, by analyzing the transition rule 'if $HasQualRole(Root(o), RootClass(r), q) \neq$ "undef" ...' in Figure 8 we can conclude that the qualifier q must be unique among all instances of a qualified role type[7] having the same root (and not only among all instances having the same ancestor).

Evolving algebras have been used to specify the operational semantics of several programming languages [B90a, B90b, B90c, Gur88a, GM90, RB92, Bla92, Gur92]. We have seen that the approach is also very fruitful and promising for specifying the semantics of novel object-oriented concepts.

References

[ABGO93] A. Albano, R. Bergamini, G. Ghelli, and R. Orsini. An object data model with roles. In *Proceedings of the International Conference on Very Large Databases*, pages 39–51, Dublin, 1993.

[B90a] E. Börger. A logical operational semantics of full Prolog, part I: Selection core and control. In E. Börger, H. Kleine Büning, and M. Richter, editors, *CSL '89*. Springer LCNS, 1990.

[B90b] E. Börger. A logical operational semantics of full Prolog, part II: Built-in predicates for database manipulations. In *MFCS '90*. Springer LCNS, 1990.

[B90c] E. Börger. A logical operational semantics of full Prolog, part III: Built-in predicates for files, terms, arithmetic and input-output. In Y. Moschovakis, editor, *Proceedings of the Workshop on Logic for Computer Science*, 1990.

[Bee90] C. Beeri. A formal approach to object-oriented databases. *Data & Knowledge Enigneering (5)*, pages 353–382, 1990.

[Bla92] B. Blakley. *A Smalltalk Evolving Algebra and its Uses*. PhD thesis, University of Michigan, 1992.

[GKS90] G. Gottlob, G. Kappel, and M. Schrefl. Semantics of object-oriented data models - the evolving algebra approach. In J. W. Schmidt and A. A. Stogny, editors, *First International East/West Database Workshop - LNCS*, page 504. Springer Verlag, 1990.

[GM88] Y. Gurevich and J. M. Morris. Algebraic operational semantics and Modula-2. In E. Börger, H. Kleine Büning, and M. Richter, editors, *CSL '87*, pages 81–101. Springer, LNCS 329, 1988.

[GM90] Y. Gurevich and L. S. Moss. Algebraic operational semantics and Occam. Rc15352, IBM Research Division, T. J. Watson Research Center, Yorktown Heights, 1990.

---

[7] and its subclasses

[GSR96]   G. Gottlob, M. Schrefl, and B. Röck. Extending object-oriented systems with roles. *In: ACM Transactions on Information Systems*, pages pp. 268–296, July 1996.

[Gur88a] Y. Gurevich. Algorithmus in the world of bounded resources. In R. Herken, editor, *The universal Turing machine - a half-century story*, pages 407–416. Oxford University Press, 1988.

[Gur88b] Y. Gurevich. Logic and the challenge of computer science. In E. Börger, editor, *Trends in Theoretical Computer Science*, pages 1–57. Computer Science Press, 1988.

[Gur92]   Y. Gurevich. The evolving algebra semantics of C. Cse-tr-141-92, EECS Department, University of Michigan, 1992.

[Mor88]   J. M. Morris. *Algebraic Operational Semantics for Modula-2*. PhD thesis, University of Michigan, 1988.

[Pap91]   M. P. Papazoglou. Roles: A methodology for representing multifaced objects. In *Proceedings of the International Conference on Database and Expert Systems Applications*, pages 7–12, 1991.

[Per90]   B. Pernici. Objects with roles. In *Proceedings of the ACM Conference on Office Information Systems*, pages 205–215, 1990.

[RB92]   E. Riccobene and E. Börger. A mathematical model of concurrent Prolog. Cstr-92-15, Dept. of Computer Science, University of Bristol, 1992.

[RS91]   J. Richardson and P. Schwarz. Aspects: Extending objects to support multiples, independent roles. In *Proceedings of the International Conference on Management of Data*, pages 298–307, 1991.

[WdJS94] R. Wieringa, W. de Jonge, and P. Spruit. Roles and dynamic subclasses: A modal logic approach. In *Proceedings of the Eighth European Conference on Object-Oriented Programming*, 1994.

Appendix: Grammar for EasyRoles

The grammar of EasyRoles is defined using Backus-Naur Form (BNF). The symbols ::= | [ ] ( ) { } " are meta-symbols belonging to the BNF formalism and not symbols of EasyRoles. All names denoted by the non-terminal symbols ⟨programName⟩, ⟨typeName⟩, ⟨varName⟩, ⟨methName⟩, and ⟨formalParName⟩ are strings, consisting of letters, digits, and some special characters. Each name starts with a letter. The terminal symbols ⟨const⟩ is a string of characters enclosed in quotes or a number consisting of digits.

⟨EasyRoles⟩	::=	⟨EasyRolesSD⟩ | ⟨EasyRolesDM⟩
⟨EasyRolesSD⟩	::=	EasyRoles define ⟨dbName⟩
		{⟨typeDef⟩} "|" {⟨varDecl⟩} "|" end.
⟨EasyRolesDM⟩	::=	EasyRoles use ⟨dbName⟩ {⟨msg⟩} end.
⟨typeDef⟩	::=	⟨classDef⟩ | ⟨simpleRoleDef⟩ | ⟨qualRoleDef⟩
⟨varDecl⟩	::=	⟨varName⟩
⟨methDef⟩	::=	⟨methName⟩ [⟨formalParName⟩] ⟨methBody⟩.
⟨methBody⟩	::=	{ ⟨msg⟩ }
⟨expr⟩	::=	⟨varName⟩ | ⟨const⟩ | ⟨msg⟩
⟨actualPar⟩	::=	⟨varName⟩ | ⟨const⟩
⟨msg⟩	::=	⟨userDefMsg⟩ | ⟨returnMsg⟩ | ⟨assignment⟩ |

```
                                ⟨newMsg⟩ | ⟨newRoleMsg⟩ | ⟨newQualRoleMsg⟩ |
                                ⟨existsAsMsg⟩ | ⟨existsAsOfMsg⟩ |
                                ⟨asMsg⟩ | ⟨asOfMsg⟩ | ⟨qualifierMsg⟩ |
                                ⟨rootMsg⟩ | ⟨roleOfMsg⟩
⟨userDefMsg⟩        ::=  ⟨addressee⟩ ⟨methName⟩ [⟨actualPar⟩].
⟨assignment⟩        ::=  ⟨varName⟩ <- ⟨expr⟩.
⟨returnMsg⟩         ::=  ^⟨expr⟩.
⟨classDef⟩          ::=  ⟨typeName⟩
                                subclass: #⟨className⟩
                                variables: ' { ⟨varName⟩ } '
                                methods: ' { ⟨methDef⟩ } '.
⟨simpleRoleDef⟩     ::=  RoleType
                                defRoleType: #⟨simpRoleTypeName⟩
                                variables: ' { ⟨varName⟩ } '
                                methods: ' { ⟨methDef⟩ } '
                                roleSuperType: #⟨typeName⟩.
⟨qualRoleDef⟩       ::=  QualifiedRoleType
                                defRoleType: #⟨qualRoleTypeName⟩
                                variables: ' { ⟨varName⟩ } '
                                methods: ' { ⟨methDef⟩ } '
                                roleSuperType: #⟨typeName⟩.
                                classOfQualifyingObj: #⟨typeName⟩.
⟨className⟩         ::=  'ObjectWithRoles' | ⟨typeName⟩
⟨newMsg⟩            ::=  ⟨className⟩ new.
⟨newSimpRoleMsg⟩    ::=  ⟨simpRoleTypeName⟩ newRoleOf: ⟨superObject⟩.
⟨newQualRoleMsg⟩    ::=  ⟨qualRoleTypeName⟩ newRoleOf: ⟨superObject⟩.
                                qualifiedBy: ⟨qualObj⟩.
⟨abandonMsg⟩        ::=  ⟨receiver⟩ abandon.
⟨existsAsMsg⟩       ::=  ⟨receiver⟩ existsAs: ⟨simpleRoleTypeName⟩.
⟨existsAsOfMsg⟩     ::=  ⟨receiver⟩ existsAs: ⟨qualRoleTypeName⟩
                                of:⟨qualObj⟩.
⟨asMsg⟩             ::=  ⟨receiver⟩ as: ⟨simpleRoleTypeName⟩.
⟨ofMsg⟩             ::=  ⟨receiver⟩ as: ⟨qualRoleTypeName⟩ of:⟨qualObj⟩.
⟨rootMsg⟩           ::=  ⟨receiver⟩ root.
⟨roleOfMsg⟩         ::=  ⟨receiver⟩ roleOf.
⟨qualifierMsg⟩      ::=  ⟨receiver⟩ qualifier.
⟨entityEquivMsg⟩    ::=  ⟨receiver⟩ entityEquiv: ⟨anotherObject⟩.
⟨simpRoleTypeName⟩  ::=  ⟨typeName⟩
⟨qualRoleTypeName⟩  ::=  ⟨typeName⟩
⟨receiver⟩          ::=  ⟨varName⟩
⟨qualObj⟩           ::=  ⟨varName⟩
⟨superObj⟩          ::=  ⟨varName⟩
⟨anotherObject⟩     ::=  ⟨varName⟩
```

Semantics in Spatial Databases

Bart Kuijpers[1], Jan Paredaens[1], and Luc Vandeurzen[2]

[1] University of Antwerp (UIA), Dept. Math. & Computer Sci.,
Universiteitsplein 1, B-2610 Antwerp, Belgium
Email: {kuijpers, pareda}@uia.ua.ac.be
[2] University of Limburg (LUC), Dept. WNI,
Universitaire Campus, B-3590 Diepenbeek, Belgium
Email: lvdeurze@alpha.luc.ac.be

Abstract. In this paper we discuss two data models for spatial database systems: the *linear data model* and the *topological data model*. Both can be used to model a wide range of applications. The linear data model is particularly suited to model spatial database applications in which exact geometrical information is required and in which this information can be approximated by linear geometrical spatial objects. The topological model on the other hand is suitable for applications in which rather than exact geometrical information the relative position of spatial objects is of importance.
We will specify in each case which types of spatial data and spatial databases are under consideration. A semantics for both data models is formally defined in terms of finite representations of spatial databases in the data models. We also present languages to query spatial databases in both models and briefly investigate their expressiveness.

1 Introduction

The number of computer applications in which database systems are used to store and manage spatial or geometric information has grown rapidly during the last decades. CAD/CAM, VLSI-design, robotics, geographical information systems, and medical imaging are only a few examples of applications that use (sometimes large amounts of) two-dimensional or three-dimensional spatial information.

Initially, spatial database management systems for such applications were build by extending traditional database management systems by introducing rather trivial spatial data types and by extending SQL in an application-dependent way. Current efforts in spatial database systems, however, aim at developing systems that are specifically suited to deal with spatial information, but which are nevertheless application-independent. This latter goal was set out in the following quote of [12]:

> "The challenge for the developers of DBMSs with spatial capabilities lies not so much in providing yet another special-purpose data structure that is marginally faster when used in a particular application, but in defining abstractions and architectures to implement systems that offer generic spatial

data management capabilities and that can be tailored to the requirements of a particular domain".

Apart from the fact that spatial database management systems are now designed as general as possible rather than for one particular application, a number of other and more theoretical concerns dominate the current research in spatial database systems:

- theoretical models are needed which support an elegant combination of spatial (or geometrical) information and non-spatial (or classical) information;
- a formally defined semantics is needed that is closed under set-theoretic, geometric and topological operations and that is defined in terms of a finite representation;
- efficient implementations of operations on n-dimensional spatial objects are desired;
- the connection with visual interfaces and multimedia must be investigated.

In this paper we describe two data models both of which are suited to model a wide class of spatial database applications: the *linear data model* and the *topological data model*. The linear data model is suited to model spatial database applications in which exact geometrical or geographical information on spatial objects is required and in which this information can be approximated by linear geometrical spatial objects. The topological model on the other hand is suitable for applications in which rather than exact geometrical information the relative position of spatial objects is of importance.

The remainder of the paper is structured as follows. In Section 2, we describe the linear data model. First, we look at a number of applications for which this data model is suited: geographical information systems, CAD/CAM and linear decision problems. We analyze the spatial data requirements of these different applications. Next, we formalize the types of data that occur in these applications into the mathematical framework of semi-linear sets in an n-dimensional Euclidean space. We conclude this section by briefly illustrating how the representation scheme of the linear data model can be extended to a language to query spatial databases in the linear data model.

In Section 3, we discuss the topological data model. First, we look at a typical example application of spatial databases in the topological data model and at the information that is characteristically contained in such spatial databases. We formally define what we mean by spatial data and spatial databases in this data model: conceptually, spatial databases consist here of points, curves between these points, and areas formed between these curves in the two-dimensional Euclidean plane. We describe a representation of spatial databases by means of a finite data structure which contains exactly the topological information of the spatial database. We conclude by giving a language to query spatial databases in the topological data model and illustrate the expressiveness of this language.

2 Linear Data Model

In this section, we concentrate on spatial database models for applications that require the knowledge of the exact geometric position in space of the spatial data they manipulate. We focus on linear spatial data, although some applications typically handle more general kinds of spatial data. The representation of a coast line, for instance, requires fractal curves. The restriction to linear data is justified however, for the following reasons:

1. at this moment there are few efficient algorithms known to implement the variety of spatial operations on curved data;
2. linear figures are perfectly suitable to approximate more general data with; and
3. the simplicity of linear data will offer us several desirable properties.

As an introduction, we discuss three different kinds of spatial applications. We briefly analyze the kind of spatial data each application requires to detect all necessary and sufficient data requirements. All these requirements together will motivate the choice of our final spatial data type.

We propose a general and natural data type that, in our opinion, covers all possible data requirements for the intended applications. The representation scheme based on this data type is complete, in the sense that it can deal with every n-dimensional, mathematically definable linear geometric figure. Once the representation of the spatial data is known, we describe formally the *linear data model* and explain its syntax and semantics. We present possible linear database instances for the discussed applications to show the effectiveness of the linear model. Finally, we conclude with extending the representation tool of linear figures to a linear spatial query language.

2.1 Data Requirements

In this section, we analyze the spatial data requirements of three totally different spatial applications. In the first example, we discuss the kind of spatial data required in geographical information systems. Next, we investigate the various spatial objects used in CAD/CAM. Finally, we show how linear (decision) problems can be interpreted as intersections, unions, differences, and projections of n-dimensional linear figures.

Geographical information systems [21] are one of the first applications that demanded a spatial database system. The task of the spatial database is to store a representation of some geographical area, e.g., a road map, together with text and number information as, for instance, speed limits and one way directions.

Representations of geographical areas are typically two-dimensional maps graphically visualizing the relevant information. Figure 1 shows a simplified representation of Belgium. On this map, we have displayed the two most important rivers, some cities, and the three regions of Belgium. Unavoidably, we grap at the polygon data type (to represent two dimensional areas), the line-segment type (to represent borders and rivers), and the point data type (to represent cities), for this purpose. Complex, not necessarily topologically connected, geographical objects are provided as compositions of these basic data types. The literature mentions various data models based on these primitive types [10, 13, 14, 15, 29, 31].

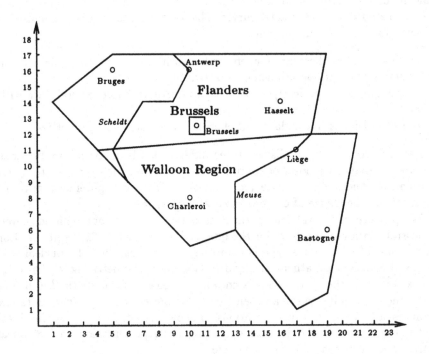

Fig. 1. Spatial information map of Belgium.

The same geographical area can be viewed from various perspectives. We can focus on the road infrastructure, the land use, and weather information, for instance. All these different *thematic layers* of the same area cannot be displayed on the same two-dimensional representation of the area. One particular way to solve this brings all these thematic layers together and considers them as one spatial data object in higher-dimensional space.

In CAD/CAM, the data requirements are somewhat different. Typically, CAD/CAM applications store and manipulate a database containing the representation and features of three-dimensional scenes and solid objects.

Up to now, constructed solid geometry (CSG), together with the boundary representation method, are the most widely propagated representation tools for CAD/CAM objects. In the CSG representation scheme, a geometric object is described as a composition of primitive objects as for instance pyramids and boxes.

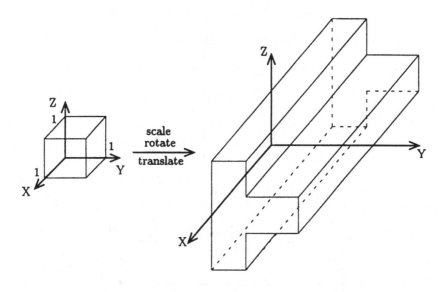

Fig. 2. Composition of two boxes into a T-shape.

The composition is achieved via motial and combinatorial operators. Under motial operators we understand affine transformations as for instance rotation and translation. Examples of combinatorial operators are the set operations union, intersection, and difference. Figure 2 shows an object with a T-shape, created via the CSG methodology.

Although solid objects are always topologically closed, it can be very helpful to use open figures to define them as illustrated by Figure 3. Two boxes are connected using a lump in the one box that precisely fits a notch in the other box. The one box can be represented as the union of the box with a small cube and the other box as the difference of the box with the topologically open interior of the same small cube.

Until now, we were only concerned about the representation of real-world objects. These could all be described using at most three free parameters. The result of linear spatial queries, however, can not always be described with three free variables. Consider, e.g., the query "Compute the position of a couple of shelves in a furnitured room such that desks can still be sit at, and doors and drawers can still be opened." The solution (the coordinates of the mass-centers of the shelves) will define an object in (at least) six-dimensional space. Moreover, that object will not be topologically closed, since open doors and drawers may not touch the shelves. In general, the solution to this kind of linear problems might be an n-dimensional, unbounded and topologically non-closed geometric figure [4].

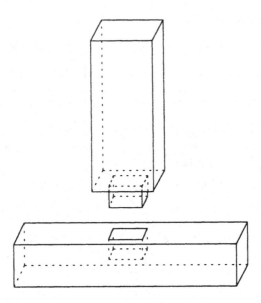

Fig. 3. A connection between two boxes.

2.2 Linear Representation Scheme

In this section, we try to formalize the various data types proposed in the previous section into a mathematical framework. This mathematical framework allows the representation of every *semi-linear set* definable in n-dimensional Euclidean space. Furthermore, the framework is safe in the sense that *only* linear figures can be represented.

As it is more natural to represent a geometrical figure as an enumeration of all its points, the representation we use will be of type "point-set." However, we have to represent our "point-sets" in a finite way to allow physical storage.

More formally, assume a totally ordered infinite set of variables over **R** called *real variables*. Define a *linear term* as a linear polynomial with rational coefficients, i.e., of the form $\sum_{i=1}^{k} a_i x_i$, where $x_1, \ldots, x_k$ are real variables and $a_1, \ldots, a_k$ are rational constants. An *atomic linear formula* is a condition of the form $T \theta a$ where T is a linear term; θ one of the following binary comparison operators $=, <, >, \leq, \geq$, and $\neq$; and a a real constant. A *linear formula* is an arbitrary well-formed formula in first-order logic with addition, i.e.,

- atomic linear formulae are linear formulae;
- if φ and ψ are linear formulae, then $\varphi \wedge \psi$; $\varphi \vee \psi$; and $\neg \varphi$ are linear formulae; and
- if x is a real variable and φ is a linear formula in which x is free, then $(\exists x)\varphi$ is a linear formula.

Every linear formula φ with n free variables, $x_1, \ldots, x_n$, defines a point-set

$$\{(x_1, \ldots, x_n) \mid \varphi(x_1, \ldots, x_n)\}$$

in n-dimensional Euclidean space $\mathbf{R}^n$. A geometrical figure in $\mathbf{R}^n$ will be called a semi-linear set if there exists a linear formula φ with n free variables such that the point-set defined by φ coincides with the geometrical figure. The representation of a semi-linear set is any linear formula, φ, that defines a point-set equal to the semi-linear set.

It is obvious that this representation scheme is not unique. In fact, any semi-linear set can be represented by an infinite number of linear formulae. On the contrary, the representation scheme is unambiguous. Every linear formula φ defines exactly one semi-linear set.

Assume in the following example that we are working in the three-dimensional Euclidean space $\mathbf{R}^3$.

Example 1. Assume we want to create a prism with height a in the z-direction. The representation of this prism is given by the linear formula

$$\varphi(x, y) \wedge (0 \leq z \leq a),$$

where φ defines the base of the prism in the xy-plane. Any prism with the same shape can now be defined in $\mathbf{R}^3$ as a composition of a translation and a rotation of this prism primitive. In general, any affine transformation can be applied to the prism primitive since affine transformations can be very simply expressed as linear formulae. If we consider, for instance, an affine transformation that does not affect the z-coordinate, the resulting prism may be described in terms of x_{new}, y_{new}, and z_{new} by the linear formula

$$(\exists x)(\exists y)(\varphi(x, y) \wedge (x_{new} = ax + by + t_x) \wedge (y_{new} = cx + dy + t_y)) \wedge (0 \leq z_{new} \leq a)$$

with a, b, c, d, e, t_x, t_y constants defining the affine transformation.

We have explored in this example a very powerful property of the linear representation scheme: the expressibility of affine transformations with linear formulae. This, together with the basic set operations union, intersection, and difference, of which semi-linear sets are closed under [33], allows the definition of linear figures using the "constructed solid geometry" method.

A practical tool to deal with semi-linear sets are *polytopes*. A *polytope* in the Euclidean space (of arbitrary dimension) is defined as the convex hull of a non-empty finite set of points in that space [5, 23, 17]. An *open polytope* is the topological interior of a polytope with respect to the smallest sub-space containing the polytope. It can be proved that bounded semi-linear sets and finite unions of open polytopes are equivalent. [33]

However, since polytopes are necessarily bounded, finite unions of polytopes can only represent bounded linear figures. Therefore, we present another tool characterizing semi-linear point-sets in all their appearances.

Günther [11] defines *polyhedral chains* as a representation scheme for geometric data. A *polyhedral chain* in the Euclidean space (of arbitrary dimension) is defined as a finite sum of *cells* each of which is a finite intersection of half-spaces. It can be shown that semi-linear sets and polyhedral chains are equivalent. [33] This property proves effectively the equivalence of semi-linear sets with mathematically definable linear figures.

The above characterizations allow us to conclude that most spatial data types found in the literature are sub-types of the semi-linear set data type. Güting [13, 14] proposes in his geo-relational algebra the spatial data types *point*, *line*, and *polygon*, which can be seen respectively as zero-, one-, and two-dimensional polytopes.[3] In his spatial data representation model Egenhofer [9] proposes *simplices* as basic objects, which are special kinds of polytopes.

In summary, semi-linear sets constitute a very general and elegant paradigm to represent linear spatial data, which are the kind of spatial data that are most often considered. We believe semi-linear sets have the potential for efficient implementation. Brodsky et al. [4, 3] introduced canonical forms for linear formulae to make efficient implementation of operations on semi-linear sets possible. Lassez et al. [20, 16] have proposed variable elimination algorithms for sets of linear constraints. The alternative characterizations we presented offer the opportunity to use polyhedral chains or polytopes as internal representation for semi-linear sets. Günther [11] has described efficient algorithms to perform set-operations on polyhedral chains. Algorithms to compute efficiently the union or intersection of n-dimensional polytopes are provided by Putnam et al. [28]. Several operations and techniques described in computational geometry, such as plane sweep and divide-and-conquer, can also be used for this purpose [22, 32, 6, 27]. Finally, the notion of semi-linear set is not bounded to any particular dimension.

2.3   The Linear Data Model

The linear spatial database model is based on the relational model, because linear spatial databases require a lot of traditional database capabilities. In particular, if the linear spatial database consists purely of non-spatial flat relations, it degenerates into a traditional database for which the relational model offers a well-accepted representation. Moreover, the relational model, and the relational calculus and algebra as well, have the interesting property of being easily extendible with new data types and operators.

More formally, a *linear spatial database scheme* consists of a finite set of relation names. Each relation name R is of some type $[n, m]$, with n and m integers. A *linear spatial database instance* is a mapping that assigns a linear relation instance to each relation name appearing in the database scheme. A *linear instance* of R, also called a *linear relation*, is a finite set of linear tuples of type $[n, m]$. A *linear tuple* of type $[n, m]$ is straightforwardly defined as a tuple

---

[3] The polygons considered by Güting are not necessary convex, but can always be decomposed into convex polygons.

of the form

$$(c_1, \ldots, c_n, \varphi(x_1, \ldots, x_m))$$

where $c_1, \ldots, c_n$ are non-spatial values from some domain U and $\varphi(x_1, \ldots, x_m)$ is a linear formula with m free real variables.

The semantics of a linear tuple $t = (c_1, \ldots, c_n, \varphi(x_1, \ldots, x_m))$ of type $[n, m]$ is the possibly infinite subset of $U^n \times \mathbf{R}^m$ defined as the Cartesian product $\{(c_1, \ldots, c_n)\} \times S$, in which $S \subseteq \mathbf{R}^m$ is the semi-linear set $\{(x_1, \ldots, x_m) \mid \varphi(x_1, \ldots, x_m)\}$. This subset of $U^n \times \mathbf{R}^m$ can be interpreted as a possibly infinite $(n + m)$-ary relation, denoted $I(t)$. The semantics of a linear relation, r, denoted $I(r)$, is defined as $I(r) = \bigcup_{t \in r} I(t)$. Finally, the semantics of a linear spatial database, DB, is the set of relations $I(r)$ with r a linear relation of DB.

In the remainder of this section, we give an example spatial database for the map of Belgium depicted in Section 2.1.

2.4 The Linear Spatial Calculus

In this section, we present a calculus-like query language, called FO + linear. The linear calculus, FO + linear, is obtained by adding to the language of linear formulae of Section 2.2 the following:

- a totally ordered infinite set of variables called *non-spatial variables*, disjoint from the set of real variables;
- atomic formulae of the form $v_1 = v_2$, with v_1 and v_2 non-spatial variables;
- atomic formulae of the form $R(v_1, \ldots, v_n; p_1, \ldots, p_m)$, with R a relation name of type $[n, m]$, $v_1, \ldots, v_n$ non-spatial variables, and $p_1, \ldots, p_m$ linear terms; and
- universal and existential quantification of non-spatial variables.

A *query* expressed in FO + linear has the form:

$$\{(x_1, \ldots, x_n) \mid \varphi(x_1, \ldots, x_n)\}$$

where $\varphi(x_1, \ldots, x_n)$ is an expression of FO+linear with $x_1, \ldots, x_n$ free variables.

Finally, we shall give some typical example queries, illustrating the expressive power of FO + linear. A precise characterization of the expressive power of FO + linear is still wide open. For a deeper investigation concerning the expressiveness and limitations of FO + linear, we refer to [33].

Example 2. An example of a (very simple) linear spatial query on the database in Example 1 is *"Find all cities that lie on a river and give their names and the names of the rivers they lie on."* This query can be expressed by the following linear calculus expression:

$$\{(c, r) \mid (\exists x)(\exists y)(\text{Cities}(c, x, y) \wedge \text{Rivers}(r, x, y))\}.$$

Cities

Name	Geometry
Antwerp	$(x = 10) \wedge (y = 16)$
Bastogne	$(x = 19) \wedge (y = 6)$
Bruges	$(x = 5) \wedge (y = 16)$
Brussels	$(x = 10.5) \wedge (y = 12.5)$
Charleroi	$(x = 10) \wedge (y = 8)$
Hasselt	$(x = 16) \wedge (y = 14)$
Liège	$(x = 17) \wedge (y = 11)$

Rivers

Name	Geometry
Meuse	$((y \leq 17) \wedge (5x - y \leq 78) \wedge (y \geq 12)) \vee$ $((y \leq 12) \wedge (x - y = 6) \wedge (y \geq 11)) \vee$ $((y \leq 11) \wedge (x - 2y = -5) \wedge (y \geq 9)) \vee$ $((y \leq 9) \wedge (x = 13) \wedge (y \geq 6))$
Scheldt	$((y \leq 17) \wedge (x + y = 26) \wedge (y \geq 16)) \vee$ $((y \leq 16) \wedge (2x - y = 4) \wedge (y \geq 14)) \vee$ $((x \leq 9) \wedge (x \geq 7) \wedge (y = 14)) \vee$ $((y \leq 14) \wedge (-3x + 2y = 7) \wedge (y \geq 11)) \vee$ $((y \leq 11) \wedge (2x + y = 21) \wedge (y \geq 9))$

Regions

Name	Geometry
Brussels	$(y \leq 13) \wedge (x \leq 11) \wedge (y \geq 12) \wedge (x \geq 10)$
Flanders	$(y \leq 17) \wedge (5x - y \leq 78) \wedge (x - 14y \leq -150) \wedge (x + y \geq 45) \wedge$ $(3x - 4y \geq -53) \wedge (\neg((y \leq 13) \wedge (x \leq 11) \wedge (y \geq 12) \wedge (x \geq 10)))$
Walloon Region	$((x - 14y \geq -150) \wedge (y \leq 12) \wedge (19x + 7y \leq 375) \wedge (x - 2y \leq 15) \wedge$ $(5x + 4y \geq 89) \wedge (x \geq 13)) \vee ((-x + 3y \geq 5) \wedge (x + y \geq 45) \wedge$ $(x - 14y \geq -150) \wedge (x \geq 13))$

Fig. 4. Representation of the spatial database of Belgium shown in Figure 1.

In all the remaining queries, we shall assume the input database consists of one relation S of type $[0, n]$. We shall also use point-variables instead of real variables, e.g., equations such as $(\mathbf{x} < \mathbf{y})$ should be interpreted as $(x_1 < y_1) \wedge \cdots \wedge (x_n < y_n)$. In particular, $(\mathbf{x} \neq 0)$ means $(x_1 \neq 0) \wedge \cdots \wedge (x_n \neq 0)$ and not $(x_1 \neq 0) \vee \cdots \vee (x_n \neq 0)$!

Example 3. The following FO + linear-expression decides whether S is bounded:

$$(\exists \mathbf{d})(\forall \mathbf{x})(\forall \mathbf{y})(S(\mathbf{x}) \wedge S(\mathbf{y}) \Rightarrow -\mathbf{d} < \mathbf{y} - \mathbf{x} < \mathbf{d}).$$

Example 4. Several topological properties of a semi-linear set can be computed in FO + linear. For instance, the topological interior of S is computed by the following FO + linear expression:

$$(\exists d)((d \neq 0) \wedge (\forall y)(x - d < y < x + d) \Rightarrow S(y)).$$

Similarly, the topological closure and topological boundary of S can be computed in FO + linear.

In spite of all this, FO+linear can not be considered as a fully adequate query language. Afrati et al. [2] proved that the query "Does the semi-linear set S lie on a line?" is not expressible in FO + linear. The list of non-expressible FO + linear-queries is further extended in [33] with the predicate $collinear(x, y, z)$, which checks if the three points x, y, and z are collinear, and the predicate $ch(x_1, \ldots, x_m, y)$, which computes all points y belonging to the convex hull of the set of points $\{x_1, \ldots, x_m\}$.

3 The Topological Data Model

In this section, we focus on a spatial database model suited for applications in which knowledge about the relative positions of spatial objects is of importance rather than exact information about the geometric position of the spatial data. We limit the discussion to spatial databases that, conceptually, consist of points, curves between these points and areas formed by these curves in the two-dimensional Euclidean plane. These databases are commonly referred to as spatial databases in the *topological data model*. We will use a railway system as an example application that can be modeled in this way.

We discuss a representation of this type of databases by means of a finite data structure that is primarily geared towards supporting queries that involve only topological properties of the spatial database. This is reflected by the fact that this data structure represents topologically equivalent spatial databases in the same way, but also represents topologically non-equivalent spatial databases in a different way. A representation that satisfies these properties corresponds to an interface which allows the user to concentrate precisely on all the topological properties of the spatial database.

Finally, to conclude this section, we present a language to query spatial databases in the topological data model.

3.1 A Typical Application

Travel information is often provided to the train traveler by means of a spatial database such as the railway map shown in Figure 5. In this map, cities (or their railway stations) are represented by points labeled with the city name and train tracks between the stations are represented by curves connecting these points.

Such spatial database (or map) does not contain exact geographic information. There is no information in this map concerning the exact position of cities or railway stations. It also contains no information to answer a metric query

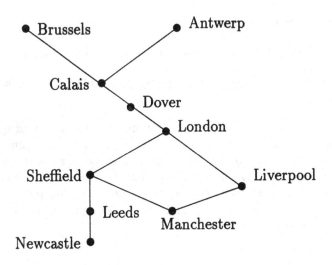

Fig. 5. A railroad map.

such as "What is the distance between London and Calais?" Since the traveler's main concern is not the longitude or latitude of cities he is also not surprised to find London shown right of Brussels in Figure 5 while in reality it is west of Brussels.

On the other hand, with the help of such maps, the traveler can answer his or her typical queries such as "Is there a connection from Brussels to Liverpool with a stop in London?" or "Do I pass Dover before passing Calais when traveling from Antwerp to London?" The class of queries which are of importance to a traveler is formed by those queries involving only properties of the map which are topological in nature. Here, concepts such as adjacency, connectivity, and containment are in the focus. The topological properties of a map are exactly those properties that are shared by any two spatial databases that can be obtained from each other by a topological deformation[4]. As an example of topologically equivalent spatial databases we take the map of Figure 5 and a representation of the same railway system by a conventional map which corresponds more closely to reality. Since in the former map the length of lines is not related to the actual length of the trajectory, length is not a topological property. Since, however, both maps show the same connections, connectedness is a topological property.

In the present section, we elaborate on the idea of topological property in the context of databases consisting of points, curves between these points, and areas formed by these curves [26]. For a survey of other application domains that can be modeled by means of a finite number of points in the plane and curves con-

---

[4] The notion of topological deformation will be made precise later.

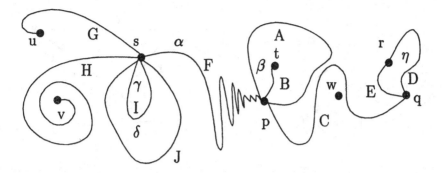

Fig. 6. An example of a spatial database in the topological data model.

necting them, we refer to Chapter 5 of the book by Laurini and Thompson [21] and references therein.

3.2 Spatial Databases in the Topological Data Model

In this section, we exactly define what we mean by spatial data and spatial databases in the topological data model. We work in the Euclidean plane $\mathbf{R}^2$.

Definition 1. A *spatial database in the topological data model* consists of a finite set of labeled points, a finite set of labeled curves, and a finite set of labeled areas. Each point label is assigned to a distinct point in $\mathbf{R}^2$. Each curve label is assigned to a distinct non-self-intersecting continuous curve[5] in $\mathbf{R}^2$ that starts and ends in a labeled point and does not contain any other labeled points except these. Two curves only intersect in a labeled point. Each area label is assigned to a distinct area formed by the labeled curves.

We remark that this definition allows curves to start and end in the same point, i.e., the database may contain loops. It also may contain multiple curves between two points. It is easily shown that for a database with n curve labels the number of area labels is bounded by $n + 1$.

We apply the following notational convention throughout the remainder of this section: Roman lower-case characters $p, q, \ldots$ denote point labels, Roman capitals $A, B, \ldots$ denote curve labels and Greek characters $\alpha, \beta, \ldots$ are used for area labels.

Figure 6 gives an example of a spatial database. This database has eight points, one of which (w) is isolated. It contains ten curves, three of which $(A, I, \text{and } J)$ are loops. There are five areas, one of which (α) is unbounded.

---

[5] In topological terms, this is a simple Jordan curve [24].

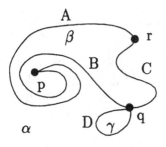
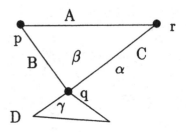

Fig. 7. Two topologically equivalent databases.

3.3 Representations of Spatial Databases in the Topological Data Model

The example application of Section 3.1 shows that in the topological data model the interpretation of spatial data is topological in nature. In other words, spatial databases in the topological data model contain information about topological properties and contain, e.g., no information about metric properties.

When we want to effectively represent spatial databases in the topological data model, and we know that only topological properties are under consideration, it may be desirable to have a representation of a spatial database which is *topologically invariant*, meaning that topologically equivalent databases will be represented in the same way. Ideally, a representation should also be *lossless*, in the sense that two databases that are *not* topologically equivalent will be represented differently.

In order to define these concepts formally, we first have to make the notion of topologically equivalent databases precise. Figure 7 gives an example of two equivalent spatial databases. Intuitively, two spatial databases are topologically equivalent if one can be obtained from the other by a continuous deformation. Mathematically, this continuous deformation is formalized by the notion of *isotopy* [24]. An isotopy h is a continuous series $(h_t \mid 0 \leq t \leq 1)$ of homeomorphisms of the plane. We thus define:

Definition 2. Two spatial databases $\mathcal{D}_1$ and $\mathcal{D}_2$ are called *topologically equivalent* if there exists an isotopy h in $\mathbf{R}^2$ such that $h_0(\mathcal{D}_1) = \mathcal{D}_1$ and $h_1(\mathcal{D}_1) = \mathcal{D}_2$, with the understanding that h respects the labels of points, curves, and areas.

Definition 3. A representation of a spatial database is called *topologically invariant* if any two topologically equivalent spatial databases are represented in the same way. A representation of a spatial database is called *lossless* if any two spatial databases that are not topologically equivalent are distinguished by the representation.

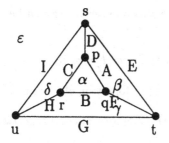

R_1	R_2	R_3	R_4
A p q	A α β	α p A 1	p A α 1
A q p	A β α	α q B 2	p C δ 2
B q r	B α γ	α r C 3	p D β 3
B r q	B γ α	β p D 1	q B α 1
C r p	C α δ	β s E 2	q A β 2
C p r	C δ α	β t F 3	q F γ 3

Fig. 8. The relations R_1, R_2, R_3 and R_4 illustrated.

Example 5. As an example of a representation of spatial databases in the topological data model we take the representation underlying the cartography system of the US Bureau of the Census [8] (see also [26]). Here a spatial database is represented by means of a classical database consisting of four relations, R_1, R_2, R_3, and R_4, on the labels of points, curves, and areas.

- R_1 gives for every curve its two endpoints;
- R_2 gives for every curve its two adjacent areas;
- R_3 give for each area its border of alternatingly curves and points; and
- R_4 gives for each point its neighborhood of alternatingly curves and areas.

For relation R_3, a clockwise order is agreed upon for outer borders of areas and a counter-clockwise order is used for holes in areas. For relation R_4, a clockwise order is used.

Figure 8 illustrates the relations R_1, R_2, R_3, and R_4 for the depicted spatial database.

The following property shows that this representation can be reduced to the relation R_4 only.

Proposition 4. $R_1, R_2,$ and R_3 can be deduced from R_4.

Proof. To deduce R_1 and R_2 we have the following algebra expressions:

$$R_1 = \Pi_{215}(\sigma_{1\neq5}(\sigma_{2=6}(R_4 \times R_4))) \cup \Pi_{215}(\sigma_{3\neq7}(\sigma_{1=5}(\sigma_{2=6}(R_4 \times R_4)))),$$

$$R_2 = \Pi_{237}(\sigma_{3\neq7}(\sigma_{2=6}(R_4 \times R_4))).$$

To deduce R_3 we have $\Pi_{123}(R_3) = \Pi_{312}(R_4)$ and

$$\left.\begin{array}{l}(\alpha p Ai) \in R_3 \\ (\alpha q B) \in \Pi_{123}(R_3) \\ (A p Q) \in R_1\end{array}\right\} \Rightarrow (\alpha q Bi + 1) \in R_3.$$

□

It is more convenient to denote the relation R_4 of Example 5 for each labeled point p as a circular alternating list of curve and area labels rather than as a set of tuples [19]. Actually, this alternating list of labels corresponds to the labels of the curves and areas that an observer, placed in the point p, sees when he makes a full clockwise circular scan of the environment of the point p. A formal definition of this alternating circular list was given in [19] and it was referred to as *the observation of a spatial database from the point p* and denoted as Obs(p). The collection of the observations of a spatial database from each of its points is called *the observation of the spatial database*. The observation of a spatial database satisfies the first requirement of a representation:

Proposition 5. [19] *The observation of a spatial database is an invariant representation of a spatial database.*

Is this representation, on the other hand, lossless? The answer is *no*. Figure 9 contains two spatial databases that can certainly not be obtained from one another by a continuous deformation. So, they are not topologically equivalent but nevertheless represented identically by means of their observation. We have for both the following:

$$\begin{array}{ll}\text{Obs}(p) = (\alpha C\delta D\beta A), & \text{Obs}(s) = (\varepsilon E\beta D\delta I), \\ \text{Obs}(q) = (\alpha A\beta F\gamma B), & \text{Obs}(t) = (\varepsilon G\gamma F\beta E), \\ \text{Obs}(r) = (\alpha B\gamma H\delta C), & \text{Obs}(u) = (\varepsilon I\delta H\gamma G).\end{array}$$

Hence, drastically different spatial databases can be represented in exactly the same way by means of their observations. In [19] it is shown, however, that there is a single cause for this phenomenon: by explicitly marking one of the areas as the unbounded area, losslessness is achieved.

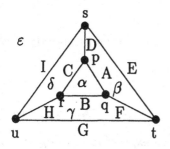 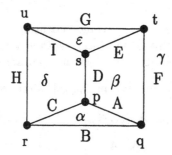

Fig. 9. Two spatial databases that are not topologically equivalent but that have the same observation.

Theorem 6. [19] *A spatial database is losslessly represented by its observation and the the label of the unbounded area.*

Indeed, the two spatial databases of Figure 9 mainly differ in the fact that for the first ε is the label of the unbounded area while it is the label for a bounded one in the second database. Theorem 6 justifies the introduction of a reserved label, α^∞, for the unbounded area.

3.4 Querying Spatial Databases in the Topological Data Model

To query spatial databases in the topological data model we introduce the following 3-sorted first-order language $\mathcal{L}_{PCA}$.

$\mathcal{L}_{PCA}$ has three sorts of *variables*:

- boldfaced lower-case characters are used for point-variables: $\mathbf{p}, \mathbf{q}, \mathbf{r}, \ldots$;
- boldfaced capitals are used for curve-variables: $\mathbf{A}, \mathbf{B}, \mathbf{C}, \ldots$; and
- boldfaced Greek characters are used for area-variables: $\alpha, \beta, \gamma, \ldots$.

The language $\mathcal{L}_{PCA}$ has one *constant*: α^∞, the label of the unbounded area. A *term* in $\mathcal{L}_{PCA}$ is

- $\mathbf{p} = \mathbf{q}$ with $\mathbf{p}$ and $\mathbf{q}$ point-variables;
- $\mathbf{A} = \mathbf{B}$ with $\mathbf{A}$ and $\mathbf{B}$ curve-variables;
- $\alpha = \beta$ with α and β area-variables;
- $\alpha = \alpha^\infty$ with α an area-variable;
- $\mathbf{A}\alpha\mathbf{B} \subset \mathrm{Obs}(\mathbf{p})$ with $\mathbf{p}$ a point-variable, $\mathbf{A}$ and $\mathbf{B}$ curve-variables and α an area-variable or the area-constant α^∞; or
- $\alpha = \mathrm{Obs}(\mathbf{p})$ with $\mathbf{p}$ a point-variable, and α an area-variable or the area-constant α^∞.

An *expression* in $\mathcal{L}_{PCA}$ is

- a term;
- a combination of expressions using $\vee, \wedge, \neg, \rightarrow$; or
- $(\exists p)\varphi$, $(\exists A)\varphi$ and $(\exists \alpha)\varphi$ with φ an expression and p a point-variable, A a curve variable and α an area-variable.

A *query* expressed in $\mathcal{L}_{PCA}$ has the form

$$\{(p_1, \ldots, p_n, A_1, \ldots A_m, \alpha_1, \ldots \alpha_k) \mid \varphi(p_1, \ldots, p_n, A_1, \ldots A_m, \alpha_1, \ldots \alpha_k)\},$$

where $\varphi(p_1, \ldots, p_n, A_1, \ldots, A_m, \alpha_1, \ldots \alpha_k)$ is an expression in $\mathcal{L}_{PCA}$ with free point-variables $p_1, \ldots, p_n$, free curve-variables $A_1, \ldots, A_m$ and free area-variables $\alpha_1, \ldots \alpha_k$.

$A\alpha B \subset Obs(p)$ means that the observation of the database from p has the form $(\ldots A\alpha B \ldots)$. The term $\alpha = Obs(p)$ is redundant if a spatial database is not allowed to contain isolated labeled points. The semantics of the expressions in $\mathcal{L}_{PCA}$ is clear. It should be noticed, however, that the language $\mathcal{L}_{PCA}$ includes $A\alpha B \subset Obs(p)$ as a term but does not include the construction $\alpha A\beta \subset Obs(p)$ as a term. The following property explains why.

Proposition 7. $\alpha A\beta \subset Obs(p)$ *if and only if* $(\exists B)B\alpha A \subset Obs(p) \wedge (\exists C)A\beta C \subset Obs(p) \wedge (\forall \gamma)(\forall D)A\gamma D \subset Obs(p) \rightarrow (\gamma = \beta \vee \gamma = \alpha)$.

Proof. If $\alpha A\beta \subset Obs(p)$, then the list $Obs(p)$ is of the form $\ldots B\alpha A\beta C \ldots$. This proofs the existence of a B and C with the desired properties. If we assume $(\exists \gamma)(\exists D)A\gamma D \subset Obs(p) \wedge \neg \gamma = \beta \wedge \neg \gamma = \alpha$, then there are three areas adjacent to A. This is clearly impossible. If $\alpha = \beta$, we have the same conclusion since $(\exists \gamma)(\exists D)A\gamma D \subset Obs(p) \wedge \neg \gamma = \alpha$ is in contradiction with the fact that A is not a loop in p.

For the other implication, we observe that the observation of the database from p looks like $\ldots B\alpha A\beta C \ldots$ or like $\ldots B\alpha A\delta_1 D_1 \ldots \delta_n A\beta C \ldots$. The first case implies $\alpha A\beta \subset Obs(p)$. In the second case, $\delta_1 = \beta$ or $\delta_1 = \alpha$. The former of these two again yields the desired result. In the case $\delta_1 = \alpha$, we have $\beta = \alpha$, whence the proposition. $\qquad\Box$

We note that the condition $(\forall \gamma)(\forall D)A\gamma D \subset Obs(p) \rightarrow (\gamma = \beta \vee \gamma = \alpha)$ is necessary in the previous proposition. If we consider a spatial database with one point p with $Obs(p) = (B\alpha^\infty A\gamma A\alpha^\infty C\alpha^\infty)$, we do not have $\alpha^\infty A\alpha^\infty \subset Obs(p)$ but still there exists a B and a C such that $B\alpha^\infty A \subset Obs(p)$ and $A\alpha^\infty C \subset Obs(p)$.

On the other hand, we have

Proposition 8. *The constructions* $A\alpha B \subset Obs(p)$ *cannot be expressed in terms of the constructions* $\alpha A\beta \subset Obs(p)$.

Proof. For both spatial databases in Figure 10, $\alpha A\alpha \subset Obs(p)$, $\alpha B\alpha \subset Obs(p)$, and $\alpha C\alpha \subset Obs(p)$ hold.

For the first, $A\alpha B \subset Obs(p)$ holds, but for the second $A\alpha B \subset Obs(p)$ does not hold. So, $A\alpha B \subset Obs(p)$ cannot be expressed in terms of the others. $\qquad\Box$

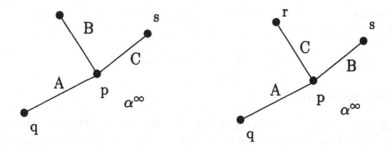

Fig. 10. Two spatial databases with the same area-curve-area information.

As a first example of a query expressed in $\mathcal{L}_{\text{PCA}}$ we take the query "Does the spatial database contain a loop?" This is a Boolean query ($n = 0, m = 0$ and $k = 0$) and it is expressed by the formula

$$(\exists\mathbf{p})(\exists\alpha)(\exists\beta)(\exists\mathbf{A}) \, \neg\alpha = \beta \wedge \alpha\mathbf{A}\beta \subset \text{Obs}(\mathbf{p}) \wedge \beta\mathbf{A}\alpha \subset \text{Obs}(\mathbf{p}),$$

in which we use the abbreviation from Proposition 7.

The relations R_1, R_2, R_3, and R_4 of Section 3.3 can all be expressed in $\mathcal{L}_{\text{PCA}}$:

- $(\mathbf{A}, \mathbf{p}, \mathbf{q}) \in R_1$ if and only if $(\neg\mathbf{p} = \mathbf{q} \wedge (\exists\alpha)(\exists\beta) \, \alpha\mathbf{A}\beta \subset \text{Obs}(\mathbf{p}) \wedge \beta\mathbf{A}\alpha \subset \text{Obs}(\mathbf{q})) \vee (\mathbf{p} = \mathbf{q} \wedge (\exists\alpha)(\exists\beta) \, \neg\alpha = \beta \wedge \alpha\mathbf{A}\beta \subset \text{Obs}(\mathbf{p}) \wedge \beta\mathbf{A}\alpha \subset \text{Obs}(\mathbf{p}))$;
- $(\mathbf{A}, \alpha, \beta) \in R_2$ if and only if $(\exists\mathbf{p}) \, \alpha\mathbf{A}\beta \subset \text{Obs}(\mathbf{p})$;
- $(\alpha, \mathbf{p}, \mathbf{A}, i) \in R_3$ if and only if $(\exists\beta) \, \beta\mathbf{A}\alpha \subset \text{Obs}(\mathbf{p})$ and to determine the order of the tuples in R_3: $(\alpha, \mathbf{p}, \mathbf{A}, i) \in R_3$ and $(\alpha, \mathbf{q}, \mathbf{B}, i+1) \in R_3$ if and only if $(\exists\beta) \, \beta\mathbf{A}\alpha \subset \text{Obs}(\mathbf{p}) \wedge (\exists\beta) \, \beta\mathbf{B}\alpha \subset \text{Obs}(\mathbf{q}) \wedge \mathbf{B}\alpha\mathbf{A} \subset \text{Obs}(\mathbf{q})$;
- $(\mathbf{p}, \mathbf{A}, \alpha, i) \in R_4$ if and only if $(\exists\mathbf{B})\mathbf{A}\alpha\mathbf{B} \subset \text{Obs}(\mathbf{p})$ and to determine the order of the tuples in R_4: $(\mathbf{p}, \mathbf{A}, \alpha, i) \in R_4$ and $(\mathbf{p}, \mathbf{B}, \beta, i+1) \in R_4$ if and only if $\mathbf{A}\alpha\mathbf{B} \subset \text{Obs}(\mathbf{p}) \wedge \alpha\mathbf{B}\beta \subset \text{Obs}(\mathbf{p}) \wedge (\exists\mathbf{C}) \, \mathbf{B}\beta\mathbf{C} \subset \text{Obs}(\mathbf{p})$.

An important query in the context of spatial databases in the topological data model is "Is the database connected?" Connectivity for a binary relation is not expressible in the first-order calculus for relational databases (see, e.g., Chapter 17 of [1]). For spatial databases in the topological data model we have

Open Problem: Is connectivity expressible in $\mathcal{L}_{\text{PCA}}$?

Again following the results for the classical case, we see that connectivity *is* expressible in $\mathcal{L}_{\text{PCA}}+$ fixpoint. We define the relation C_i for points $\mathbf{p}$ and $\mathbf{q}$ as follows: $C_i(\mathbf{p}, \mathbf{q})$ is true if and only if there is a path from $\mathbf{p}$ to $\mathbf{q}$ of length at most i in the spatial database. Clearly, C_1 is expressible in $\mathcal{L}_{\text{PCA}}$. Let

$$\varphi(T) = C_1(\mathbf{p}, \mathbf{q}) \vee T(\mathbf{p}, \mathbf{q}) \vee (\exists\mathbf{r})(T(\mathbf{p}, \mathbf{r}) \vee C_1(\mathbf{r}, \mathbf{q})).$$

Then clearly $C_{i+1} = \varphi(C_i)$. For non-inflationary fixpoint semantics, the least fixpoint C of φ can be used to express "Is the database connected?":

$$(\forall \mathbf{p})(\forall \mathbf{q}) \; \neg \mathbf{p} = \mathbf{q} \to C(\mathbf{p}, \mathbf{q}).$$

Acknowledgements

The results in this paper were presented by the three authors at the EDBT Summer School "Advances in Database Technology" in Gubbio, Italy, September 4–8, 1995. The authors are indebted to Marc Gyssens, Jan Van den Bussche, and Dirk Van Gucht for the collaborative research that has lead to several of the results discussed in this paper. The authors also thank Marc Gyssens for carefully proofreading the paper.

References

1. S. Abiteboul, R. Hull, and V. Vianu, *Foundations of Databases*, Addison-Wesley Publishing Company, 1995.
2. F. Afrati, S. Cosmadakis, S. Grumbach, and G. Kuper, "Linear Versus Polynomial Constraints in Database Query Languages," in Proceedings *2nd Int'l Workshop on Principles and Practice of Constraint Programming* (Rosario, WA), A. Borning, ed., *Lecture Notes in Computer Science*, vol. 874, Springer-Verlag, Berlin, 1994, 181–192.
3. A. Brodsky, J. Jaffar, and M.J. Maher, "Toward Practical Constraint Databases," in Proceedings *19th Int'l Conf. on Very Large Databases* (Dublin, Ireland), 1993, 567–580.
4. A. Brodsky and Y. Kornatzky, "The LyriC Language: Querying Constraint Objects," in Proceedings *Post-ILPS'94 Workshop on Constraints and Databases* (Ithaca, NY), 1994.
5. A. Brøndsted, *An Introduction to Convex Polytopes, Graduate Texts in Mathematics*, vol. 90, Springer-Verlag, New York, 1983.
6. I. Carlbom, "An Algorithm for Geometric Set Operations Using Cellular Subdivision Techniques," *IEEE Computer Graphics and Applications*, 7:5, 1987, 44–55.
7. A. Chandra and D. Harel, "Computable Queries for Relational Database Systems," *Journal of Computer and System Sciences*, 21:2, 1980, 156–178.
8. J.P. Corbett. Topological Principles of Cartography. Technical Paper No. 48, US Bureau of the Census, Washington, DC, USA: US Government Printing Office, 1979.
9. M.J. Egenhofer, "A Formal Definition of Binary Topological Relationships," in Proceedings *Foundations of Data Organization and Algorithms*, W. Litwin and H.-J. Schek, eds., *Lecture Notes in Computer Science*, vol. 367, Springer-Verlag, Berlin, 1989, 457–472.
10. M.J. Egenhofer, "Why not SQL!", *Int'l J. on Geographical Information Systems*, 6:2, 1992, 71–85.
11. O. Günther, ed., *Efficient Structures for Geometric Data Management, Lecture Notes in Computer Science*, vol. 337, Springer-Verlag, Berlin, 1988.
12. O. Günther and A. Buchmann, *Research Issues in Spatial Databases*, in Sigmod Record, vol. 19, 4, 61-68, 1990.

13. R.H. Güting, "Geo-Relational Algebra: A Model and Query Language for Geometric Database Systems," in *Advances in Database Technology—EDBT '88*, Proceedings *Int'l Conf. on Extending Database Technology* (Venice, Italy), J.W. Schmidt, S. Ceri, and M. Missikoff, eds., *Lecture Notes in Computer Science*, vol. 303, Soringer-Verlag, Berlin, 1988, 506–527.

14. R.H. Güting, "Gral: An Extensible Relational Database System for Geometric Applications," in Proceedings *15th Int'l Conf. on Very Large Databases* (Amsterdam, the Netherlands), 1989, 33–34.

15. R.H. Güting, "An Introduction to Spatial Database Systems," *VLDB-Journal*, 3:4, 1994, 357–399.

16. T. Huynh, C. Lassez, and J.-L. Lassez. Fourier Algorithm Revisited. In Proceedings *2nd Int'l Conf. on Algebraic an Logic Programming*, H. Kirchner and W. Wechler, eds. *Lecture Notes in Computer Science*, vol. 463. Springer Verlag, Berlin, 1990, 117–131.

17. P.J. Kelly and M.L. Weiss. *Geometry and Convexity: a Study in Mathematical Methods*, J. Wiley and Sons, New York, 1979.

18. P.C. Kanellakis, G.M. Kuper and P.Z. Revesz, "Constraint Query Languages," *Journal of Computer and System Sciences*, to appear, also in Proceedings *9th ACM SIGACT-SIGMOD-SIGART Symposium on Principles of Database Systems* (Nashville, TN), 1990, 299–313.

19. B. Kuijpers, J. Paredaens, and J. Van den Bussche "Lossless representation of topological spatial data," in Proceedings *4th Symposium on Advances in Spatial Databases*, M. J. Egenhofer and J. R. Herring, eds., *Lecture Notes in Computer Science*, vol. 951. Springer Verlag, Berlin, 1995, 1–13.

20. J.-L. Lassez, "Querying Constraints," in Proceedings *9th ACM SIGACT-SIGMOD-SIGART Symposium on Principles of Database Systems* (Nashville, TN), 1990, 288–298.

21. R. Laurini and D. Thompson. *Fundamentals of Spatial Information Systems*. The A.P.I.C. Series, 37, Academic Press, 1992.

22. M. Liebling and A. Prodon, "Algorithmic Geometry," in *Scientific Visualization and Graphics Simulation*, D. Thalmann, ed., J. Wiley and Sons. 14–25.

23. P. McMullen and G.C. Shephard, *Convex Polytopes and the Upper Bound Conjecture*, University Press, Cambridge, 1971.

24. E.E. Moise. *Geometric Topology in Dimensions 2 and 3. Graduate Texts in Mathematics*, vol. 47, Springer-Verlag, 1977.

25. J. Paredaens, J. Van den Bussche, and D. Van Gucht, "Towards a Theory of Spatial Database Queries," in Proceedings *13th ACM SIGACT-SIGMOD-SIGART Symposium on Principles of Database Systems* (Minneapolis, MN), 1994. 279–288.

26. J. Paredaens. Spatial Databases. The Final Frontier. *Database Theory - ICDT '95, Lecture Notes in Computer Science*, vol. 893, 14–32, Springer-Verlag, 1995.

27. F.P. Preparata and D.E. Muller. "Finding the Intersection of n Half-Spaces in Time $O(nlogn)$," *Theoretical Computer Science*, 8, 1979, 45–55.

28. L.K. Putnam and P.A. Subrahmanyam, "Boolean Operations on n-Dimensional Objects," *IEEE Computer Graphics and Applications*, 6:6, 1986, 43–51.

29. N. Roussopoulos, C. Faloutsos, and T. Sellis, "An Efficient Pictorial Database System for PSQL," *IEEE Transactions on Software Engineering*, 14:5, 1988, 639–650.

30. W. Schwabhauser, W. Szmielew, and A. Tarski. *Metamathematische Methoden in der Geometrie*, Springer-Verlag, Berlin, 1983.

31. P. Svensson and Z. Huang, "Geo-Sal: A Query Language for Spatial Data Analysis," in Proceedings *2nd Symposium on Advances in Spatial Databases*, O. Günther

and H.-J. Schek, eds. *Lecture Notes in Computer Science*, vol. 525. Springer-Verlag, Berlin, 1991, 119–140.

32. B. Tilove, "Set Membership Classification: a Unified Approach to Geometric Intersection Problems," *IEEE Transactions on Computers*, C-29:10, 1980, 874–883.

33. L. Vandeurzen, M. Gyssens, and D. Van Gucht, "On the Desirability and Limitations of Linear Spatial Query Languages," in Proceedings *4th Symposium on Advances in Spatial Databases*, M. J. Egenhofer and J. R. Herring, eds., *Lecture Notes in Computer Science*, vol. 951. Springer Verlag, Berlin, 1995, 14-28.

The Additivity Problem for Data Dependencies in Incomplete Relational Databases

Mark Levene[1] and George Loizou[2]

[1] University College London, Gower Street, London WC1E 6BT, U.K.
E-Mail: mlevene@cs.ucl.ac.uk
[2] Birkbeck College, Malet Street, London WC1E 7HX, U.K.
E-Mail: george@dcs.bbk.ac.uk

Abstract. Functional dependencies (FDs) and inclusion dependencies (INDs) are the most fundamental integrity constraints that arise in practice in relational databases. We introduce null functional dependencies (NFDs) and null inclusion dependencies (NINDs) to cater for the situation when a database is incomplete and thus contains null values. If a NFD or NIND is weakly satisfied in a database, then there exists a possible world of this database in which the NFD or NIND is satisfied in the standard way. Additivity is the property of the equivalence of the weak satisfaction of a set of NFDs and NINDs, Σ, with the individual weak satisfaction of each member of Σ in the said database. We show that in general satisfaction of NFDs and NINDs is not additive. The problem that arises is: under what conditions is weak satisfaction of NFDs and NINDs additive. We solve this problem for the following cases: when Σ is a set of NFDs, when Σ is a set of unary NINDs and when Σ is a set of NFDs and unary NINDs. We show that, when the set of NINDs is unary, checking whether Σ is additive can be done in time polynomial in the size of Σ.

1 Introduction

Functional dependencies (FDs) [39,5] generalise the notions of *entity integrity* and *keys* [10] and inclusion dependencies (INDs) [35,9] generalise the notions of *referential integrity* and *foreign keys* [10,12]. In this sense FDs and INDs are the most fundamental data dependencies that arise in practice.

Codd [10] suggested the addition to the database domains of an unmarked null value, whose meaning is "value at present unknown", which we denote by *unk*, in order to extend relations so that they can model situations when the information is incomplete. We call such relations, whose tuples may contain the null value *unk*, *incomplete relations* (or simply relations) and we call a set of incomplete relations an *incomplete database* (or simply a database). Following Codd's proposal, incomplete information is represented in SQL by using *unk* as a distinguished null value [13].

The theory of data dependencies in relational databases has been generalised in order to deal with incomplete databases. In particular, FDs have been generalised to *null functional dependencies* (NFDs) [31,4,24], multivalued dependencies [39,5] have been generalised to *null multivalued dependencies* [31] and join dependencies [39,5] have been generalised to *null join dependencies* [23]. More recently INDs have been generalised to *null inclusion dependencies* (NINDs) [25].

A database schema **R** is a collection of relation schemas $\{R_1, \ldots, R_n\}$ and each relation schema R_i has an associated sequence of attributes, denoted by schema(R_i). Correspondingly, a database d over **R** is a collection $\{r_1, \ldots, r_n\}$ of relations such that each r_i is a relation over R_i. We define the semantics of an incomplete database, d, in terms of the *possible worlds* relative to d, which we denote by POSS(d). POSS(d) is the set of all databases that emanate from all possible substitutions of occurrences of *unk* in d by nonnull values in the database domains.

Intuitively, a NFD R : X → Y is *weakly satisfied* (or simply satisfied) in a database d over **R**, if there exists a database d' in POSS(d) such that the relation over R in d' satisfies the NFD on using the standard definition of FD satisfaction [39,5].

Correspondingly, we now explain the meaning of a NIND R[X] ⊆ S[Y] being *weakly satisfied* (or simply satisfied) in a database. Intuitively, an occurrence of *unk* is *less informative* than an occurrence of a nonnull value, and a tuple t_1 over a relation schema R_1, with schema(R_1) = $< A_1, \ldots, A_m >$, is less informative than a tuple t_2 over a relation schema R_2, with schema(R_2) = $< B_1, \ldots, B_m >$, written $t_1 \sqsubseteq t_2$, if ∀ i ∈ {1,...,m}, $t_1[A_i]$ is less informative than $t_2[B_i]$. The NIND R[X] ⊆ S[Y] is satisfied in a database, d, containing relations r over R and s over S, if ∀t_1 ∈ r, ∃t_2 ∈ s such that $t_1[X] \sqsubseteq t_2[Y]$. This definition of a NIND can be seen to faithfully generalise the definition of an IND, since it implies that there exists a database in POSS(d) which satisfies the NIND on using the standard definition of IND satisfaction [35,9].

We write d $\approx$ α to denote the fact that an incomplete database, d, *weakly satisfies* a NFD or a NIND α (or simply satisfies α). We say that d *weakly satisfies* a set of NFDs and NINDs Σ (or simply satisfies Σ), written d $\approx \Sigma$, if d satisfies all the NFDs and NINDs in Σ and, in addition, ∃d' ∈ POSS(d) such that d' satisfies all the NFDs and NINDs in Σ.

Weak satisfaction (or simply satisfaction) is defined in terms of possible worlds. Intuitively, if an incomplete database, d, satisfies a set of data dependencies, say Σ, then there exists a sequence of updates, each update modifying a null value to a nonnull value, such that the resulting complete database satisfies all the data dependencies α ∈ Σ. The problem that arises is that although there may exist such a sequence of updates for every single data dependency α ∈ Σ, two or more such sequences may lead to different possible worlds. In particular, there may not exist a single sequence of updates that leads to one possible world that satisfies all of the data dependencies α in Σ. From the user's point of view, when d $\not\approx \Sigma$, it is natural to view such a database, d, as contradictory. Even if d is a true reflection of the current available information the user may still view Σ as contradictory. We call this problem the *additivity problem*. The aim of this paper is to determine how Σ can be syntactically restricted so that this problem does not arise.

We next give the formal definition of additive satisfaction and present some motivating examples. Satisfaction is said to be *additive* [5,24] with respect to a class of databases, say DBC, and a class of sets of NFDs and NINDs, say $DEPC$, whenever: for all databases d in DBC and for all sets of NFDs and NINDs Σ in $DEPC$, d $\models \Sigma$ if and only if $\forall \alpha \in \Sigma$, d $\models \alpha$.

It is easy to verify that satisfaction is additive with respect to the class of complete databases (i.e., databases without nulls) and the class of sets of NFDs and NINDs. That is, when the information is complete and there is only a single possible database then the additivity problem does not arise.

We next give three motivating examples each exhibiting typical counterexample databases showing that satisfaction is not additive with respect to the class of incomplete databases and a class of sets of NFDs and/or NINDs. The first example shows that satisfaction is not additive with respect to the class of incomplete databases and the class of all sets of NFDs. The second example shows that satisfaction is not additive with respect to the class of incomplete databases and the class of all sets of NINDs. The third example shows that satisfaction is not additive with respect to the class of incomplete databases and the class of all sets of NFDs and NINDs that contain only a single NFD and a single NIND.

Example 1. Let $d_1 = \{r_1\}$ be a database, where r_1 over R is the well-known incomplete relation [4] shown in Table 1. It can easily be verified that $d_1 \models$ R : A $\rightarrow$ B and $d_1 \models$ R : B $\rightarrow$ C but $d_1 \not\models \{$R: A $\rightarrow$ B, R : B $\rightarrow$ C$\}$. Also, let $d_2 = \{r_2\}$ be a database, where r_2 over R is shown in Table 2. It can easily be verified that $d_2 \models$ R : A $\rightarrow$ C and $d_2 \models$ R : B $\rightarrow$ C, but $d_2 \not\models \{$R : A $\rightarrow$ C, R: B $\rightarrow$ C$\}$. Finally, let $d_3 = \{r_3\}$, where r_3 over R is shown in Table 3. It can easily be verified that $d_3 \models$ R : B $\rightarrow$ A and $d_3 \models$ R: AC $\rightarrow$ B, but $d_3 \not\models \{$R : B $\rightarrow$ A, R : AC $\rightarrow$ B$\}$.

A	B	C
0	unk	0
0	unk	1

Table 1. The counterexample relation r_1

A	B	C
0	unk	0
0	0	unk
unk	0	1

Table 2. The counterexample relation r_2

A	B	C
0	0	unk
unk	0	0
0	1	0

Table 3. The counterexample relation r_3

Example 2. Let r, s and z be the relations shown in Tables 4, 5 and 6, respectively, and let d = $\{$r, s, z$\}$ be a database over **R**, with **R** = $\{$R, S, T$\}$ and schema(R) = <A>, schema(S) = <B> and schema(T) = <C>. It can easily be verified that $d \not\approx R[A] \subseteq S[B]$ and $d \not\approx R[A] \subseteq T[C]$ but $d \not\approx \{R[A] \subseteq S[B], R[A] \subseteq T[C]\}$.

A
unk

Table 4. The counterexample relation r

B
0

Table 5. The counterexample relation s

C
1

Table 6. The counterexample relation z

Example 3. Let r be the relation shown in Table 7 and let $d = \{r\}$ be a database over **R**, with **R** $= \{R\}$ and schema(R) $=$ <A, B>. It can easily be verified that $d \not\approx A \rightarrow B$ and $d \not\approx R[A] \subseteq R[B]$ but $d \not\approx \{A \rightarrow B, R[A] \subseteq R[B]\}$.

A	B
0	0
1	0
unk	1

Table 7. A counterexample relation

We are interested in finding the largest class of sets of NFDs and NINDs for which satisfaction is additive. We solve the problem for NFDs and unary NINDs separately, and for NFDs and unary NINDs together. (A NIND $R[X] \subseteq S[Y]$ is *unary* if both X and Y are single attributes [11].) We now briefly describe the solution to the additivity problem.

We show that a set of NFDs, F, is additive if and only if it is *monodependent*. Informally, F is monodependent if for each attribute A there is a unique NFD that functionally determines A, and in addition only trivial cycles involving A arise between any two NFDs one of which functionally determines A (see Definition 36).

We also show that a set of unary NINDs, I, is additive if and only if it is *monodirectional*. Informally, I is monodirectional if for every pair of unary NINDs that have a common left-hand side, there exists at least one compensating unary NIND that is logically implied by I (see Definition 42).

We further show that a set of NFDs and unary NINDs, $\Sigma = F \cup I$, is additive if and only if F is monodependent, I is monodirectional and Σ satisfies the *cyclicity condition*. Informally, Σ satisfies the cyclicity condition if whenever the left-hand side of a NIND is contained in the left-hand side of a NFD or vice versa, then there exist a compensating NFD and a compensating unary NIND that are logically implied by Σ (see Definition 48).

Finally, we show that as long as the set of NINDs is unary additive satisfaction can be checked in polynomial time in the size of the set of NFDs and NINDs under consideration.

The rest of the paper is organised as follows. In Section 2 we formalise incomplete relations and incomplete databases, and define a partial order on tuples of such relations. In Section 3 we define the notions of NFD and NIND and their satisfaction in a database. In Section 4 we extend the *chase procedure*, defined over complete databases with respect to FDs [32,18,5] and INDs [21,34], to incomplete databases with respect to NFDs and NINDs. In order to establish our results we make extensive use of the chase procedure as a theorem proving tool. In Section 5 we formalise the additivity problem for data dependencies. In Section 6 we solve the additivity problem for NFDs, in Section 7 we solve the additivity problem for unary NINDs, and in Section 8 we solve the additivity problem for NFDs and unary NINDs. In Section 9 we relate our work to previous research pertaining to incomplete information as it affects the satisfaction of data dependencies in relations. Finally, in Section 10 we give our concluding remarks.

2 Relations that Model Incomplete Information

In this section we briefly introduce the underlying database model used throughout the paper.

Definition 4 (Relation and database schema). Let Att be a countably infinite set of attributes. A *relation schema* is a relation symbol R together with an associated similarity type, denoted by type(R), such that type(R) $\in \omega$, where ω is the set of all natural numbers. We refer to such a schema simply as R. For convenience we associate with each relation schema R a total and one-to-one mapping, att: $\{1, \ldots, \text{type}(R)\} \rightarrow$ Att, which allows us to name the type(R) components of a relation schema R; we denote the sequence $<$att(1), $\ldots$, att(type(R))$>$ by schema(R).

A *database schema* is a set $\mathbf{R} = \{R_1, \ldots, R_n\}$, $n \in \omega$, such that each $R_i \in \mathbf{R}$ is a relation schema.

From now on we will refer to a sequence of attributes as a shorthand for a sequence of distinct attributes (we assume that sequences of attributes do not contain any repeated attributes). As usual uppercase letters appearing at the end of the alphabet will be used to denote sequences of attributes, while those at the beginning of the alphabet will be used to denote single attributes. When convenient we will write $A_1, \ldots, A_n$ instead of $< A_1, \ldots, A_n >$ to describe a sequence and when no ambiguity arises we will refer to a sequence of attributes as a set of attributes. We take A $\in < A_1, \ldots, A_m >$ to mean A $\in \{A_1, \ldots, A_m\}$ and $< A_1, \ldots, A_m > \subseteq < B_1, \ldots, B_k >$, with m $\leq$ k, to mean $\{A_1, \ldots, A_m\} \subseteq \{B_1, \ldots, B_k\}$. The difference between two sequences of attributes, denoted by

X−Y, is the sequence resulting from removing all the common attributes in X and Y from X while maintaining the original order of the attributes remaining in X. The concatenation of two sequences X and Y is denoted by XY; if the sequences X, Y are *not* disjoint we define their concatenation XY to be (X−Y)Y.

For a set or a sequence X, |X| will denote the cardinality of X. Finally, the *size* of a set or sequence X is defined to be the cardinality of a standard encoding [15] of X.

Definition 5 (Relation and database). Let *Dom* be a countably infinite set of values and let *unk, inc* ∈ *Dom* be two distinguished values, denoting the null values "unknown" and "inconsistent", respectively.

A *type(R)-tuple* (or simply a tuple whenever type(R) is understood from context) is a member of $Dom \times \ldots \times Dom$ (type(R) times).

An *incomplete relation* (or simply a relation) over R is a finite (possibly empty) set of type(R)-tuples. An *incomplete database* (or simply a database) over $\mathbf{R} = \{R_1, \ldots, R_n\}$ is a set $d = \{r_1, \ldots, r_n\}$ such that each $r_i \in d$ is a relation over $R_i \in \mathbf{R}$.

We call values in $Dom − \{unk, inc\}$ nonnull values and the values *unk* and *inc* (unmarked) null values. We let DB(**R**) denote the countably infinite set of all databases over **R**. From now on we will assume that $d = \{r_1, \ldots, r_n\}$ is a database over a database schema $\mathbf{R} = \{R_1, \ldots, R_n\}$ and that r is a relation over a relation schema R.

Definition 6 (Projection). The *projection* of a tuple $t \in r$ onto the attribute $A_i = att(i)$, denoted by $t[A_i]$, is the i-coordinate of t, i.e., t(i). Projection is extended to a sequence of attributes $Y = < A_1, \ldots, A_m > \subseteq$ schema(R), denoted by t[Y] (also called the Y-value of t), and to relations, denoted by $\pi_Y(r)$, in the usual manner [39,5].

Definition 7 (Active domain). The *active domain* of a relation r over R, denoted by adom(r), is defined by

$$adom(r) = \{v \mid \exists A \in schema(R), \exists t \in r \text{ such that } t[A] = v\} \cup \{unk, inc\}.$$

The active domain of a database $d = \{r_1, \ldots, r_n\}$ over **R**, denoted by adom(d), is defined by

$$adom(d) = \bigcup \{adom(r_i) \mid r_i \in d\}.$$

Definition 8 (Complete and consistent relations and databases). A type(R)-tuple t is said to be *complete* if $\forall A_i \in$ schema(R), $t[A_i] \neq unk$ and $t[A_i] \neq inc$, i.e., $t[A_i]$ is a nonnull value, otherwise t is said to be *incomplete*; t is said to be *inconsistent* if $\exists A_i \in$ schema(R), such that $t[A_i] = inc$, otherwise t is said to be *consistent*.

A relation r over R is said to be *complete* if $\forall t \in r$, t is complete, otherwise r is said to be *incomplete*. A relation r over R is said to be *inconsistent* if $\exists t \in r$ such that t is inconsistent, otherwise r is said to be *consistent*.

A database d over R is said to be *complete* if all the relations r in d are complete, otherwise d is said to be *incomplete*. A database d over R is said to be *inconsistent* if there exists a relation r in d such that r is inconsistent, otherwise d is said to be *consistent*.

We let COMPLETE(R) denote the countably infinite set of all complete databases over R.

Definition 9 (Less informative values). Let r be a relation over R. We define a partial order in *Dom*, denoted by $\sqsubseteq$, as follows: where $u, v \in Dom$,

$$u \sqsubseteq v \text{ if and only if } u = v \text{ or } u = unk \text{ or } v = inc.$$

Definition 10 (Less informative tuples). Let schema$(R_1) = <A_1, \ldots, A_m>$ and schema$(R_2) = <B_1, \ldots, B_m>$, i.e., type$(R_1)$ = type(R_2) = m. We extend $\sqsubseteq$ to be a partial order in the set of type(R_1)-tuples and type(R_2)-tuples, as follows: where t_1 is a type(R_1)-tuple and t_2 is a type(R_2)-tuple, t_1 is *less informative than* t_2 (or equivalently t_2 is *more informative than* t_1), written $t_1 \sqsubseteq t_2$, if

$$\forall i \in \{1, \ldots, m\}, t_1[A_i] \sqsubseteq t_2[B_i].$$

We observe that the set of all type(R)-tuples is a *lattice* having no infinite chains [14], whose bottom element is $<unk, \ldots, unk>$ and whose top element is $<inc, \ldots, inc>$. We next define the *join* operator [14] of this complete lattice of tuples.

Definition 11 (The join operator). Let r be a relation over R. We define the *join* operator, denoted by $\sqcup$, as a mapping from an ordered pair, (v_1, v_2), of values in *Dom* $\times$ *Dom* to a single value in *Dom* as follows:

$v_1 \sqcup v_2$ is the least upper bound of v_1 and v_2 with respect to $\sqsubseteq$.

We extend $\sqcup$ to be a mapping from an ordered pair, (t_1, t_2), of type(R)-tuples to a single type(R)-tuple as follows:

$t_1 \sqcup t_2 = t$, where t is a type(R)-tuple and $\forall A_i \in$ schema(R), $t[A_i] = t_1[A_i] \sqcup t_2[A_i]$.

It can easily be verified that $t_1 \sqcup t_2$ returns the least upper bound of t_1 and t_2, i.e., the join operator indeed implements the lattice-theoretic join.

Definition 12 (The set of possible worlds of a relation). The set of all *possible worlds* relative to a relation r over R, denoted by POSS(r), is defined by

$$POSS(r) = \{s \mid s \text{ is a relation over } R \text{ and there exists a total and onto mapping}$$
$$f : r \rightarrow s \text{ such that } \forall t \in r, t \sqsubseteq f(t) \text{ and } f(t) \text{ is complete}\}.$$

We extend POSS to a database $d = \{r_1, \dots, r_n\}$ over **R**, as follows:

$$POSS(d) = \{\{s_1, \dots, s_n\} \mid s_1 \in POSS(r_1) \text{ and } \dots \text{ and } s_n \in POSS(r_n)\}.$$

The following proposition states the relationship between the concept of possible worlds and consistency.

Proposition 13. The following two statements are true:

1. A relation r over R is inconsistent if and only if POSS(r) = $\emptyset$.
2. A database d over **R** is inconsistent if and only if POSS(d) = $\emptyset$. □

From now on we assume that unless otherwise stated relations and databases are consistent.

3 Null functional and null inclusion dependencies

In this section we introduce the null data dependencies we investigate in the paper.

Definition 14 (Null Functional Dependency). A *null functional dependency* (or simply a NFD) over a database schema **R** is a statement of the form $R : X \rightarrow Y$ (or simply $X \rightarrow Y$ whenever R is understood from context), where $R \in \mathbf{R}$ and X, Y $\subseteq$ schema(R).
  A NFD $X \rightarrow Y$ is said to be *trivial* if $Y \subseteq X$; it is said to be *standard* if X $\neq \emptyset$.

Hereafter *we will assume that all NFDs are standard*. We also assume that a database schema **R** has a set of NFDs associated with it, denoted by F. We let F(R) be the subset of NFDs in F over a relation schema $R \in \mathbf{R}$, that is F(R) = $\{R : X \rightarrow Y \mid R : X \rightarrow Y \in F\}$. We let NFD(**R**) be the finite set of all possible sets F of NFDs over **R**.
  The following definition is a syntactic definition of NFD satisfaction.

Definition 15 (Satisfaction of a NFD). A NFD $R : X \rightarrow Y$ over **R** is satisfied in a database d, over **R**, denoted by $d \models R : X \rightarrow Y$, if, where $r \in d$ is the relation over $R \in \mathbf{R}$, r is consistent and $\forall t_1, t_2 \in r$, if $t_1[X]$ and $t_2[X]$ are complete and $t_1[X] = t_2[X]$, then $t_1[Y] \sqcup t_2[Y]$ is consistent.

From now on we will assume that when $R : X \to Y \in F$ and d is a database over R, then $r \in d$ is the relation over $R \in \mathbf{R}$. We observe that if $r \in d$ is a complete relation then $d \approx X \to Y$ if and only if the standard definition of functional dependency (FD) is satisfied, i.e., $\forall t_1, t_2 \in r$, if $t_1[X] = t_2[X]$, then $t_1[Y] = t_2[Y]$ [39,5].

The following proposition gives a semantic characterisation of NFD satisfaction in terms of possible worlds.

Proposition 16. Let d be a database over $\mathbf{R}$ and $r_1 \in d$ be the relation over $R_1 \in \mathbf{R}$ such that r_1 is consistent. Then $d \approx R_1 : X \to Y$ if and only if $\exists r_2 \in \text{POSS}(r_1)$ such that $\forall t_1, t_2 \in r_2$, if $t_1[X] = t_2[X]$, then $t_1[Y] = t_2[Y]$. $\square$

As a result of Proposition 16, whenever appropriate, we assume without loss of generality that the left-hand and right-hand sides of NFDs are disjoint, and moreover that the right-hand sides of NFDs are singletons.

Definition 17 (Null Inclusion Dependency). A *null inclusion dependency* (or simply a NIND) over a database schema $\mathbf{R}$ is a statement of the form $R[X] \subseteq S[Y]$, where $R, S \in \mathbf{R}$ and $X \subseteq \text{schema}(R)$, $Y \subseteq \text{schema}(S)$ are sequences of attributes such that $|X| = |Y|$.

A NIND $R[X] \subseteq S[Y]$ is said to be unary if $|X| = 1$. A NIND is said to be *trivial* if it is of the form $R[X] \subseteq R[X]$.

We assume that a database schema $\mathbf{R}$ has a set of NINDs associated with it, denoted by I, and let $\text{NIND}(\mathbf{R})$ be the finite set of all possible sets I of NINDs over $\mathbf{R}$.

The following definition is a syntactic definition of NIND satisfaction.

Definition 18 (Satisfaction of a NIND). A NIND $R[X] \subseteq S[Y]$ over $\mathbf{R}$ is satisfied in a database d over $\mathbf{R}$, denoted by $d \approx R[X] \subseteq S[Y]$, if d is consistent and $\forall t_1 \in r$, $\exists t_2 \in s$ such that $t_1[X] \sqsubseteq t_2[Y]$, where $r \in d$ is the relation over $R \in \mathbf{R}$ and $s \in d$ is the relation over $S \in \mathbf{R}$.

From now on we will assume that when $R[X] \subseteq S[Y] \in I$ and d is a database over $\mathbf{R}$, then $r \in d$ is the relation over $R \in \mathbf{R}$ and $s \in d$ is the relation over $S \in \mathbf{R}$. We observe that if d is a complete database then $d \approx R[X] \subseteq S[Y]$ if and only if the standard definition of inclusion dependency (IND) is satisfied, i.e., $\pi_X(r) \subseteq \pi_Y(s)$ [9]. The justification for Definition 18 is that the partial order of less informative tuples extended to relations generalises set inclusion in a natural way.

The following proposition gives a semantic characterisation of NIND satisfaction in terms of possible worlds.

Proposition 19. Let d_1 be a database over $\mathbf{R}$ and $R[X] \subseteq S[Y]$ be a NIND over $\mathbf{R}$. If $d_1 \approx R[X] \subseteq S[Y]$ then $\exists d_2 \in \text{POSS}(d_1)$ such that $\pi_X(r) \subseteq \pi_Y(s)$, where $r \in d_2$ is the relation over $R \in \mathbf{R}$ and $s \in d_2$ is the relation over $S \in \mathbf{R}$. $\square$

We note that the converse of the above proposition does not hold. For example, let $d_1 = <r_1, r_2>$ be a database over $\mathbf{R} = \{R_1, R_2\}$, where $r_1 = \{<\text{a, b}>\}$ is the relation over R_1, with schema$(R_1) = <\text{A, B}>$, and $r_2 = \{<unk, \text{c}>\}$ is the relation over R_2, with schema$(R_2) = <\text{C, D}>$. Then $d_1 \not\approx R_1[A] \subseteq R_2[C]$ but $d_2 \approx R_1[A] \subseteq R_2[C]$, where $d_2 = <r_1, s_2> \in \text{POSS}(d_1)$ is a database over $\mathbf{R}$, with $s_2 = \{<\text{a, c}>\}$ being a relation over R_2, and $\pi_{<A>}(r_1) \subseteq \pi_{<C>}(s_2)$. Thus the existence of a possible world of a database, say d, that satisfies an IND is not sufficient for a corresponding NIND to be satisfied in d. Consequently, it is not possible to relax Definition 18 so that the converse of Proposition 19 would hold, since in that case, in general, referential integrity would be violated.

From now on we will assume that $\Sigma = F \cup I$ is a set of NFDs and NINDs over $\mathbf{R}$. We will also assume without loss of generality that Σ does not contain any trivial NFDs or NINDs.

Definition 20 (Logical implication). We say that Σ *logically implies* a NFD or a NIND α over $\mathbf{R}$, written $\Sigma \approx \alpha$, whenever $\forall$ d $\in$ DB($\mathbf{R}$), the following condition is true:

$$\text{if } \forall \beta \in \Sigma, d \approx \beta \text{ holds then } d \approx \alpha \text{ also holds.}$$

The implication problem is to determine the computational complexity of the logical implication $\Sigma \approx \alpha$, where as before $\Sigma = F \cup I$ and α is a NFD or a NIND. In the special case where $\Sigma = F$ the implication problem can be solved in linear time in the size of F [6,4] and in the special case when $\Sigma = I$ the implication problem is PSPACE-complete [9] (in [25] it was shown that the implication problems for INDs and NINDs coincide). In the case where Σ may contain both NFDs and NINDs the implication problem is decidable and EXPTIME-complete [25] (for FDs and INDs it was shown that the implication problem is undecidable [35]).

We close this section by presenting a relevant result pertaining to unary NINDs. We say that a set of NFDs F over $\mathbf{R}$ and a set of NINDs I over $\mathbf{R}$ have *no interaction* if for each NFD α over $\mathbf{R}$ and for each NIND β over $\mathbf{R}$, $F \cup I \approx \alpha$ if and only if $F \approx \alpha$ and $F \cup I \approx \beta$ if and only if $I \approx \beta$.

Theorem 21. Let $\Sigma = F \cup I$ be a set of NFDs and unary NINDs over $\mathbf{R}$. Then F and I have no interaction.

Proof. The result follows immediately by the soundness and completeness of the axiom system for NFDs and NINDs given in [25]. We now present an alternative proof, which does not utilise this result.

Suppose that $F \not\approx R : X \rightarrow Y$. Then $\exists$ d $\in$ DB($\mathbf{R}$) such that $\forall \alpha \in F$, d $\approx \alpha$ but d $\not\approx R : X \rightarrow Y$. The database d can always be made to satisfy all the NINDs in I by adding tuples to s, where s $\in$ d is the relation over S, of the form $\{< unk, \ldots, unk, v, unk, \ldots, unk >\}$, with the B-value being v, whenever a unary NIND of the form R[A] $\subseteq$ S[B] is violated in d. Suppose that $I \not\approx R[A] \subseteq S[B]$. Then $\exists$ d $\in$ DB($\mathbf{R}$) such that $\forall \beta \in I$, d $\approx \beta$ but d $\not\approx R[A] \subseteq S[B]$. Let

d' be a database consisting of $r = \{< unk, \ldots, unk, 0, unk, \ldots, unk >\}$, with the A-value being 0, $s = \{< unk, \ldots, unk, 1, unk, \ldots, unk >\}$, with the B-value being 1, and all other relations being empty. The database d' can be made to satisfy all the NINDs in I by adding tuples, having at most a single nonnull value, to the relations in d' thus obtaining the required database d. The result follows, since $\forall \alpha \in F$, d $\not\approx \alpha$ due to the fact that the tuples in d do not have more than one nonnull value. $\square$

The implication problem for unary NINDs can be solved in linear time in the size of the input set of NINDs [11]. On using Theorem 21 the next corollary follows.

Corollary 22. Let $\Sigma = F \cup I$ be a set of NFDs and unary NINDs. The implication problem for F and I can be solved in linear time in the size of Σ.
$\square$

4 The chase procedure for NFDs and NINDs

Herein we extend the standard chase procedure defined over complete databases with respect to FDs [32,18,5] and INDs [21,34] to incomplete databases with respect to NFDs and NINDs. In order to establish our results in the following sections we make extensive use of the chase procedure as a theorem proving tool.

Let Dum $= \{\perp_1, \perp_2, \ldots, \perp_q\}$ be a set of distinguished nonnull values in *Dom*, which do not appear in d, where q denotes the finite number of distinct occurrences of *unk* in d. For the purpose of defining the chase procedure we extend the partial order in *Dom* as follows: $\forall\, i,j \in \{1,\ldots,q\}$, $\perp_i \sqsubseteq \perp_j$, and for all nonnull values v appearing in d, we have that $\forall \perp_i \in$ Dum, $\perp_i \sqsubseteq v$ but $v \not\sqsubseteq \perp_i$. Furthermore, we extend $\sqcup$ as follows: if $i \leq j$ then $\perp_i \sqcup \perp_j = \perp_i$, otherwise $\perp_i \sqcup \perp_j = \perp_j$.

We now define two *chase rules*, which are applied to a database d over **R**.

NFD rule: if $R : X \rightarrow Y \in F$ and $\exists t_1, t_2 \in r$ such that $t_1[X] = t_2[X]$ and $t_1[Y] \neq t_2[Y]$, then $\forall A \in Y$, change all occurrences of $t_1[A]$ and $t_2[A]$ *in d* to $t_1[A] \sqcup t_2[A]$.

NIND rule: if $R[X] \subseteq S[Y] \in I$, and $\exists\, t_1 \in r$, $\exists\, t_2 \in s$, with $t_1[X] \sqsubseteq t_2[Y]$ or $t_2[X] \sqsubseteq t_1[Y]$, but $\not\exists\, t_3 \in s$ with $t_1[X] = t_3[Y]$, then $\forall\, i \in \{1,\ldots,m\}$, change all occurrences of $t_1[A_i]$ and $t_2[B_i]$ *in d*, to $t_1[A_i] \sqcup t_2[B_i]$, where $X = < A_1 \ldots, A_m >$ and $Y = < B_1 \ldots, B_m >$.

We now give the pseudo-code of an algorithm designated, CHASE(d, F, I), which, given an input d, F and I, applies the NFD and NIND rules to d as long as possible and returns the resulting database over **R**. CHASE(d, F, I) will also denote the database resulting from the ensuing Algorithm 23.

Algorithm 23 (CHASE(d, F, I)).
1. **begin**
2.   Result := d;
3.   i := 1;
4.   **for each** r ∈ Result, with r over R, **do**
5.   **for each** t ∈ r and A ∈ schema(R) such that t[A] = *unk* **do**
6.   t[A] := $\perp_i$;
7.   i := i + 1;
8.   **end for**
9.   **end for**
10.   Tmp := ∅;
11.   **while** Tmp ≠ Result **do**
12.   Tmp := Result;
13.   Apply the NFD rule or the NIND rule to Result;
14.   **end while**
15.   **return** Result;
16. **end.**

The following proposition states an important property of the chase procedure [32,40,18,5] with respect to NFDs, which will be useful in Section 6. In the sequel we call an execution of line 13 in Algorithm 23 a *chase step* and we say that the chase step *applies* the NFD or NIND rule to the current state of d.

Proposition 24. Let d be a consistent database over **R** and let F be a set of NFDs over **R**. Then $\exists d_1 \in$ POSS(d) such that $\forall$ R : X → Y ∈ F, $d_1 \not\approx$ R : X → Y if and only if CHASE(d, F, ∅) is consistent, or equivalently, CHASE(d, F, ∅) ∈ POSS(d).   □

It can be verified that CHASE(d, F, ∅) is unique only up to the order in which the values in Dum are assigned to the null attribute values in d (cf. [32,5]). This is due to the fact that the for loops beginning at lines 4 and 5 of Algorithm 23 do not specify the order in which these statements are to be executed.

On the other hand, CHASE(d, ∅, I) is *not* necessarily unique even up to the order in which the values in Dum are assigned to the null attribute values in d. For example, let d = {r, s} be a database, where r over R, with schema(R) = <A>, is the relation shown in Table 8 and s over S, with schema(S) = <B>, is the relation shown in Table 9. Furthermore, let I = {R[A] ⊆ S[B]}. Then the occurrence of $\perp_i$ in r may be changed to 0 or to 1 depending on whether the NIND rule for R[A] ⊆ S[B] chooses the first or second tuple in s.

From now on we will assume that the for loops beginning at lines 4 and 5 of Algorithm 23 assign the values in Dum to the null attribute values in d in some arbitrary but fixed order. Moreover, we will denote the set of all consistent databases resulting from executing Algorithm 23 by SETOF(CHASE(d, F, I)).

The following proposition can be proved by utilising the same technique used in [1, Theorem 1], since each application of a chase step reduces the number of distinct values in the database by at least one.

B
0
1

A
$\perp_i$

Table 8. The counterexample relation r

Table 9. The counterexample relation s

Proposition 25. CHASE(d, F, I) can be computed in time polynomial in the sizes of d, F and I. $\square$

On the negative side SETOF(CHASE(d, F, I)) may contain an exponential number of databases in the sizes of d and I due to the nonuniqueness of CHASE(d, $\emptyset$, I). For example, let d = {r} be a database with schema(R) = < $A_1, A_2, \ldots, A_m$, B, C>, where r is shown in Table 10. Also, let I = $\cup_{i=1}^m$ {R[A_i] $\subseteq$ R[B], R[A_i] $\subseteq$ R[C]} be a set of unary NINDs. It follows that |SETOF(CHASE(d, $\emptyset$, I))| = 2^n but the only database that satisfies all the NINDs in I is the database resulting from modifying all the occurrences of $\perp_i$, for $i = 1, \ldots, m$, to 0.

A_1	A_2	...	A_m	B	C
$\perp_1$	$\perp_2$	...	$\perp_m$	0	0
0	0	...	0	1	0

Table 10. A relation inducing an exponential number of distinct chases

Proposition 26. Let d be a consistent database over **R** and let I be a set of NINDs over **R**. Then $\exists d_1 \in$ POSS(d) such that $\forall$ R[X] $\subseteq$ S[Y] $\in$ I, $d_1 \not\approx$ R[X] $\subseteq$ S[Y] if and only if $\exists d_2 \in$ SETOF(CHASE(d, $\emptyset$, I)) such that $\forall$ R[X] $\subseteq$ S[Y] $\in$ I, $d_2 \not\approx$ R[X] $\subseteq$ S[Y].

Proof. (If.) Let $d_2 \in$ SETOF(CHASE(d, $\emptyset$, I)) be a database such that $\forall$ R[X] $\subseteq$ S[Y] $\in$ I, $d_2 \not\approx$ R[X] $\subseteq$ S[Y]. Moreover, let us replace all occurrences of $\perp_i \in$ adom(d_2), where i $\in$ {1,...,q}, by a distinct nonnull value $v_i \in$ Dom that does not appear in adom(d_2), thus obtaining the database d_1. The result follows, since $d_1 \in$ POSS(d) and $\forall$ R[X] $\subseteq$ S[Y] $\in$ I, $d_1 \not\approx$ R[X] $\subseteq$ S[Y].

(Only if.) Suppose that $\not\exists d_2 \in$ SETOF(CHASE(d, $\emptyset$, I)) such that $\forall$ R[X] $\subseteq$ S[Y] $\in$ I, $d_2 \not\approx$ R[X] $\subseteq$ S[Y]. Equivalently, $\forall d_2 \in$ SETOF(CHASE(d, $\emptyset$, I)), $\exists$ R[X] $\subseteq$ S[Y] $\in$ I such that $d_2 \not\approx$ R[X] $\subseteq$ S[Y]. Let $d_2 \in$ SETOF(CHASE(d, $\emptyset$, I)) and R[X] $\subseteq$ S[Y] $\in$ I be a database and a NIND, respectively, such that $d_2 \not\approx$ R[X] $\subseteq$ S[Y]. Furthermore, let us replace all occurrences of $\perp_i \in$ adom(d_2), where i $\in$ {1,...,q}, by a distinct nonnull value $v_i \in$ Dom that does not appear in Dum, thus obtaining the database d_1. Obviously, $d_1 \not\approx$ R[X] $\subseteq$ S[Y] independently of the choice of v_i for each i $\in$ {1,...,q}. Now d_1 is an arbitrary element of

POSS(d) realising a possible sequence of assignments of the null values in d to nonnull values in *Dom*. The result follows, since this implies that no sequence of assignments of the null values in d to nonnull values in *Dom* is possible for which $\forall$ R[X] $\subseteq$ S[Y] $\in$ I, $d_1 \not\approx$ R[X] $\subseteq$ S[Y] obtains. □

We next show that the chase for NFDs and NINDs can be computed by first applying the NIND rule as long as possible and then applying the NFD rule as long as possible (cf. [34] for a similar result concerning noncircular sets of INDs, that is sets of nontrivial INDs, which do not logically imply INDs of the form R[X] $\subseteq$ R[Y]).

Proposition 27. Let d be a consistent database over **R** and let $\Sigma = F \cup I$ be a set of NFDs and NINDs over **R**. Then $\exists d_1 \in$ SETOF(CHASE(d, F, I)) such that $\forall \alpha \in \Sigma$, $d_1 \not\approx \alpha$ if and only if $\exists d_2 \in$ SETOF(CHASE(CHASE(d, $\emptyset$, I), F, $\emptyset$)) such that $\forall \alpha \in \Sigma$, $d_2 \not\approx \alpha$ and $d_1 = d_2$.

Proof. The if part is immediate, since SETOF(CHASE(CHASE(d, $\emptyset$, I), F, $\emptyset$)) $\subseteq$ SETOF(CHASE(d, F, I)). For the only if part assume that $d_1 \in$ SETOF(CHASE (d, F, I)) is such that $\forall \alpha \in \Sigma$, $d_1 \not\approx \alpha$ and therefore d_1 is consistent. We need to show that $\exists d_2 \in$ SETOF(CHASE(CHASE(d, $\emptyset$, I), F, $\emptyset$)) such that $\forall \alpha \in \Sigma$, $d_2 \not\approx \alpha$. The result is obtained by induction on the minimal number of chase steps required to arrive at d_1 during the computation of the chase. The basis step is vacuously true when zero chase steps are required to compute d_1. In the induction step there are two cases to consider.

Firstly, the last chase step is an application of the NFD rule. The result follows by inductive hypothesis which implies that the state of d_1 prior to the last chase step can be computed by applying the NIND rule first as long as possible.

Secondly, the last chase step is an application of the NIND rule for, say R[X] $\subseteq$ S[Y]. By inductive hypothesis the state of d_1 prior to the last chase step can be computed by applying the NIND rule first as long as possible. Thus we can assume that the penultimate chase step is an application of the NFD rule for T : W → Z.

Let d' be the state of d_1 prior to the application of the last two chase steps associated with the NFD rule for T : W → Z and the NIND rule for R[X] $\subseteq$ S[Y] in that order. It can be verified that the equality with respect to the left-hand side of the NFD T : W → Z is not affected by the said NIND rule. Thus the NFD rule may be applied after the NIND rule has been applied to d'. Furthermore, by examining all the possibilities, the entries in the relations of d_1 attain their highest values with respect to $\sqsubseteq$ whether the aforesaid rules are interchanged or not. The result now follows by inductive hypothesis. □

The next proposition is a consequence of Proposition 27 on using Propositions 24 and 26.

Proposition 28. Let d be a consistent database over **R** and let $\Sigma = F \cup I$ be a set of NFDs and NINDs over **R**. Then $\exists d_1 \in$ POSS(d) such that $\forall \alpha \in \Sigma$, $d_1 \not\approx \alpha$ if and only if $\exists d_2 \in$ SETOF(CHASE(d, F, I)) such that $\forall \alpha \in \Sigma$, $d_2 \not\approx \alpha$. □

The next proposition, whose proof is left to the reader, shows that the chase procedure is invariant with respect to sets of NFDs and NINDs that are equivalent with respect to logical implication.

Proposition 29. Let d be a consistent database over $\mathbf{R}$ and let $\Sigma = F \cup I$ be a set of NFDs and NINDs over $\mathbf{R}$. In addition, let $F \subseteq F'$ and $I \subseteq I'$ be sets of NFDs and NINDs over $\mathbf{R}$, respectively, where $\forall \beta \in (F' \cup I') - \Sigma$, $\Sigma \not\approx \beta$. Then $\exists d_1 \in \text{SETOF}(\text{CHASE}(d, F, I))$ such that $\forall \alpha \in \Sigma$, $d_1 \approx \alpha$ if and only if $\exists d_2 \in \text{SETOF}(\text{CHASE}(d, F', I'))$ such that $\forall \alpha \in \Sigma$, $d_2 \approx \alpha$. $\square$

From now on we will assume that when computing the chase we apply the NIND rule first as long as possible and then do not apply it any further, i.e., we compute $\text{CHASE}(\text{CHASE}(d, \emptyset, I), F, \emptyset)$.

We close the section by defining a transformation, denoted by TR, which when applied to a database d over $\mathbf{R}$ returns a database $\text{TR}(d, I)$ over $\mathbf{R}$ which satisfies all the NINDs in I by adding tuples to the relations in d. Specifically, $\text{TR}(d, I)$ transforms d by applying the following transformation rule, initially to d, and then to the resulting states of d as long as possible, where d' is a state of d during the transformation, r' is the relation in d' over R and s' is the relation in d' over S.

Transformation rule: if $R[X] \subseteq S[Y] \in I$ and $\exists t_1 \in r'$ such that $\not\exists t_2 \in s'$ with $t_1[X] \subseteq t_2[Y]$, then add a tuple t_2 over S to s', with $t_2[Y] = t_1[X]$ and $\forall A \in \text{schema}(S) - Y$, $t_2[A] = unk$.

It can be verified that $\forall \alpha \in I$, $\text{TR}(d, I) \approx \alpha$, by the definition of the satisfaction of a NIND, since otherwise the transformation rule would not have been applied as long as possible leading to a contradiction. We observe that the above transformation rule is utilised in Sections 7 and 8.

5 The additivity problem for null data dependencies

Herein we define the additivity problem referred to in the introduction.

Definition 30 (Satisfaction of a set of NFDs and NINDs). Let d be a database over $\mathbf{R}$ and Σ be a set of NFDs and NINDs. Then d satisfies Σ, denoted by $d \approx \Sigma$, whenever:

1. $\forall \alpha \in \Sigma$, $d \approx \alpha$, and
2. $\exists d' \in \text{POSS}(d)$ such that $\forall \alpha \in \Sigma$, $d' \approx \alpha$.

We note that by Proposition 16 if Σ consists of NFDs only then in the above definition condition (1) is implied by condition (2).

Following [5] and [24] we now define additive satisfaction of a class of sets of NFDs and NINDs with respect to a class of databases.

Definition 31 (Additive satisfaction). Satisfaction is said to be *additive* with respect to a class of databases, say *DBC*, and a class of sets of NFDs and NINDs, say *DEPC*, whenever:

$$\forall d \in DBC, \forall \Sigma \in DEPC, d \not\approx \Sigma \text{ if and only if } \forall \alpha \in \Sigma, d \not\approx \alpha.$$

Obviously, the only if part of the above definition trivially holds, since, by Definition 30, if $d \not\approx \Sigma$ then $\forall \alpha \in \Sigma, d \not\approx \alpha$. Thus in order to show that satisfaction is additive with respect to a class of databases and a class of sets of NFDs and NINDs we need to show that if $\forall \alpha \in \Sigma, d \not\approx \alpha$, then $\exists d' \in POSS(d)$ such that $\forall \alpha \in \Sigma, d' \not\approx \alpha$.

The next lemma follows immediately from Definitions 20 and 30.

Lemma 32. Let d be a database over **R** and Σ be a set of NFDs and NINDs over **R**. Then $d \not\approx \Sigma$ if and only if $d \not\approx \{\alpha \mid \Sigma \not\approx \alpha\}$. □

The following lemma is immediate, since condition (2) of Definition 30 vacuously holds for complete databases.

Lemma 33. Satisfaction is additive with respect to COMPLETE(**R**) and NFD(**R**) ∪ NIND(**R**). □

6 The additivity problem for null functional dependencies

Herein we investigate the additivity problem for NFDs on their own. The next lemma follows from the counterexamples provided in Example 1 of the introduction.

Lemma 34. Satisfaction is not additive with respect to DB(**R**) and NFD(**R**). □

We assume that the reader is familiar with Armstrong's axiom system for FDs [2,39,5]. The closure of a set of NFDs F over **R** with respect to Armstrong's axiom system, denoted by F^+, is defined by

$$F^+ = \bigcup \{F(R)^+ \mid R \in \mathbf{R}\},$$

where $F(R)^+$ is the closure of $F(R)$ with respect to Arsmtrong's axiom system. A set of NFDs G over R is a *cover* of a set of NFDs F over R if $G^+ = F^+$.

Definition 35 (Reduced and canonical sets of NFDs). A NFD $X \to Y \in F^+$ is *reduced* [6] if there does not exist a set of attributes $W \subset X$ such that $W \to Y \in F^+$. A set of NFDs F is *reduced* if all the NFDs in F are reduced.

A set of FDs F is *canonical* if it is reduced and the right-hand sides of all the FDs in F are singletons.

We further note that reduced and canonical covers G of a set of NFDs F can be obtained in polynomial time in the size of F [6]. From now on for the rest of the paper we will restrict our attention to reduced sets of NFDs and assume that *all the sets of NFDs in* NFD(R) *are reduced.*

Definition 36 (Monodependent sets of NFDs). Two nontrivial NFDs of the forms $R : X \to A$ and $R : Y \to A$, where $A \in$ schema(R), are said to be *incomparable* if X and Y are incomparable (i.e., $X \not\subseteq Y$ and $Y \not\subseteq X$). Two nontrivial NFDs of the forms $R : XB \to A$ and $R : YA \to B$, where $A,B \in$ schema(R), are said to be *cyclic*.

A set of NFDs F over R is *monodependent* if $\forall R \in \mathbf{R}$, $\forall A \in$ schema(R), the following two conditions are true:

1. Whenever there exist incomparable NFDs, $X \to A$, $Y \to A \in F(R)^+$, then $X \cap Y \to A \in F(R)^+$.
2. Whenever there exist cyclic NFDs, $XB \to A$, $YA \to B \in F(R)^+$, then either $Y \to B \in F(R)^+$ or $(X \cap Y)A \to B \in F(R)^+$.

An immediate consequence of the above definition is that if G is a cover of a set of NFDs F over R, then F is monodependent if and only if G is monodependent.

We observe that the two defining conditions of monodependent sets of NFDs correspond to the two defining properties of *conflict-free* sets of *multivalued dependencies* (MVDs) [37,31,7]. In particular, condition (1) corresponds to the *intersection property* and condition (2) corresponds to the *split-freeness property*. We further observe that the set of MVDs that are logically implied by a monodependent set of NFDs may not be conflict-free and thus monodependence is a weaker notion than conflict-freeness. For example, let $F(R) = \{A \to B, B \to A\}$ be a set of NFDs over R, with schema(R) = <A, B, C>. It can easily be verified that $F(R)$ is monodependent but that the set of MVDs logically implied by $F(R)$ is not conflict-free.

The next lemma shows that monodependence for NFDs implies additivity. In particular, the *pseudo-transitivity inference rule* will be utilised, where if $R : X \to Y \in F(R)^+$ and $R : WY \to Z \in F(R)^+$, then $R : XW \to Z \in F(R)^+$ can be derived.

Lemma 37. Let F be a set of monodependent NFDs over R. Then $\forall d \in$ DB(R), $\forall R \in \mathbf{R}$, if $\forall R : X \to Y \in F$, $d \approx R: X \to Y$, then $d \approx F$.

Proof. Assume without loss of generality that F is a canonical set of NFDs noting that a canonical set of NFDs is reduced. Also assume that all the NFDs in F are of the form $R : X \to Y$ for a fixed $R \in \mathbf{R}$.

We show that if $\exists d \in$ DB(R) such that $\forall R : X \to Y \in F$, $d \approx R: X \to Y$, but $d \not\approx F$, then F cannot be monodependent as assumed. Let d be such a database. By Proposition 24 it follows that CHASE(d, F, ∅) is inconsistent.

We conclude the result by induction on the minimal number of chase steps, k, required to show that CHASE(d, F, $\emptyset$) is inconsistent.

(*Basis*): At least two chase steps are needed to show that CHASE(d, F, $\emptyset$) is inconsistent, since by assumption $\forall\, X \to Y \in F$, $d \not\approx X \to Y$. Thus consider the case when $k = 2$. Suppose the second chase step applies the NFD $X \to A \in F$ to the tuples $t_1, t_2 \in r$, where $r \in d$ is the relation over R. Then after the first chase step is applied $t_1[X] = t_2[X]$ but $t_1[A] \sqcup t_2[A]$ is inconsistent. Without loss of generality assume that the first chase step applies the NFD $R: Y \to B \in F$ to the tuples t_2 and t_3 in r. There are two cases to consider.

Case1: $B = A$. In this case the first chase step applies the NFD $Y \to A$ to t_2 and t_3 in r resulting in $t_1[A] \sqcup t_2[A]$ being inconsistent. It follows that $t_1[A] \sqcup t_3[A]$ is inconsistent in r, since otherwise $t_1[A] \sqcup t_2[A]$ is inconsistent in r implying that one chase step is sufficient to show that CHASE(d, F, $\emptyset$) is inconsistent. Now, if $X = Y$ then one chase step which applies the NFD $X \to A$ to the tuples t_1 and t_3 in r is sufficient to show that CHASE(d, F, $\emptyset$) is inconsistent, thus $X \neq Y$. The result that F is not monodependent now follows by the assumption that F is canonical, since $X \to A$ and $Y \to A$ must be incomparable NFDs and $X \cap Y \to A \notin F^+$.

Case2: $B \neq A$. In this case the first chase step applies the NFD $Y \to B$ to t_2 and t_3 in r resulting in $t_1[B] = t_2[B]$. Furthermore, $t_1[A] \sqcup t_2[A]$ is inconsistent in r, since $k = 2$. It follows that $B \in X$, otherwise one chase step would suffice to show that CHASE(d, F, $\emptyset$) is inconsistent.

Now suppose that $A \notin Y$. Then we can derive $(X - B)Y \to A \in F^+$ by the pseudo-transitivity rule, where $X \not\subseteq (X - B)Y$, since $B \notin Y$. Now, if $(X - B)Y \not\subseteq X$ then $(X - B)Y \to A$ and $X \to A$ are incomparable. Furthermore, $(X - B)$ is a proper subset of X and therefore $(X - B) \to A \notin F^+$, since F is canonical. Thus, there exists a canonical set of NFDs G such that $W \to A$, $X \to A \in G$, where $W \subseteq (X - B)Y$. The result that F is not monodependent follows from Case1 by replacing F with G. Therefore, we assume that $(X - B)Y \subseteq X$, implying that $(X - B)Y$ is a proper subset of X, since $B \notin Y$. This contradicts the fact that F is canonical, since $(X - B)Y \to A \in F^+$.

We therefore suppose that $A \in Y$. The result that F is not monodependent now follows, since $Y \to B$ and $X \to A$ are cyclic NFDs and in addition the following two assertions are true.

Firstly, $(X - B) \to A \notin F^+$ due to the fact that by assumption F is canonical. Secondly, $t_1[B] = t_3[B]$ in r, since $Y \to B$ was applied to t_2 and t_3 and $k = 2$. Moreover, $t_1[(X \cap Y)] = t_3[(X \cap Y)]$ in r, since both $t_1[(X \cap Y)] = t_2[(X \cap Y)]$ in r and $t_2[(X \cap Y)] = t_3[(X \cap Y)]$ in r. Furthermore, $t_2[A] = t_3[A]$ in r, since $A \in Y$, and therefore $t_1[A] \sqcup t_3[A]$ is inconsistent in r. Thus, if $(X \cap Y)B \to A \in F^+$, then due to the assumption that F is canonical one chase step which applies the NFD $(X \cap Y)B \to A$ to t_1 and t_2 would suffice to show that CHASE(d, F, $\emptyset$) is inconsistent. It therefore follows that $(X \cap Y)B \to A \notin F^+$ which is equivalent to $((X - B) \cap (Y - A))B \to A \notin F^+$, since $B \notin Y$ and $A \notin X$. (Recall that $(X - B) \to A \notin F^+$.) The result that F is not monodependent follows.

(Induction): Assume the result holds when the minimal number of chase steps required to show that CHASE(d, F, $\emptyset$) is inconsistent is k, with k $\geq$ 2; we then need to prove that the result holds when the minimal number of chase steps required to show that CHASE(d, F, $\emptyset$) is inconsistent is k+1. Suppose the last chase step applies the NFD X $\rightarrow$ A $\in$ F to the tuples t_1 and t_2 in the penultimate state of r during the execution of CHASE(d, F, $\emptyset$). Then after the penultimate chase step is applied $t_1[X] = t_2[X]$ but $t_1[A] \sqcup t_2[A]$ is inconsistent. Without loss of generality assume that the penultimate chase step applies the NFD Y $\rightarrow$ B $\in$ F to the tuples t_2 and t_3 in the state prior to the penultimate state of r during the execution of CHASE(d, F, $\emptyset$).

The result follows by a similar argument to the basis step noting that if k or less chase steps are sufficient to show that CHASE(d, F, $\emptyset$) is inconsistent, then the result follows by inductive hypothesis. $\square$

The next lemma shows that additivity for NFDs implies monodependence.

Lemma 38. Let F be a set of NFDs over **R** and assume that $\forall$ d $\in$ DB(**R**), $\forall$ R $\in$ **R**, if $\forall$ R : X $\rightarrow$ Y $\in$ F, d $\not\approx$ R : X $\rightarrow$ Y, then d $\not\approx$ F. Then F is monodependent.

Proof. We show that if F is not monodependent, then $\exists$ d $\in$ DB(**R**) such that $\forall$ R : X $\rightarrow$ Y $\in$ F, d $\not\approx$ R : X $\rightarrow$ Y but d $\not\approx$ F. We assume without loss of generality that F(R) is not monodependent, where R $\in$ **R**, and $\forall$ S $\in$ **R** $-$ {R}, F(S) is monodependent. Furthermore, we will assume for the rest of the proof that all NFDs are of the form R : X $\rightarrow$ Y. There are two cases to consider.

Case1: There exist incomparable NFDs X $\rightarrow$ A, Y $\rightarrow$ A $\in$ F^+ but X $\cap$ Y $\rightarrow$ A $\notin$ F^+. Let Rest = schema(R) $-$ XYA and let d $\in$ DB(**R**) be a database, where the relation r $\in$ d over R is shown in Table 11 and $\forall$ s $\in$ d $-$ {r}, s = $\emptyset$.

It can be verified that $\forall$ V $\rightarrow$ T $\in$ F, d $\not\approx$ V $\rightarrow$ T, since the only NFDs that are not satisfied in d are of the form W $\rightarrow$ A, where W $\subseteq$ X $\cap$ Y, due to the assumption that X $\cap$ Y $\rightarrow$ A $\notin$ F^+. The result now follows due to the fact that d $\not\approx$ F, since it can easily be verified that $\forall d' \in$ POSS(d), either $d' \not\approx$ X $\rightarrow$ A or $d' \not\approx$ Y $\rightarrow$ A.

X $\cap$ Y	X $-$ Y	Y $-$ X	A	Rest
0 ... 0	0 ... 0	*unk...unk*	0	*unk...unk*
0 ... 0	0 ... 0	0 ... 0	*unk*	*unk...unk*
0 ... 0	*unk...unk*	0 ... 0	1	*unk...unk*

Table 11. The relation pertaining to Case1

Case2: There exist cyclic NFDs, XB $\rightarrow$ A, YA $\rightarrow$ B $\in$ F^+, but both Y $\rightarrow$ B $\notin$ F^+ and (X $\cap$ Y)A $\rightarrow$ B $\notin$ F^+ obtain. Let Rest = schema(R) $-$ XYAB and let d $\in$ DB(**R**) be a database, where the relation r $\in$ d over R is shown in Table 12 and $\forall$ s $\in$ d $-$ {r}, s = $\emptyset$.

The only NFDs that are not satisfied in d are of the form $W \to B$, where $W \subseteq Y$, or of the form $W \to B$, where $W \subseteq (X \cap Y)A$. These violations are justified due to the assumption that $Y \to B \notin F^+$ and $(X \cap Y)A \to B \notin F^+$. The result now follows due to the fact that $d \not\models F$, since it can easily be verified that $\forall d' \in POSS(r)$, $d' \not\models YA \to B$. $\quad\square$

$X \cap Y$	$X - Y$	$Y - X$	A	B	Rest
$0 \ldots 0$	$0 \ldots 0$	$unk \ldots unk$	0	0	$unk \ldots unk$
$0 \ldots 0$	$0 \ldots 0$	$0 \ldots 0$	unk	0	$unk \ldots unk$
$0 \ldots 0$	$unk \ldots unk$	$0 \ldots 0$	0	1	$unk \ldots unk$

Table 12. The relation pertaining to Case2

The following theorem summarises Lemmas 37 and 38.

Theorem 39. Satisfaction is additive with respect to DB(R) and a class of sets of NFDs **FC** if and only if all the sets of NFDs in **FC** are monodependent. $\quad\square$

Theorem 40. Monodependence of a set of NFDs F over **R** can be checked in time polynomial in the size of F.

Proof. In [24] it was shown that a canonical set of NFDs F(R) over R is monodependent if and only if $\forall A \in schema(R)$, the following two conditions are true:

1. There exists at most one NFD in F(R) of the form $X \to A$, and if $X \to A \in F(R)$ then $\forall B \in X$, $(schema(R) - AB) \to A \notin F(R)^+$.
2. Whenever $X \to A$, $Y \to B \in F(R)$, then either $A \notin Y$ or $Y \subseteq (X \cap Y)A$.

The result follows by [33], where it was shown that given a set of NFDs, G(R), a canonical set of NFDs, F(R), such that $F(R)^+ = G(R)^+$, can be obtained in time polynomial in the size of G(R). $\quad\square$

7 The additivity problem for unary null inclusion dependencies

Herein we investigate the additivity problem for unary NINDs on their own. The next lemma follows from the counterexample provided in Example 2 of the introduction.

Lemma 41. Satisfaction is not additive with respect to DB(R) and NIND(R). $\square$

Definition 42 (Monodirectional sets of unary NINDs). A set of unary N-INDs I over **R** is *monodirectional* if for every pair of nontrivial NINDs, R[A] ⊆ S[B] and R[A] ⊆ T[C], that are logically implied by I, at least one of the following conditions is true:

1. S = T and B = C, or
2. I |≈ S[B] ⊆ T[C], or
3. I |≈ T[C] ⊆ S[B], or
4. I |≈ S[B] ⊆ R[A], or
5. I |≈ T[C] ⊆ R[A].

The next lemma shows that monodirectionality implies additivity for unary NINDs.

Lemma 43. Let I be a set of monodirectional unary NINDs over **R**. Then ∀ d ∈ DB(**R**), if ∀ R[A] ⊆ S[B] ∈ I, d |≈ R[A] ⊆ S[B], then d |≈ I.

Proof. We show that if ∃ d ∈ DB(**R**) such that ∀ R[A] ⊆ S[B] ∈ I, d |≈ R[A] ⊆ S[B], but d |̸≈ I, then I is not monodirectional. Let d be such a database. Then by Proposition 26, ∀d' ∈ SETOF(CHASE(d, ∅, I)), ∃ R[A] ⊆ S[B] ∈ I such that d' |̸≈ R[A] ⊆ S[B]. Let d' be a database in SETOF(CHASE(d, ∅, I)) and R[A] ⊆ S[B] ∈ I be a unary NIND such that d' |̸≈ R[A] ⊆ S[B].

We conclude the proof by induction on the minimal number, k, of chase steps required in the computation of d' to derive the fact that d' |̸≈ R[A] ⊆ S[B].

(*Basis*): Assume that k = 1 and thus the chase step applies the NIND rule for R[A] ⊆ T[C] ∈ I to d. The application of this NIND rule must cause a distinguished nonnull value, say $\perp_i$, in Dum to be modified to a nonnull value, say v, in Dom − Dum. Furthermore, d' |≈ R[A] ⊆ T[C], as a result of applying the NIND rule for R[A] ⊆ T[C]. We now show that all the conditions of monodirectionality given in Definition 42 are violated, otherwise a contradiction arises.

1. If S = T and B = C then it follows that d' |≈ R[A] ⊆ S[B].
2. Assume that I |≈ S[B] ⊆ T[C] and thus d |≈ S[B] ⊆ T[C] by the definition of logical implication. By modifying $\perp_i$, instead of to v, to an appropriate nonnull value in the active domain of the relation over S in d we obtain d' |≈ R[A] ⊆ S[B], since d |≈ R[A] ⊆ S[B].
3. Assume that I |≈ T[C] ⊆ S[B] and thus d |≈ T[C] ⊆ S[B] by the definition of logical implication. It follows that d' |≈ R[A] ⊆ S[B], since d |≈ R[A] ⊆ S[B].
4. Assume that I |≈ S[B] ⊆ R[A] and thus d |≈ S[B] ⊆ R[A] by the definition of logical implication. Therefore, I |≈ S[B] ⊆ T[C] by the transitivity rule for NINDs [9,25] and thus d |≈ S[B] ⊆ T[C]. The result follows as in (2).
5. Assume that I |≈ T[C] ⊆ R[A] and thus d |≈ T[C] ⊆ R[A] by the definition of logical implication. Therefore, I |≈ T[C] ⊆ S[B] by the transitivity rule for NINDs and thus d |≈ T[C] ⊆ S[B]. The result follows as in (3).

(*Induction*): Assume the result holds when the minimal number of chase steps required to compute d' is k, with $k \geq 1$; we then need to prove that the result holds when the minimal number of chase steps required to derive the fact that $d' \not\approx R[A] \subseteq S[B]$ is k+1. Let d_1 be the state of d' prior to applying the (k+1)th chase step and let the (k+1)th chase step be an application of the NIND rule for a NIND $Q[D] \subseteq T[C] \in I$. By inductive hypothesis $d_1 \approx R[A] \subseteq S[B]$; moreover, $d' \approx Q[D] \subseteq T[C]$. There are two cases to consider.

Case1: $I \approx R[A] \subseteq Q[D]$ obtains. By inductive hypothesis $d_1 \approx R[A] \subseteq Q[D]$, since otherwise we can replace $R[A] \subseteq S[B]$ by $R[A] \subseteq Q[D]$ and obtain the result in k chase steps. By the transitivity rule for NINDs it follows that $I \approx R[A] \subseteq T[C]$ and thus $d' \approx R[A] \subseteq T[C]$. The result is now obtained by an argument analogous to that made in the basis step utilising Proposition 29.

Case2: $I \not\approx R[A] \subseteq Q[D]$ obtains. There are two subcases to consider.

Firstly, $I \approx Q[D] \subseteq R[A]$ obtains. By inductive hypothesis $d_1 \approx Q[D] \subseteq R[A]$, since otherwise we can replace $R[A] \subseteq S[B]$ by $Q[D] \subseteq R[A]$ and obtain the result in k chase steps. By the transitivity rule for NINDs it follows that $I \approx Q[D] \subseteq S[B]$ and thus $d_1 \approx Q[D] \subseteq S[B]$. Next, suppose that the (k+1)th chase step causes a distinguished nonnull value, say $\perp_i$, in d_1 to be modified to a nonnull value, say v, in $Dom - $ Dum. It follows that $\perp_i$ is an A-value in the relation over R in d_1 and that v is not a B-value in the relation over S in d', since $d' \not\approx R[A] \subseteq S[B]$. Therefore, $d' \not\approx Q[D] \subseteq S[B]$, since v is a D-value in the relation over Q in d'. The result follows by replacing $R[A] \subseteq S[B]$ by $Q[D] \subseteq S[B]$ and arguing that I is not monodirectional in a manner analogous to that made in the basis step on utilising Proposition 29.

Secondly, $I \not\approx Q[D] \subseteq R[A]$ obtains. There must therefore exist a distinguished nonnull value, say $\perp_i$, in Dum that is both an A-value of the relation over R in d_1 and a D-value of the relation over Q in d_1, since $d' \not\approx R[A] \subseteq S[B]$. There are two final subcases to consider.

Firstly, for some relation schema P and an attribute $E \in schema(P)$, both $I \approx P[E] \subseteq R[A]$ and $I \approx P[E] \subseteq Q[D]$ obtain. The result that I is not monodirectional follows by an argument analogous to that made in the basis step, where $R[A]$ is replaced by $P[E]$, on utilising Proposition 29.

Secondly, for some relation schema P and an attribute $E \in schema(P)$, both $I \approx R[A] \subseteq P[E]$ and $I \approx Q[D] \subseteq P[E]$ obtain. By inductive hypothesis, $d_1 \approx R[A] \subseteq P[E]$, since otherwise we can replace $R[A] \subseteq S[B]$ by $R[A] \subseteq P[E]$ and obtain the result in k or less chase steps. Furthermore, $P[E] \neq S[B]$ and $d' \approx Q[D] \subseteq P[E]$, since otherwise the result that I is not monodirectional follows by an argument analogous to that made in the basis step, where $R[A]$ is replaced by $Q[D]$ and $S[B]$ is replaced by $P[E]$, on utilising Proposition 29. We can therefore assume without loss of generality that $P[E] = T[C]$, since an application of the NIND $Q[D] \subseteq P[E]$ at the appropriate stage during the computation of d' will cause the violation $d' \not\approx R[A] \subseteq S[B]$. It follows that $d' \approx R[A] \subseteq P[E]$, since the application of $Q[D] \subseteq P[E]$ replaces $\perp_i$ by an E-value in the relation over P in d_1. The result that I is not monodirectional follows by an argument analogous to that made in the basis step, where $R[A] \subseteq T[C]$ is replaced by $R[A] \subseteq P[E]$, on utilising Proposition 29. $\square$

The next lemma shows that additivity for unary NINDs implies monodirectionality.

Lemma 44. Let I be a set of unary NINDs over **R** and assume that $\forall\ d \in DB(\mathbf{R})$, if $\forall\ R[A] \subseteq S[B] \in I$, $d \models R[A] \subseteq S[B]$, then $d \models I$. Then I is monodirectional.

Proof. We show that if I is not monodirectional, then $\exists\ d \in DB(\mathbf{R})$ such that $\forall\ R[A] \subseteq S[B] \in I$, $d \models R[A] \subseteq S[B]$ but $d \not\models I$. Now, if I is not monodirectional then there exists a pair of nontrivial unary NINDs $R[A] \subseteq S[B]$ and $R[A] \subseteq T[C]$ that are logically implied by I, such that either $S \neq T$ or $B \neq C$ and *none* of the following conditions is true:

1. $I \models S[B] \subseteq T[C]$.
2. $I \models T[C] \subseteq S[B]$.
3. $I \models S[B] \subseteq R[A]$.
4. $I \models T[C] \subseteq R[A]$.

Let d be a database over **R**, where $r \in d$ is the relation over R shown in Table 13, $s \in d$ is the relation over S shown in Table 14, $z \in d$ is the relation over T shown in Table 15, and all the other relations in $d - \{r, s, z\}$ are empty.

schema(R)
$unk \ldots unk$

B	schema(S)$-$B
0	$unk \ldots unk$

C	schema(T)$-$C
1	$unk \ldots unk$

Table 13. The counterexample relation r over R

Table 14. The counterexample relation s over S

Table 15. The counterexample relation z over T

Let r_1 in TR(d, I) be the relation over R, s_1 in TR(d, I) be the relation over S and z_1 in TR(d, I) be the relation over T, where TR is the transformation defined at the end of Section 4.

We claim that *none* of the following statements is true:

1. $0 \in \pi_C(z_1)$.
2. $1 \in \pi_B(s_1)$.
3. $0 \in \pi_A(r_1)$.
4. $1 \in \pi_A(r_1)$.

The claim follows, since if one or more of the above statements is true, then I would be monodirectional. More specifically, by a straightforward induction on the number of times the transformation rule was applied to d it can be shown that:

1. if (1) is true then I $\approx$ S[B] $\subseteq$ T[C],
2. if (2) is true then I $\approx$ T[C] $\subseteq$ S[B],
3. if (3) is true then I $\approx$ S[B] $\subseteq$ R[A] and
4. if (4) is true then I $\approx$ T[C] $\subseteq$ R[A].

The result now follows, since TR(d, I) $\not\approx$ I is evident. $\quad\square$

The following theorem summarises Lemmas 43 and 44.

Theorem 45. Satisfaction is additive with respect to DB(**R**) and a class of sets of unary NINDs **IC** if and only if all the sets of NINDs in **IC** are monodirectional. $\square$

The following theorem is an immediate consequence of Definition 42 and Corollary 22.

Theorem 46. Monodirectionality of a set I of unary NINDs over **R** can be checked in time polynomial in the size of I. $\quad\square$

We conclude this section by showing that when the NINDs are not unary then we cannot just replace A by X, B by Y and C by W in Definition 42. Let r, s and z be the relations shown in Tables 16, 17 and 18, respectively, and let d = {r, s, z} be a database over **R**, with **R** = {R, S, T}, schema(R) = <A, B>, schema(S) = <C, D> and schema(T) = <E>. Furthermore, let I = {R[AB] $\subseteq$ S[CD], R[B] $\subseteq$ T[E], T[E] $\subseteq$ S[C], T[E] $\subseteq$ S[D]}. It can easily be verified that $\forall \alpha \in I$, d $\approx \alpha$ but d $\not\approx$ I. Moreover, the set of unary NINDs implied by I is monodirectional.

Table 16. The counterexample relation r

Table 17. The counterexample relation s

Table 18. The counterexample relation z

8   The mixed additivity problem

Herein we investigate the additivity problem for NFDs and unary NINDs. The next lemma follows from the counterexample provided in Example 3 of the introduction.

Lemma 47. Satisfaction is not additive with respect to DB(**R**) and the class of sets of NFDs and NINDs that contains only a single NFD and a single NIND. $\square$

We now solve the mixed additivity problem for a set $\Sigma = F \cup I$, where I is a set of unary NINDs. Without loss of generality we assume that Σ does not contain any trivial NFDs or NINDs and that the right-hand sides of NFDs in F are singletons. Moreover, we will assume that all the NFDs and NINDs mentioned from now on are nontrivial.

Definition 48 (The cyclicity condition). Σ satisfies the *cyclicity condition* if whenever $\Sigma \not\approx R : XA \to B$, $\Sigma \not\approx R : X \to A$, $\Sigma \not\approx R : X \to B$ and $\Sigma \approx R[A] \subseteq S[C]$, then $\Sigma \approx R : B \to A$ and $\Sigma \approx R[B] \subseteq S[C]$.

We observe that if $X = \emptyset$ then, since we have assumed that NFDs are standard, the if part of Definition 48 can be simplified to: whenever $\Sigma \approx R : A \to B$ and $\Sigma \approx R[A] \subseteq S[C]$. Furthermore, if F is monodependent and $\Sigma \approx R : XA \to B$, $\Sigma \not\approx X \to B$ and $\Sigma \approx R : B \to A$, then it must be the case that $\Sigma \approx R : A \to B$.

The next lemma shows that monodependence and monodirectionality together with the cyclicity condition imply additivity for NFDs and unary NINDs.

Lemma 49. Let $\Sigma = F \cup I$ be a set of NFDs and unary NINDs over R, where F is monodependent, I is monodirectional and Σ satisfies the cyclicity condition. Then $\forall\, d \in DB(R)$, if $\forall \alpha \in \Sigma$, $d \approx \alpha$, then $d \approx \Sigma$.

Proof. Assume, without loss of generality, that F is a canonical set of NFDs noting that a canonical set of NFDs is reduced. We show that if $\exists\, d \in DB(R)$ such that $\forall \alpha \in \Sigma$, $d \approx \alpha$ but $d \not\approx \Sigma$, then either F is not monodependent, or I is not monodirectional or Σ violates the cyclicity condition. Let d be such a database. If I is not monodirectional then the result follows by Theorem 45 on using Proposition 27. If F is not monodependent (assuming that I is monodirectional) then the result follows by Theorem 39, since there is no interaction between F and I by Theorem 21 due to the fact that I is a set of unary NFDs. (See the example at the end of this section which shows how monodependence needs to be modified when the NINDs may not be unary.)

So assume that F is monodependent and that I is monodirectional. Thus by Proposition 28, $\forall d' \in$ SETOF(CHASE(d, F, I)), $\exists \beta \in \Sigma$ such that $d' \not\approx \beta$. Moreover, by Proposition 27 $\forall d' \in$ SETOF(CHASE(CHASE(d, $\emptyset$, I), F, $\emptyset$)), $\exists \beta \in \Sigma$ such that $d' \not\approx \beta$. Let $d_2 \in$ SETOF(CHASE(CHASE(d, $\emptyset$, I), F, $\emptyset$)) be such a database, with $d_1 =$ CHASE(d, $\emptyset$, I), and thus $d_2 =$ CHASE(d_1, F, $\emptyset$). Now, since I is monodirectional it must be the case that $\forall \alpha \in I$, $d_1 \approx \alpha$. Furthermore, there exists a NFD or NIND $\beta \in \Sigma$ such that $d_2 \not\approx \beta$. It follows that d_2 is inconsistent, i.e., that β is a NFD, due to the fact that I is a set of unary NINDs which implies that no application of the NFD rule for a NFD in F can lead to a NIND in I being violated. Moreover, $\exists \beta \in F$ such that $d_1 \not\approx \beta$, since otherwise d_2 must be consistent due to the fact that F is monodependent, leading to a contradiction. Thus only one chase step for a NFD in F need be applied to d_1 during the computation of CHASE(d_1, F, $\emptyset$) in order to show that d_2 is inconsistent.

Assume that the NFD in F leading to d_2 being inconsistent by applying one chase step to d_1 is R : XA → B. Therefore, $\Sigma \not\models$ R : X → B and $\Sigma \not\models$ R : X → A, due to our assumption that F is canonical. Furthermore, assume that R : XA → B is applied to the tuples $t_1, t_2 \in$ r, with $t_1[XA] = t_2[XA]$ and $t_1[B] \sqcup t_2[B]$ being inconsistent, where r $\in d_1$ is the relation over R. Without loss of generality we assume that the inconsistency arises due to a modification of a prior state u_1 of t_1 by an application of the NIND rule for a NIND in I. There are two cases to consider.

Case1: In the first case an application of the NIND rule causes $u_1[B]$ to be modified to $t_1[B]$, where $u_1[B] = \perp_i \in$ Dum and $t_1[B] = 1 \in Dom -$ Dum are two B-values of the relation r over R in the state of d_1 prior to the application of the NIND rule. We show that this case cannot occur by contradiction to the fact that $d_1 \not\models$ R : XA → B.

There are two subcases to consider, where, without loss of generality, $u_1[AB]$ and $t_2[AB]$ are shown in Table 19 and a C-value, in the active domain of a relation s over S in the state of d_1 prior to the application of the NIND rule, is shown in Table 20.

Firstly, the NIND rule for S[C] ⊆ R[B] is applied, assuming that this NIND is in I. But then the nonnull value 1 is the B-value in the active domain of r, so $d_1 \approx$ S[C] ⊆ R[B]. Thus the NIND rule for S[C] ⊆ R[B] need not be applied, leading to a contradiction.

Secondly, the NIND rule for R[B] ⊆ S[C] is applied, assuming that this NIND is in I. But then the nonnull value 0 must be a C-value in the active domain of s, since $d_1 \approx$ R[B] ⊆ S[C]. Thus we can modify $\perp_i$ to 0, also leading to a contradiction of the fact that $d_1 \not\models$ R : XA → B.

A	B
0	$\perp_i$
0	0

C
1

Table 19. The counterexample tuples in r   Table 20. The counterexample tuple in s

Case2: In the second case an application of the NIND rule for R[A] ⊆ S[C], assuming that this NIND is in I, causes $u_1[A]$ to be modified to $t_1[A]$, where $u_1[A] = \perp_i \in$ Dum and $t_1[A] = 0 \in Dom -$ Dum are two A-values of the relation r over R in the state of d_1 prior to the application of the NIND rule. We show by contradiction that this case cannot occur unless the cyclicity condition is violated. Again, there are two subcases to consider.

Firstly, without loss of generality, $u_1[AB]$ and $t_2[AB]$ are shown in Table 21 and a C-value, in the active domain of a relation s over S in d_1 prior to the application of the NIND rule, is shown in Table 22. We assume in this case that if $\perp_i$ can be modified to 1, then the contradiction pertaining to $d_1 \not\models$ R : XA → B will not arise. Now, by the cyclicity condition, $\Sigma \approx$ R[B] ⊆ S[C] and thus $d_1 \approx$ R[B] ⊆ S[C] by the definition of logical implication due to the fact that

$\forall \alpha \in I$, $d_1 \not\approx \alpha$. Therefore, 1 must also be a C-value in the active domain of s and thus we can modify $\perp_i$ to 1 because of the NIND rule associated with R[A] $\subseteq$ S[C], leading to a contradiction of the fact that $d_1 \not\models R : XA \to B$.

A	B
$\perp_i$	0
0	1

C
0

Table 21. The counterexample tuples in r   **Table 22.** The counterexample tuple in s

Secondly, without loss of generality, $u_1[AB]$, $t_2[AB]$ and a third AB-value $t_3[AB]$ are shown in Table 23, and two C-values, in the active domain of a relation s over S in d_1 prior to the application of the NIND rule, are shown in Table 24. Furthermore, assume that the state of d_1, prior to the application of the NIND rule for R[A] $\subseteq$ S[C], satisfies R[B] $\subseteq$ S[C] and that $\perp_i$ must be modified either to 0 or to 1. It can be verified that this state of d_1 violates $R : B \to A$. Now, $d \not\approx R : B \to A$ by the definition of logical implication due to the fact that $\forall \alpha \in F$, $d \not\approx \alpha$ and furthermore by the cyclicity condition $\Sigma \not\approx R : B \to A$. Therefore, in a manner similar to that concerning the violation of $R : XA \to B$ in d_1, a NIND rule in I must have caused d_1 to violate $R : B \to A$. The result now follows, since if $t_2[A] = 0$ then $u_1[A]$ can be modified to 1 and if $t_3[A] = 1$ then $u_1[A]$ can be modified to 0, both modifications leading to a contradiction of the fact that $d_1 \not\models R : XA \to B$. (The modifications are due to the NIND rule for R[A] $\subseteq$ S[C].) $\square$

A	B
$\perp_i$	0
0	1
1	1

C
0
1

Table 23. The counterexample tuples in r   **Table 24.** The counterexample tuples in s

The next lemma shows that additivity for NFDs and unary NINDs implies monodependence, monodirectionality and the cyclicity condition.

Lemma 50. Let Σ be a set of NFDs and unary NINDs over R and assume that $\forall d \in DB(R)$, if $\forall \alpha \in \Sigma$, $d \not\approx \alpha$, then $d \not\approx \Sigma$. Then F is monodependent, I is monodirectional and Σ satisfies the cyclicity condition.

Proof. We show that if F is not monodependent, or if I is not monodirectional, or if the cyclicity condition is violated, then $\exists d \in DB(R)$ such that $\forall \alpha \in \Sigma$ $d \not\approx \alpha$ but $d \not\models \Sigma$. In order to prove the result we consider the three cases in turn.

Case1. Suppose that F is not monodependent. We define an auxiliary relation, designated R(0, 1), over R $\in$ **R**. Let R(i), where i $\in \{0,1\}$, be defined by R(i)

$= \cup_{A \in schema(R)} \{t_A \mid \forall B \in schema(R)-A, t_A[B] = unk$ and $t_A[A] = i\}$. We define $R(0, 1)$ by $R(0, 1) = R(0) \cup R(1)$. The result now follows by unioning $R(0, 1)$ to all the relations constructed in Lemma 38, noting that r satisfies all the NFDs in $F(R)$ if and only if $r \cup R(0, 1)$ also satisfies all the NFDs in $F(R)$.

Case2. Suppose that I is not monodirectional. The result follows by Lemma 44 noting that $TR(d, I)$ constructed in the proof of that lemma also satisfies all the NFDs in F.

Case3. Suppose that Σ does not satisfy the cyclicity condition. Then there exists a NFD $R : XA \rightarrow B$ and a NIND $R[A] \subseteq S[C]$ such that $\Sigma \not\approx R : XA \rightarrow B$, $\Sigma \not\approx R : X \rightarrow A$, $\Sigma \not\approx R : X \rightarrow B$ and $\Sigma \not\approx R[A] \subseteq S[C]$, but either $\Sigma \not\approx R : B \rightarrow A$ or $\Sigma \not\approx R[B] \subseteq S[C]$.

Firstly, suppose that $\Sigma \not\approx R : B \rightarrow A$. Let d be a database over **R**, with $r \in d$ being the relation over R shown in Table 25, $s \in d$ being the relation over S shown in Table 26, and all the other relations in $d - \{r, s\}$ being empty. It can be verified that $\forall \alpha \in \Sigma$, $TR(d, I) \approx \alpha$, where TR is the transformation defined at the end of Section 4. It is also evident that $TR(d, I) \not\approx \Sigma$ as required.

X	A	B	schema(R)−XAB
0 ... 0	0	0	unk ... unk
0 ... 0	1	0	unk ... unk
0 ... 0	unk	1	unk ... unk

Table 25. The first counterexample relation r over R

schema(S)
0 ... 0
1 ... 1

Table 26. The first counterexample relation s over S

Secondly, suppose that $\Sigma \not\approx R[B] \subseteq S[C]$. Let d be a database over **R**, with $r \in d$ being the relation over R shown in Table 27, $s \in d$ being the relation over S shown in Table 28, and all the other relations in $d - \{r, s\}$ being empty. It can be verified that $\forall \alpha \in \Sigma$, $TR(d, I) \approx \alpha$. It is also evident that $TR(d, I) \not\approx \Sigma$ as required. $\square$

X	A	B	schema(R)−XAB
0 ... 0	0	0	unk ... unk
0 ... 0	unk	1	unk ... unk

Table 27. The second counterexample relation r over R

schema(S)
0 ... 0

Table 28. The second counterexample relation s over S

The following theorem summarises Lemmas 49 and 50.

Theorem 51. Satisfaction is additive with respect to DB(**R**) and a class of sets of NFDs and unary NINDs **FC** $\cup$ **IC**, where **FC** and **IC** are classes of sets of NFDs and unary NINDs, respectively, if and only if all the sets of NFDs in **FC**

are monodependent, all the sets of NINDs in **IC** are monodirectional and all the sets of NFDs and NINDs in **FC** ∪ **IC** satisfy the cyclicity condition. □

The next theorem is an immediate consequence of Definition 48, Corollary 22, Theorem 40 and Theorem 46.

Theorem 52. Whether or not a set Σ of NFDs and unary NINDs satisfies the cyclicity condition can be checked in time polynomial in the size of Σ. □

We conclude this section by demonstrating that when the NINDs are not unary the solution to the mixed additivity problem requires the extension of the definition of monodependence. Let F = {S : D → E} and I = {R[AC] ⊆ S[DE], R[BC] ⊆ S[DE]}, with schema(R) = <A, B, C> and schema(S) = <D, E>. The NFDs R : A → C and R : B → C can be derived from F ∪ I by the *pullback inference rule* [35,25]. In addition, F is not monodependent, since F ∪ I $\not\approx$ ∅ → C (in any case we have assumed that all NFDs are standard). Next, let d = {r, s} be a database where r over R is shown in Table 29 and s over S is shown in Table 30; we assume that $\perp_1$ and $\perp_2$ are distinguished nonnull values in *Dom*. It can easily be verified that d $\not\approx$ R : B → C, d $\not\approx$ R : A → C, d $\not\approx$ R[BC] ⊆ S[DE] and d $\not\approx$ R[AC] ⊆ S[DE]. Moreover, d $\not\approx$ S : D → E if and only if $\perp_1 = \perp_2$ and thus d $\not\approx$ F ∪ I if and only if $\perp_1 = \perp_2$. Therefore, if d $\not\approx$ S : D → E then d $\not\approx$ F ∪ I. We have thus exhibited a set F ∪ I of NFDs and NINDs in which F is not monodependent but for which satisfaction is additive.

A	B	C
0	unk	$\perp_1$
0	0	unk
unk	0	$\perp_2$

Table 29. The counterexample relation r over R

D	E
0	$\perp_1$
0	$\perp_2$

Table 30. The counterexample relation s over S

9 A Brief Survey of Related Work

Herein we review the history of FDs in the context of incomplete relational databases as it relates to the results presented in this paper.

Grant [17] was one of the pioneers in considering the effect of null values on the satisfaction of FDs. Translating Grant's definition of a *maybe* FD into our terminology, X → Y is satisfied in a relation r over R, if whenever $t_1[X] \sqcup t_2[X]$ is consistent, then $t_1[Y] \sqcup t_2[Y]$ is also consistent, where $t_1, t_2 \in$ r. Grant did not consider either the axiomatisation of NFDs or the satisfaction of a set of NFDs in a relation.

Vassiliou [40] and Honeyman [18] considered the satisfaction of a set of NFDs in a relation, their main results being Propositions 24 and 25. Vassiliou also considered the axiomatisation of NFDs but only in the restricted case when the FDs are *strong*, namely in the sense that they are required to be satisfied in all possible worlds. It is interesting to note that the context of Honeyman's work is not incomplete information but rather that of determining the satisfaction of a set of FDs defined over a relation schema R, with respect to a database d over R, and where schema(R) $= \bigcup_{i=1}^{n}$ schema(R_i).

Lien [31] as well as Atzeni and Morfuni [3] considered the axiomatisation of NFDs. In particular, they showed that the inference rules: reflexivity, augmentation, decomposition and union, are sound and complete for NFDs; we call this axiom system, Lien and Atzeni's axiom system. That is, by dropping the transitivity rule from Armstrong's axiom system and adding the decomposition and union rules, we obtain Lien and Atzeni's axiom system. In [24] we have shown that when a set of NFDs is monodependent then the closure of such a set of NFDs, with respect to Lien and Atzeni's axiom system, is the same as its closure with respect to Armstrong's axiom system. In contrast to our work, Atzeni and Morfuni considered the semantics of unmarked nulls to be "no information", and Lien considered the semantics of unmarked nulls to be "does not exist" or "inapplicable". Lien and Atzeni's sound and complete axiom system was preempted by [30], wherein the axiomatisation of multivalued dependencies in incomplete relations is considered. In [26] we have shown that Lien and Atzeni's axiom system can be viewed in terms propositional implications holding in a subset of a three-valued propositional logic. In [4] the interaction of *existence constraints* with NFDs is also considered.

As far as we are aware the first explicit and unambiguous formulation of the additivity problem was given in [5, page 243], but a solution to this problem was not forthcoming with respect to the implication problem. We consider the solution of the additivity problem to be an important prerequisite for any relational database system supporting NFDs, since otherwise semantic anomalies may arise. The results obtained herein make a contribution in this direction.

A formalisation of functional and multivalued dependencies in incomplete relations from a domain theoretic point of view was carried out by Libkin [28], thus extending the work of [8]. The motivation behind Libkin's research is to establish the semantics of types in database programming languages. Additionally, Levene and Loizou [23] investigate join dependencies in the context of incomplete relations. The main result in [23] is that a variant of the chase procedure, called the *or-chase*, is a sound and complete inference procedure for null join dependencies. Finally, Levene and Loizou [25] introduced the NIND and exhibited a sound and complete axiom system for NFDs and NINDs. Moreover, Levene and Loizou showed that the implication problem for NFDs and NINDs is decidable and EXPTIME-complete (for FDs and INDs it was shown that the implication problem is undecidable [35]).

An extension of the concept of keys, which relaxes entity integrity in the context of incomplete information, was investigated by Thalheim [38]. A family

K of subsets of schema(R) is called a *key set* for a relation r over **R**, if $\forall t_1, t_2 \in$ r, $\exists K \in \mathbf{K}$ such that $t_1[K]$ and $t_2[K]$ are complete and $t_1[K] = t_2[K]$.

Imielinski and Lipski [19] consider the more general framework of tuple and equality generating dependencies and Grahne [16] extends their work building on [20]. Both Imielinski and Lipski, and Grahne deal mainly with *marked* nulls as opposed to the unmarked nulls considered herein, and are interested in the problem of finding the most suitable representation for incomplete databases. The additivity problem does not arise in their work as such.

Our definition of NFD embodies the *Closed World Assumption* (CWA) [20,29], since our definition of the set of possible worlds of a database, d, (Definition 12) allows only completed tuples from the relations in d to be present in POSS(d). On the other hand, if we had taken the *Open World Assumption* (OWA) [20,29], Definition 12 would have to be relaxed to allow additional tuples to be present in POSS(d), which do not result from completed tuples in the relations of d. It can be shown that the results obtained herein also hold when the OWA approach is taken, by considering the following argument. Suppose that d $\models \Sigma$, where d is a database over **R** and Σ is a set of NFDs and NINDs over **R**, and let $d_1 \in$ POSS(d) be a database such that $\forall \alpha \in \Sigma, d_1 \models \alpha$; the existence of d_1 is guaranteed by Definition 30. Then, we can always add complete tuples to the relations in d_1 resulting, say in d_2, as long as $d_2 \models \Sigma$ still holds. In this case, the closed world, in the form of d_1, can be viewed as the greatest lower bound of all open worlds emanating from d_1.

To conclude this brief survey we mention a recent approach taken by Keen and Rajasekar [22] who formalise the partitions arising from data dependencies such as FDs in the context of *rough sets* [36].

10 Concluding Remarks

We have investigated the additivity problem for NFDs and NINDs. The largest class of sets of NFDs for which additivity holds with respect to DB(**R**) is the class of monodependent sets of NFDs. In addition, checking whether a set of NFDs is monodependent can be done in time polynomial in the size of F. The largest class of sets of unary NINDs for which additivity holds with respect to DB(**R**) is the class of monodirectional sets of NINDs. Moreover, checking whether a set of unary NINDs is monodirectional can be done in time polynomial in the size of I. Finally, the largest class of sets of NFDs and unary NINDs for which additivity holds with respect to DB(**R**) is the class of monodependent sets of NFDs and monodirectional sets of unary NINDs which satisfy the cyclicity condition. Furthermore, checking whether a set of data dependencies, Σ, is in this last subclass can be done in time polynomial in the size of Σ.

In all of the situations when additivity is lacking this is due to some ambiguity in the specification of the set of data dependencies. In the case of NFDs either two sets of attributes determine the same attribute or there is some nontrivial cyclic behaviour between two NFDs. In the case of unary NINDs the left-hand side of a NIND is included in two distinct NINDs. Finally, in the case of NFDs and unary NINDs an attribute in the left-hand side of a NFD is also the left-hand side of a unary NIND. The subclasses of data dependencies which were shown to be additive resolve the ambiguity either by removing the offending data dependencies or by adding other data dependencies to the original set in order to neutralise the problem.

Suppose the user would like to maintain d $\not\approx$ Σ for all database states d. If Σ is an additive set of data dependencies, then the database system need only check d $\not\approx$ α, $\forall \alpha \in \Sigma$. This can be done in time polynomial in the sizes of d, F and I. On the other hand, if Σ is not an additive set of data dependencies the database system needs to check, in addition, that $\exists d' \in$ POSS(d) such that $\forall \alpha \in \Sigma, d' \not\approx \alpha$. It is not obvious that this can be done in polynomial time, since as was shown in the example following Proposition 25, SETOF(CHASE(d, F, I)) may contain an exponential number of databases and only one of these databases actually satisfies all the data dependencies in Σ.

We conjecture that the results obtained herein can be extended to the general class of sets of NFDs and NINDs with the aid of the observations made at the end of Sections 7 and 8. In any case, when the set of NINDs is not necessarily unary, it does not seem likely that there is a polynomial time algorithm for checking whether satisfaction is additive for a set of NINDs or a set of NFDs and NINDs due to the intractability of the respective implication problems for NINDs on their own and for NFDs and NINDs together. It would be interesting to investigate the additivity problem for null join dependencies, thus covering all the data dependencies that arise in practice. Finally, in [27] we study the impact of assuming that sets of FDs are monodependent on normalisation theory in relational databases.

References

1. A.V. Aho, C. Beeri and J.D. Ullman, The theory of joins in relational databases. *ACM Transactions on Database Systems* 4, (1979), 297-314.
2. W.W. Armstrong, Dependency structures of data base relationships. In: *Proceedings of the IFIP Congress*, Stockholm, pp. 580-583, 1974.
3. P. Atzeni and N.M. Morfuni, Functional dependencies in relations with null values. *Information Processing Letters* 18, (1984), 233-238.
4. P. Atzeni and N.M. Morfuni, Functional dependencies and constraints on null values in database relations. *Information and Control* 70, (1986), 1-31.
5. P. Atzeni and V. De Antonellis, *Relational Database Theory*. Redwood City, Ca., Benjamin/Cummings, 1993.
6. C. Beeri and P.A. Bernstein, Computational problems related to the design of normal form relational schemas. *ACM Transactions on Database Systems* 4, (1979), 30-59.
7. C. Beeri, R. Fagin, D. Maier and M. Yannakakis, On the desirability of acyclic database schemes. *Journal of the ACM* 30, (1983), 479-513.
8. P. Buneman, A. Jung and A. Ohori. Using powerdomains to generalize relational databases. *Theoretical Computer Science* 91, (1991), 23-55.

9. M.A. Casanova, R. Fagin and C.H. Papadimitriou, Inclusion dependencies and their interaction with functional dependencies. *Journal of Computer and System Sciences* **28**, (1984), 29-59.

10. E.F. Codd, Extending the database relational model to capture more meaning. *ACM Transactions on Database Systems* **4**, (1979), 379-434.

11. S.S. Cosmadakis, P.C. Kanellakis and M.Y. Vardi, Polynomial-time implication problems for unary inclusion dependencies. *Journal of the ACM* **37**, (1990), 15-46.

12. C.J. Date, Referential integrity. In: *Relational Database: Selected Writings*. Reading, Ma., Addison-Wesley, pp. 41-63, 1986.

13. C.J. Date and H. Darwen, *A Guide to the SQL Standard*, third edition. Reading, Ma., Addison-Wesley, 1993.

14. B.A. Davey and H.A. Priestly, *Introduction to Lattices and Order*. Cambridge, U.K., Cambridge University Press, 1990.

15. M.R. Garey and D.S. Johnson, *Computers and Intractability: A Guide to the Theory of NP-completeness*. New York, Freeman, 1979.

16. G. Grahne, *The Problem of Incomplete Information in Relational Databases*, Lecture Notes in Computer Science, Volume 554. Berlin, Springer Verlag, 1991.

17. J. Grant, Incomplete information in a relational database. *Fundamenta Informaticae* **3**, (1980), 363-378.

18. P. Honeyman, Testing satisfaction of functional dependencies. *Journal of the ACM* **29**, (1982), 668-677.

19. T. Imielinski and W. Lipski Jr., Incomplete information and dependencies in relational databases. In: *Proceedings of the ACM SIGMOD Conference on Management of Data*, San Jose, pp. 177-184, 1983.

20. T. Imielinski and W. Lipski Jr., Incomplete information in relational databases. *Journal of the ACM* **31**, (1984), 761-791.

21. D.S. Johnson and A. Klug, Testing containment of conjunctive queries under functional and inclusion dependencies. *Journal of Computer and System Sciences* **28**, (1984), 167-189.

22. D. Keen and A. Rajasekar, Rough sets and data dependencies. In: *Proceedings of the Workshop on Incompleteness and Uncertainty in Information Systems*, Montreal, pp. 87-101, 1993.

23. M. Levene and G. Loizou, Inferring null join dependencies in relational databases. *BIT* **32**, (1992), 413-429.

24. M. Levene and G. Loizou , The additivity problem for functional dependencies in incomplete relations. *Acta Informatica* **34**, (1997), 135-149.

25. M. Levene and G. Loizou, Null inclusion dependencies in relational databases. *Information and Computation* **134**, (1997) in press.

26. M. Levene and G. Loizou, A correspondence between variable relations and three-valued propositional logic. *International Journal of Computer Mathematics* **55**, (1995), 29-38.

27. M. Levene and G. Loizou, Database design for incomplete relations. Research Note RN/95/18, Department of Computer Science, University College London, 1995.

28. L. Libkin, A relational algebra for complex objects based on partial information. In: *Proceedings of the Symposium on Mathematical Foundations of Database and Knowledge Base Systems*, Rostock, Germany, pp. 29-43, 1991.

29. L. Libkin, A semantics-based approach to design of query languages for partial information. Research report MS-CIS-94-38. Computer and Information Science Department, School of Engineering and Applied Science, Univerity of Pennsylvania, 1994.

30. Y.E. Lien, Multivalued dependencies with null values in relational databases. In: *Proceedings of the International Conference on Very Large Data Bases*, Rio de Janeiro, pp. 61-66, 1979.

31. Y.E. Lien, On the equivalence of database models. *Journal of the ACM* 29, (1982), 333-362.

32. D. Maier, A.O. Mendelzon and Y. Sagiv, Testing implications of data dependencies. *ACM Transactions on Database Systems* 4, (1979), 455-469.

33. D. Maier, Minimum covers in the relational database model. *Journal of the ACM* 27, (1980), 664-674.

34. H. Mannila and K.-J. Räihä, *The Design of Relational Databases*. Reading, Ma., Addison-Wesley, 1992.

35. J.C. Mitchell, The implication problem for functional and inclusion dependencies. *Information and Control* 56, (1983), 154-173.

36. Z. Pwalak, Rough sets. *International Journal of Computer and Information Sciences* 11, (1982), 341-356.

37. E. Sciore, Real world MVD's. In: *Proceedings of the ACM SIGMOD Conference on Management of Data*, Ann Arbor, pp. 121-132, 1981.

38. B. Thalheim, On semantic issues connected with keys in relational databases permitting null values. *Journal of Information Processing Cybernetics* 25, (1989), 11-20.

39. J.D. Ullman, *Principles of Database and Knowledge-Base Systems*, Vol. I. Rockville, Md., Computer Science Press, 1988.

40. Y. Vassiliou, Functional dependencies and incomplete information. In: *Proceedings of the International Conference on Very Large Data Bases*, Montreal, pp. 260-269, 1980.

A Semantics-Based Approach to Design of Query Languages for Partial Information

Leonid Libkin

Bell Laboratories
600 Mountain Ave., Murray Hill, NJ 07974, USA
email: libkin@bell-labs.com

Abstract. Most of work on partial information in databases asks which operations of standard languages, like relational algebra, can still be performed correctly in the presence of nulls. In this paper a different point of view is advocated. We believe that the semantics of partiality must be clearly understood and it should give us new design principles for languages for databases with partial information.

There are different sources of partial information, such as missing information and conflicts that occur when different databases are merged. In this paper, we develop a common semantic framework for them which can be applied in a context more general than the flat relational model. This ordered semantics, which is based on ideas used in the semantics of programming languages, cleanly intergrates all kinds of partial information and serves as a tool to establish connections between them.

Analyzing properties of semantic domains of types suitable for representing partial information, we come up with operations that are naturally associated with those types, and we organize programming syntax around these operations. We show how the languages that we obtain can be used to ask typical queries about incomplete information in relational databases, and how they can express some previously proposed languages. Finally, we discuss a few related topics such as mixing traditional constraints with partial information and extending semantics and languages to accommodate bags and recursive types.

1 Partial Information in Databases

Many aspects of database systems whose importance is evident in a variety of applications are yet to be adequately represented in practical database management systems. In many cases the reason for this is the lack of underlying theory. One of such problems is handling partial information in databases. While no one doubts that it must be dealt with, simply because in most applications we can not assume that the information stored in a database is perfect, the field has not been satisfactorily explored. Most results about partial information in databases are negative in their nature. They show what can *not* be done – efficiently or at all – if standard tools are used in the presence of partial information.

The main goal of this paper is to make a step toward a general theory of partial information. Partiality of information can be viewed as giving additional meaning to values that can be stored. Alternatively, one can regard it as constraining those values. Note, however, that such constraints are imposed on values that can be stored, and not on the whole database. Our goal is to represent these constraints in an adequately chosen mathematical framework, so that they can be reasoned about. Having found such a framework, we must demonstrate its usefulness. In this paper we concentrate on developing languages for partial information.

The main thesis of this paper is that, rather than showing what can not be done with standard tools, one should concentrate on designing new tools specifically for handling partial information. This thesis can be subdivided into two.

1. In order to understand partial information in databases, we have to know exactly what it means. That is, we have to have a *semantics* for partial information. We develop a formalism, whose roots can be found in [Bis81, BJO91, Gra91, IL84, JLP92, Lib91, Vas79], and whose main idea is that *partiality is represented via orderings on objects.*
2. We are not interested in semantics *per se*; the semantics that we define will help us find the right programming constructs for query languages for partial information. Our approach is based on [Car88, BBN91, BBW92, BLS+94], and its gist is that operations *naturally* associated with datatypes should be used as the basis for the language design. The word "naturally" has a precise mathematical meaning, and it has to do with the properties of semantic domains of the datatypes used. Thus, we can formulate our second main principle, which says that *semantics suggests programming constructs.*

In the rest of this section we give a brief survey of the field of partial information in databases – to the extent we shall need it to motivate and substantiate our study.

1.1 Classical approach – null values

Name	Salary	Room	Telephone
John	15K	075	ni
Ann	17K	ni	ni
Mary	ni	351	x-1595

Name	Salary	Room	Telephone
John	15K	075	ne
Ann	17K	un	ni
Mary	un	351	x-1595

Fig. 1. Relations with nulls

Soon after Codd introduced his relational model, people realized that in real applications not all values may be present. For example, in the first relation in figure 1 that might be a part of a university or a corporation database, some values are missing and the symbol **ni** (no information) is used. Note that there could be several different reasons for using **ni**. This is reflected in the second relation in figure 1 where three kinds of nulls are used (cf. [LL86, RKS89, Zan84]). **ne** means nonexistent; that is, John does not have a phone. **un** means existing unknown; Mary is on payroll but the precise figure of her salary is unknown. And **ni** still means no information. For other kinds of nulls see [GZ88, LL93].

One of the most important achievements of the early work on partial information was an observation made in [Cod79]. Since every null value can be potentially replaced by a non-null value, each relation with nulls is represented by a *set* of relations without partial information. Moreover, this set could be considered as the *semantics* of the given incomplete relation. This idea was central to the seminal study [IL84] in which querying databases with nulls using standard languages like relational algebra was examined. The family of all complete relations that a relation R with nulls can represent was called a representation of R; we prefer the term semantics of R and denote it by $[\![R]\!]$. If q is a relational algebra query, we can ask q on $[\![R]\!]$, obtaining $q([\![R]\!]) = \{q(T) \mid T \in [\![R]\!]\}$. If we could find an relation R' such that $[\![R']\!] = q([\![R]\!])$, then we would be able to call R' the answer to q on R, that is, $q(R)$. However, for most classes of queries this is impossible. In fact, even milder definition of $q(R)$ leads to similar negative results.

Very little is known about null values in complex objects or nested relations, that is, relations whose attributes can be relation-valued themselves. An attempt to extend the results of [IL84] was made in [RKS89] (only for a restricted subclass of complex objects, those in partitioned normal form, cf. [AB86]), but later an error was found [LL91]. It was then shown [LL93] that some of the results can be recovered if equality of representations of incomplete complex objects is replaced by the Hoare equivalence, which will be defined later. However, [LL93] used the standard presentation of languages for complex objects, like in [TF86, SS86, Col90], and consequently inherited all of its problems and drawbacks. In particular, the description of the notion of null-extended join operator is almost one-page long, and many other operations are rather hard to grasp. The algebra for complex objects proposed in [Lib91] does not have adequate power to work with set-valued attributes. Thus, the problem of incorporating partial information into data models more complex than the standard (flat) relational model remains open.

1.2 Semantics of partiality

Order and partiality The key idea of our approach to semantics of partial information is that partiality is represented via orderings on objects. For the first time this idea appeared probably in [Vas79], and two years later it was further explored in [Bis81]. As a simple example, consider values that may occur in a database. Then **ni** is more partial, or less informative, than any total (nonpartial) value v such as 15K or 'Mary'. Therefore, we impose an order according to which **ni** $\leq v$ for any total value v.

Most databases are obtained from base values by applying record and set constructors, so we need to extend the orderings respectively. For records the most natural way to do it is componentwise. For records with fields labeled by $l_1, \ldots, l_n$, we define

$$[l_1 : v_1, \ldots, l_n : v_n] \leq [l_1 : v_1', \ldots, l_n : v_n'] \quad \text{iff} \quad \forall i = 1, \ldots, n : v_i \leq v_i'$$

For sets there are various ways to extend a partial order, and typically the following one, perceived as a generalized subset ordering, $X \sqsubseteq Y$ iff $\forall x \in X \, \exists y \in Y : x \leq y$, was considered.

The idea of representing partiality via orders is central to our study. At this point, we would like to note that it can also be viewed as imposing certain constraints on *values* that can be stored, rather than the whole database, as is the case with most standard constraints. That is, **ni** and 123 are not just symbols; there is a certain semantic relationship between them, that is often not taken into account in the theory of partial information.

Constraints on null values Codd [Cod75] proposed to use three-valued logic to query databases with nulls, but serious problems with this approach were exemplified in [Gra77]. Instead, in [Gra77, Bis81] and a number of other papers it was suggested that one use Skolem variables to represent different occurrences of nulls. To represent various interconnections between those nulls, it was suggested to use constraints on the Skolem variables. For example, in the simplest case, called Codd tables, all Skolem variables are distinct. Inequality tables allow conditions like $x \neq y$ or $x \neq 4$ where x and y are variables. In conditioned tables, in addition to such constrains, a variable may occur more than once, and each tuple may have a constraint associated only with it.

In [AKG91] complexity of querying relational databases with incomplete information and constraints on nulls is studied thoroughly. A typical problem considered in [AKG91] is the following. Given a query q, a relation R with nulls and a set of constraints C, and a total relation (that is, relation without any occurrences of nulls) T, is it possible that one can find a relation T' in $[R]$ such that T' satisfies all the constraints in C and $q(T') = T$. It was shown in [AKG91] that for many classes of constrained tables problems of this kind are very hard (i.e. NP, coNP or Π_2^p-complete), but in some restricted cases they are polynomial.

1.3 Semantics of collections

Assume we are given a collection of database objects with partial information. What is the semantics of such collection? It turns out that this question can not be answered unless we make certain assumptions about what kinds of collections can be supported. In what follows, we discuss three which are of particular importance for this paper: sets under closed and open world assumptions and disjunctive sets (or-sets). In section 4 we shall also consider bags.

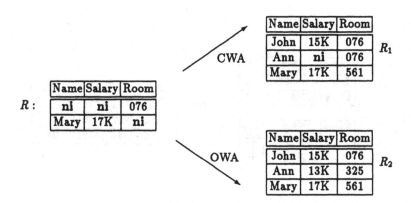

Fig. 2. Illustration to CWA and OWA

Open and closed worlds It was observed in [Rei78] that certain assumptions on the nature of partiality are to be made if we want to provide a notion of correctness of query evaluation algorithms. To explain these assumptions, consider relation R in figure 2. Once all or some information about missing values (ni's) is known, we have a relation that represents better knowledge than R. However, there may be different assumptions about the values that are allowed in the new relation.

One possible interpretation, called the *closed world assumption* or *CWA*, states that we can only improve our knowledge about records that are already stored but can not invent new ones. For example, it is legal to add any record $\boxed{v_1 | v_2 | 076}$ which improves upon the first record in R. It is also possible to add a record $\boxed{\text{Mary} | 17K | 561}$ which is better knowledge than that represented by the second record in R. However, it is *not* possible to add a record $\boxed{\text{Ann} | \text{ni} | 561}$ as it does not improve any of the records already in the database. That is, the database is *closed* for adding new records.

Contrary to that, the *open world assumption* or *OWA* allows adding records to database as well as improving already existing records. Under the open world assumption, adding any record considered above to the database is perfectly legal. That is, the database is *open* for adding new records.

To summarize, Figure 2 shows how to replace missing values according to both assumptions. This interpretation of OWA and CWA is similar to the one typically used in databases with incomplete informations (cf. [IL84, Var86]) but slightly different from [Rei78] who used a logical setting. However, later we shall show that analogs of most of the results from [Rei78] hold in our setting as well.

D_1:

Name	SS#	Age
John	123456789	24
Mary	987654321	32

D_2:

Name	SS#	Age
John	123456789	27
Ann	564738291	25

$\xrightarrow{merge}$

Name	SS#	Age
John	123456789	$\langle 24, 27 \rangle$
Mary	987654321	32
Ann	564738291	25

Fig. 3. Example of or-sets arising in merging databases

Disjunctive information The idea of using disjunctive information as a means to express partiality was already present in [Lip79, Lip81]. But it was not until almost ten years later that the first attempt was made to introduce disjunctions *explicitly* into the standard relational model. Consider the following example. Suppose we have two databases, D_1 and D_2 shown in figure 3. Assume that we merge D_1 and D_2. It is clear that records `Mary 987654321 32` and `Ann 564738291 25` should be in the resulting database. But what is the value of the Age field for John? Since SS# identifies people uniquely, we have *conflicting* information coming from two databases, and this conflict must be recorded in the newly created database until one finds out if John is 24 or 27 years of age. Therefore, both ages – 24 and 27 – are stored in the new database. However, the semantics of the Age attribute (which is now set-valued) is different from the usual interpretation of sets in databases. Rather than suggesting that John is both 24 and 27 years old, it says that John is 24 *or* 27.

Since such disjunctive sets, also called *or-sets*, have semantics that differs from the ordinary sets, we shall use a special notation $\langle \rangle$ for them. That is, in the result of merging D_1 and D_2, the value of the Age attribute for John is $\langle 24, 27 \rangle$, see figure 3. While structurally just a set, it denotes an integer, which is either 24 or 27. That is, there are two different views of or-sets: structural, that concerns *representation*, and conceptual, that concerns *meaning*. This idea was present in the initial papers on or-sets [INV91a, INV91b] and later was formalized and worked out in [LW96].

1.4 Toward a general theory

There are a number of models for partial information in the database literature. Some of them are quite ad-hoc, based on specific needs arising in particular applications. We have seen two sources of partiality: null values and disjunctive information. (There are others; see, for example, [BDW91, Lib95a].) There are no solid theoretical foundations for any of these, nor are there any results that show how they are connected. Moreover, most models of partiality are developed only for the flat relational model, and virtually nothing is known for more complicated database models. This situation in the field of partial information was summarized in a recent survey [Kan90]:

> "... for the representation and querying of incomplete information databases, there are many partial solutions but no satisfactory full answer. It seems that the further away we move from the relational data model, the fewer analytical and algebraic tools are available."

Thus, to address the problem of partial information in databases and to move closer to satisfactory solutions that work for a large class of data models, one has to come up with new analytical tools and show their applicability not only in the study of the extended data models but also in the development of new query languages for databases with partial information. Making progress in this direction is the major motivation for this work. In this paper we develop a new approach to partial information that integrates all kinds of partiality within the same semantic framework. In addition to giving us necessary analytical and algebraic tools to study various kinds of partial information, this framework also naturally suggests operations that should be included into the language that works with partial information. Techniques that are developed for analyzing the structure of partial information can be applied to the study of the languages that deal with it.

Organization. In Section 2 we explore the first main principle of our approach saying that *partiality is represented via orders on objects*. First we briefly describe the main ideas of the approach of [BJO91, Lib91] that treats database objects as elements of certain partially ordered spaces of descriptions. Then we apply it in a typed setting, obtaining orderings for various kinds of collection type constructors. Thus, for the first time choosing orderings is tied with semantics of collections. Then we explain the difference between structural and conceptual representation of disjunctive information from the semantic point of view, and list some of the properties of semantic domains of collections which will be used for the language design.

In Section 3 we develop the second idea which says that *semantics suggests programming constructs*. We start by explaining the approach to the language design based on [Car88, BBN91, BBW92, BLS⁺94] that suggests building languages for data around datatypes involved. Specifically, for each datatype constructor one needs introduction and elimination operations, and those can be obtained if one looks at the operations *naturally* – in the categorical sense – associated with the semantics of the datatypes. We show how to apply this approach to languages with partial information, and disjunctive information in particular. As two examples of applicability of obtained languages, we show that the algebra of [Zan84] can be viewed as a sublanguage of our language for sets, and we show how this language can be used to query equational tables, in which equality constraints are imposed on null values.

Finally, in Section 4, we discuss topics that should be further explored, but with some initial results already obtained. These include mixing traditional database constraints with partial information; recursive types and values in the presence of incompleteness of information; and extending our approach to bags (multisets).

All proofs can be found in [Lib94] (which is available by ftp). In those cases when proofs can also be found in journal or conference proceedings articles, additional references are given.

2   Semantics of Partial Information

The purpose of this section is to study the semantics of partial data. The unifying theme for various kinds of partial information is using ordered sets as their semantics, where the meaning of the order is "being more informative". Once orderings on values come into play, there is a need in new basic models for incomplete databases. We first describe an approach suggested in [BJO91] and further developed in [JLP92, Lib91, LL90] that, in a very general way, treats database objects as elements of certain ordered sets. Then we adapt this approach to the typed setting. For that we need to choose orderings on various kinds of collections. To do so, we formalize elementary updates on collections which improve our knowledge about the real world situation represented by that data, that is, add information. Then we characterize transitive closures of those updates, thus obtaining the orderings. We carry out this program for OWA and CWA sets and or-sets. We use the orderings to define the semantics of collections of partial objects. It will be shown that the semantics and the orderings agree naturally. We study important properties of semantic domains of partial data which will later be used to organize programming syntax.

2.1   Partial information and orderings on objects

It was discovered in [BJO91] that a representation of the underlying principles of relational database theory can be found in the theory of domains which has been developed as the basis of the denotational semantics of programming languages.

A database is a collection of descriptions, and the meaning $[d]$ of a description d is the set of all possible objects described by it. Therefore, we can order descriptions by saying that a description d_1 is better than a description d_2 if it describes fewer objects, i.e. if it is a more precise description. For example, let d_1 and d_2 be the records in a relational database: $d_1 = [\text{Dept: CIS}, \text{Office: } 176]$, and $d_2 = [\text{Name: John}, \text{Dept: CIS}, \text{Office: } 176]$. If name, department and office are the only attributes, then the meaning of d_1 is the set of all possible records that refer to CIS people in office 176, in particular, d_2. Therefore, d_2 is better than d_1 because $[d]_2 \subseteq [d]_1$.

If all descriptions of objects come from the same domain A which is partially ordered by $\leq$, then we define $[d] \overset{\text{def}}{=} \{d' \in D \mid d' \geq d\} = \uparrow d$. Then $d_1 \leq d_2$ iff $[d_2] \subseteq [d_1]$. Sometimes it is helpful to restrict domains A to those in which every element $x \in A$ is bounded above by a maximal element $x_m \geq x$. The collection of maximal elements is denoted by $A^{\max}$, and the new semantic function then is $[x]_{\max} = [x] \cap A^{\max}$. This semantic function was used in [AKG91, Gra91, IL84].

Consistency in posets is another useful notion. Two elements $x, y \in A$ are called *consistent* if there exists $z \in A$ such that $x, y \leq z$. In the case of records this means *joinable* as in [Zan84] (i.e. they do not contradict each other): for example, [Name: John, Dept: ni, Office: 176] and [Name: John, Dept: CIS, Office: ni] are consistent as both of them are below d_2.

Note that if both d_1 and d_2 in our example above are stored in a relational database, then d_1 could be removed as it does not add any information. Generally, in the usual set interpretation of databases, if $x \leq y$, then x could be removed. Removing redundant elements leaves us with a collection of incomparable elements. Such collections are called *antichains*. That is, a subset X of an ordered set A is an antichain if $x \not< y$ for any $x, y \in A$.

The main idea of [BJO91] was that database objects are represented as antichains in domains, which are special kinds of posets used in semantics of programming languages. This was later refined in [Lib94] by requiring that database objects be antichains of compact elements; we shall return to this distinction later when we discuss recursive types. The approach has proved very fruitful. The concept of scheme was introduced in such a generalized setting, relational algebra operators were reconstructed, and functional and multivalued dependencies were defined and shown to possess the expected properties, see [BJO91, JLP92, Lib91].

However, this approach is too general, and we would like to adapt it to a typed setting. Complex objects. or nested relations, are constructed from values of base types (such as integers, strings etc.) by applying the record and the set type constructor. That is, their *types* are given by the following grammar:

$$t ::= b \mid [l_1 : t, \ldots, l_n : t] \mid \{t\}$$

where b ranges over a collection of base types, $[l_1 : t_1, \ldots, l_n : t_1]$ is the record type whose instances are records with fields l_is such that the value of the l_i field has type t_i, and $\{t\}$ is the set type constructor whose values are (for now) finite sets of values of type t.

Therefore, to obtain orderings for complex objects, we need to order base objects, records and sets. Orderings on base values are determined by null values that a given datatype allows. For example, in the case of three nulls **ne**, **ni** and **un** allowed for the type of naturals, the ordering is shown in figure 4. As was mentioned already, records are ordered componentwise. However, there is no "universal" way of ordering sets. The purpose of the next section is to identify some ways of doing it and associate them with various kinds of collections.

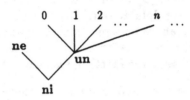

Fig. 4. Order on null values

2.2 Orderings on collections

Our general problem is the following. Given a poset $\langle A, \leq \rangle$ and the family of all collections (sets, or-sets etc.) over A, how do we order those? As usual, our interpretation of the partial order is "being more informative". What does it mean to say that one collection of partial descriptions is more informative than another? As two examples of families of collections over A that we would like to order, we consider $\mathbb{A}_{\text{fin}}(A)$, the family of finite antichains of A, and $\mathbb{P}_{\text{fin}}(A)$, the family of finite subsets of A.

A similar problem arises in the semantics of programming languages, most notably in the semantics of concurrency, cf. [Gun92]. Three orderings, called the *Hoare*, the *Smyth* and the *Plotkin* ordering have been proposed ([Gun92, Smy78, Plo76]):

(Hoare) $$X \sqsubseteq^\flat B \Leftrightarrow \forall x \in X \exists y \in Y : x \leq y$$

(Smyth) $$X \sqsubseteq^\natural Y \Leftrightarrow \forall y \in Y \exists x \in Y : x \leq y$$

(Plotkin) $$X \sqsubseteq^\natural Y \Leftrightarrow X \sqsubseteq^\flat Y \text{ and } X \sqsubseteq^\natural Y$$

All of them have been used for databases with partial information: the Hoare ordering in [Bis81, IL84, Lib91], the Smyth ordering in [BJO91, Oho90], the

Plotkin ordering in [PS93]. However, none of these papers addressed the question whether the chosen ordering is appropriate for the intended semantics of collections. Choosing the right orderings is the main purpose of this subsection. Our main claims are summarized in the table below.

Kind of collection	Ordering
Sets under CWA	Plotkin ($\sqsubseteq^\natural$)
Sets under OWA	Hoare ($\sqsubseteq^\flat$)
Or-sets	Smyth ($\sqsubseteq^\sharp$)

The technique we use to justify these claims is the following. We define "elementary updates" that add information. For example, for CWA databases such updates should add information to individual records. For OWA we may have additional updates that add records to a database. For or-sets, reducing the number of possibilities adds information as an or-sets denotes one of its elements. We formalize those updates and then look at their transitive closure. That is, a collection C_1 is more informative than C_2 if C_1 can be reached from C_2 by a sequence of elementary updates that add information. There are two ways to perform updates that add information, because redundancies represented by comparable elements could be removed. That is, one way is to keep all elements, even those that are comparable, and the other way is to remove redundancies, that is, to make sure that the result of each elementary update is an antichain again. These two ways lead to some orderings on either antichains of ordered sets or arbitrary subsets thereof. We shall consider both and show that they coincide.

Ordering CWA databases. In a closed world database, it is possible to update individual records but it is impossible to add new records. To understand what the elementary updates are, recall the example in figure 2. We view R_1 as more informative than R under the CWA. There could be more than one person in 076. That is, an incomplete record can be updated in various ways that give rise to a number of new records, and this is consistent with the closed world assumption, and this is how the first two records in R_1 are obtained. The third record in R_1 is obtained from the second record in R by adding the salary value. Thus, we see that the way the closed world databases are made more informative is by getting more information about individual records. The first picture in figure 5 illustrates those updates. We simply remove an element (record) from a database and replace it by a number of more informative elements (records).

There are two ways to formalize those updates, depending on whether arbitrary sets or only antichains are allowed. Let $X \subseteq A$ be a finite subset of the poset A. Let $x \in X$ and $X' \subseteq A$ be a finite nonempty subset of A such that $x \leq x'$ for all $x' \in X'$. Then we allow the following update:

$$X \overset{\text{CWA}}{\longmapsto} (X - x) \cup X'$$

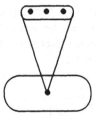 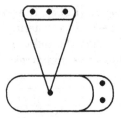

Fig. 5. Updates for CWA and OWA

For antichains, we need to impose two additional restrictions. First, X' must be an antichain, and second, the result must be an antichain. To ensure the second requirement is satisfied, we keep only maximal elements. That is, in the case of antichains the legitimate updates are

$$X \xrightarrow{\text{CWA}}_a \max((X - x) \cup X')$$

We now say that $X \sqsubseteq^{\text{CWA}} Y$ if $X, Y \subseteq A$ and Y can be obtained from X by a sequence of updates $\xrightarrow{\text{CWA}}$, that is, $\sqsubseteq^{\text{CWA}}$ is the transitive closure of $\xrightarrow{\text{CWA}}$ on $\mathbb{P}_{\text{fin}}(A)$. Similarly, $X \sqsubseteq_a^{\text{CWA}} Y$ if X, Y are finite antichains of A and Y can be obtained from X by a sequence of updates $\xrightarrow{\text{CWA}}_a$, that is, $\sqsubseteq_a^{\text{CWA}}$ is the transitive closure of $\xrightarrow{\text{CWA}}_a$ on $\mathbb{A}_{\text{fin}}(A)$. To justify the claim that the closed world databases must be ordered by the Plotkin ordering, we prove the following.

Theorem 1. a) *Let* $X, Y \in \mathbb{P}_{\text{fin}}(A)$. *Then* $X \sqsubseteq^{\text{CWA}} Y$ *iff* $X \sqsubseteq^\natural Y$.
b) *Let* $X, Y \in \mathbb{A}_{\text{fin}}(A)$. *Then* $X \sqsubseteq_a^{\text{CWA}} Y$ *iff* $X \sqsubseteq^\natural Y$. $\square$

Corollary 2. *Let* X *and* Y *be finite antichains in* A *such that* $X \sqsubseteq^\natural Y$. *Then it is possible to find a sequence of antichains* $X_1, \ldots, X_n$ *such that* $X_1, \ldots, X_n \subseteq X \cup Y$ *and* $X \xrightarrow{\text{CWA}}_a X_1 \xrightarrow{\text{CWA}}_a \ldots \xrightarrow{\text{CWA}}_a X_n \xrightarrow{\text{CWA}}_a Y$. $\square$

Ordering OWA databases. In an open world database, it is possible to update individual records and add new records. As in the case of the CWA databases, consider a simple example of relations R and R_2 in figure 2. Some of the records in R_2, that we view as a more informative one, are obtained by modifying records of R. However, one record, $\boxed{\text{Ann} \mid \perp \mid 325}$ can not be obtained by modifying any record in R. The reason it was put there is that the database is open for new records. Under this interpretation, we view adding records as an update that adds information. In the above example, adding that record improves our knowledge about what can be a university or a company database of employees. This is illustrated by the second picture in figure 5. Not only do we allow replacing a record by a number of more informative records, but we also allow adding new records.

Similarly to the CWA case, there are two ways to formalize these updates, depending on whether arbitrary sets or only antichains are allowed. Let $X \subseteq A$ be a finite nonempty subset of the poset A. Let $x \in X$ and $X' \subseteq A$ be a finite subset of A such that $x \leq x'$ for all $x' \in X'$. Let X'' be an arbitrary finite subset of A. Then we allow the following updates:

$$X \xmapsto{\text{OWA}} (X - x) \cup X' \quad \text{and} \quad X \xmapsto{\text{OWA}} X \cup X''$$

For antichains, we impose an additional restriction that the result always be an antichain. We do it by keeping only maximal elements in the results. Therefore, in the case of antichains the legitimate updates are

$$X \xmapsto{\text{OWA}}_a \max((X - x) \cup X') \quad \text{and} \quad X \xmapsto{\text{OWA}} \max(X \cup X'')$$

We say that $X \sqsubseteq^{\text{OWA}} Y$ if $X, Y \subseteq A$ and Y can be obtained from X by a sequence of updates $\xmapsto{\text{OWA}}$, that is, $\sqsubseteq^{\text{OWA}}$ is the transitive closure of $\xmapsto{\text{OWA}}$ on $\mathbb{P}_{\text{fin}}(A)$. Similarly, $X \sqsubseteq^{\text{OWA}}_a Y$ if X, Y are finite antichains of A and Y can be obtained from X by a sequence of updates $\xmapsto{\text{OWA}}_a$, that is, $\sqsubseteq^{\text{OWA}}_a$ is the transitive closure of $\xmapsto{\text{OWA}}_a$ on $\mathbb{A}_{\text{fin}}(A)$. To justify the claim that the OWA databases must be ordered by the Hoare ordering, we prove

Theorem 3. a) *Let* $X, Y \in \mathbb{P}_{\text{fin}}(A)$. *Then* $X \sqsubseteq^{\text{OWA}} Y$ *iff* $X \sqsubseteq^\flat Y$.
b) *Let* $X, Y \in \mathbb{A}_{\text{fin}}(A)$. *Then* $X \sqsubseteq^{\text{OWA}}_a Y$ *iff* $X \sqsubseteq^\flat Y$. $\square$

Corollary 4. *Let* X *and* Y *be finite antichains in* A *such that* $X \sqsubseteq^\flat Y$. *Then it is possible to find a sequence of antichains* $X_1, \ldots, X_n$ *such that* $X_1, \ldots, X_n \subseteq X \cup Y$ *and* $X \xmapsto{\text{OWA}}_a X_1 \xmapsto{\text{OWA}}_a \ldots \xmapsto{\text{OWA}}_a X_n \xmapsto{\text{OWA}}_a Y$. $\square$

Ordering or-sets. We now define update rules for or-sets. We start with a simple example.

$$X_1 : \left\langle \begin{array}{|c|c|c|} \hline \text{Name} & \text{Salary} & \text{Room} \\ \hline \text{John} & \perp & 076 \\ \hline \text{Ann} & \perp & \perp \\ \hline \text{Mary} & 17\text{K} & \perp \\ \hline \end{array} \right\rangle \quad \xrightarrow{\text{or} - \text{set}} \quad X_2 : \left\langle \begin{array}{|c|c|c|} \hline \text{Name} & \text{Salary} & \text{Room} \\ \hline \text{John} & \perp & 076 \\ \hline \text{Ann} & 13\text{K} & \perp \\ \hline \end{array} \right\rangle$$

There are two reasons why we view X_2 as a more informative or-set than X_1. First, additional information about Ann was obtained. It is now known that her salary is 13K. Second, one of the records was removed. Note that removing an element from an or-set makes it more informative. Indeed, while $\langle 1, 2, 3 \rangle$ is an integer which is either 1 or 2 or 3, $\langle 1, 2 \rangle$ is an integer which is 1 or 2, so we have additional information that it can not be 3.

Therefore, we consider two types of updates on or-sets: improving information about individual records and removing elements:

$$X \xmapsto{\text{or}} (X - x) \cup X' \qquad \text{if } x \in X \text{ and } x \leq x' \text{ for all } x' \in X' \text{ and } X' \neq \emptyset$$

$$X \xmapsto{\text{or}} X - x \qquad \text{if } x \in X \text{ and } X - x \neq \emptyset$$

To redefine these updates for antichains, we must decide how redundancies in or-sets are removed. We suggest that only minimal elements be kept in the results. To see why, consider the following or-set with two comparable records:

$$\left\langle \begin{array}{|c|c|} \hline \text{Name} & \text{Room} \\ \hline \text{John} & 076 \\ \hline \text{John} & \textbf{un} \\ \hline \end{array} \right\rangle$$

This or-set denotes a person whose name is John and who is either in room 076 or in an unknown room. The semantics of this is exactly as having one record for John in an unknown room. (This will be made precise in the next section.) Hence, we retain the minimal elements. Then the updates for antichains become

$$X \xmapsto{\text{or}} \min((X - x) \cup X') \qquad \text{if } x \in X \text{ and } x \leq x' \text{ for all } x' \in X' \text{ and } X' \neq \emptyset$$

$$X \xmapsto{\text{or}} X - x \qquad \text{if } x \in X \text{ and } X - x \neq \emptyset$$

Define $\sqsubseteq^{\text{or}}$ and $\sqsubseteq^{\text{or}}_a$ as the transitive closure of $\xmapsto{\text{or}}$ and $\xmapsto{\text{or}}_a$ respectively. To justify the last claim that the or-sets must be ordered by the Smyth ordering, we prove the following.

Theorem 5. a) *Let $X, Y \in \mathbb{P}_{\text{fin}}(A)$, $X, Y \neq \emptyset$. Then $X \sqsubseteq^{\text{or}} Y$ iff $X \sqsubseteq^{\natural} Y$.*
   b) *Let $X, Y \in \mathbb{A}_{\text{fin}}(A)$, $X, Y \neq \emptyset$. Then $X \sqsubseteq^{\text{or}}_a Y$ iff $X \sqsubseteq^{\natural} Y$.* $\square$

Corollary 6. *Let X and Y be finite antichains in A such that $X \sqsubseteq^{\natural} Y$. Then it is possible to find a sequence of antichains $X_1, \ldots, X_n$ such that $X_1, \ldots, X_n \subseteq X \cup Y$ and $X \xmapsto{\text{or}}_a X_1 \xmapsto{\text{or}}_a \ldots \xmapsto{\text{or}}_a X_n \xmapsto{\text{or}}_a Y$.* $\square$

2.3 Semantics of collections

We will need some notation. Recall that the family of finite antichains of a poset A is denoted by $\mathbb{A}_{\text{fin}}(A)$. By $\mathcal{P}^{\natural}(A)$ we mean the poset $\langle \mathbb{A}_{\text{fin}}(A), \sqsubseteq^{\natural} \rangle$, and by $\mathcal{P}^{\sharp}(A)$ we denote $\langle A_{\text{fin}}(A), \sqsubseteq^{\sharp}\rangle$. These two constructions are the bases for the Hoare and the Smyth powerdomains used in semantics of concurrency, see [Gun92]. Note that $\mathcal{P}^{\flat}(A)$ is a join-semilattice, where the join operation is given by $X \sqcup^{\flat} Y = \max(X \cup Y)$, and $\mathcal{P}^{\sharp}(A)$ is a meet-semilattice, where the meet operation is given by $X \sqcap^{\sharp} Y = \min(X \cup Y)$.

Recall that the semantics of a database object d, which is an element of an ordered set A, is defined as the set of all elements of A that it can possibly denote, that is, $[d] = \uparrow d = \{d' \in A \mid d' \geq d\}$. Following this definition and the results of the previous section, we can define the semantics of sets under OWA and CWA. Assume that elements of sets are taken from a partially ordered set A. Then we define the semantic functions $[\cdot]_{\text{set}}^{\text{OWA}}, [\cdot]^{\text{OWA}}, [\cdot]_{\text{set}}^{\text{CWA}}, [\cdot]^{\text{CWA}}$ where index "set" stands for the set semantics (as opposed to the antichain semantics for which we do not use an index), as follows:

$$[X]_{\text{set}}^{\text{OWA}} = \{Y \in \mathbb{P}_{\text{fin}}(A) \mid X \sqsubseteq^{\flat} Y\} \qquad [X]^{\text{OWA}} = \{Y \in A_{\text{fin}}(A) \mid X \sqsubseteq^{\flat} Y\}$$
$$[X]_{\text{set}}^{\text{CWA}} = \{Y \in \mathbb{P}_{\text{fin}}(A) \mid X \sqsubseteq^{\natural} Y\} \qquad [X]^{\text{CWA}} = \{Y \in A_{\text{fin}}(A) \mid X \sqsubseteq^{\natural} Y\}$$

In what follows, we shall mostly consider the open world assumption. Hence, if no superscript is used, it is assumed that we deal with the OWA. That is, $[X] = [X]^{\text{OWA}}$ and $[X]_{\text{set}} = [X]_{\text{set}}^{\text{OWA}}$.

A number of useful properties of these functions are summarized in the following proposition.

Proposition 7. *1. If $X, Y \subseteq_{\text{fin}} A$, then $[Y]_{\text{set}}^{\text{OWA}} \subseteq [X]_{\text{set}}^{\text{OWA}}$ iff $X \sqsubseteq^{\text{OWA}} Y$ iff $X \sqsubseteq^{\flat} Y$.*

2. If $X, Y \in A_{\text{fin}}(A)$, then $[Y] \subseteq [X]$ iff $X \sqsubseteq_a^{\text{OWA}} Y$ iff $X \sqsubseteq^{\flat} Y$.

3. If $X \subseteq_{\text{fin}} A$, then $[X] = [\max X]$ and $[X]_{\text{set}}^{\text{OWA}} = [\max X]_{\text{set}}^{\text{OWA}}$.

4. If $X, Y \subseteq_{\text{fin}} A$, then $[Y]_{\text{set}}^{\text{CWA}} \subseteq [X]_{\text{set}}^{\text{CWA}}$ iff $X \sqsubseteq^{\text{CWA}} Y$ iff $X \sqsubseteq^{\natural} Y$.

5. If $X \subseteq_{\text{fin}} A$, then $[X]_{\text{set}}^{\text{CWA}} = [\max X \cup \min X]_{\text{set}}^{\text{CWA}}$ and $[X]^{\text{CWA}} = [\max X \cup \min X]^{\text{CWA}}$. □

Closed world databases were initially defined in the logical setting. In particular, [Rei78] defined a CWA answer to a query as a certain set of tuples without incomplete information. In our terminology, this corresponds to finding an answer to a query with respect to the $[\,]_{\max}^{\text{CWA}}$ semantic function. It was proved in [Rei78] that the CWA query evaluation distributes over union and intersection, and that whenever a database is consistent with the negations of the facts stored in it, the OWA and the CWA query evaluation algorithms produce the same result. It was also proved that the minimal CWA answers contain exactly one tuple.

The following proposition shows that analogs of these results hold in our setting. Note that to say that a database X is consistent with negation of any fact stored in it, is the same as to say that any $y \notin X$ is consistent with some $x \in X$. In other words, if every $z \in A$ lies under some $z_m \in A^{max}$, then $X \sqsubseteq^\flat A^{max}$. Finally, a domain of n-ary relations with one kind of nulls is the product of n copies of an infinite flat domain. In view of this, the proposition below says that the results of [Rei78] are preserved, at least in the spirit.

Proposition 8. *Let A be a poset such that each element is under an element of A^{max}. Then*

1) If A is a product of n copies of infinite flat domains and $Y \in [X_1 \cap X_2]^{CWA}_{max}$, then $Y = Y_1 \cap Y_2$ where $Y_1 \in [X_1]^{CWA}_{max}$ and $Y_2 \in [X_2]^{CWA}_{max}$.
2) For any poset A, $[X_1 \cup X_2]^{CWA}_{max} = \{Y_1 \cup Y_2 \mid Y_1 \in [X_1]^{CWA}_{max}, Y_2 \in [X_2]^{CWA}_{max}\}$.
3) If $X \sqsubseteq^\flat A^{max}$, then $[X]^{CWA}_{max} = [X]^{OWA}_{max}$.
4) If X is bounded above in A, then a minimal nonempty $Y \in [X]^{CWA}_{max}$ is a singleton. □

Or-sets can be treated at both structural and conceptual levels. At the structural level we just define $[X]^{or} = \{Y \in \mathbb{P}_{fin}(A) \mid X \sqsubseteq^\flat Y\}$ (or using $A_{fin}(A)$ if we need an antichain semantics.) The following proposition is the counterpart of proposition 7 for or-sets.

Proposition 9. *1. If $X, Y \subseteq_{fin} A$, then $[Y]^{or} \subseteq [X]^{or}$ iff $X \sqsubseteq^{or} Y$ iff $X \sqsubseteq^\flat Y$.*

2. If $X, Y \in A_{fin}(A)$, then $[Y]^{or} \subseteq [X]^{or}$ iff $X \sqsubseteq^{or}_a Y$ iff $X \sqsubseteq^\flat Y$.

3. If $X \subseteq_{fin} A$, then $[X]^{or} = [\min X]^{or}$. □

Note that propositions 7 and 9 justify using maximal elements to remove redundancies from sets under OWA and using minimal elements to remove redundancies from or-sets. For sets under CWA, it is necessary to retain both minimal and maximal elements; the elements which are strictly in between can be removed as the fifth item in proposition 7 suggests.

Semantics of types and typed objects. The semantic functions above could also be used to define the semantic domains of *types*. For simplicity, assume that we have the following type system:

$$t ::= b \mid t \times t \mid \{t\} \mid \langle t \rangle$$

and that we are dealing with the open world assumption. Notice that we use pairs instead of records. Pairs are sufficient to simulate records and are easier to work with as notation does not become too complicated. We now define the *structural semantics* $[]_s$ that corresponds to the structural interpretation of or-sets.

Suppose that for each base type b its semantic domain $[b]_s$ is given. We define the semantic domains of all types inductively. Suppose we want to deal with antichains. Then

- $[t \times s]_s = [t]_s \times [s]_s.$
- $[\{t\}]_s = \langle \mathbb{A}_{\text{fin}}([t]_s), \subseteq^\flat \rangle = \mathcal{P}^\flat([t]_s).$
- $[\langle t \rangle]_s = \langle \mathbb{A}_{\text{fin}}([t]_s), \subseteq^\natural \rangle = \mathcal{P}^\natural([t]_s).$

The structural semantics of objects is defined inductively.

- For each base type b and an element x of this type, $[x]_s = \uparrow x = \{x' \in [b]_s \mid x' \geq x\}$.
- If $x = (x_1, x_2)$, then $[x]_s = [x_1]_s \times [x_2]_s$.
- If X is of type $\{t\}$, then $[X]_s = [X]^{\text{OWA}}$.
- If X is of type $\langle t \rangle$, then $[X]_s = [X]^{\text{or}}$.

Note that the last clauses in the definitions of type and object semantics say that we have defined the *structural semantics* of or-sets. That is, we viewed or-sets as collections and not as single elements they could represent. Our next goal is to define the *conceptual* semantics $[]_c$ of or-sets.

First, for base types both semantics coincide, i.e. $[b]_c = [b]_s$. For other type constructors $[]_c$ is defined as follows. Note that there are two possibilities for the semantics of the set type constructor, but the definition of the semantics of objects will work with both of them.

- $[t \times s]_c = [t]_c \times [s]_c.$
- $[\{t\}]_c = \langle \mathbb{A}_{\text{fin}}([t]_c), \subseteq^\flat \rangle = \mathcal{P}^\flat([t]_c)$ or $[\{t\}]_c = \langle \mathbb{P}_{\text{fin}}([t]_c), \subseteq^\flat \rangle.$
- $[\langle t \rangle]_c = [t]_c.$

The last clause corresponds to the fact that conceptually an or-set is just one of its elements. Semantics of each object is now going to be a finitely generated filter $F = \uparrow \{f_1, \ldots, f_n\} = \uparrow f_1 \cup \ldots \cup \uparrow f_n$. Again, we define it inductively.

- For each base type b and an element x of this type, $[x]_c = \uparrow x = \{x' \in [b]_c \mid x' \geq x\}$.
- If $x = (x_1, x_2)$, then $[x]_c = [x_1]_c \times [x_2]_c$.
- Let $X = \{x_1, \ldots, x_n\}$ be a set of type $\{t\}$. Then $[X]_c = \{Y \mid \forall i = 1, \ldots, n : Y \cap [x_i]_c \neq \emptyset\}$. Here Y is taken from $\mathbb{P}_{\text{fin}}([t]_c)$ or $\mathbb{A}_{\text{fin}}([t]_c)$ depending on the definition of the semantics of types.
- Let $X = \langle x_1, \ldots, x_n \rangle$ be an or-set of type $\langle t \rangle$. Then $[X]_c = [x_1]_c \cup \ldots \cup [x_n]_c$.

Before we prove that this semantic function possesses the desired properties, let us make a few observations. First, the definition of the semantics of or-sets coincides with the intended semantics of or-sets: an or-set denotes one of its elements. Second, to understand the semantics of pairs and sets, consider two simple examples. Let $x_1 = \langle 1, 2 \rangle$, $x_2 = \langle 3, 4 \rangle$. Assume that there is no ordering involved. The semantics of x_1 is then a set $\{1, 2\}$ and the semantics of x_2 is $\{3, 4\}$.

Therefore, $[(x_1, x_2)]_c = \{(1,3),(1,4),(2,3),(2,4)\}$. Now consider (x_1, x_2). It is a pair whose first component is 1 or 2 and whose second component is 3 or 4. Hence, it is one of the following pairs: $(1,3),(1,4),(2,3),(2,4)$. And this is exactly what the semantic function $[]_c$ tells us. For semantics of sets, consider $X = \{x_1, x_2\} = \{(1,2),(3,4)\}$. It is is a set that has at least two elements: one is 1 or 2, and the other is 3 or 4. Hence, it must contain one of the following sets (since we believe in OWA): $\{1,3\}, \{1,4\}, \{2,3\}, \{2,4\}$. Now look at $[X]_c$. A set Y belongs to $[X]_c$ if $Y \cap [(1,2)]_c = Y \cap \{1,2\} \neq \emptyset$ and $Y \cap [(3,4)]_c = Y \cap \{3,4\} \neq \emptyset$ which happens if and only if Y contains one of the four sets above. This justifies our definition of the conceptual semantics of sets.

Now we can prove the following.

Theorem 10. *For every object x of type t, $[x]_c$ is a finitely generated filter in $[t]_c$. Furthermore, if x and y are of type t and $x \leq y$ in $[t]_s$, then $[y]_c \subseteq [x]_c$.*
□

Corollary 11. *If x and y are objects of the same type, then $[x]_s = [y]_s$ implies $[x]_c = [y]_c$.*
□

The converse is not true: $\langle(1,2),\langle 3\rangle\rangle$ and $\langle\langle 1\rangle,\langle 2\rangle,\langle 3\rangle\rangle$ are structurally different objects of type $\langle\langle int\rangle\rangle$, but $[\langle(1,2),\langle 3\rangle\rangle]_c = [\langle\langle 1\rangle,\langle 2\rangle,\langle 3\rangle\rangle]_c = \{1,2,3\}$.

Relationship between CWA sets, OWA sets and or-sets. There is a naturally arising question: do we really need all three kinds of collections – OWA sets, CWA sets and or-sets? Can not we just represent some of them using the others? The answer to this question is that we do need all three kinds of collections and no such representations exist. First, let us see what could be a representation of, say, OWA sets with or-sets. It could be a procedure that, given a poset A and $X \in \mathbb{A}_{fin}(A)$, calculates $Y \in \mathbb{A}_{fin}(A)$ such that $Z \in [X]$ iff $Z \in [Y]^{or}$. The following proposition tells us that it is impossible to do so.

Proposition 12. *For every poset A which is not a chain and has at least two elements, there exists $X \in \mathbb{A}_{fin}(A)$ such that for no $Y \in \mathbb{A}_{fin}(A)$ the following holds: 1) $[X] = [Y]^{or}$; 2) $[X]^{or} = [Y]$; 3) $[X] = [Y]^{CWA}_{set}$; 4) $[X]^{CWA}_{set} = [Y]$; 5) $[X]^{or} = [Y]^{CWA}_{set}$; 6) $[X]^{CWA}_{set} = [Y]^{or}$.*
□

2.4 Properties of semantic domains of types

We did not define the semantics of types and objects for nothing. Our goal is to use the semantics as a guideline for the language design. In this subsection we establish a number of useful properties of semantic domains of types which be used extensively in the next section.

Recall that the structural semantics of types $\{t\}$ and $\langle t \rangle$ was defined as $\mathcal{P}^\flat([t])$ and $\mathcal{P}^\natural([t])$ respectively. Let $\eta : A \to \mathcal{P}^\flat(A)$ or $\mathcal{P}^\natural(A)$ be the singleton function: $\eta(x) = \{x\}$. Then both $\mathcal{P}^\flat(\cdot)$ and $\mathcal{P}^\natural(\cdot)$ have nice characterizations as follows.

Proposition 13. *Let A be a poset. Then $\langle \mathcal{P}^\flat(A), \sqcup^\flat, \emptyset \rangle$ ($\langle \mathcal{P}^\natural(A), \sqcap^\natural, \emptyset \rangle$) is the free join-semilattice with bottom (free meet-semilattice with top) generated by A. That is, for every join-semilattice with bottom $\langle S, \vee, \bot \rangle$ (meet-semilattice with top $\langle S, \wedge, \top \rangle$) and every monotone map $f : A \to S$, there exists a unique semilattice homomorphism $f^+ : \mathcal{P}^\flat(A) \to S$ ($f^+ : \mathcal{P}^\natural(A) \to S$) that makes the first (second) diagram below commute.*

So far the only semantic distinction between or-sets and sets showed up in different orderings for those and in different interpretations for conceptual semantics. We have not yet seen any results suggesting how these may interact. This is important for a language design, so that we would be able to distinguish between sets and or-sets. A natural way to study the connection between sets and or-sets is to look at the semantic domains of iterated types, that is, $\{\langle t \rangle\}$ and $\langle \{t\} \rangle$, and see how they are related. In other words, one has to find out what the relationship between $\mathcal{P}^\flat(\mathcal{P}^\natural(A))$ and $\mathcal{P}^\natural(\mathcal{P}^\flat(A))$ is. Here we have the following useful fact.

Theorem 14. (see also [Lib92, LW96]) *Given a finite set of finite sets $\mathcal{X} = \{X_1, \ldots, X_n\}$ where $X_i = \{x_1^i, \ldots, x_{k_i}^i\}$, let $F_{\mathcal{X}}$ be the set of functions $f : \{1, \ldots, n\} \to \mathbb{N}$ such that for any $i: 1 \leq f(i) \leq k_i$. If all X_i's are subsets of A, define two maps α_a and β_a as follows:*

$$\alpha_a(\mathcal{X}) = \min_{f \in F_{\mathcal{X}}} \sqsubseteq^\flat (\max\{x_{f(i)}^i \mid i = 1, \ldots, n\})$$

$$\beta_a(\mathcal{X}) = \max_{f \in F_{\mathcal{X}}} \sqsubseteq^\natural (\min\{x_{f(i)}^i \mid i = 1, \ldots, n\})$$

Then for any poset A, α_a restricted to $\mathcal{P}^\flat(\mathcal{P}^\natural(A))$ and β_a restricted to $\mathcal{P}^\natural(\mathcal{P}^\flat(A))$ are mutually inverse isomorphisms between $\mathcal{P}^\flat(\mathcal{P}^\natural(A))$ and $\mathcal{P}^\natural(\mathcal{P}^\flat(A))$. □

Now, let us see what α_a does if there is no order involved. In this case an input to α_a can be considered as a set of or-sets:

$$\mathcal{X} = \{\langle x_1^1, \ldots, x_{k_1}^1 \rangle, \ldots, \langle x_1^n, \ldots, x_{k_n}^n \rangle\}$$

Assume all x_j^is are distinct. Then $\alpha_a(\mathcal{X})$ is the or-set of sets

$$\langle\{x_{f(1)}^1, \ldots, x_{f(n)}^n\} \mid f \in F\mathcal{X}\rangle$$

That is, all possible choices encoded by or-sets are explicitly listed. We shall use α_a as a programming primitive extensively in the next section.

The iterated construction $\mathcal{P}^{\flat\natural}(A) = \mathcal{P}^\flat(\mathcal{P}^\natural(A)) \cong \mathcal{P}^\natural(\mathcal{P}^\flat(A))$ possesses the following important property. Both join and meet operations can be defined on $\mathcal{P}^\flat(\mathcal{P}^\natural(A))$ and supply it with the lattice structure: $\mathcal{X} \sqcup^\flat \mathcal{Y} = \max^\flat(\mathcal{X} \cup \mathcal{Y})$ where $\max^\flat$ is taking maximal elements with respect to $\sqsubseteq^\flat$, and $\mathcal{X} \sqcap^\flat \mathcal{Y} = \max^\flat\{X \sqcap^\natural Y \mid X \in \mathcal{X}, Y \in \mathcal{Y}\}$. Moreover, it can be described via a well-known mathematical construction. This description will prove useful later, when we discuss programming primitives for or-sets.

Theorem 15. *For an arbitrary poset A, $\mathcal{P}^{\flat\natural}(A)$ is the free distributive lattice with top and bottom generated by A.* $\square$

This result is quite robust and holds when some changes are made in the definitions of $\mathcal{P}^\flat(\cdot)$ and $\mathcal{P}^\natural(\cdot)$. In particular, if $\mathcal{P}^\flat_{\neq\emptyset}(A)$ and $\mathcal{P}^\natural_{\neq\emptyset}$ are defined as $\mathcal{P}^\flat$ and $\mathcal{P}^\natural$ except that the empty antichain is not allowed and $\mathcal{P}^{\flat\natural}_{\neq\emptyset}$ and $\mathcal{P}^{\natural\flat}_{\neq\emptyset}$ are respective compositions of $\mathcal{P}^\flat_{\neq\emptyset}$ and $\mathcal{P}^\natural_{\neq\emptyset}$, then the following holds.

Corollary 16. *For an arbitrary poset A, $\mathcal{P}^{\flat\natural}_{\neq\emptyset}(A)$ and $\mathcal{P}^{\natural\flat}_{\neq\emptyset}(A)$ are isomorphic. Moreover, $\mathcal{P}^{\flat\natural}_{\neq\emptyset}(A)$ is the free distributive lattice generated by A.* $\square$

This fact is the key of the normalization process suggested in [LW96] as a means of incorporating conceptual semantics into the language. We shall come to it again later.

3 Languages for partial information

3.1 The Tannen-Cardelli thesis

In this subsection we give an overview of two principles of language design, which, when combined, provide a uniform way of organizing programming syntax around datatypes involved.

Suppose we want to design a language that works with objects given by some type system, like the one we had for complex objects. How do we choose primitives of such a language? The idea of Cardelli (see [Car88]) is that one should use *introduction* and *elimination* operations associated with type constructors as primitives of a programming language. The introduction operations are needed to construct objects of a given type whereas the elimination operations are used for doing computations over them. For example, record formation is the introduction operation for records, and projections are the elimination operations.

How does one find those introductions and elimination operations? Databases work with various kinds of collections. One approach (due to Tannen [BBW92, BTS91]) to finding the introduction and elimination operations for those collections is to look for operations *naturally* associated with them. To do so, one often characterizes the semantic domains of collection types via *universality properties*, which tell us what the introduction and the elimination operations are.

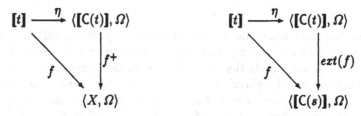

Fig. 6. Operations naturally associated with collection types

Assume that we have a collection type constructor (like sets, bags, lists etc.) that we denote by $C(\cdot)$. Then, for any type t, $C(t)$ is the type of collections of elements of type t (e.g. sets or bags of type t). By *universality property* we mean that the following is true about $[C(t)]$, the semantic domain of type $C(t)$. It is possible to find a set Ω of operations on $[C(t)]$ and a map $\eta : [t] \to [C(t)]$ such that for any other Ω-algebra $\langle X, \Omega \rangle$ and a map $f : [t] \to X$ there exists a unique Ω-homomorphism f^+ such that the first diagram in figure 6 commutes. If we are successful in identifying η and Ω, then we can make them the *introduction* operations. The reason is that now any object of type $C(t)$ can be constructed from objects of type t by first embedding them into type $C(t)$ by means of η, and then constructing more complex objects using the operations from Ω. The *elimination* operation is given by the universality property. That is, the general elimination operation is a higher-order operation that takes f as an input and returns f^+.

Combining these two ideas by Cardelli and Tannen gives us languages for many kinds of collections. Consider sets, assuming that the semantic domain of $\{t\}$ is the finite powerset of elements of t, that is, $\mathbb{P}_{fin}([t])$. For any set X, its finite powerset $\mathbb{P}_{fin}(X)$ is the free semilattice generated by X. That is, the operations of Ω are $\emptyset$ and $\cup$ and η is the singleton formation: $\eta(x) = \{x\}$. Moreover, these operations can be applied for arbitrary types. That is, η is the *polymorphic singleton*; its type is $t \rightarrow \{t\}$ for any t. Similarly, $\cup$ is the polymorphic union of type $\{t\} \times \{t\} \rightarrow \{t\}$. Any set of type $\{t\}$ can be constructed from elements of type t using $\emptyset, \cup$ and η: $\{x_1, \ldots, x_n\} = \eta(x_1) \cup \ldots \cup \eta(x_n)$.

The operation that takes f into f^+ is the following

$$
\begin{aligned}
fun \; f^+[e, u](\emptyset) \quad &= e \\
| \quad f^+[e, u](\{x\}) \quad &= f(x) \\
| \quad f^+[e, u](A \cup B) &= u(f^+[e, u](A), f^+[e, u](B))
\end{aligned}
$$

This operation f^+, often called *structural recursion* [BBN91, BBW92], depends on e and u which are interpretations of the operations of Ω on its range. Notice that if e and u do not supply the range of f^+ with the structure of a semilattice, then f^+ may not be well-defined. For example, if e is 0, f is the constant function that always returns 1, and u is $+$, then retaining duplicates may easily lead to a wrong cardinality function: $1 = f^+[0, +](\{1\}) = f^+[0, +](\{1, 1\}) = 2$. To overcome this problem, one should require that e be interpreted as $\emptyset$ and u as $\cup$. Generally, the simplest way to ensure well-definedness is to require that $\langle X, \Omega \rangle$ be $\langle [\![C(s)]\!], \Omega \rangle$ for some type s. Thus, we obtain the second diagram in figure 6.

The unique completing homomorphism is called $ext(f)$, the extension of f. Its semantics in the case of sets is $ext(f)\{x_1, \ldots, x_n\} = f(x_1) \cup \ldots \cup f(x_n)$. This justifies the name because $ext(f)$ "extends" f to sets. It is a polymorphic higher-order operation that takes f of type $t \rightarrow \{s\}$ and returns $ext(f) : \{t\} \rightarrow \{s\}$. This function is well-defined. Using ext together with $\eta, \emptyset, \cup$, projections and record formation, conditional and the equality test gives us precisely the nested relational algebra [BBW92] but the presentation is nicer than the standard ones, such as in [SS86, TF86]. Instead of ext one can use two functions: $map(f) : \{t\} \rightarrow \{s\}$ provided f is of type $t \rightarrow s$ (this function maps f over its input: $map(f)(\{x_1, \ldots, x_n\}) = \{f(x_1), \ldots, f(x_n)\}$) and $\mu : \{\{t\}\} \rightarrow \{t\}$ that flattens a set of sets: $\mu(\{X_1, \ldots, X_n\}) = X_1 \cup \ldots \cup X_n$. Diagrams in figure in 6 represent a well-known mathematical construction, which is going from an adjunction to the Kleisli category of its monad, and the fact that ext and map and μ are interchangeable follows from the general properties of the categorical notion of a monad, see [BW90].

This approach to the language design was shown to be extremely useful in the past few years, see [LW94a, LW94b, Suc94]. Here we apply it to partial information; the reader has probably already noticed the similarity between diagrams in figure 6 and proposition 13, which will give us the operations of the language.

General operators and pairs

$$\frac{g:u\to s \quad f:s\to t}{f\circ g:u\to t} \qquad \frac{c:bool \quad f:s\to t \quad g:s\to t}{if\ c\ then\ f\ else\ g:s\to t} \qquad \frac{f:u\to s \quad g:u\to t}{(f,g):u\to s\times t}$$

$$\overline{\pi_1^{s,t}:s\times t\to s} \qquad \overline{\pi_2^{s,t}:s\times t\to t} \qquad \overline{!^t:t\to unit}$$

$$\overline{Kc:unit\to Type(c)} \qquad \overline{id^t:t\to t} \qquad \overline{\leq_s:s\times s\to bool}$$

Set operators for partial information (given by $\mathcal{P}^{\flat}$)

$$\overline{\rho_2^{s,t}:s\times\{t\}\to\{s\times t\}} \qquad \overline{\eta^t:t\to\{t\}} \qquad \overline{\sqcup_t^{\flat}:\{t\}\times\{t\}\to\{t\}}$$

$$\overline{\mu_a^t:\{\{t\}\}\to\{t\}} \qquad \overline{empty^t:unit\to\{t\}} \qquad \frac{f:s\to t}{map_a(f):\{s\}\to\{t\}}$$

Set operators without partial information (given by $\mathbb{P}_{fin}$)

$$\overline{\rho_2^{s,t}:s\times\{t\}\to\{s\times t\}} \qquad \overline{\eta^t:t\to\{t\}} \qquad \overline{\cup_t:\{t\}\times\{t\}\to\{t\}}$$

$$\overline{\mu^t:\{\{t\}\}\to\{t\}} \qquad \overline{empty^t:unit\to\{t\}} \qquad \frac{f:s\to t}{map(f):\{s\}\to\{t\}}$$

Fig. 7. Expressions of $\mathcal{NRL}$ and $\mathcal{NRL}_a$.

3.2 Language for sets and its sublanguages

Consider sets under the OWA. Since the semantic domain of type $\{t\}$ is $\mathcal{P}^{\flat}(\llbracket t\rrbracket)$, proposition 13 gives us the universality property and consequently introduction and elimination operations. Introduction operations are $\eta(x)=\{x\}$ and $X\sqcup^{\flat}Y = \max(X\cup Y)$, while the restricted form of elimination operation ext_a is given by $ext_a(f)(\{x_1,\ldots,x_n\}) = f(x_1)\sqcup^{\flat}\ldots\sqcup^{\flat}f(x_n) = \max(f(x_1)\cup\ldots\cup f(x_n))$. We prefer using the map-μ presentation. The semantics of those operations is given by $\mu_a(\{X_1,\ldots,X_n\}) = \max(X_1\cup\ldots\cup X_n)$ and $map_a(f)(\{x_1,\ldots,x_n\}) = \max(\{f(x_1),\ldots,f(x_n)\})$. The index "a" stands for antichains.

If no order (partiality) is involved, then the semantics of $\{t\}$ is $\mathbb{P}_{fin}(\llbracket t\rrbracket)$ which is the free join-semilattice with bottom generated by $[t]$. Hence, the operations given by this universality property are the same as those for the language for OWA sets, except that max is not taken. For instance, $\cup$ is used instead of $\sqcup^b$. The resulting language, $\mathcal{NRL}$ is precisely the nested relational algebra as has been mentioned (see [BBW92]).

Figure 7 contains expressions of two languages: $\mathcal{NRL}$ (nested relational language) of [BBW92] and $\mathcal{NRL}_a$ ($\mathcal{NRL}$ on antichains). Both languages share the general operators (the only exception is $\mathcal{NRL}$'s equality test instead of comparability test of $\mathcal{NRL}_a$). In the figure, we annotate expressions with their most general types. Since those types can be inferred, in what follows we shall omit them. $\mathcal{NRL}$ has all operations from the group of operations not dealing with partial information, and $\mathcal{NRL}_a$ has operations from the "set operations for partial information" group. Let us briefly recall the semantics of the operators that have not been explained already. $\leq_s$ is the comparability test at type s; that is, $\leq_s (x,y)$ evaluates to true if x, y are of type s and $x \leq y$ in $[s]_s$. In other words,

- $(x, y) \leq_{s \times t} (x', y)' \Leftrightarrow x \leq_s x'$ and $y \leq_t y'$.
- $x \leq_{\{s\}} y \Leftrightarrow x \leq^\flat_s y$ (i.e. $\forall o \in x\ \exists o' \in y : o \leq_s o'$).

ρ_2 is the pair-with operation: $\rho_2(x, \{x_1, \ldots, x_n\}) = \{(x, x_1), \ldots, (x, x_n)\}$. $unit$ is a special base type that has only one element. Its presence here is dictated by the fact that $\mathcal{NRL}$ is an algebra of *functions*. That is, to make a constant like $\emptyset$ into a function, we make it a function of type $unit \to \{t\}$ that always returns $\emptyset$. Composition of functions is denoted by $\circ$, pairing of functions is denoted by (f, g) and π_1 and π_2 are first and second projections.

Note that the languages are parameterized by an unspecified family of base types. That is, we view $\mathcal{NRL}$ and $\mathcal{NRL}_a$ as analog of relational algebra or calculus, which is the starting point for most languages for flat relations. Should one need additional types and operations on them (like real numbers and real arithmetic), they can be added easily. But the most important step in language design is to choose the operations that manipulate data, and this is what the operations of $\mathcal{NRL}$ and $\mathcal{NRL}_a$ are.

Now we are going to establish some properties of the languages. First, we do not need $\leq_s$ as a primitive at all types because it can be defined.

Proposition 17. *Assume that $\leq_b$ is given for any base type b. Then $\leq_s$ is definable in $\mathcal{NRL}_a$ without using $\leq_s$ as a primitive. Furthermore, under the assumption that $\leq_b$ can be tested in $O(1)$ time, the time complexity of verifying $x \leq_s y$ is $O(n^2)$, where n is the total size of x and y.* □

Using this, we can show that $\mathcal{NRL}$ is sufficient to simulate $\mathcal{NRL}_a$.

Theorem 18. *NRC$_a$ is a sublanguage of NRC augmented with $\leq_b$ for all base types.* □

However, there is one subtle point. Assume that we have two sets X_1 and X_2 of type $\{t\}$ such that $\max X_1 = \max X_2$. That is, X_1 and X_2 represent the same object in $[\![\{t\}]\!]_s$. Let $f : \{t\} \to t'$ be a function definable in NRC. Is it true that $f(X_1)$ and $f(X_2)$ represent the same object in $[\![t']\!]_s$? Unfortunately, the answer to this question is negative. To see why, consider x and y of type t such that $x \leq_t y$ and $x \neq y$. Assume that $g : t \to t'$ is such that $g(x)$ and $g(y)$ are not comparable by $\leq_{t'}$. Then $map(g)(\{y\}) = \{g(y)\}$ and $map(g)(\{x,y\}) = \{g(x), g(y)\}$. Even though $\max\{y\} = \max\{x,y\}$, we have $\max(map(g)(\{y\})) \neq \max(map(g)(\{x,y\}))$. The reason why this happens is that g is not a monotone function. Requiring monotonicity is sufficient to repair this problem. Define the following translation function $(\cdot)^\circ$ on objects that forces objects in the set-theoretic semantics into the objects in the antichain semantics:

- For x of base type b, $x^\circ = x$.
- For $x = (x_1, x_2)$, $x^\circ = (x_1^\circ, x_2^\circ)$.
- For $X = \{x_1, \ldots, x_n\}$, $X^\circ = \max\{x_1^\circ, \ldots, x_n^\circ\}$.

We say that a function $f : s \to t$ definable in NRC *agrees with the antichain semantics* if $x^\circ = y^\circ$ implies $f(x)^\circ = f(y)^\circ$. We say that it is *monotone* iff $x \leq_s y$ implies $f(x) \leq_t f(y)$.

Proposition 19. *A monotone function f definable in NRC agrees with the antichain semantics. If f is not monotone, then $map(f)$ does not agree with the antichain semantics.* □

Therefore, we would like to identify the subclass of monotone functions definable in NRC. Unfortunately, it is not possible to do it algorithmically. Not being able to decide monotonicity is another reason why we prefer to view NRC$_a$ as a sublanguage of NRC in which the antichain semantics can be modeled, rather than a separate language.

Theorem 20. *It is undecidable whether a function f definable in NRC is monotone.* □

There are some intersting anomalies of the antichain semantics. The most surprising of all is that $[\![\eta]\!]_s = [\![powerset]\!]_s$ or, in other words, $NRC_a(powerset) = NRC_a$. Indeed, since for any $Y \in \mathbb{P}_{fin}(X)$ we have $Y \subseteq X$ and hence $Y \sqsubseteq^\flat X$, then under the antichain semantics $[\![\mathbb{P}_{fin}(X)]\!]_s = [\![\max \mathbb{P}_{fin}(X)]\!]_s = [\![\{X\}]\!]_s = [\![\eta(X)]\!]_s$. There are two lessons we learn from this interesting collapse. First, as we have said already, it is better to view NRC$_a$ as a sublanguage of NRC rather than a separate language. Second, *powerset* is *not* a good candidate to enrich expressiveness of the language. (Of course, the result of [SP94] which states that even very simple algorithms expressed with *powerset* need at least exponential space to be evaluated is a much stronger argument against *powerset*).

The next question we are going to address is that of conservativity of $\mathcal{NRL}$ over $\mathcal{NRL}_a$. Given a family of primitives p interpreted for both set theoretic and antichain semantics, we say that $\mathcal{NRL}(\leq_b, \mathbf{p})^1$ is *conservative* over $\mathcal{NRL}_a(\mathbf{p})$ if for any function f definable in $\mathcal{NRL}(\leq_b, \mathbf{p})$ and satisfying the condition that $f(x) = f(x)^\circ$ for any $x = x^\circ$, such f is definable in $\mathcal{NRL}_a(\mathbf{p})$. We do not know if $\mathcal{NRL}(\leq_b)$ is conservative over $\mathcal{NRL}_a$. However, we can show that it is conservative when augmented with aggregate functions. Instead of choosing a restricted set of aggregates, we use a general template suggested by [LW94a, LW94b]. This is the higher-order function $\sum(f)$ that takes a function $f : t \to \mathbb{N}$ and returns $\sum(f) : \{t\} \to \mathbb{N}$ given by $\sum(f)(\{x_1, \ldots, x_n\}) = f(x_1) + \ldots + f(x_n)$. Other operations on the type of naturals include multiplication and modified subtraction (monus) $\dot{-}$. The key idea in the proof of the proposition below is that using these additional functions we can encode objects using only natural numbers, cf. [LW94c].

Proposition 21. $\mathcal{NRL}(\mathbb{N}, \sum, \cdot, \dot{-}, \leq_b)$ *is conservative over* $\mathcal{NRL}_a(\mathbb{N}, \sum, \cdot, \dot{-})$. $\square$

Example: Zaniolo's language In one of the first languages for partial information [Zan84] there is only one kind of nulls – **ni**. The ordering on records is defined component-wise and it is lifted to relations by using the Hoare ordering. Zaniolo's language was initially designed for flat relations only but here we show how to extend it to the nested relations. We shall use the notation $\downarrow x$ for $\{y \mid y \leq x\}$.

The main notion in the language is that of x-relation which is an equivalence class with respect to the Hoare ordering. That is, R_1 and R_2 are equivalent if $R_1 \sqsubseteq^\flat R_2$ and $R_2 \sqsubseteq^\flat R_1$. In our terminology this means that $\downarrow R_1 = \downarrow R_2$. Therefore, we can pick a canonical representative of each equivalence class: the canonical representative of the equivalence class of R is $\max R$. Clearly, $\downarrow R_1 = \downarrow R_2$ implies $\max R_1 = \max R_2$.

The next notion used for defining the operations in the language is that of generalized membership: $r \hat{\in} R$ iff $r \leq r'$ for some $r' \in R$. In other words, $r \hat{\in} R$ iff $r \in \downarrow R$ or $\{r\} \sqsubseteq^\flat R$. Using this notion, Zaniolo defined the following main operations:

$$R_1 \hat{\cup} R_2 = \max\{r \mid r \hat{\in} R_1 \text{ or } r \hat{\in} R_2\}$$

$$R_1 \hat{\cap} R_2 = \max\{r \mid r \hat{\in} R_1 \text{ and } r \hat{\in} R_2\}$$

$$R_1 \hat{-} R_2 = \max\{r \mid r \hat{\in} R_1 \text{ and } \neg(r \hat{\in} R_2)\}$$

---

[1] We use parenthesis to list types and operations added to the language.

Now we can see how operations are translated into the standard order-theoretic language we advocate in this paper:

$$R_1 \hat{\cup} R_2 \;=\; \max\{t \mid t \in \downarrow R_1 \text{ or } t \in \downarrow R_2\} \;=\; \max \downarrow R_1 \cup \downarrow R_2 \;=\; R_1 \sqcup^{\flat} R_2$$

$$R_1 \hat{\cap} R_2 \;=\; \max \downarrow R_1 \cap \downarrow R_2 \;=\; \max\{r_1 \wedge r_2 \mid r_1 \in R_1, r_2 \in R_2\} \;=\; R_1 \sqcap^{\flat} R_2$$

$$R_1 \hat{-} R_2 \;=\; \max\{t \mid t \in \downarrow R_1 \text{ and } \neg(t \in \downarrow R_2)\} \;=\; R_1 - \downarrow R_2$$

Thus, Zaniolo's union, intersection and difference are order-theoretic analogs of the usual set-theoretic union, intersection and difference. Next we notice that these operations are definable in $\mathcal{NRL}_a$ and hence in $\mathcal{NRL}$ augmented with orderings at base types. We have seen already that max is definable, so we only need the following lemma which is proved by an easy induction and definitions of $\sqcup^{\flat}$ and $\sqcap^{\flat}$.

Lemma 22. *If the least upper bound* $\vee_b : b \times b \to b$ *and the greatest lower bound* $\wedge_b : b \times b \to b$ *are given for any base type* b, *then the least upper bound* $\vee_s : s \times s \to s$ *and the greatest lower bound* $\wedge_s : s \times s \to s$ *are definable in* $\mathcal{NRL}_a$ *for every type* s. □

The last operation of Zaniolo's language is the join (we omit projection and selection as these are standard and of course definable in $\mathcal{NRL}_a$). The join with respect to a set X of attributes was defined as

$$R_1 \bowtie_X R_2 \;:=\; \max\{t_1 \vee t_2 \mid t_1 \hat{\in} R_1, \quad t_2 \hat{\in} R_2, \quad t_1 \text{ and } t_2 \text{ are total on } X\}$$

Without the condition that t_1 and t_2 must be total on X that translates into $\max\{t_1 \vee t_2 \mid t_1 \in R_1, t_2 \in R_2\}$ and hence is definable in $\mathcal{NRL}_a$ by taking cartesian product of R_1 and R_2 and mapping $\vee$ over it. In the case of flat relations, it is also possible to check if the value of a projection is **ni** since **ni** is available as a constant of base types now. Hence, the totality condition can be checked, and since selection is definable, so is $\bowtie_X$. Summing up, we have

Theorem 23. *The language of Zaniolo is a sublanguage of* $\mathcal{NRL}_a$, *and hence* $\mathcal{NRL}$. □

Notice that in the case of model with one null **ni** we do not have to require orderings on base types as these are definable using just equality test.

3.3 Language for sets and or-sets

Proposition 13 gives us the properties of semantic domains of or-set types which are necessary to find the programming primitives. Notice that if no ordering is involved, then structurally or-sets and sets are indistinguishable. Hence, in this case all or-set operations are the same as in the case of sets, and we only add prefix or and change types $\{t\}$ to $\langle t \rangle$. In the case of ordered semantics, it is only the ordering and removal of redundancies that are different. Hence, we shall have analogs of all operations of the set language but the semantics is different: $or\_map_a(f)(\langle x_1, \ldots, x_n \rangle) = \min(\langle f(x_1), \ldots, f(x_n) \rangle)$, $or\_\mu_a(\langle X_1, \ldots, X_n \rangle) = \min(X_1 \cup \ldots \cup X_n)$ and $X \sqcap^! Y = \min(X \cup Y)$.

So far there is no interaction of sets and or-sets present in the language. Since any operator providing such interaction must have source and target types involving both sets and or-sets, theorem 14 suggests what this operator could be. Its type is $\{\langle t \rangle\} \rightarrow \langle \{t\} \rangle$. For the ordered case, it is α_a of theorem 14. For unordered case, it is the following operator α:

$$\alpha(\{\{x^i_j \mid 1 \le j \le k_i\} \mid i = 1, \ldots, n \rangle)$$
$$= \langle \{x^i_{f(i)} \mid i = 1, \ldots, n\} \mid f : \{1, \ldots, n\} \rightarrow \mathbb{N}, \forall i : 1 \le f(i) \le k_i \rangle$$

(or, compactly, $\alpha(\mathcal{X}) = \langle \{x^i_{f(i)} \mid i = 1, \ldots, n\} \mid f \in \mathcal{F}_{\mathcal{X}} \rangle$ using the notation of theorem 14).

Since or-sets are ordered by the Smyth ordering and redundancies are removed by taking minimal elements, we augment the definitions of orderings on complex objects and forcing sets into antichains from the previous section as follows:

- $x \le_{(s)} y \Leftrightarrow x \le^!_s y$ (i.e. $\forall o' \in y \; \exists o \in x : o \le_s o'$)
- $\langle x_1, \ldots, x_n \rangle^{\circ} = \min \langle x_1^{\circ}, \ldots, x_n^{\circ} \rangle$

Definition. *The language or-$\mathcal{NRL}$ is defined as $\mathcal{NRL}$ augmented by the or-set constructs without ordering from figure 8 and α, see [LW96]. The language or-$\mathcal{NRL}_a$ is defined as $\mathcal{NRL}_a$ augmented by the or-set constructs for ordered domains from figure 8 and α_a.*

Some useful properties of or-$\mathcal{NRL}$ and or-$\mathcal{NRL}_a$ are summarized in the theorem below.

Theorem 24. *1. If $\le_b$ is given at any base type b, then $\le_s$ is definable in or-$\mathcal{NRL}_a$ without using $\le_s$ as a primitive.*

2. Under the assumption that $\le_b$ can be tested in $O(1)$ time, the time complexity of verifying $x \le_s y$ is $O(n^2)$, where n is the total size of x and y.

3. or-$\mathcal{NRL}_a$ is a sublanguage of or-$\mathcal{NRL}(\le_b)$.

4. For any two objects x, y of type s, $x \le_s y$ iff $x^{\circ} \le_s y^{\circ}$.

5. For any operator g_a of or-$\mathcal{NRL}_a$ and the corresponding operator g of or-$\mathcal{NRL}$ the following holds: $g_a(x) = g(x)^{\circ}$ whenever x is a legitimate input to g_a (that is, $x = x^{\circ}$).

Or-Set operartions without ordering

$$\overline{or\_\rho_2{}^{s,t} : s \times \langle t \rangle \to \langle s \times t \rangle} \quad \overline{or\_\eta^t : t \to \langle t \rangle} \quad \overline{or\_\cup^t : \langle t \rangle \times \langle t \rangle \to \langle t \rangle}$$

$$\overline{or\_\mu^t : \langle\langle t \rangle\rangle \to \langle t \rangle} \quad \overline{or\_empty^t : unit \to \langle t \rangle} \quad \frac{f : s \to t}{or\_map\ f : \langle s \rangle \to \langle t \rangle}$$

Or-Set operations for ordered domains (given by $\mathcal{P}^!$)

$$\overline{or\_\rho_2{}^{s,t} : s \times \langle t \rangle \to \langle s \times t \rangle} \quad \overline{or\_\eta^t : t \to \langle t \rangle} \quad \overline{\sqcap_t^! : \langle t \rangle \times \langle t \rangle \to \langle t \rangle}$$

$$\overline{or\_\mu_a^t : \langle\langle t \rangle\rangle \to \langle t \rangle} \quad \overline{or\_empty^t : unit \to \langle t \rangle} \quad \frac{f : s \to t}{or\_map_a\ f : \langle s \rangle \to \langle t \rangle}$$

Interaction of sets and or-sets without ordering

$$\overline{\alpha^t : \{\langle t \rangle\} \to \langle\{t\}\rangle}$$

Interaction of sets and or-sets for ordered domains

$$\overline{\alpha_a^t : \{\langle t \rangle\} \to \langle\{t\}\rangle}$$

Fig. 8. Expressions of or-$\mathcal{NRL}$ and or-$\mathcal{NRL}_a$

6. *Any monotone function f definable in or-$\mathcal{NRL}$ agrees with the antichain semantics. If f is not monotone, then $map(f)$ and $or\_map(f)$ do not agree with the antichain semantics.*

7. *It is undecidable whether a function f definable in or-$\mathcal{NRL}$ is monotone.* □

Not let us look at the conceptual semantics $[\![\,]\!]_c$ of the or-set operators of or-$\mathcal{NRL}$ and or-$\mathcal{NRL}_a$.

Theorem 25. *The following equations hold:*

1. $[or\_\mu_a(x)]_c = [x]_c$.

2. $[\alpha_a(x)]_c = [x]_c$.

3. $[or\_\rho_2(x)]_c = [x]_c$.

4. $[x \sqcap^! y]_c = [x]_c \cup [y]_c$.

5. $[or\_map_a(f)(\{x_1, \ldots, x_n\})]_c = [f(x_1)]_c \cup \ldots \cup [f(x_n)]_c$.

Moreover, for or-NRL the same equations hold if finite powerset is used instead of $\mathcal{P}^b(\cdot)$ to give semantics of $\{t\}$. □

The intuition behind the first three equations is that or_μ, or_ρ_2 and α do not change the meaning. Indeed, consider $x = \langle\langle 1, 2\rangle, \langle 2, 3\rangle\rangle$. The meaning of x is an or-set which is either $\langle 1, 2\rangle$ or $\langle 2, 3\rangle$. Hence, x is an integer which is either 1 or 2 or 3. But this is the same as the meaning of $\langle 1, 2, 3\rangle = or\_\mu(x)$. For α, the meaning of $y = \{\langle 1, 2\rangle, \langle 3\rangle\}$ is a set whose first element is 1 or 2 and whose second element is 3. That is, y is either $\{1, 2\}$ or $\{2, 3\}$, and its meaning is the same as that of $\langle\{1, 2\}, \{2, 3\}\rangle = \alpha(y)$.

It was shown in [LW96] that if or_μ, α and or_ρ_2 are repeatedly applied to subobjects of an object x while possible, then a) the process will eventually terminate and b) the result of this process does not depend on the sequence in which those operations were applied to subobjects of x. (As explained in more detail in [Lib95b], it is important that duplicates obtained during this process be retained until the very last application.) The result uniquely determined by such a process is called a *normal form* and denoted by $normalize(x)$. It can be seen that if x has or-sets in it, then the type of $normalize(x)$ is $\langle t \rangle$ where t does not have any or-set brackets. The intuitive meaning of $normalize(x)$ is listing all possibilities encoded by x. Of course this should not change the meaning. Now, with the help of theorem 25 we can formulate this precisely.

Corollary 26. $[normalize(x)]_c = [x]_c$. □

This corollary is formulated for the set theoretic semantics, because existence and well-definedness of *normalize* was proved only for the set semantics in [LW96]. Extending this result in various ways, including antichain semantics, is the subject of a separate paper [Lib95b].

Concluding this section, we give a simple example of applicability of or-NRL to classical problems of incomplete information in relational databases by showing how to use it to solve the membership problem for equational tables.

Example: Membership problem for equational tables in or-NRL Recall that equational tables are relations where variables can be used as well as total values, and each variable may occur more than once. The membership problem is to determine, given an equational table and a relation without variables, if the relation is a possible world for the table. That is, if it is possible to instantiate variables to values such that the table will be instantiated into the given relation. It is known that this problem is $\mathcal{NP}$-complete [AKG91], so we can not hope to give a solution that does not use the expensive α.

For simplicity of exposition, assume that we have a base type b having both variables $x_1, \ldots$ and values $v_1, \ldots$ and that it is possible to distinguish between variables and values. A relation R is an object of type $\{b \times b\}$ such that no variable occurs in it. A table T is also an object of type $\{b \times b\}$ but now variables may occur. It is possible to find the set of all variables that occur in T using the fact that $select$ is defiable in $\mathcal{NRL}$ (cf. [BBW92]):

$$\text{VAR}_T \quad := \quad select(is\_variable) \circ map(\pi_1)(T) \ \cup \ select(is\_variable) \circ map(\pi_2)(T)$$

All values that occur in R can be found as

$$\text{VAL}_R \quad := \quad map(\pi_1)(R) \ \cup \ map(\pi_2)(R)$$

In or-$\mathcal{NRL}$ it is possible to define $powerset_{or} : \{t\} \to \langle\{t\}\rangle$ which lists all subsets of a given set. This is done by first taking a set $\{x_1, \ldots, x_n\}$ and producing a new object $\{\langle\{x_1\}, \{\}\rangle, \ldots, \langle\{x_n\}, \{\}\rangle\}$ and then applying α to it and mapping μ over the result. So, the next step is to compute $powerset_{or}(cartprod(\text{VAR}_T \times \text{VAL}_R))$ and select those sets in it in which every variable from VAR_T occurs exactly once. We denote this resulting object of type $\langle\{b \times b\}\rangle$ by ASSIGN. Each element of ASSIGN can be viewed as an assignment of values to variables, so it can be applied to T in the following sense. For every x in ASSIGN (which is a set of pairs variable-value), we can write a function that substitutes each variable in T by the corresponding value, and then map this function over ASSIGN. The reader is invited to see how such a function can be written in or-$\mathcal{NRL}$.

The resulting object is now X of type $\langle\{b \times b\}\rangle$ which is the or-set of all possible relations that can be obtained from T by using valuation maps whose values are in VAL_R. Therefore, R is a possible world for T if and only if R is a member of X. To verify this, we write $or\_map(\lambda x.eq(x, R))(X)$ and then check if $true$ is in the result. This gives us the membership test.

It is interesting to note that the membership problem for Codd tables, while being of polynomial time complexity, requires solving the bipartite matching problem which can be reformulated as a problem of finding a system of distinct representatives, see [AKG91]. Therefore, the power of $\mathcal{NRL}$ is too limited to solve the membership problem even for Codd tables, because the bipartite matching problem can not be solved in it [Lib94]. However, with the power of α, the language can solve a much more complicated membership for equational tables.

4 New directions

4.1 Traditional constraints and partial information

In this paper we developed type systems and languages for databases with partial information. The next important step will be to accommodate traditional database constraints into the model. Relatively little is known about constraints in relational databases with nulls (see [AM86, Gra91, PDGV89, Tha91, Tha89]) and virtually nothing is known about constraints for other kinds of partial information. To the best of our knowledge, no work has been done on understanding how the ordering interacts with constraints.

There are several possible approaches to the study of interaction of traditional constraints with partial information. Since we advocate the order-theoretic models of databases and consider rather complicated type systems, we believe one should try to apply the approach that formalizes constraints independently of the particular kind of data structures involved. For example, one may use the lattice theoretic approach to dependencies and normalization developed in [DLM92, Day92] or define dependencies as certain classes of first order formulae as in [Fag82].

Another useful idea is to introduce analogs of some constrains for databases with partial information in a "disjunctive" manner [AM86, Tha89]. Following [Tha89], we consider keys. In a usual relational database, a set K of attributes is a key if $\pi_K(t_1) \neq \pi_K(t_2)$ for any two distinct tuples t_1 and t_2. Suppose we have a relational database in which only one kind of nulls, **ni**, is allowed, and the order is given by $\mathbf{ni} \leq v$ for any v. Then a family $\mathcal{K} = \{K_1, \ldots, K_n\}$ of sets of attributes is called a *key set* [Tha89] if for any two distinct tuples t_1 and t_2, there exists a $K_i \in \mathcal{K}$ such that t_1 and t_2 are defined on K_i (that is, none of the K_i-values is **ni**) and $\pi_{K_i}(t_1) \neq \pi_{K_i}(t_2)$. For relations without null values this simply means that $\bigcup \mathcal{K}$ is a key. A key set if minimal if all K_is are singletons. The disjunctive nature of such constraints matches the usual key constrains in the closed world semantics.

Proposition 27. *For any relation R with **ni** null values and a set K of attributes, $\mathcal{K} = \{\{k\} \mid k \in K\}$ is a minimal key set iff $\pi_{K \cap \text{def}(t,t')}(t) = \pi_{K \cap \text{def}(t,t')}(t')$ implies $t = t'$, where $\text{def}(t,t')$ is the set of attributes on which both t and t' are defined. Furthermore, this implies that for any $T \in [R]_{\max}^{\text{CWA}}$ with card $T \leq$ card R, K is a key of T.* $\square$

The converse to the last statement is not true. Consider $R = \{(\mathbf{ni}, 1), (2, 1)\}$. Then for any T as in the statement of the proposition, the first attribute is a key, but it is not a key set for R.

We believe that this idea of making one constraint into a family while maintaining a close connection with the intended semantics can be quite productive. The concept of a key set can be reformulated as $\forall t, t' \ \forall K \in \mathcal{K} : (K \subseteq \mathrm{def}(t, t') \Rightarrow \pi_K(t) = \pi_K(t')) \Rightarrow t = t'$. This in turn implies that $\bigcup \mathcal{K}$ is a key for any $T \in [R]_{\max}^{\mathrm{CWA}}$ and shows that keys can be further generalized to functional dependencies and probably a to greater class of dependencies given in a first order language with equality.

4.2 Recursive types and values

The discussion in this subsection assumes some knowledge of the formal semantics of programming languages. The complex object data model, which was the main object of study in this paper, usually serves as the underlying model for object-oriented databases. But object-oriented databases include more than that. In particular, they often deal with recursive values. In many models recursive values are represented by oids; in practice, these are implemented as pointers. However, the formal semantics of recursive types and values, and in particular recursive types and values in the presence of partial information, must be worked out.

Since semantics of recursive types is usually obtained as a limit construction, this suggests using domains instead of arbitrary posets. Assume that we add a recursive type constructor to the type system:

$$t := x \mid b \mid unit \mid t \times t \mid \{t\} \mid \mu x.t$$

where x ranges over type variables, and $\mu x.t$ is the recursive type constructor (x must be free in t). Since semantics of recursive types is usually obtained as a solution to an equation, which in turn is a (co)limit in some category, we have to switch to categories of domains from categories of posets. A *domain* is a poset in which every directed set has a least upper bound and compact elements form a basis. A compact element is characterized by the property that $c \leq \bigsqcup X$ implies $c \leq x$ for some $x \in X$. Compact elements form a basis of D if for every $x \in D$, $\mathbf{K}_x = \{c \mid c \leq x, c \text{ compact}\}$ is directed and $x = \bigsqcup \mathbf{K}_x$.

It was suggested in [Gun85] that one formulate a number of requirements on the category of domains in which the semantics of types is to be found. In [Gun85] such requirements were formulated for type systems suitable for traditional functional languages, but those do not use the set type constructor. Following [Gun85], let us try to formulate a number of requirements on the category of domains $\mathbf{C}$ in which a semantics of recursive complex object types can be found. First of all, its objects must be closed under $\times$ (product type) and $\wp^{\flat}(\cdot)$ which is $\mathsf{Idl}(\mathcal{P}^{\flat}(\mathbf{K}\cdot))$, the ideal completion of $\mathcal{P}^{\flat}(\mathbf{K}\cdot)$. Second, it must contain the domains of base types (which are usually flat domains or those similar to posets in figure 4). Third, equations of form $D = \mathbb{F}(D)$, where $\mathbb{F}$ is a functor composed from the constant base type functors, products and $\wp^{\flat}(\cdot)$, must have a solution in $\mathbf{C}$. This guarantees that the semantics of recursive types can still be found in $\mathbf{C}$.

Of course a number of categories satisfy these requirements, but most of them contain too many domains that never arise as domains of types. If we interpret compact elements as objects that can actually be stored in a database, then having an object x that can be stored and an object y that is less informative than x, we should be able to store y as well, provided or-sets are not used. That is, there is one additional condition saying that the compact elements must form an ideal, i.e. $\downarrow KD = KD$. Now we call a category of domains that satisfy all these conditions a *database category*.

Proposition 28. *The following are examples of database categories:*
1) C_1, *the category of domains in which there is no infinite chain under any compact element.*
2) C_2, *the category of domains in which the number of elements under any compact element is finite.*
3) Subcategories of C_1 *and* C_2 *in which all ideals are distributive lattices and/or maps are required to preserve compactness.*
4) The category of dI-domains and stable maps (see [Gun92] for the definition).
□

So, we have a number of categories in which semantics of recursive complex object types can be found. But this is not the end of the story, because there are two major issues that must be addressed. First, these conditions are no longer satisfied if we add the or-set type constructor. Second, all recursive database objects have finite representation and could be stored in a database. But we can easily see that they are not necessarily compact elements in the domains of their types. For example, consider $\mu x.string \times x$. Its elements are infinite sequences of strings, and compact elements are those in which almost all entries are $\bot_{string}$. We can think of this type as, for example, *type person = [Name:string, spouse:person]*. Its elements certainly have finite representation, but are not compact elements of the domain of *person*. Therefore, we need to identify elements of the domains which have a finite representation. This identification must be done order-theoretically. Therefore, a proper definition of elements having a finite representation and identification of elements of solutions of recursive domain equations having finite representations remain open problems. We believe that progress towards solving these problems will suggests the right operations to be used for programming with recursive complex objects.

4.3 Bags and partial information

So far we have tacitly assumed that we deal with sets and duplicates are always removed. However, most practical database management systems use bags as the underlying data model. There has been some interest in languages for bags recently [GM93, LW94a, LW94b]. A standard bag language, called BQL or BALG, was obtained. It is supposed to play the same role for bags as (nested) relational algebra plays for set (or complex objects). One can also transfer the results on orderings from sets to bags. To define elementary updates, we should keep in mind that having a bag rather than a set means that each element of a bag represents an object and if there are many occurrences of some element, then at the moment certain objects are indistinguishable.

In view of this, we define updates on bags as follows. First, if b is an element of bag B, and $b \leq b'$, then $B \overset{\text{CWA}}{\rightsquigarrow}$ (and $\overset{\text{OWA}}{\rightsquigarrow}$)$(B - \{|b|\}) \uplus \{|b'|\}$. Here $-$ is bag difference, $\uplus$ is additive union and $\{|\ |\}$ are bag brackets. In the case of OWA we also add $B \overset{\text{OWA}}{\rightsquigarrow} B \uplus \{|b|\}$. Transitive closures of these relations are denoted by $\unlhd^{\text{CWA}}$ and $\unlhd^{\text{OWA}}$. It was shown by the author how to describe $\unlhd^{\text{CWA}}$ and $\unlhd^{\text{OWA}}$ algorithmically. For a finite bag B and an injective map $\phi : B \to \mathbb{N}$, also called *labeling*, by $\phi(B)$ we denote the set $\{(b, \phi(b)) \mid b \in B\}$. In other words, ϕ assigns a unique label to each element of a bag. If B is a finite bag of elements of a poset, then the ordering on pairs (b, n) where $b \in B$ and $n \in \mathbb{N}$ is the following: $(b, n) \leq (b', n')$ iff $b \leq b'$ and $n = n'$.

Proposition 29. (see also [LW95]) *The binary relations $\unlhd^{\text{CWA}}$ and $\unlhd^{\text{OWA}}$ on bags are partial orders. Given two bags B_1 and B_2, $B_1 \unlhd^{\text{CWA}} B_2$ ($B_1 \unlhd^{\text{OWA}} B_2$) iff there exist labelings ϕ and ψ on B_1 and B_2 respectively such that $\phi(B_1) \sqsubseteq^\natural \psi(B_2)$ (respectively $\phi(B_1) \sqsubseteq^\flat \psi(B_2)$).* □

That is, the correspondence between OWA and the Hoare ordering and CWA and the Plotkin ordering continues to hold.

We saw that that $\sqsubseteq^\natural$ and $\sqsubseteq^\flat$ are definable in our basic set language $\mathcal{NRL}$. However, for bags the situation is different. It was shown in [LW95] that neither $\unlhd^{\text{CWA}}$ nor $\unlhd^{\text{OWA}}$ is definable in the basic bag language BQL. Hence, any implementation of a bag language that supports incomplete information must provide orderings at all types, as these can not be lifted from base types if powerful primitives like fixpoints are not used.

4.4 Language implementation

The core language for sets and or-sets has been implemented as a library of modules in Standard ML, see [GL94]. It was useful in several application such as querying incomplete design databases, or querying independent databases to obtain approximate answers. We believe that in the future implementations several changes must be made. For example, an algebraic syntax of or-$\mathcal{NRL}$, which is reflected by the syntax of OR-SML, should be changed to a more user friendly syntax, such as comprehensions [BLS+94]. This poses a few problems, such as incorporating normalization of disjunctive objects into the comprehension syntax. It is also important that a user be able to add any collection of null values to any preexisting type and define orderings on them. Currently this is possible only with user-defined new types. Finally, it would be interesting to see if using partial information leads to any new optimizations.

Acknowledgements. This paper is based on the results from my handwritten notes from 1992-1994, and a few results from two conference papers (the conference version of [LW96], that appeared in PODS'93, and [LW94b]). Most results can also be found in my thesis [Lib94]. While working on those notes and papers, I had numerous opportunities to discuss the results with a number of people, and the feedback I received from them was very helpful. I would like to thank Peter Buneman, Carl Gunter, Elsa Gunter, Achim Jung, Paris Kanellakis, Val Tannen, Victor Vianu and Limsoon Wong. I am also grateful to anonymous referees for helpful comments.

References

[AB86]   S. Abiteboul and N. Bidoit. Non-first normal form relations: An algebra allowing data restructuring. *Journal of Computer and System Sciences*, 33(3):361–371, 1986.

[AKG91] S. Abiteboul, P. Kanellakis, and G. Grahne. On the representation and querying of sets of possible worlds. *Theoretical Computer Science*, 78:159–187, 1991.

[AM86]   P. Atzeni and N. Morfuni. Functional dependencies and constraints on null values in database relations. *Information and Control*, 70(1):1-31, July 1986.

[BBW92] V. Breazu-Tannen, P. Buneman, and L. Wong. Naturally embedded query languages. In J. Biskup and R. Hull, editors, *LNCS 646: Proceedings of 4th International Conference on Database Theory, Berlin, Germany, October, 1992*, pages 140–154. Springer-Verlag, October 1992.

[BDW91] P. Buneman, S. Davidson, and A. Watters. A semantics for complex objects and approximate answers. *Journal of Computer and System Sciences*, 43(1):170–218, August 1991.

[Bis81] J. Biskup. A formal approach to null values in database relations. In *Advances in Data Base Theory: Volume 1*. Plenum Press, New York, 1981.

[BLS+94] P. Buneman, L. Libkin, D. Suciu, V. Tannen, and L. Wong. Comprehension syntax. *SIGMOD Record*, 23(1):87–96, March 1994.

[BJO91] P. Buneman, A. Jung and A. Ohori. Using powerdomains to generalize relational databases. *Theoretical Computer Science*, 91:23–55, 1991.

[BBN91] V. Breazu-Tannen, P. Buneman, and S. Naqvi. Structural recursion as a query language. In *Proceedings of 3rd International Workshop on Database Programming Languages, Naphlion, Greece*, pages 9–19. Morgan Kaufmann, August 1991.

[BTS91] V. Breazu-Tannen and R. Subrahmanyam. Logical and computational aspects of programming with Sets/Bags/Lists. In *LNCS 510: Proceedings of 18th International Colloquium on Automata, Languages, and Programming, Madrid, Spain, July 1991*, pages 60–75. Springer Verlag, 1991.

[BW90]   M. Barr and C. Wells. *Category Theory for Computing Science*. Series in Computer Science. Prentice Hall International, New York, 1990.

[Car88]   L. Cardelli. Types for data-oriented languages. In J. W. Schmidt, S. Ceri, and M. Missikoff, editors, *LNCS 303: Advances in Database Technology — International Conference on Extending Database Technology, Venice, Italy, March 1988*. Springer-Verlag, 1988.

[Cod75]   E. F. Codd. Understanding relations. *Bulletin of ACM SIGMOD*, pages 23–28, 1975.

[Cod79]   E. F. Codd. Extending the database relational model to capture more meaning. *ACM Transactions on Database Systems*, 4(4):397–434, December 1979.

[Col90]   L. S. Colby. A recursive algebra for nested relations. *Information Systems*, 15(5):567–582, 1990.

[Day92]   A. Day, The lattice theory of functional dependencies and normal decompositions. *Intern. J. of Algebra and Computation*, 2:409–431, 1992.

[DLM92]   J. Demetrovics, L. Libkin and I. Muchnik. Functional dependencies in relational databases : a lattice point of view. *Discrete Applied Mathematics*, 40:155–185, 1992.

[Fag82]   R. Fagin. Horn clauses and database dependencies. *Journal of ACM*, 29:952–985, 1982.

[GL94]   E. Gunter and L. Libkin, OR-SML: A functional database programming language for disjunctive information and its applications. In D. Karagiannis, ed., *LNCS 856: Proceedings of Conference on Database and Expert Systems Applications, Athens, 1994*, Springer Verlag, 1994, pages 841–850.

[GM93]   S. Grumbach and T. Milo. Towards tractable algebras for bags. *Proceedings of the 12th Conference on Principles of Database Systems*, Washington DC, 1993, pages 49–58.

[Gra77]   J. Grant. Null values in relational databases. *Information Processing Letters*, 6:156–157, 1977.

[Gra91]   G. Grahne. *The Problem of Incomplete Information in Relational Databases*. Springer-Verlag, Berlin, 1991.

[Gun85]   C. Gunter. Comparing categories of domains. In *"Mathematical Foundations of Programming Semantics"* (A. Melton ed), Springer Lecture Notes in Computer Science, vol. 239, Springer, Berlin, 1985, pages 101–121.

[Gun92]   C. Gunter. *Semantics of Programming Languages: Structures and Techniques*. Foundations of Computing. MIT Press, 1992.

[GZ88]   G. Gottlob and R. Zicari. Closed world databases opened through null values. In *Proceedings of Very Large Databases*, pages 50–61, Cambridge, Massachusetts, 1988.

[IL84]   T. Imielinski and W. Lipski. Incomplete information in relational databases. *Journal of the ACM*, 31:761–791, October 1984.

[INV91a]   T. Imielinski, S. Naqvi, and K. Vadaparty. Incomplete objects — a data model for design and planning applications. In J. Clifford and R. King, editors, *Proceedings of ACM-SIGMOD International Conference on Management of Data, Denver, Colorado, May 1991*, pages 288–297. ACM Press, 1991.

[INV91b]   T. Imielinski, S. Naqvi, and K. Vadaparty. Querying design and planning databases. In C. Delobel, M. Kifer, and Y. Masunaga, editors, *LNCS 566: Deductive and Object Oriented Databases*, pages 524–545, Berlin, 1991. Springer-Verlag.

[JLP92]   A. Jung, L. Libkin, and H. Puhlmann. Decomposition of domains. In *LNCS 598: Proceedings of 1991 Conference on Mathematical Foundations of Programming Semantics*, pages 235–258, Berlin, 1992. Springer-Verlag.

[Kan90] P. Kanellakis. Elements of relational database theory. In *Handbook of Theoretical Computer Science, Volume B*, pages 1075–1156. North Holland, 1990.

[Lib91] L. Libkin. A relational algebra for complex objects based on partial information. In J. Demetrovics and B. Thalheim, editors, *LNCS 495: Proceedings of Symposium on Mathematical Fundamentals of Database Systems, Rostock, 1991*, pages 36–41. Springer-Verlag, 1991.

[Lib92] L. Libkin. An elementary proof that upper and lower powerdomain constructions commute. *Bulletin of the EATCS*, 48:175–177, 1992.

[Lib94] L. Libkin. *Aspects of Partial Information in Databases*. PhD thesis, Department of Computer and Information Science, University of Pennsylvania, 1994.

[Lib95a] L. Libkin. Approximation in databases. In G. Gottlob and M. Vardi, editors, *LNCS 893: Proceedings of International Conference on Database Theory, Prague, 1995*, pages 411–424. Springer-Verlag, 1995. Full version to appear in *Theoretical Computer Science*.

[Lib95b] L. Libkin. Normalizing incomplete databases. In *Proceedings of 14th ACM Symposium on Principles of Database Systems*, pages 219–230, San Jose, CA, May 1995.

[Lip79] W. Lipski. On semantic issues connected with incomplete information databases. *ACM Transactions on Database Systems*, 4(3):262–296, September 1979.

[Lip81] W. Lipski. On databases with incomplete information. *Journal of ACM*, 28:41–70, 1981.

[LL86] N. Lerat and W. Lipski. Nonapplicable nulls. *Theoretical Computer Science*, 46:67–82, 1986.

[LL90] M. Levene and G. Loizou. The nested relation type model: An application of domain theory to databases. *The Computer Journal*, 33:19–30, 1990.

[LL91] M. Levene and G. Loizou. Correction to "Null values in nested relational databases" by M. A. Roth, H. F. Korth, and A. Silberschatz. *Acta Informatica*, 28:603–605, 1991.

[LL93] M. Levene and G. Loizou. A fully precise null extended nested relational algebra. *Fundamenta Informaticae*, 19:303–343, 1993.

[LW94a] L. Libkin and L. Wong. New techniques for studying set languages, bag languages, and aggregate functions. In *Proceedings of 13th ACM Symposium on Principles of Database Systems*, pages 155–166, Minneapolis, Minnesota, May 1994. Full version to appear in *Journal of Computer and System Sciences*.

[LW94b] L. Libkin and L. Wong. Some properties of query languages for bags. In C. Beeri, A. Ohori, and D. Shasha, editors, *Proceedings of 4th International Workshop on Database Programming Languages, New York, August 1993*, pages 97–114. Springer-Verlag, January 1994.

[LW94c] L. Libkin and L. Wong. Conservativity of nested relational calculi with internal generic functions. *Information Processing Letters*, 49:273–280, 1994.

[LW95] L. Libkin and L. Wong. On representation and querying incomplete information in databases with bags. *Information Processing Letters*, 56:209–214, 1995.

[LW96] L. Libkin and L. Wong. Semantic representations and query languages for or-sets. *Journal of Computer and System Sciences*, 52(1):125–142, 1996.

[Oho90] A. Ohori. Semantics of types for database objects. *Theoretical Computer Science*, 76(1):53–91, 1990.

[PDGV89] J. Paredaens, P. De Bra, M. Gyssens and D. Van Gucht, *"The Structure of the Relational Data Model"*, Springer, Berlin, 1989.

[Plo76] G. D. Plotkin. A powerdomain construction. *SIAM Journal of Computing*, 5, September 1976.

[PS93] A. Poulovassilis and C. Small. A domain theoretic approach to integrating functional and logical database languages. In *Proceedings of VLBD*, pages 416–428, 1993.

[Rei78] R. Reiter. On closed world databases. In H. Gallaire and J. Minker, editors, *Logic and Databases*. Plenum Press, 1978.

[RKS89] M. A. Roth, H. F. Korth, and A. Silberschatz. Null values in nested relational databases. *Acta Informatica*, 26(7):615–642, 1989.

[Smy78] M. B. Smyth. Power domains. *Journal of Computer and System Sciences*, 16(1):23–36, 1978.

[SP94] D. Suciu and J. Paredaens. Any algorithm in the complex object algebra needs exponential space to compute transitive closure. In *Proceedings of 13th ACM Symposium on Principles of Database Systems*, pages 201–209, Minneapolis, Minnesota, May 1994.

[SS86] H.-J. Schek and M. H. Scholl. The relational model with relation-valued attributes. *Information Systems*, 11(2):137–147, 1986.

[Suc94] D. Suciu. Fixpoints and bounded fixpoints for complex objects. In C. Beeri, A. Ohori, and D. Shasha, editors, *Proceedings of 4th International Workshop on Database Programming Languages, New York, August 1993*, pages 263–281. Springer-Verlag, January 1994.

[Tha89] B. Thalheim. On semantic issues connected with keys in relational databases permitting null values. *J. Inf. Process. and Cybernet.*, 25(1/2):11–20, 1989.

[Tha91] B. Thalheim. *"Dependencies in Relational Databases"*, Teubner-Texte zur Mathematik, Band 126, Stuttgart-Leipzig, 1991.

[TF86] S. J. Thomas and P. C. Fischer. Nested relational structures. In P. C. Kanellakis and F. P. Preparata, editors, *Advances in Computing Research: The Theory of Databases*, pages 269–307, London, England, 1986. JAI Press.

[Var86] M. Y. Vardi. On the integrity of databases with incomplete information. In *Proceedings of 5th ACM Symposium on Principles of Database Systems*, pages 252–266, 1986.

[Vas79] Y. Vassiliou. Null values in database management – a denotational semantics approach. In *Proceedings of SIGMOD*, 1979.

[Zan84] C. Zaniolo. Database relation with null values. *Journal of Computer and System Sciences*, 28(1):142–166, 1984.

Constraint Databases: A Survey[*]

Peter Z. Revesz
Department of Computer Science and Engineering
University of Nebraska–Lincoln
revesz@cse.unl.edu

Abstract. Constraint databases generalize relational databases by finitely representable infinite relations. This paper surveys the state of the art in constraint databases: known results, remaining open problems and current research directions. The paper also describes a new algebra for databases with integer order constraints and a complexity analysis of evaluating queries in this algebra.

In memory of Paris C. Kanellakis

1 Introduction

There is a growing interest in recent years among database researchers in constraint databases, which are a generalization of relational databases by finitely representable infinite relations. Constraint databases are parametrized by the type of constraint domains and constraint used. The good news is that for many parameters constraint databases leave intact most of the fundamental assumptions of the relational database framework proposed by Codd. In particular,

1. Constraint databases can be queried by constraint query languages that
   (a) have a semantics based on first-order or fixpoint logics with constraints.
   (b) can be evaluated in closed-form.
   (c) can be algebraic and (efficiently) evaluated set-at-a-time.
2. Constraint databases can be efficiently indexed.
3. Integrity constraints can be enforced on constraint databases.
4. Aggregate operators can be applied to constraint databases.
5. Constraint databases can be extended with indefinite information.
6. Constraint databases can be extended with sets, nesting and complex objects.

---

[*] This work was supported by NSF grants IRI-9625055, IRI-9632871 and by a Gallup Research Professorship.

This survey will emphasize points 1(b) and 1(c), and give extensive references for points 2-6. For point 1(a) one can find several good books on first-order logic, for example [53], or good surveys on constraint logic programming and fixpoint semantics [42, 75, 153, 154]. There are also good introductions to logic programming (without constraints) in [10, 50, 101] and to database query languages (also without constraints) in [3, 79, 149]. One can also find an earlier tutorial on constraint databases in [80], and an applications-oriented survey in [61].

Points 1(b) and 1(c) will be illustrated by a new algebra for constraint databases with integer order constraints. It also analyses the computational complexity of evaluating relational calculus queries with integer order constraints.

The survey is organized as follows. Section 2 reviews first-order theories. Section 3 reviews relational databases and query languages. This section contains a comparison between relational databases and logic programming. Section 4 reviews constraint databases and query languages. This section contains a comparison of constraint databases and constraint logic programming. Section 5 summarizes known complexity results. Section 6 lists results on expressive power of languages. Section 7 discusses various semantic extensions of constraint databases. Section 8 mentions some prototype constraint database systems. Finally Section 8 lists some outstanding open problems.

2 First-Order Theories

2.1 Predicate Calculus

First we define the *first-order predicate calculus* language. The *alphabet* of this language consists of the following:

- A countably infinite set of variables. We usually denote variables by $x, y, z, v, u, \ldots$
- A countably infinite set δ of constants. We usually denote constants by $a, b, c, \ldots$. The domain of each variable is δ.
- A set $\mathcal{R}$ of relation symbols. We usually denote relation symbols by $P, Q, R, \ldots$.
- Connectives $\wedge$ (conjunction), $\vee$ (disjunction), $\neg$ (negation).
- Quantifiers, $\exists$ (there exists) and $\forall$ (for all).

It is usual in the literature to restrict consideration in the definitions and proofs only to the connectives $\neg, \wedge$ and the quantifier $\exists$ because using only these all the others can be expressed. It is also possible to express implication $\rightarrow$ and double implication $\leftrightarrow$ using only those connectives.

Each relation symbol R has a fixed *arity*, that is, number of arguments. We denote the arity of R by $\alpha(R)$. 0-ary relations are permitted.

We define *predicate calculus formulas*, abbreviated PC formulas, inductively as follows:

- If R is an n-ary relation symbol and $x_1, \ldots, x_n$ are variables or constants, then $R(x_1, \ldots, x_n)$ is a PC formula.
- If ϕ is an PC formula, then $\neg\phi$ is an PC formula.
- If ϕ_1 and ϕ_2 are PC formulas, then $\phi_1 \wedge \phi_2$ and $\phi_1 \vee \phi_2$ are PC formulas.
- If ϕ is a PC formula and x is a variable, then $\exists x(\phi)$ and $\forall x(\phi)$ are PC formulas.

In the last line of the above definition, we call each occurrence of variable x within ϕ a *bound* variable. Variables that are not bound are called *free* in a formula.

One of the older problems that was considered by logicians is to decide whether a given predicate calculus formula is satisfiable, that is, whether there are relations that can be assigned to the relation symbols within the formula so that the formula becomes true. Another problem of interest in the area of theorem proving is whether all possible assignments make the formula true. Formulas with this property are called valid.

It was shown by Church that whether an unrestricted (both finite and infinite assignments are permitted) predicate calculus sentence (formula without free variables) is valid is undecidable. More precisely, the set of valid sentences is r.e. (recursively enumerable) but not co-r.e. Even if we restrict all relations to be finite, the problem remains undecidable. Here the set of valid sentences is co-r.e. and not in r.e. [140]. The satisfiability problem is also undecidable because a formula is satisfiable if and only if its negation is not valid. These negative results imply that there is no hope of using first-order predicate calculus as a query language. Fortunately, satisfiability can be solved for many subsets of the predicate calculus described later in the survey.

2.2 First Order Theories with Constraints

In this survey by constraints we mean special named relations. For example, let's suppose that our domain is the set of integers. Then the equality constraint $=$ means the infinite binary relation $\{(i, i) : i \in \mathbf{Z}\}$. (In the paper we use $\mathbf{R}$ for reals, $\mathbf{Q}$ for rationals, $\mathbf{N}$ for natural numbers, and $\mathbf{Z}$ for integers.) Similarly, the addition constraint $+$ means the infinite ternary relation such that the sum of the first two arguments is equal to the third argument. In the following we will keep using the usual infix notation for common constraints.

By first-order theories with constraints we mean various subsets of first-order predicate calculus in which the only relations are constraints. In these theories there is only one assignment of interest: for each constraint symbol the corresponding constraint relation is assigned.

During the past hundred years many quantifier elimination procedures were developed for various first-order theories with constraints. By quantifier elimination we mean rewriting a formula with quantifiers into an equivalent one without quantifiers. It is out of the scope of this survey to review quantifier elimination procedures. However, we give a chronological outline of the major results in this area.

Some works considered only existentially quantified formulas. In the following table we indicate this as ∃QE. (For example, we mark as ∃QE Fourier's method even though it can be easily extended to deal with universal quantifiers.) It should be remembered that the following is only a partial list.

1828: ∃QE for $Th(\mathbf{R}, <, +)$ by Fourier [58].
1856: ∃QE for boolean algebras by Boole.
1927: QE for $Th(\mathbf{Q}, <)$ by Langford [99].
1929: QE for $Th(\mathbf{Z}, <, +)$ by Presburger [113].
1931: no QE for $Th(\mathbf{Z}, +, *)$ by Gödel [62].
1951: QE for $Th(\mathbf{R}, <, +, *)$ by Tarski [141].
1970: no ∃QE for $Th(\mathbf{Z}, +, *)$ by Matiyasevich [104].
1976: ∃QE for integers with modulus constraints by Williams [157].
1982: no QE for $Th(\mathbf{R}, +, *, exp)$ by van den Dries [150].

The decision problem is the problem of identifying whether a first-order formula without free variables is true or false. It is clear that the elimination of all quantifiers from a formula without free variables should leave as value either true or false. Hence the decision problem reduces to the quantifier elimination problem. Most negative results for quantifier elimination follow via reduction from the undecidability of the decision problem for the corresponding theories.

3 Relational Databases and Query Languages

3.1 Relational Databases and Their Problems

It is well-known that the relational data model enjoys great success in the business world. However, the causes of its success are less well-known. Sometimes it is wrongly assumed that its success is solely due to being based on logic. In reality the relational data model provides solutions to many practical problems that more complex logics often do not solve. Let's see some of these problems.

In the information market there are three important problems that databases need to solve.

1. **Ad-Hoc User's Problem:** Many database users want to enter ad-hoc queries that they improvise on-the-fly. They also want answers to every syntactically correct ad-hoc query.

2. **Application Vendor's Problem:** Application vendors sell libraries of queries to users. Application vendors must guarantee termination of the queries on each valid database input. In theory they may use any programming language for writing queries. However, guaranteeing termination is difficult in many programming languages. Hence they also want a restricted language in which any query they write terminates.

3. **Data Vendor's Problem:** Data vendors buy raw data in the form of databases and produce refined data in the form of databases which they sell to other data vendors. In the information market, there is often a long chain of data vendors from raw data to the users. The data model must serve as a common data communication standard. Each data vendor uses queries to transform raw data to the data product. Often these queries are secret or patented.

By looking at the context of how database systems are used in practice we can see that two important requirements have to be met. First, each query must terminate. Second, each query must give as output a database. We might call these the termination and the constructibility requirements.

Both of the above requirements are satisfied in the relational data model [41, 3, 79, 149], which is illustrated in Figure 1. Each relational database is a finite set of tables. Each table is an abstract data type and is a relation containing a finite set of tuples. A requirement in the relational data model is that queries be evaluable functions from finite databases to finite databases. That requirement is met by three relational query languages that we review in the next three subsection: (1) Relational Calculus, (2) Datalog, and (3) Stratified Datalog.

Fig. 1. The Relational Data Model

3.2 Relational Calculus

Syntactically relational calculus and predicate calculus are the same. However, in relational calculus –like in first-order theories with constraints– we are interested in only one assignment to the relations. We assign to each relation symbol an input relation given by the user.

The semantics of any relational calculus query ϕ is a mapping from relational databases to relational databases. Let $x_1, \ldots, x_n$ be the set of free variables of ϕ in some fixed order and let $\phi(a_1, \ldots, a_n)$ denote the formula obtained by substituting a_i for x_i for each $1 \leq i \leq n$.

Each input database d is an assignment of a finite or infinite number of tuples over $\delta^{\alpha(R_i)}$ to each R_i. The output database is a single relation of arity n defined as $\{(a_1, \ldots, a_n) :< \delta, d > \models \phi(a_1, \ldots, a_n)\}$. Here $< \delta, d > \models$ means *satisfaction* with respect to a domain δ and database d and is defined as follows. If r_i is the set of tuples assigned to relation symbol R_i, then

$$< \delta, d > \models R_i(a_1, \ldots, a_k) \text{ iff } (a_1, \ldots, a_k) \in r_i \tag{1}$$
$$< \delta, d > \models (\phi \wedge \psi) \text{ iff } < \delta, d > \models \phi \text{ and } < \delta, d > \models \psi \tag{2}$$
$$< \delta, d > \models (\neg \phi) \text{ iff not } < \delta, d > \models \phi \tag{3}$$
$$< \delta, d > \models (\exists x_i \phi) \text{ iff } < \delta, d > \models \phi[x_i/a_j] \text{ for some } a_j \in \delta \tag{4}$$

where $[x_i/a_j]$ means the instantiation of the free variable x_i by a_j.

Remark: Unfortunately, not all relational calculus queries preserve finiteness. For example, if r is any finite unary relation assigned to relation symbol R and δ is any infinite domain, then the query $\{(a) :< \delta, r > \models \neg R(a)\}$ defines an infinite relation. There are several approaches to guarantee finiteness by syntactically restricting relational calculus queries to various "safe" subsets [13, 72, 86, 149]. Safe relational calculus queries are translatable to relational algebra, a procedural language.

3.3 Datalog

Datalog [3, 11, 50, 101, 149] is a fragment of predicate calculus extending relational calculus with intensionally defined relations. In relational calculus each query defines a single output relation which is not named explicitly and all other relations are inputs. In contrast in Datalog a query may define several output relations which are referred to by name within the query. Hence in Datalog the output relations are defined using references to themselves.

Syntactically a *Datalog* program Π is a finite set of rules of the form:

$$R_0(x_1, \ldots, x_k) :\!- R_1(x_{1,1}, \ldots, x_{1,k_1}), \ldots, R_n(x_{n,1}, \ldots, x_{n,k_n}).$$

where the Rs are relation symbols and the xs are either variables or constants.

Semantically each Datalog program is a mapping. To explain this mapping, we first associate with each rule of the above form the formula:

$$\forall v_1 \ldots \forall v_m (R_0(x_1, \ldots, x_k) \vee \neg R_1(x_{1,1}, \ldots, x_{1,k_1}) \vee \ldots \vee \neg R_n(x_{n,1}, \ldots, x_{n,k_n}))$$

where $v_1, \ldots, v_m$ are the variables in the rule. We also associate with Π the conjunction of the formulas associated with each rule in Π. Let F_Π denote this formula.

We call *extensional database relations*, or EDBs, those relations whose symbol occurs only on the right hand side of rules. We call the other relation symbols the *intensional database relations*, or IDBs. In each Datalog query the EDBs are the input relations assigned by the user and the IDBs are the output relations to which assignments are sought. The EDBS and IDBs are disjoint in each Datalog program.

We call an *interpretation* of Π any assignment I of a finite or infinite number of tuples over $\delta^{\alpha(R_i)}$ to each R_i that occurs in Π. A *model* of Π is an interpretation of Π satisfying F_Π. A model I is a *minimum model* if and only if $I \subseteq J$ for all models J.

We call an interpretation an *input database* if it assigns to each R_i that occurs at least once on the left hand side of a rule in Π the empty set of tuples.

Each Datalog program Π is a mapping from input databases to interpretations. Let d be an input database. Then the output of Π on d, denoted $\Pi(d)$, is the minimum model of Π containing d. The following theorem assures us that we really have a mapping.

Proposition 3.1 Let Π be any Datalog program and d be any input database. Then there exists a minimum model of Π containing d. $\Box$

Alternative Operational Semantics An important alternative definition of the semantics of Datalog programs is called *fixpoint* semantics.

We call *valuation* any function from (tuples of) variables to (tuples of) constants satisfying the following: for all tuples t_1 and t_2, $\nu(t1, t2) = (\nu(t_1), \nu(t_2))$, and for all constants c, $\nu(c) = c$.

The *immediate consequence operator* of a Datalog program Π, denoted T_Π, is a mapping from interpretations to interpretations as follows. For each interpretation I:

$R_0(a_1, \ldots, a_n) \in T_P(I)$ iff there is a valuation ν and a rule of the form $R_0(x_1, \ldots, x_k) :\!- R_1(x_{1,1}, \ldots, x_{1,k_1}), \ldots, R_n(x_{n,1}, \ldots, x_{n,k_n})$ in Π such that $\nu(x_1, \ldots, x_n) = (a_1, \ldots, a_n)$ and $< \delta, d >\models R_i(\nu(x_{i,1}, \ldots, x_{i,k_i}))$ for each $1 \leq i \leq n$.

An interpretation I is called a *fixpoint* of a program Π iff $T_\Pi(I) = I$.

Proposition 3.2 Let Π be any Datalog program and d be any input database. Each fixpoint of Π is a model of F_Π. Moreover, there is a minimum fixpoint of Π containing d. $\square$

The following states that the model-theoretic and the fixpoint semantics coincide.

Proposition 3.3 Let Π be any Datalog program and d be any input database. The minimum fixpoint of Π containing d equals $\Pi(d)$. $\square$

3.4 Stratified Datalog

Stratified Datalog [3, 50, 149] extends Datalog with negation. Intuitively, an expression like $R_0 :\!- R_1 \wedge \neg R_2$ means that R_0 is the set difference of the relations R_1 and R_2. The problem is that to say anything definite about R_0 we must know the full value of the negated relation. That motivates the following definitions.

We call *semipositive* those Datalog programs with negation that only allow negation of EDBs. (See [3, 50] for more discussion.)

Semantically, each semipositive Datalog program is a mapping from databases to interpretations. We can define F_Π similarly to the case of Datalog. We have that:

Proposition 3.4 Let Π be any semipositive Datalog program and d be any input database that assigns non-empty relations only to the EDBs. Then there exists a minimum model of Π containing d. $\square$

Another extension of Datalog is the class of *stratified Datalog* programs. Each stratified Datalog program Π is the union of semipositive programs $\Pi_1, \ldots, \Pi_k$ satisfying the following property: no relation symbol R that occurs negated in a Π_i is an IDB in any Π_j with $j \geq i$.

It is usual to associate with each stratified Datalog program Π a function σ from rules to positive integers. The function σ indicates the grouping of the rules into semipositive programs in an order that satisfies the above property. We will assume that a σ is associated with each stratified Datalog program.

Each stratified Datalog program is a mapping from databases to interpretations. In particular, if Π is the union of the semipositive programs $\Pi_1, \ldots, \Pi_k$ with the above property, then the composition $\Pi_k(\ldots \Pi_1() \ldots)$ is its semantics.

Proposition 3.5 Let Π be any stratified Datalog program consisting of the union of some semipositive programs $\Pi_1, \ldots, \Pi_k$ with the above property. Let d be any database that assigns non-empty relations only to the EDBs of Π_1. Then there exists a minimum model of Π containing d. $\Box$

Remark: An explicit specification of σ is not required. [12] describes an algorithm to find a σ satisfying the above property. Moreover, [12] also shows that all σ's satisfying the above property are semantically equivalent.

Remark 2: Datalog programs with negation on the right hand side of the rules can be assigned an *inflationary* semantics [4, 64, 89]. This semantics is not equivalent to the one given here and seems less frequently used.

3.5 Relational Databases vs. Logic Programming

It is not our goal here to review logic programming [52, 11], which has known similarities with relational database queries. We would like only to point out some essential differences between these two concepts.

Each logic program is a mapping from a finite set of facts to a least model. Logic programs do not always terminate and least models are not always a finite set of facts. Therefore, logic programs do not satisfy the termination and constructibility requirements, which as we saw are crucial problems in databases.

Every relational query can be expressed as a logic program, but the reverse is not true. Unfortunately, from the database point of view the higher expressive power of logic programs is at the expense of some practicality. The following is a brief historical summary of the developments in the two areas, based on [10]:

1970: Relational Algebra proposed by Codd [41].
1972: Relational Calculus shown equivalent to Relational Algebra by Codd.
1973-74: Prolog by Colmerauer, Kanoui, and Van Caneghem [44] and Kowalski.
1976: Fixpoint Semantics for Prolog by Van Emden and Kowalski.
1979-80: Datalog by Aho and Ullman [7] and Chandra and Harel [31].
1985-88: Stratified Datalog by Chandra and Harel [33] and Prolog by Apt, Blair and Walker [12].

4 Constraint Databases and Query Languages

Constraint programming, or programming with constraints as primitives in the programming language, was first investigated in the early 1960's by Sutherland in the SKETCHPAD system [139]. Since then constraint programming was applied to various problems in artificial intelligence [60, 102, 105, 135], graphical-interfaces [22, 131], and in logic programming and databases. We review only the developments in the latter two areas, and even in logic programming we mention only on those developments that have a relationship to databases. The reader may find detailed surveys on constraint logic programming in [42, 75, 96, 153, 154].

4.1 Constraint Databases and Their Problems

Many database applications have to deal with infinite concepts like time and space. However, in practice only those databases can be used which can be finitely represented. Fortunately, many infinite data can be finitely represented using constraint databases. A general framework for using constraint databases is presented in [82]. The following three definitions are from that paper.

A *generalized k-tuple* is a quantifier-free conjunction of constraints on k variables ranging over a domain δ. Each generalized k tuple represents in a finite way an infinite set of regular k-tuples. For example, suppose that relation R contains the set of points on the line that passes through the origin and has slope two. While R has in it an infinite number of tuples, it can be finitely represented by the generalized 2-tuple $R(x, y) :- y = 2 * x$.

A *generalized relation of arity* k is a finite set of generalized k-tuples, with each k-tuple over the same variables.

A *generalized database* is a finite set of generalized relations.

If we use generalized databases, then all the definitions of query language semantics still apply except that we have to also generalize the meaning of $\models$. That can be done as follows.

Let r_i be the generalized relation assigned to R_i. We associate with each r_i a formula F_{r_i} that is the disjunction of the formulas on the right hand side of each generalized k-tuple of r_i. Let ϕ be any relational calculus formula. Satisfaction with respect to a domain δ and database d, denoted $< \delta, d > \models$, is defined recursively as follows:

$$< \delta, d > \models R_i(a_1, \ldots, a_k) \text{ iff } F_{r_i}(a_1, \ldots, a_k) \text{ is true} \tag{5}$$

$$< \delta, d > \models (\phi \wedge \psi) \text{ iff } < \delta, d > \models \phi \text{ and } < \delta, d > \models \psi \qquad (6)$$
$$< \delta, d > \models (\neg \phi) \text{ iff not } < \delta, d > \models \phi \qquad (7)$$
$$< \delta, d > \models (\exists x_i \phi) \text{ iff } < \delta, d > \models \phi[x_i/a_j] \text{ for some } a_j \in \delta \qquad (8)$$

The following alternative semantics that is equivalent to the above is discussed in [82]:

Let $\phi = \phi(x_1, \ldots, x_m)$ be a relational calculus program with free variables $x_1, \ldots, x_m$. Let relation symbols $R_1, \ldots, R_n$ in ϕ be assigned the generalized relations $r_1, \ldots, r_n$ respectively. Let $\phi[R_1/F_{r_1}, \ldots, R_n/F_{r_n}]$ be the formula that is obtained by replacing in ϕ each database atom $R_i(z_1, \ldots, z_k)$ by the formula $F_{r_i}[x_1/z_1, \ldots, x_k/z_k]$ where $F_{r_i}(x_1, \ldots, x_k)$ is the formula associated with r_i. The output database of ϕ on input database $r_1, \ldots, r_n$ is the relation $\{(a_1, \ldots, a_m) :< \delta, d > \models \phi_1(a_1, \ldots, a_m)$ where $\phi_1 = \phi[R_1/F_{r_1}, \ldots, R_n/F_{r_n}]\}$.

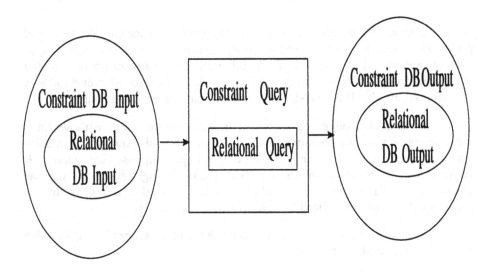

Fig. 2. The Constraint Data Model

In the generalized database model of [82] queries are functions from generalized databases to generalized databases using the same type of constraints. This *closed-form* requirement is the analogue of the termination and constructibility requirements in relational databases and stems from the same practical considerations that were discussed in Section 3.1. Constraint query languages are generalizations of relational query languages with constraints, i.e., reference to built-in relations are allowed in them. These ideas of the constraint data model are summarized in Figure 2. We present an example constraint query language and closed-form evaluation in Section 4.2.

As a consequence of the alternative semantics above we have:

Proposition 4.1 Let $\mathcal{T}$ be any first-order theory with constraint relations. If $\mathcal{T}$ admits quantifier elimination, then the output of each relational calculus query on generalized relations containing only constraints in $\mathcal{T}$ can be evaluated in finite time. Moreover, the output can be represented as a generalized relation containing only constraints in $\mathcal{T}$. □

Proposition 4.1 implies that all of the quantifier elimination results in Section 2.2 help realize the goal of closed-from evaluation. Hence they are very much relevant for querying generalized databases. Because of them relational calculus on many types of constraint databases can be used without any restriction, i.e. not even the "safety" problem is a concern. For Datalog and stratified Datalog queries however closed-form evaluation is more difficult and sometimes impossible (see Section 5). Recently [145] presented broadly applicable sufficient conditions for termination and closed-form evaluation of Datalog queries with constraints.

4.2 An Example Closed-Form Evaluation

Quantifier elimination algorithms provide closed-form evaluations for queries. Unfortunately, many quantifier elimination algorithms are computationally inefficient. Efficiency can be improved by algebrizing the quantifier elimination procedure. Algebraic operators are desirable because they provide efficient set-at-a-time computations with generalized relations. The idea of using algebras instead of simple quantifier elimination goes back to Tarski and Thompson [142]. Codd's *relational algebra* [41] is another example of algebrization of query evaluation. Relational algebra is a procedural language that is equivalent in expressive power to safe Relational Calculus. Relational Calculus queries are translated to relational algebra for quicker evaluation [3, 149].

More recently some algebraic operators are considered in the case of linear constraint databases in [23], in the case of dense order constraints in [81], and in the case of discrete order constraints in [120], which shows a partial algebra with only select, project, and join operators. Next we extend those to the full set of the relational algebra operators and give that as an illustration of algebras for generalized databases. Our definitions will follow mainly [120].

Definition 4.1 Let x and y be any two integer variables or constants. Given some assignment to the variables, a *minimum gap-order* constraint $x <_g y$ for some gap-value $g \in \mathbf{N}$ holds if and only if $g < y - x$ holds in the given assignment. A *minimum gap-order* constraint $x = y$ holds if and only if x and y are equal in the given assignment. A *maximum gap-order* constraint $x <^h y$ for some gap-value $h \in \mathbf{N}$ holds if and only if $0 < y - x < h$ holds in the given assignment. □

Definition 4.2 Let $x_1, \ldots, x_n$ be integer variables and $c_1, \ldots, c_m$ be integer constants. Any graph with vertices labeled $x_1, \ldots, x_n, c_1, \ldots, c_m$ and at most one undirected edge labeled by $=$ or at most one directed edge labeled by $<_g^h$ for some $g \in \mathbf{N}$ and $h \in \mathbf{N} \cup +\infty$ between any pair of distinct vertices is called a *mm-gapgraph*. □

Remark: Any $g = 0$ and $h = +\infty$ may be considered as default values and not written out explicitly within the mm-graphs.

Definition 4.3 Any mm-gapgraph with vertices labeled with variables $x_1, \ldots, x_n$ and constant 0 is in *normal form*. Furthermore, any set of mm-gapgraphs each with vertices labeled with $x_1, \ldots, x_n, 0$ is in *normal form*. □

It is easy to see that any mm-gapgraph of size n can be put into normal form in $O(n)$ time. We have change each constraint of the form $c <_g x$ (respectively $c <^h x$) where $c > 0$ into $0 <_{c+g} x$ (respectively $0 <_c^{c+h} x$). The cases when $c < 0$ or is on the right hand side of the minimum (respectively maximum) gap-order constraint are similar.

For the rest of this section, assume that all gap-graphs are in normal form. Furthermore, assume that each order constraint has both a minimum and a maximum bound. If that is not true in some constraint than add the default values of 0 for minimum and $+\infty$ for maximum gap-values.

Definition 4.4 Let G be a mm-gapgraph with vertices $y, v_1, \ldots, v_n, 0$. Then a *shortcut* operation over vertex y transforms G into an output mm-gapgraph with vertices $v_1, \ldots, v_n, v_{n+1}$ where $v_{n+1} = 0$ as follows. First, for each $0 < i, j, \leq n+1$ do the following.

If $v_i = y$ and $y = v_j$ are edges in G, then add $v_i = v_j$ as an undirected edge to G.

If $v_i = y$ and $y <_g^h v_j$ are edges in G, then add $v_i <_g^h v_j$ as a directed edge to G.

If $v_i <_g^h y$ and $y = v_j$ are edges in G, then add $v_i <_g^h v_j$ as a directed edge to G.

If $v_i <_{g_1}^{h_1} y$ and $y <_{g_2}^{h_2} v_j$ are edges in G, then add $v_i <_{g_1+g_2+1}^{h_1+h_2-1} v_j$ as a directed edge to G.

Second, if there are two or more edges of the form $<_{g_1}^{h_1}, \ldots, <_{g_k}^{h_k}$ between vertices v_i and v_j then delete these edges and replace these with the edge $v_i <_{\max(g_1,\ldots,g_k)}^{\min(h_1,\ldots,h_k)} v_j$. If more than one edge remains between any two vertices, then the shortcut operation fails, returns an error message, and it does not produce a shortcut mm-gapgraph as output. Otherwise, y and its incident edges are deleted and the resultant mm-gapgraph is returned. □

In the above, the first part of the shortcut operation adds only constraints that follow by transitivity from the set of original constraints represented by the input mm-gapgraph. In the second part the simplification is needed to ensure that the graph remains in mm-gapgraph form and has at most one edge between any pair of vertices. Note that if after the simplification more than one edge remains between any pair of vertices, then they must be differently oriented or one directed and another undirected, i.e. equality, constraint. This clearly implies that the mm-gapgraph is not satisfiable. Note that apart from this obvious case the shortcut operation does not check the mm-gapgraph for satisfiability.

Definition 4.5 Let G_1 and G_2 be two mm-gapgraphs over some (maybe different) subsets of the variables $v_1, \ldots, v_n$ and the constant 0. Then a *merge* operation on G_1 and G_2 creates a mm-gapgraph G with vertices $v_1, \ldots, v_n, v_{n+1} = 0$ as follows. For each $0 < i, j \leq n + 1$ do the following.

If there is no edge between v_i and v_j in G_1 and G_2, then do nothing.
If there is an edge between v_i and v_j in only one of G_1 or G_2, then add that edge to G.
If $v_i = v_j$ is an edge in both G_1 and G_2, then add $v_i = v_j$ as an edge to G.
If $v_i <_{g_1}^{h_1} v_j$ in G_1 and $v_i <_{g_2}^{h_2} v_j$ in G_2 are edges, then add $v_i <_{max(g_1,g_2)}^{min(h_1,h_2)} v_j$ as an edge to G.
If $v_j <_{g_1}^{h_1} v_i$ in G_1 and $v_j <_{g_2}^{h_2} v_i$ in G_2 are edges, then add $v_j <_{max(g_1,g_2)}^{min(h_1,h_2)} v_i$ as an edge to G.
In any other case the merge operation fails, and it does not return any graph. □

In the merge operation we want any assignment that satisfies the output mm-gapgraph to satisfy both of the input mm-gapgraphs. The operation guarantees this by checking that the corresponding edges in the two input mm-gapgraphs are compatible and by combining the stricter minimum and the stricter maximum gap-order constraints in the corresponding edges and adding the combination to the output mm-gapgraph. The last condition "in any other case" includes the cases when G_1 and G_2 are not compatible, for example, when for some variables v and w, one specifies that v is less than w while the other says that v is greater than w. In these cases there is clearly no assignment that can satisfy both graphs, hence the merge operation will fail. Next we prove the semantic correctness of the operations defined, that is, we show that shortcut is a valid existential quantifier elimination procedure and join is consistency preserving.

Lemma 4.1 Let G be a mm-gapgraph over variables $y, v_1, \ldots, v_n$ and constant 0. Let G' be the mm-gapgraph obtained by shortcutting over y in G (if exists). Let $a_0, a_1, \ldots, a_n$ be any sequence of integer numbers. Then $G(a_0, a_1, \ldots, a_n)$ is true if and only if G' exists and $G'(a_0, a_1, \ldots, a_n)$ is true. □

For the merge operation we show that the *and* of the input mm-gapgraphs is consistent if and only if the output mm-gapgraph is consistent.

Lemma 4.2 Let G_1 and G_2 be two mm-gapgraphs over some (maybe differ-ent) subsets of the variables $v_1, \ldots, v_n$ and over 0. Let G be the mm-gapgraph obtained by merging G_1 and G_2 (if exists). Let $a_1, \ldots, a_n$ be any sequence of integer numbers. Then $G_1(a_0, a_1, \ldots, a_n)$ and $G_2(a_0, a_1, \ldots, a_n)$ are true if and only if G exists and $G(a_0, a_1, \ldots, a_n)$ is true. $\square$

Based on the above operators, we define the generalized project $\dot{\pi}$ and the generalized join $\bowtie$ operators. Let R_1 and R_2 be two relations that are both in normal form. Then the generalized join of R_1 and R_2, denoted $R_1 \bowtie R_2$ is the set $\{merge(G_1, G_2) : G_1 \in R_1, G_2 \in R_2\}$. Assume that R_1 is a k-ary relation with argument symbols $S = \{x_1, \ldots, x_k\}$. Then the generalized project of R_1 onto a subset $S' = S \setminus \{x_i\}$ of the arguments is the set $\{shortcut(x_i, G) : G \in R_1\}$.

The generalized selection operation on R, denoted $\dot{\sigma}_C R$, where C is any selection condition that is the conjunction of minimum and maximum gap-order constraints, is the set $\{merge(G, graph(C)) : G \in R\}$. Here $graph$ is a function that transforms each conjunction of gap-order constraints into an mm-gapgraph.

The generalized rename operation $\dot{\rho}$ just renames the argument vertices in each mm-gapgraph in the given generalized relation.

Now let R_1 and R_2 be two k-ary generalized relations with the same scheme. Then the generalized union operation $\dot{\cup}$ is defined as the union of the mm-gapgraphs in R_1 and R_2.

Also, the generalized difference of R_1 and R_2, denoted $R_1 \dot{-} R_2$, is defined to be the set $\{R_1 \bowtie R_3 : R_3 = \neg R_2\}$ where $\neg R_2$ is the *complement* of R_2 in the standard sense. That is, if R_2 represents any set of regular tuples $\mathcal{B} \subseteq \delta^k$, then $\neg R_2$ is the set of regular tuples $\delta^k \setminus \mathcal{B}$. The following can be proven using De Morgan's laws.

Lemma 4.3 Let R be a k-ary relation represented by a set of mm-gapgraphs of size n. Then a generalized relation representing the complement of R can be found in $O(n^{k^2})$ time. $\square$

We have defined the generalized versions of all the fundamental relational algebra operators. (Note that cross product is the case of join when there are no overlaps in the arguments of the two input relations. Our definition of join allows that possibility.) Next we give an example of the use of the generalized algebraic operators.

Example 4.1 Suppose that two persons want to schedule a meeting during a given month. The first person is free from the 3rd to the 6th and from the 16th to the 26th. The second person is free from the 6th to the 18th and from the 25th to the 30th. Also suppose that they don't want to meet on the 6th and the 13th. Which days could they meet?

The relation FREE telling which person is free on which days and the relation BAD_DAYS can be represented in normal form as follows.

FREE	Person-ID	Day	
	p	t	$0 <^2 p \wedge 0 <^7_2 t$
	p	t	$0 <^2 p \wedge 0 <^{27}_{15} t$
	p	t	$0 <^3_1 p \wedge 0 <^{19}_5 t$
	p	t	$0 <^3_1 p \wedge 0 <^{31}_{24} t$

BAD_DAYS	Day	
	t	$0 <^7_5 t$
	t	$0 <^{14}_{12} t$

The query that finds the good days for meeting is the following:

$$((\dot{\pi}_{Day}\,\dot{\sigma}_{0<^2 p}\,FREE) \bowtie (\dot{\pi}_{Day}\,\dot{\sigma}_{0<^3_1 p}\,FREE)) \doteq BAD\_DAYS$$

Here $\dot{\sigma}_{0<^2 p}FREE$ will be the first two tuples of FREE. (Note that the selection condition when added to the other tuples will result in an inconsistency.) That projected into Day will give a temporary relation $R_1(t) = \{G_1, G_2\}$ where G_1 represents $0 <^7_2 t$ and G_2 represents $0 <^{27}_{15} t$.

Similarly, $\dot{\pi}_{Day}\dot{\sigma}_{0<^3_1 p}FREE$ will yield $R_2(t) = \{G_3, G_4\}$ where G_3 represents $0 <^{19}_5 t$ and G_4 represents $0 <^{31}_{24} t$. The generalized join of R_1 and R_2 will be $\{merge(G_1, G_3),$
$merge(G_1, G_4), merge(G_2, G_3), merge(G_2, G_4)\}$. The temporary output will be the following generalized relation:

R_3	Day	
	t	$0 <^7_5 t$
	t	$0 <^{19}_{15} t$
	t	$0 <^{27}_{24} t$

In the above we do not show the merge of G_1 and G_4 because it is inconsistent. Next we take the complement of BAD_DAYS. This will yield:

$$\neg((0 <^7_5 t) \vee (0 <^{14}_{12} t))$$
$$\equiv \neg((0 <_5 t \wedge 0 <^7 t) \vee (0 <_{12} t \wedge 0 <^{14} t))$$
$$\equiv (\neg(0 <_5 t) \vee \neg(0 <^7 t)) \wedge (\neg(0 <_{12} t) \vee \neg(0 <^{14} t))$$
$$\equiv ((t < 0 \vee t = 0 \vee 0 <^6 t) \vee (t < 0 \vee t = 0 \vee 0 <_6 t)) \wedge$$
$$\quad ((t < 0 \vee t = 0 \vee 0 <^{13} t) \vee (t < 0 \vee t = 0 \vee 0 <_{13} t))$$
$$\equiv (t < 0 \vee t = 0 \vee 0 <^6 t \vee 0 <_6 t) \wedge (t < 0 \vee t = 0 \vee 0 <^{13} t \vee 0 <_{13} t)$$
$$\equiv (t < 0 \vee t = 0 \vee 0 <^6 t \vee 0 <^{13}_6 t \vee 0 <_{13} t)$$

Hence the complement of BAD_DAYS is a generalized relation with five tuples. Finally, we take the generalized join of R_3 and the complement of BAD_DAYS. We obtain:

R_5	Day
t	$0 <_{15}^{19} t$
t	$0 <_{24}^{27} t$

The above generalized relation expresses that the two persons could meet any day from the 16th to the 18th and from the 25th to the 26th inclusive.

4.3 Constraint Databases vs. Constraint Logic Programming

Let us briefly compare constraint databases and constraint logic programming [42, 75, 153, 154].

Each constraint logic program is a mapping from a finite set of constraint facts to a least model. The most general framework for constraint logic programming was given by Jaffar and Lassez [74] who show that under very mild assumptions about the constraint predicates, the semantics of Prolog-like languages with constraints changes only slightly, in particular queries can still be given a least model semantics.

Constraint query languages are a subset of constraint logic programs. However, Jaffar and Lassez do not give any criteria for effectively evaluating the least model or even whether the least model is finitely representable. For constraint query languages the least models are effectively computable and finitely representable. Therefore, constraint query languages solve the user's constructibility requirement and the data vendor's problem, which are NOT solved by constraint logic programs in general. The main contribution of constraint database research is the set of algorithmic solutions to these problems.

Some important constraint programming languages are the following: Prolog III which allows constraints over the 2-valued Boolean algebra and linear arithmetic constraints over the rationals [43]. CHIP [49] which allows linear arithmetic constraints over both the rationals and bounded subsets of the integers. $CLP(\mathcal{R})$ [76] which provides polynomial constraints over the reals. LIFE [8] which allows constraints over feature trees and also provides a notion of objects. Trilogy [156] which allows constraints over strings, integers, and real numbers. The following is a brief historical outline of the developments in constraint logic programming and constraint databases:

1982: Prolog II, first instance of CLP.
1987: CLP semantics by Jaffar and Lassez [74].
1990: CQL database framework by Kanellakis, Kuper and Revesz [82].

5 Complexity Issues

In this section, we first review the known complexity results for first-order theories with constraints in Section 5.1. Then we review the known data complexity results for both relational and constraint query languages in Section 5.2. We discuss how data complexity is related to closed-form evaluation in Section 5.3. Finally Section 5.4 discusses optimization techniques to speed up query evaluation.

5.1 The Decision Problem for First-Order Theories with Constraints

The computational complexity of the decision problem for first-order theories was investigated in depth during the past twenty years. We list only some of the important results in this area.

The computational complexity of $Th(\mathbf{R}, <, +, *)$ is investigated in [19, 45, 92, 119]. The complexity of $Th(\mathbf{R}, <, +)$, a subset of the previous theory, is in DSPACE(2^{cn}) where n is the size of the formula [55] and also in alternating Turing machine class $TA(2^{cn}, n)$ [29]. (See [77] for definitions of various complexity classes.) Another interesting subset of the above theory allows only difference constraints, i.e. only constraints of the form $x_i - x_j > c$ for x_i, x_j variables and c constant. The complexity of this language is considered in [90, 91] and is shown to be PSPACE-complete in general and to be Σ_k^p-complete for k alternation of $\exists$ and $\forall$ quantifiers in the prenex form. The complexity of the theory of rational order is considered in [54] and is shown to be in DSPACE($n \log n$). The complexity of Presburger arithmetic is considered in [21, 57, 118].

In the above complexity analyses the Ehrenfeucht-Fraïssé game technique [51, 59] plays a major role. In this section, we illustrate a simple case of this important technique by applying it to the first-order theory of integer order.

In general, Ehrenfeucht-Fraïssé games are used to show that quantifiers ranging over all elements of a domain of a theory may be restricted to small finite subsets of the domain. This makes the validity of formulas of a theory decidable by exhaustive search. Upper bounds on the size of the finite subsets yield upper bounds on the time or space required to evaluate the formulas. The theory of integer order provides a simple case of the power of this general technique. Ferrante and Rackoff [55] used Ehrenfeucht-Fraïssé games in a compact proof to show an $O(n^2)$ space upper bound for deciding formulas of size n that have no constants other than possibly 0. Their analysis is more complex than necessary because they are concerned with several theories at once. In the following we simplify their proof for the case of the theory of integer order only and also add a means to deal with constants other than 0.

First, the infinite set of possible integer tuples that may satisfy a first-order formula is divided into a finite number of equivalence classes. The goal is to show that any member of an equivalence class satisfies a formula if and only if every member of the equivalence class satisfies that formula. This limits the number of possible cases that needs to be considered during evaluation, because it is enough to pick just one member from each equivalence class to test whether it is a solution. At first we look at the case when the formulas have no constants in them.

Definition 5.1 Let $\bar{a}_k = (a_1, \ldots, a_k)$ and $\bar{b}_k = (b_1, \ldots, b_k)$ be tuples of integers. For each $k, d \in N$ we write that $\bar{a}_k \sim_{k,d} \bar{b}_k$ if and only if for each $1 \leq i, j \leq k$, if $\mid a_i - a_j \mid \leq 2^{d-k}$, then $a_i - a_j = b_i - b_j$, and if $a_i - a_j > 2^{d-k}$, then $b_i - b_j > 2^{d-k}$. □

In the next lemma, we use $\models$ to mean satisfaction in the standard sense.

Lemma 5.1 Let $F(x_1, \ldots, x_k)$ be any formula of the theory of integer order, and let d be the quantifier depth in F. Then for any tuples $\bar{a}_k, \bar{b}_k$, if $\bar{a}_k \sim_{k,d} \bar{b}_k$, then $\bar{a}_k \models F(x_1, \ldots, x_k)$ if and only if $\bar{b}_k \models F(x_1, \ldots, x_k)$.

Proof: We prove the lemma by induction on the number of $\vee, \neg, \exists$ operators in F. Assume that $\bar{a}_k \sim_{k,d} \bar{b}_k$. For the base case, we have a single order constraint of the form $x_i < x_j$ or $x_i = x_j$. Clearly, each of these is either true or false in both $\bar{a}_k$ and $\bar{b}_k$. For more complex formulas we have the following cases:

(1) $F(\bar{x}) \equiv F'(\bar{x}) \vee F''(\bar{x})$. Suppose $\bar{a}_k \models F'(\bar{x}) \vee F''(\bar{x})$. Then, without loss of generality $a_k \models F'(\bar{x})$. By induction, $\bar{b}_k \models F'(\bar{x})$. Hence, $\bar{b}_k \models F'(\bar{x}) \vee F''(\bar{x})$.

(2) $F(\bar{x}) \equiv \neg F'(\bar{x})$. Suppose $\bar{a}_k \models \neg F'(\bar{x})$. Then, $\bar{a}_k \not\models F'(\bar{x})$. By induction, $\bar{b}_k \not\models F'(\bar{x})$. Hence, $\bar{b}_k \models \neg F'(\bar{x})$.

(3) $F(\bar{x}) \equiv \exists z F'(\bar{x}, z)$. Suppose $a_k \models \exists z F'(\bar{x}, z)$. Then for some a_{k+1}, $\bar{a}_k, a_{k+1} \models F'(\bar{x}, z)$. If $a_{k+1} = a_j$ for some $1 \leq j \leq k$, then we choose $b_{k+1} = b_j$. Otherwise, let $a_{j_1} < a_{k+1} < a_{j_2}$ be the pair of integers within $\bar{a}_k$ between which a_{k+1} lies. If $a_{j_2} - a_{j_1} \leq 2^{d-k}$, then choose $b_{k+1} = b_{j_1} + a_{k+1} - a_{j_1}$. If $a_{j_2} - a_{j_1} > 2^{d-k}$, then choose $b_{k+1} = b_{j_1} + 2^{d-k}$. Since $\bar{a}_k \sim_{k,d} \bar{b}_k$, it is easy to see that in both cases the choices make $\bar{a}_{k+1} \sim_{k+1,d} \bar{b}_{k+1}$. By induction, $\bar{b}_{k+1,d} \models F'(\bar{x}, z)$. Hence, $\bar{b}_k \models F(\bar{x})$.

These cases prove the "if" part of the lemma. By arguing similarly for $\bar{b}_k$ we prove the "only if" part of the lemma. □

The above lemma can be generalized to the case when there are constants in the formula. Moreover it can be turned into an effective quantifier elimination procedure. The quantifier-free formula that is returned however, will have to use *gap-order* constraints, that is atomic formulas of the form $x_i - x_j > k$ where k is a nonnegative integer number.

Theorem 5.1 Let $F(x_1, \ldots, x_k)$ be a formula in the first-order theory of integer order. Then we can find a quantifier-free formula $F'(x_1, \ldots, x_k)$ in the theory of integer gap-order such that $F \leftrightarrow F'$ is true.

Furthermore, the size of F' is at most $O((k!(k-1)^{2^d+2}((2^{d+1}+3)m)^k)n)$ where d is the quantifier depth of F, m is the number of distinct integer constants in F and n is the total size of F.

Proof: We want to find one member from each equivalence class – in the sense of Definition 5.1– whose members satisfy F. By Lemma 5.1, if F had no constants in it, then we would have to try only $O(k!(k-1)^{2^d+2})$ sequences of integers, i.e., $k!$ ordering of the variables in $\bar{a}_k$ and between each adjacent pair trying out only equalities and gaps of size 1 to $2^d + 1$. However, if F contains constants, then the relative ordering and gap-sizes among the constants and the variables have to be also known to be able to evaluate atomic formulas that contain constants, e.g., $x_i = c$, $x_i < c$, or $x_i \geq c$.

We can extend Definition 5.1 as follows. We write that $\bar{a}_k \sim_{k,d} \bar{b}_k$ if and only if for each constant or variable u in F the following condition holds: for each $1 \leq i \leq k$, if $\mid a_i - u \mid \leq 2^{d-k}$, then $a_i - u = b_i - u$, if $a_i - u > 2^{d-k}$, then $b_i - u > 2^{d-k}$, and if $u - a_i > 2^{d-k}$, then $u - b_i > 2^{d-k}$.

Hence we would need for each of the possible ordering-gaping of the variables only a gap assignment with respect to the constants that occur in the formula. With respect to each constant c, a variable x_i can be placed into $2^{d+1} + 3$ distinguishable positions, that is, x_i less than c by $1, \ldots, 2^d + 1$, x_i equal to c, or x_i greater than c by $1, \ldots, 2^d + 1$. With m constants in F, this leaves $(2^{d+1} + 3)m$ choices for each variable. Hence we have the upper bound of $O(k!(k-1)^{2^d+2}((2^{d+1}+3)m)^k)$ many different equivalence classes with constants. (Actually, we may have much less, as only a part of the gap choices will be consistent with the variable orderings, and only part of the gap assignments with respect to the constants will be consistent with the variable orderings and gap choices.)

Similarly to Lemma 5.1 it can be shown that if any member of an equivalence class satisfies the formula, then each member of the equivalence class satisfies the formula. Moreover, we can pick a representative from each equivalence class and test whether it satisfies the formula. It is clear that each equivalence class can be written as a quantifier-free formula over the free variables that is a conjunction of gap-order constraints. The formula F' will be the disjunction of the conjunctive formulas representing the equivalence classes that satisfy F. Clearly the size of each conjunctive formula is less than the size of F. This proves the theorem. $\square$

Lemma 5.1 shows that the formulas with integer order cannot distinguish between gaps than are more than exponential in their size. We show in the following example as a lower bound a formula which does distinguish between gaps that are up to an exponential in the size of the formula.

Many possible formulas can be found with that property. Our example is quite simple and is in disjunctive normal form. That is an improvement over previous examples of hard formulas. That is, Ferrante and Rackoff's method of writing short formulas that define complicated properties exactly exploit the fact that the formula is not in normal form. If their example were put into normal form its size would increase exponentially.

Example 5.1

$$Gap_{2^n}(s,t) \equiv \exists x \forall y \; Gap_{2^{n-1}}(x,y) \vee (s < y < t) \vee (t < y < s)$$

$$Gap_1(s,t) \equiv s \neq t$$

The formula $Gap_{2^n}(s,t)$ is satisfied if and only if $\mid t - s \mid \geq 2^n$. This is easy to prove by induction as follows. For $n = 0$, $Gap_{2^0}(s,t) \equiv Gap_1(s,t)$ is satisfied if and only if $\mid t - s \mid \geq 1$, as claimed. For Gap_{2^n} without loss of generality let $s < t$. We reason as follows.

(if) Suppose that $t - s \geq 2^n$. Then let $x = s + 2^{n-1}$. Then for all $y \leq s$ the condition $x - y \geq 2^{n-1}$ holds. Also, for all $y \geq t$ the condition $y - x \geq 2^{n-1}$ holds. For all $s < y < t$ the second condition holds. Hence $Gap_{2^n}(s,t)$ holds.

(only if) Suppose that $t - s < 2^n$. For any x if $s < x < t$, then either $x - s < 2^{n-1}$ and $Gap_{2^{n-1}}(x,t)$ is false or $t - x < 2^{n-1}$ and $Gap_{2^{n-1}}(x,s)$ is false, and since $s < s < t$ and $s < t < t$ are both false, the formula must be false when either $y = s$ or $y = t$. If $x \leq s$ or $x \geq t$, then the formula is false because each of the three disjuncts fails when $y = x$. $\Box$

5.2 Query Evaluation Formulated as a Decision Problem

When analyzing the complexity of query evaluation, it is common to reformulate the query evaluation problem as a decision problem.

Data Complexity: For each fixed program Π we define a language $L_\Pi = \{(t,d) : t \in \Pi(d)\}$. The language L_Π consists of the set of strings which are pairs of a regular relational database tuple t and an input database d (written as a string of generalized relational database tuples) such that t is in the semantically defined output of Π on d (that is, independent of any particular representation). Following Chandra and Harel [31] and Vardi [155] we call *data complexity* the computational complexity of deciding whether a pair (t,d) is in the language L_Π. Data complexity is a commonly used measure in databases because it expresses the intuition that usually the size of the database dominates by several orders of magnitude the size of the query program.

δ	Constraints	Relational Calculus	Datalog	Stratified Datalog
D		AC_0 (s) [81] LOGSPACE (s) [31]	PTIME-comp (s) [7, 31]	PTIME-comp (s) [12, 33]
Q	$\neq, \leq, <$	AC_0 [81] LOGSPACE [82, 54]	PTIME-comp [82]	PTIME-comp [82]
N, Z	$\equiv_k$ for fixed set of k's	in PTIME [78, 157]	PTIME-comp [147]	PTIME-comp [145]
N, Z	$1S$	in NC [120]	PSPACE-comp (s) [38]	PSPACE-comp (s) [36]
$P(D)$	$\subseteq, k \in, k \notin$	in PTIME ($\exists$ only) [134]	DEXPTIME-comp [122]	DEXPTIME-comp (s) [124]
B_m	$=_{B_m}$	in PTIME ($\exists$ only) [82]	2^{2^n}-comp [82, 125]	in $2^{2^{2^n}}$ (s) [125]
Z	$\neq, \leq, <, <_k$	in NC [120]	DEXPTIME-comp [121, 122]	non-elem-comp (s) [123]
R	$<, +$	in NC [55]	undec.	undec.
N, Z	$<, +, \equiv_k$	in $O(2^{n^{c^n}})$ [118, 21]	undec.	undec.
R	$+, *$	NC [82, 19, 119]	undec.	undec.
Z	$+, *$	undec. [62]	undec.	undec.
Q	$+, *$	undec. [128]	undec.	undec.

Fig. 3. The Data Complexity of Constraint Query Languages

Figure 3 summarizes some of the known data complexity results for relational and constraint query languages. The yet unmentioned domain symbols in the table are: D for any discrete domain (for example the integers), B_m for free Boolean algebra with m elements, and $P(Z)$ for sets of integers. In the figure ($\exists only$) means that only relational calculus without $\neg$ and $\forall$ is considered and (s) means other syntactical restrictions. The $=$ is not listed as a constraint in any row of the table, but it is assumed to be present in each row.

Most of the complexity results in Figure 3 assume Turing machines as the computational model. The exceptions are the NC-ness results which assume the PRAM model of computation and the AC_0 results which assume random-access alternating Turing machines [14, 30].

The known data complexity results for relational databases are shown in the first row. For relational databases (safe) relational calculus has LOGSPACE [31] and AC_0 [81] data complexity in the PRAM and Alternating Turing machine models, respectively. Also, for relational databases both Datalog [7, 31] and Stratified Datalog [12, 33] have PTIME-complete data complexity.

In the Figure 3 the constraint $<_k$ where k is a nonnegative integer is called a gap-order constraint. For variables x_i and x_j, the constraint $x_i <_k x_j$ is true if and only if $x_i + k < x_j$ is true.

[120] considered relational calculus with $\neq, \leq, <$ constraints on the integers in the input database and showed it to be decidable within PTIME data complexity. Theorem 5.2 in this paper is an improvement of that result to NC and with the remarks after it an extension with gap-order constraints within the input database. (Note that without the extension the closed-form requirement is not satisfied.)

Koubarakis [91] considered the first-order language of difference constraints, i.e. only constraints of the form $x_i - x_j > c$ for x_i, x_j integer variables and c integer constant. Koubarakis shows that the expression complexity of this language is PSPACE-complete and provides a quantifier elimination method. When the reals are considered as the domain, the expression complexity remains the same.

It turns out that the expressive power of the languages in [120] and [91] in the case of integers is the same. That is because $x_i - x_j > c$ is equivalent to $x_j <_c x_i$ if $c \geq 0$ and is equivalent to $\neg(x_i <_{(-c-1)} x_j)$ if $c < 0$. Furthermore, any gap-order constraint $x_i <_c x_j$ can be expressed by the subformula $\exists z_1 \ldots \exists z_c (x_i < z_1 \land z_1 < \ldots < z_c \land z_c < x_j)$.

The constraint $\equiv_k$ is the usual modulus constraint on integers, that is, $x_i \equiv_k x_j$ is true if and only if the remainder of x_i divided by k equals the remainder of x_j divided by k where k is a positive integer. The set of solutions $\{c + kn : n \in \mathbf{Z}\}$ of a modulus constraint of the form $x \equiv_k c$ is called a linear repeating point.

Datalog with a successor function, which is denoted $1S$ in the table, has the safety requirement that addition is applied only to the first argument of each relation. This distinguished argument of relations is called a temporal argument. The languages of [78, 38, 39] can express many interesting temporally recurring events. For example, they can express that employees in a company get paid every week. In the language of [39] this would be:

$$paid(t, p) :- employee(p, c), paid(t_2, p), t = t_2 + 1 + 1 + 1 + 1 + 1 + 1 + 1$$

However, the languages are different in expressive power. [78] cannot express transitive closure queries, while [39] cannot express the difference of relations. The expressive power of these languages is compared in [16] which also present an undecidable language. The expressive power of point and interval-based query languages is compared in [146].

[147] also combines modulus constraints with integer gap-order constraints. Datalog with gap-order constraints is shown to have a closed form and a DEXPTIME-complete data complexity in [121, 122]. The expression complexity of the same

language is shown to be in DEXPTIME in [47]. Recent work adds stratified nega-tion to Datalog with gap-order constraints with some syntactical safety restric-tions. The resultant language has a non-elementary data complexity [123]. The relationship between syntactical safety as given in [123] and semantical safety is discussed in [136] and it is shown that syntactical safety cannot be extended to include all semantically safe queries.

Datalog with set order constraints of the form $U \subseteq V$, $k \in U$, and $k \notin U$, where k is an integer (or element of some other infinite domain D) and U, V are set variables or sets of constants, is considered in [134, 122, 124]. The first reference shows that conjunctive queries have PTIME, and the other two show that Datalog and safe stratified Datalog have a DEXPTIME-complete data complexity.

The data complexity of relational calculus and Datalog queries with Boolean equality constraints over a free Boolean algebra with m generators is analyzed in [82, 125].

Some related results that do not appear in the table are works on decid-ing set constraints. The set constraints considered in [5] are much more general than the ones in the table. Quantifier elimination is not possible in the more general case considered there. There sets appear as leaves of functional terms and unification and other methods are considered for the decision problem only.

When we have addition and multiplication, then we can express the order relation in both the **R** and the **Z** case. When the domain is **Z**, then we can also express exponentiation. The undecidability results in the table are based in part on these observations.

5.3 From the Decision Problem to Closed-Form Evaluation

Next we give an example of how one can translate the complexity results for the decision problem of a first-order theory with constraints to a closed-form evaluation result for relational calculus queries.

Theorem 5.2 Let Π be any fixed Relational Calculus program. Then Π can be evaluated in NC in the size of any generalized database with integer order constraints such that the output will be a generalized relation with integer gap-order constraints.

Proof: First using Proposition 4.1 translate the query evaluation problem into a quantifier elimination problem in the theory of integer order. Also trans-form the formula into a prenex normal form, i.e. where all the quantifiers occur only at the front. A formula can be put into prenex-form in NC.

The theorem follows from Theorem 5.1 taking advantage of the fact that the quantifier depth and the number of free variables are fixed constants. When we test a representative of each equivalence class whether it satisfies the formula for each new existential variable a_{k+i} we need to test only $O((2(k-i)+1)2^d(2^{d+1} + 3)m)$ many choices depending where a_{k+i} is inserted into the current order of the variables $a_1, \ldots, a_{k+i-1}$ and the m constants. Since d and k are fixed constants, employing an exhaustive search on these possibilities the total number of cases is still only $O(m^d)$. Since $m < n$ the total number of cases is only a polynomial in the size of the generalized database input. Each case should be tested on a quantifier-free formula which can be done individually in NC and all of them in parallel in NC. Once the value of each case is known, the quantifiers can be evaluated in NC too. $\square$

Remark 1: It is possible to improve the above result by allowing the generalized database input to contain gap-order constraints. If the maximum gap-value in the input database is some constant c then similarly to Example 5.1 we can express it by a formula which adds only $\log c$ quantifier-depth and size. That is, the problem with gap-order constraints in the input generalized database can be still reduced to evaluating in the theory of integer order a formula that has $O(k + \log c)$ quantifier depth. Hence this problem is also in NC.

Remark 2: The theory of integers with a successor relation, i.e. $+1$, can be also reduced to case of the theory of integer order. That is because any constraint of the form $x+1 = y$ in the former can be expressed by the subformula $(x < y) \wedge \neg \exists z (x < z \wedge z < y)$ in the latter. This implies that with successor constraints also query evaluation is in NC.

The following is the analogue of Theorem 5.2 in the case of algebraic queries.

Theorem 5.3 Let Π be any fixed generalized relational algebra query. Then Π can be evaluated in NC in the size of any generalized database input that is in normal form.

Proof: The proof is by induction on the parse tree of the relational algebra expression showing that the temporary relation T_i associated with each internal node i has a size that is polynomial in the size of the input relations (at the leaves) below it and that T_i can be evaluated in NC. To show polynomial size is easy because generalized select, project, and rename can only decrease the number of mm-gapgraphs in the temporary relation and join can only return at most $n * m$ mm-gapgraphs where n and m are the number of mm-gapgraphs in the two input relations. By Lemma 4.3 the number of mm-gapgraphs can also grow only polynomially by each negation (and therefore difference). Since the relational algebra expression is fixed the output relation at the root node must have a number of mm-graphs that is polynomial in the size of the input generalized database. Finally, we note that the size of each mm-gapgraph is bounded by a constant because the number of arguments in each relation is fixed.

To show NC-ness of the evaluation it is enough to show that each generalized algebra operation can be evaluated in NC in the size of the input relation(s). For select, project, and rename and join that is obvious. Negation can be done in NC similarly to Theorem 5.2, that is, we precompute and test in parallel all $O(n^{k^2})$ mm-gapgraphs whether it satisfies the negated formula that is the disjunction of all the mm-gapgraphs in the input relation. $\square$

Unfortunately, there are no general techniques to use data complexity results for Datalog and Stratified Datalog to bound the time required by a closed-form evaluation algorithm. Even worse, for constraint query languages a finite data complexity does not imply that there is a closed-form evaluation.

5.4 Optimization Problems

Many optimization methods are based on the idea of transforming programs into semantically equivalent ones that however can be evaluated faster. Transformation from a relational calculus query to an algebra discussed above is one example. Other examples includes the propagation of selection and projection operators and the ordering of join operators in both relational calculus and similarly by magic set techniques in Datalog. Recent extensions of these techniques for constraint queries can be found in [26, 27, 71, 97, 98, 106, 133, 144, 152].

The testing for equivalence during program transformations often is accomplished by testing for query containment first. Recall that each relational calculus program ϕ defines a mapping from any input database d (which may be represented finitely) to an output database $\phi(d)$ (which may also be represented finitely). We say that a program ϕ_1 is contained in program ϕ_2, denoted $\phi_1 \subseteq \phi_2$, if and only if for each input database d, all the tuples in $\phi_1(d)$ are also in $\phi_2(d)$. The *containment* problem is: Given two programs ϕ_1, ϕ_2 decide whether $\phi_1 \subseteq \phi_2$.

The containment problem is particularly important for a subclass of relational calculus queries that are formed without the connectives $\neg$ and $\vee$ and the quantifier $\forall$. These queries are called *Conjunctive Queries*.

The containment problem is NP-complete for conjunctive queries without constraints [34]. It remains NP-complete with only linear equality constraints [82]. The problem becomes Π_2^p-complete with dense linear order constraints [151]. The containment problem for conjunctive queries with quadratic equation constraints over the reals is Π_2^p-hard [82].

Besides query transformations, good indexing techniques on the generalized tuples in the input database relations can also improve the efficiency of query evaluation. A typical problem in query evaluation is 1-dimensional range searching, which asks to return all tuples that have an x attribute with values between two constants.

Range searching on regular relations can be implemented by B-trees and and B$^+$-trees [17, 46] which are good in minimizing the number of accesses to secondary storage. Range searching requires $O(\log_B N + K/B)$ secondary memory accesses in the worst case, where B is the number of tuples in a block, N is the total number of tuples in the relation searched, and K is the number of tuples returned.

The problem of range searching on generalized relations can be implemented using grid-files, quad-trees, and R-trees (see the books [112, 129, 130] for a review of these and other spatial data structures). The idea is to index each generalized tuple by the interval that is the projection of the tuple onto the x axis. The data structures mentioned above can easily accommodate insertions and deletions as well as range searching. Unfortunately, they work well only with main-memory storage but do not give worst-case guarantees on the number of accesses to secondary storage. [84] gives a data structure and an algorithm with optimal worst-case performance with regard to secondary storage accesses. The data structure is static in the sense that it allows insertions but no deletions. [117, 116] also considers multi-dimensional searching, i.e. range searching when several attributes are involved.

6 Expressive Power

Relational calculus queries without constraints (see Section 3.2) can be evaluated using a quantifier elimination procedure over the first-order theory of equality if in the input database each relation is a finite set of regular tuples. However, a quantifier elimination procedure may be slow compared to the usual evaluation of "safe" relational calculus queries (see [3, 149] for definition of safe). The efficiency of "safe" queries is due primarily to the fact that in them the quantifiers can be restricted to range over the set of constants occurring explicitly in the query, called the *active domain*, denoted δ_A, without a change in the output relation.

Using a version of Ehrenfeucht-Fraïssé games, Aylamazyan, Gilula, Stolboushkin and Schwartz showed that in any relational calculus query (safe or unsafe) it suffices to let quantifiers range over the active domain plus q number of additional constants from the full domain δ where q is the number of quantified variables [13]. This means that we can evaluate "unsafe" relational calculus queries with almost the same efficiently as safe relational queries.

Let's call active-domain semantics the mapping defined as in Section 3.2 but δ replaced by δ_A. Hull and Su considered whether relational calculus queries under the unrestricted and the active-domain semantics have the same expressive power. They found that when the input database consists of relations with a finite set of regular tuples, then the answer is yes, that is, for each unrestricted query it is possible to find an active-domain query that gives always the same output [72]. Paredaens, Van den Bussche and Van Gucht show the equivalence when the input database consists of generalized relations with linear inequality constraints over the reals [111].

Another interesting question is the relative expressibility of relational calculus queries over different types of generalized databases. The problem of finding a *convex hull* and a *voronoi diagram* is expressible in relational calculus with polynomial inequality constraints over the reals. These queries cannot be expressed in relational calculus without generalized databases and constraints. That is because the latter queries are always *generic* or isomorphism preserving, that is, if two input databases are isomorphic, then their outputs are also isomorphic [31]. Clearly, this property of genericity is lost when constraints are added. Necessary modifications of the concept of genericity are investigated in [95, 109, 111].

Negative results are also interesting. The strongest negative result is that relational calculus with polynomial constraints over the real numbers cannot express even simple recursive queries like connectivity, transitive closure and parity of a relation [18]. This results extends earlier work on linear inequality constraints [6, 68, 94], and on rational numbers and order constraints [65, 137].

Finally, another negative result from [65] is that valid sentences of the first-order predicate calculus when relations range over finitely representable databases is undecidable. This case is similar to the finite relations case, that is, validity here is also co-r.e. and not in r.e.

7 Further Extensions

There are a number of recent extensions of the constraint data model. Among these are the addition of (1) integrity constraints, (2) aggregation operators, (3) indefinite information (4) complex objects, and (5) spatial and topological databases.

Integrity constraints play an important part in regular relational database design and have been investigated in great detail (see [143]). Dependency theory among integrity constraints for generalized databases is however a fairly open area, which was investigated only recently [15, 103]. [15] defines *constraint generating dependencies* and studies the computational complexity of their implication and consistency problems. Let $emp(name, salary, boss)$ be a relation storing information about employees in a company. An example of a simple case of constraint generating dependency is

$$\forall n_1 \forall s_1 \forall b_1 \forall n_2 \forall s_2 \forall b_2 ((emp(n_1, s_1, b_1) \wedge emp(n_2, s_2, b_2) \wedge b_1 = n_2) \to (s_1 < s_2))$$

meaning that bosses always earn more than their employees. Even this is more general than typical integrity constraints on relational databases because it assumes that the domain of the second attribute is an interpreted domain with order. (The usual assumption is an uninterpreted domain with no constraint relations defined on it.)

Aggregation operators [87] have an important use in practical database query languages such as SQL. It is a challenging problem to define meaningful and efficiently evaluable aggregation operators on generalized databases. Maximum, minimum and area were proposed as aggregation operators in [95]. More recent work on this problem appears in [40, 37, 67].

Indefinite information represented by null values is also a practical concern. Null values represent either unknown or unexisting values. Evaluation of constraint queries with null values is considered in [90, 91, 134].

Complex values are important for the convenient representation of many kind of real-life data [3]. Values such as Booleans, strings, integer, real or rational numbers are all scalar values. Complex values are built from scalar values using in a nested way set and tuple constructors. It is a challenge to define constraints and find good constraint solving algorithms for complex objects. The introduction of set constraints and a quantifier elimination algorithm on set variables in [134, 122] can be considered as a preliminary step in that direction. In [134] complex values are further enhanced by object identifiers, leading to an interesting combination of constraint and object-oriented programming. Another proposal to combine constraints and objects is presented in [24]. Nested databases with dense order constraints are considered in [66].

Recent work on spatial and topological databases that extend the constraint data model can be found in [93, 108, 126]. In [108] constraint queries where variables range over regions instead of points are considered. In [126] constraint database and knowledge-base change operators, including revision, update, and arbitration are described. A survey on spatial databases can be found in [110].

8 Prototype Systems

It is encouraging to see that some prototype constraint database systems are just starting to appear. The constraint database system DISCO (short for Datalog with integer and set constraints) [25] implements two data types: integers and (finite and cofinite) sets of integers. In DISCO the following constraint relations are allowed: (1) between integers variables and constants: $=, \neq, <, \leq, >, \geq$ and gap-order constraint $<_k$ (see Section 5.2), (2) between set variables and constants: $=, \subseteq$, and (3) between integer constants c and set variables or constants $X: c \in X$ and $c \notin X$. Seminaive evaluation and projection and selection pushing is implemented in DISCO. The DISCO system was used recently for example in genomic database applications [127].

An implementation of Datalog with periodicity constraints was described recently in [144] . Also, a compile-time constraint-solving method is implemented within the DeCoR database system in [63]. The C^3 constraint object-oriented system is also being implemented recently [28]. These prototype systems are important feasibility demonstrations for the theoretical ideas about constraint databases. They also may give interesting feedback for further theoretical study.

9 Open Problems

There are obviously many research topics that need further consideration. The list below collects only some of the most interesting and it seems difficult open problems concerning constraint query languages and generalized databases.

(1) What is the relative expressive power of relational calculus queries over generalized databases with polynomial inequality constraints over the reals under the unrestricted vs. the active-domain semantics? This problem was studied in [109].

(2) What is the size of the generalized database output for Datalog queries with integer order constraints, i.e. in $Th(Z, <)$? This problem was studied in [121]. Note that without constraints, this problem reduces in an obvious way to the data complexity problem. A similar reduction however still needs to be shown when constraints are present.

(3) What is the data complexity of relational calculus with only linear inequality constraints, i.e., in $Th(R, +, <)$? For *k-bounded* queries, that is, queries where the number of occurrences of the addition symbol in each constraint is bounded, it was shown that the problem is in AC_0 in [65]. Is the data complexity still in AC_0 without this restriction?

(4) Ajtai and Gurevich [9] showed that the queries that are expressible in both Datalog and relational calculus over regular databases are those that are *bounded*. Here bounded means that the number of iterations needed in the naive evaluation of the query is always a constant for any input database [3, 79]. Is this result true also if we allow generalized databases?

(5) What is the upper bound for the computational complexity of testing containment of conjunctive queries with quadratic equation constraints? The lower bound of Π_2^p-hard is shown in [82].

(6) Can we design a data structure that implements insertion, deletion, and range searches with optimal worst-case access to secondary storage? This problem is investigated in [84, 117, 116].

Acknowledgement: I thank the editors, Leonid Libkin and Bernhard Thalheim, for their encouragement in writing this survey. I also thank the referees for numerous helpful comments.

References

1. S. Abiteboul, C. Beeri. On the Power of Languages for the Manipulation of Complex Objects. *INRIA Research Report 846*, 1988.
2. S. Abiteboul and P. Kanellakis. Database Theory Column: Query Languages for Complex Object Databases. *SIGACT News*, 21, pp. 9–18, 1990.
3. S. Abiteboul, R. Hull and V. Vianu. Foundations of Databases. *Addison-Wesley*, 1994.
4. S. Abiteboul and V. Vianu. Datalog Extensions for Database Queries and Updates. *J. Comput. System Sci.*, **43** (1991), pp. 62–124.
5. A. Aiken. Set Constraints: Results, Applications and Future Directions. *Proc. 2nd Workshop on Principles and Practice of Constraint Programming*, 171–179, 1994.
6. F. Afrati, S.S. Cosmadakis, S. Grumbach, G.M. Kuper. Linear vs. Polynomial Constraints in Database Query Languages. *Proc. 2nd Workshop on Principles and Practice of Constraint Programming*, 152–160, 1994.
7. A.V. Aho, J.D. Ullman. Universality of Data Retrieval Languages. *Proc. 6th ACM Symp. on Principles of Programming Languages*, 110–117, 1979.
8. H. Aït-Kaci, A. Podelski. Towards a Meaning of LIFE. *Journal of Logic Programming*, 16, 195–234,1993.
9. M. Ajtai, Y. Gurevich. Datalog vs. First Order. *Journal of Computer and Systems Sciences*, 1994.
10. K.R. Apt. Logic Programming. *Handbook of Theoretical Computer Science*, Vol. B, chapter 10, (J. van Leeuwen editor), North-Holland, 1990.
11. K.R. Apt, M.H. van Emden. Contributions to the Theory of Logic Programming. *J. ACM*, Vol. 29 (3), 841–862, 1982.
12. K.R. Apt, H.A. Blair, A. Walker. Towards a Theory of Declarative Knowledge, in: J. Minker, ed., Foundation of Deductive Databases and Logic Programming. Morgan Kaufmann, 1988.
13. A.K. Aylamazyan, M.M. Gilula, A.P. Stolboushkin, G.F. Schwartz. Reduction of the Relational Model with Infinite Domain to the Case of Finite Domains (in Russian). *Proc. USSR Acad. of Science (Doklady)*, 286(2):308–311, 1986.
14. D.A. Barrington, N. Immerman, H. Straubing. On Uniformity within NC^1. *Journal of Computer and System Sciences*, 41:274–306,1990.
15. M. Baudinet, J. Chomicki, P. Wolper. Constraint-Generating Dependencies. *Proc. 5th Int. Conf. on Database Theory*, 322–337, 1995.
16. M. Baudinet, M. Niezette, P. Wolper. On the Representation of Infinite Temporal Data and Queries. *Proc. 10th ACM Symp. on Principles of Database Systems*, 280–290, 1991.
17. R. Bayer, E. McCreight. Organization of Large Ordered Indexes. *Acta Informatica*, 1:173–189, 1972.
18. M. Benedikt, G. Dong, L. Libkin, L. Wong. Relational Expressive Power of Constraint Query Languages. *Proc. 15h ACM Symp. on Principles of Database Systems*, 5–16, 1996.
19. M. Ben-Or, D. Kozen, J. Reif. The Complexity of Elementary Algebra and Geometry. *Journal of Computer and System Sciences*, 32:251–264, 1986.
20. C. Bell, A. Nerode, R. Ng, V.S. Subrahmanian. Implementing Deductive Databases by Linear Programming. *Proc. 11h ACM Symp. on Principles of Database Systems*, 283–292, 1992.

21. L. Berman. Precise Bounds for Presburger Arithmetic and the Reals with Addition. *Proc. 18th IEEE FOCS*, pp. 95-99, 1977.

22. A.H. Borning. The Programming Language Aspects of ThingLab, A Constraint-Oriented Simulation Laboratory. *ACM TOPLAS* 3:4:353–387, 1981.

23. A. Brodsky, J. Jaffar, M.J. Maher. Toward Practical Constraint Databases. *Proc. 19th VLDB*, 322–331, 1993.

24. A. Brodsky, Y. Kornatzky. The *Lyric* Language: Querying Constraint Objects. *Proc. SIGMOD*, 35–46, 1995.

25. J. Byon, P.Z. Revesz. DISCO: A Constraint Database System with Sets. *Proc. Workshop on Constraint Databases and Applications*, Springer-Verlag LNCS 1034, 68–83, 1995.

26. A. Brodsky, C. Lassez, J.L. Lassez, M.J. Maher. Separability of Polyhedra for Optimal Filtering of Spatial and Constraint Data. *Proc. 14th Symp. on Principles of Database Systems*, 1995.

27. A. Brodsky, Y. Sagiv. Inference of Inequality Constraints in Logic Programs. *Proc. 10th ACM Symp. on Principles of Database Systems*, 227–241, 1991.

28. A. Brodsky and V. Segal. The C^3 Constraint Object-Oriented Database System: An Overview, 134–159, In: [61].

29. A.R. Bruss, A.R. Meyer. On Time-Space Classes and their Relation to the Theory of Real Addition. *Proc. 10th ACM STOC*, pp. 233-239, 1978.

30. S.R. Buss. The Formula Value Problem is in ALOGTIME. *Proc. 19th ACM STOC*, pp. 123-131, 1987.

31. A.K. Chandra, D. Harel. Computable Queries for Relational Data Bases. *Journal of Computer and System Sciences*, vol. 21, 156–178, 1980.

32. A.K. Chandra, D. Harel. Structure and Complexity of Relational Queries. *Journal of Computer and System Sciences*, vol. 25, 99–128, 1982.

33. A.K. Chandra, D. Harel. Horn Clause Queries and Generalizations. *Journal of Logic Programming*, vol. 2, 1–15, 1985.

34. A.K. Chandra, P.M. Merlin. Optimal Implementation of Conjunctive Queries in Relational Databases. *Proc. ACM STOC*, 77–90, 1977.

35. J. Chomicki. Polynomial Time Query Processing in Temporal Deductive Databases. *Proc. 9th ACM Symp. on Principles of Database Systems*, 379–391, 1990.

36. J. Chomicki. *Functional Deductive Databases: Query Processing in the Presence of Limited Function Symbols*, Ph.D. Thesis. Rutgers University, 1990.

37. J. Chomicki, D. Goldin, G. Kuper. Variable Independence and Aggregation Closure. *Proc. 15th ACM Symp. on Principles of Database Systems*, 40–48, 1996.

38. J. Chomicki, T. Imielinski. Relational Specifications of Infinite Query Answers. *Proc. ACM SIGMOD*, 174–183, 1989.

39. J. Chomicki, T. Imielinski. Finite Representation of Infinite Query Answers. *ACM Transactions of Database Systems*, 181–223, vol. 18, no. 2, 1993.

40. J. Chomicki, G. Kuper. Measuring Infinite Relations. *Proc. 14th ACM Symp. on Principles of Database Systems*, 78-85, 1995.

41. E.F. Codd. A Relational Model for Large Shared Data Banks. *CACM*, 13:6:377–387, 1970.

42. J. Cohen. Constraint Logic Programming Languages. *CACM*, 33:7:52–68, 1990.

43. A. Colmerauer. An Introduction to Prolog III. *CACM*, 33:7:69–90, 1990.

44. A. Colmerauer, H. Kanoui, and M. Van Caneghem. Prolog, Bases Th'eoriques et D'evelopements Actuels. *Techniques et Sciences Informatiques*, 2:4:271–311, 1983.

45. G.E. Collins. Quantifier Elimination for Real Closed Fields by Cylindrical Algebraic Decomposition. *Proc. 2nd GI conference on Automata Theory and Languages*, LNCS 33, pp. 512-532, Springer-Verlag, 1975.

46. D. Comer. The Ubiquitous B-Tree. *Computing Surveys*, 11:2:121–137, 1979.

47. J. Cox, K. McAloon. Decision Procedures for Constraint Based Extensions of Datalog. In: *Constraint Logic Programming*, MIT Press, 1993.

48. J. Cox, K. McAloon, C. Tretkoff. Computational Complexity and Constraint Logic Programming. *Annals of Math. and AI*, 5:163–190, 1992.

49. M. Dincbas, P. Van Hentenryck, H. Simonis, A. Aggoun, T. Graf, F. Berthier. The Constraint Logic Programming Language CHIP. *Proc. Fifth Generation Computer Systems*, Tokyo Japan, 1988.

50. K. Doets, *From Logic to Logic Programming*. MIT PRess, 1994.

51. A. Ehrenfeucht. An application of games to the completeness problem formalized theories. *Fund. Math*, 49, 1961.

52. M.H. van Emden, R.A. Kowalski. The Semantics of Predicate Logic as a Programming Language. *J. ACM*, Vol. 23 (4), 733–742, 1976.

53. H.B. Enderton. *A Mathematical Introduction to Logic*. Academic Press, 1972.

54. J. Ferrante, J.R. Geiser. An Efficient Decision Procedure for the Theory of Rational Order. *Theoretical Computer Science*, 4:227–233, 1977.

55. J. Ferrante, C. Rackoff. A Decision Procedure for the First Order Theory of Real Addition with Order. *SIAM J. Comp*, 4:1:69–76, 1975.

56. J. Ferrante, C.W. Rackoff. *The Computational Complexity of Logical Theories*, Springer-Verlag (No. 718), 1979.

57. M.J. Fischer, M.O. Rabin. Super-Exponential Complexity of Presburger Arithmetic. *SIAM-AMS Proc. volume VII*, American Mathematical Society, 1974.

58. J-B.J. Fourier. Reported in: Analyse des travaux de l'Acadamie Royale des Sciences, pendant l'annee 1824, Partie mathematique, Histoire de l'Academie Royale des Sciences de l'Institut de France, Vol. 7, xlvii-lv, 1827. (Partial English translation in: D.A. Kohler. Translation of a Report by Fourier on his work on Linear Inequalities. Opsearch, Vol. 10, 38–42, 1973.)

59. R. Fraïssé. Sur les classifications des systèmes de relations. *Publ. Sci. Univ Alger*, I:1, 1954.

60. E. Freuder. Synthesizing Constraint Expressions. *CACM*, 21:11, 1978.

61. V. Gaede, A. Brodsky, O. Günther, D. Srivastava, V. Vianu, M. Wallace, (Eds.), *Constraint Databases and Applications*, Proc. Second Int. Workshop on Constraint Database Systems, Delphi, Greece, January 1997, and Workshop on Constraints and Databases, Cambridge, MA August 1996, Springer-Verlag LNCS 1191.

62. K. Gödel. Über formal unentscheidbare Sätze der Principia Mathematica und verwandter Systeme I. *Monatshefte für Mathematik und Physik*. vol. 38, 173–198, 1931.

63. R. Gross, R. Marti. Compile-time Constraint Solving in a Constraint Database System. *Proc. Post-ILPS'94 Workshop on Constraints and Databases*, 13–25, 1994.

64. Y. Gurevich, S. Shelah. Fixed-Point Extensions of First-Order Logic. *Annals of Pure and Applied Logic*, 32, 265–280, 1986.

65. S. Grumbach, J Su. Finitely Representable Databases. *Proc. 13th ACM Symp. on Principles of Database Systems*, 289–300, 1994.

66. S. Grumbach, J Su. Dense-Order Constraint Databases. *Proc. 14th ACM Symp. on Principles of Database Systems*, 66-77, 1995.

67. S. Grumbach, J Su. Towards Practical Constraint Databases. *Proc. 15h ACM Symp. on Principles of Database Systems*, 28–39, 1996.

68. S. Grumbach, J Su, C. Tollu. Linear Constraint Databases. *Proc. LCC*, 1994.

69. M.R. Hansen, B.S. Hansen, P. Lucas, P. van Emde Boas. Integrating Relational Databases and Constraint Languages. *Computer Languages*, 14:2:63–82, 1989.

70. N. Heintze, J. Jaffar. Set Constraints and Set-Based Analysis. *Proc. 2nd Workshop on Principles and Practice of Constraint Programming*, 1-17, 1994.

71. R. Helm, K. Marriott, M. Odersky. Constraint-based Query Optimization for Spatial Databases. *Proc. 10th ACM Symp. on Principles of Database Systems*, 181–191, 1991.

72. R. Hull, J. Su. Domain Independence and the Relational Calculus. *Acta Informatica*, 31, 513–524, 1994.

73. N. Immerman. Relational Queries Computable in Polynomial Time. *Information and Control*, 68:86-104, 1986.

74. J. Jaffar, J.L. Lassez. Constraint Logic Programming. *Proc. 14th ACM POPL*, 111–119, 1987.

75. J. Jaffar, M.J. Maher. Constraint Logic Programming: A Survey. *J.Logic Programming*, 19 & 20, 503–581, 1994.

76. J. Jaffar, S. Michaylov, P.J. Stuckey, R.H. Yap. The CLP(R) Language and System. *ACM Transactions on Programming Languages and Systems*, 14:3, 339-395, 1992.

77. D.S. Johnson. A Catalogue of Complexity Classes. *Handbook of Theoretical Computer Science*, Vol. A, chapter 2, (J. van Leeuwen editor), North-Holland, 1990.

78. F. Kabanza, J-M. Stevenne, P. Wolper. Handling Infinite Temporal Data. *Proc. 9th ACM Symp. on Principles of Database Systems*, 392–403, 1990. Final version to appear in *Journal of Computer and System Sciences*.

79. P.C. Kanellakis. Elements of Relational Database Theory. *Handbook of Theoretical Computer Science*, Vol. B, chapter 17, (J. van Leeuwen editor), North-Holland, 1990.

80. P.C. Kanellakis. Tutorial: Constraint Programming and Database Languages. *Proc. 14th ACM Symp. on Principles of Database Systems*, 46-53, 1995.

81. P.C. Kanellakis, D.Q. Goldin. Constraint Programming and Database Query Languages. *Proc. 2nd TACS*, 1994.

82. P.C. Kanellakis, G.M. Kuper, P. Z. Revesz. Constraint Query Languages. *Journal of Computer and System Sciences*, vol. 51, no. 1, pp. 26-52, August 1995. (Preliminary version in *Proc. 9th ACM Symp. on Principles of Database Systems*, 299–313, 1990.)

83. P.C. Kanellakis, J.L. Lassez, V.J. Saraswat, eds., *Proc. Workshop on the Principles and Practice of Constraint Programming*, 1993.

84. P. C. Kanellakis, S. Ramaswamy, D. E. Vengroff, J. S. Vitter. Indexing for Data Models with Constraints and Classes. *Proc. 12th ACM Symp. on Principles of Database Systems*, 233–243, 1993.

85. L.G. Khachian. A Polynomial Algorithm in Linear Programming. *Soviet Math. Dokl.*, 20(1), 191-194, 1979.

86. M. Kifer. On Safety, Domain Independence, and Capturability of Database Queries. *Proc. International Conference on Databases and Knowledge Bases*, Jerusalem Israel, 1988.

87. A. Klug. Equivalence of Relational Algebra and Relational Calculus Query Languages having Aggregate Functions. *JACM*, 29:3:699–717, 1982.

88. A. Klug. On Conjunctive Queries Containing Inequalities. *JACM*, 35:1:146–160, 1988.

89. P. Kolaitis, C.H. Papadimitriou. Why not Negation by Fixpoint? *Proc. 7th ACM Symp. on Principles of Database Systems*, 231–239, 1988.

90. M. Koubarakis. Representing and Querying in Temporal Databases: the Power of Temporal Constraints. *Proc. Ninth International Conference on Data Engineering*, 1993.

91. M. Koubarakis. Complexity Results for First-Order Theories of Temporal Constraints. *Int. Conf. on Knowledge Representation and Reasoning*, 1994.

92. D. Kozen, C. Yap. Algebraic Cell Decomposition in NC. *Proc. 26th IEEE FOCS*, 515–521, 1985.

93. B. Kuipers, J. Paredaens, Jan Van den Bussche. On Topological Elementary Equivalence of Spatial Databases. *Proc. 6th Int. Conf. on Database Theory*, 432–446, Springer-Verlag LNCS 1186, 1997.

94. G.M. Kuper. On the Expressive Power of the Relational Calculus with Arithmetic Constraints. *Proc. 3rd Int. Conf. on Database Theory*, 202–211, 1990.

95. G.M. Kuper. Aggregation in Constraint Databases. *Proc. Workshop on the Principles and Practice of Constraint Programming*, 176–183, 1993.

96. W. Leler. *Constraint Programming Languages*. Addison Wesley, 1987.

97. A. Levy, I.S. Mumick, Y. Sagiv, O. Shmueli. Equivalence, Query Reachability and Satisfiability in Datalog Extensions. *Proc. 12h ACM Symp. on Principles of Database Systems*, 109–122, 1993.

98. A. Levy, Y. Sagiv. Constraints and Redundancy in Datalog. *Proc. 11h ACM Symp. on Principles of Database Systems*, 67–80, 1992.

99. C. Langford. Some Theorems on Deducibility. *Annals of Mathematics*. vol. 28, 16–40, 459–471, 1927.

100. L. Libkin, L. Wong. New Techniques for Studying Set Languages, Bag Languages and Aggregate Functions. *Proc. 13h ACM Symp. on Principles of Database Systems*, 155–166, 1994.

101. J.W. Lloyd. *Foundations of Logic Programming*. Spring, Berlin, 2nd ed., 1987

102. A.K. Mackworth. Consistency in Networks of Relations. *AI*, 8:1, 1977.

103. M. J. Maher and D. Srivastava. Chasing Constraint-Tuple Generating Dependencies. *Proc. 15h ACM Symp. on Principles of Database Systems*, 128–138, 1996.

104. Y. Matiyasevich. Enumerable Sets are Diophantine. *Doklady Akademii Nauk SSR*. vol. 191, 279–282, 1970.

105. U. Montanari. Networks of Constraints: Fundamental Properties and Application to Picture Processing. *Information Science*, 7, 1974.

106. I. S. Mumick, S. J. Finkelstein, H. Pirahesh, R. Ramakrishnan. Magic Conditions. *Proc. 9th ACM Symp. on Principles of Database Systems*, 314–330, 1990.

107. I.S. Mumick, O. Shmueli. Universal Finiteness and Satisfiability. *Proc. 13h ACM Symp. on Principles of Database Systems*, 190–200, 1994.

108. C.H. Papadimitriou, D. Suciu, V. Vianu. Topological Queries in Spatial Databases. *Proc. 15h ACM Symp. on Principles of Database Systems*, 81–92, 1996.

109. J. Paredaens, J.V.D. Bussche, D.V. Gucht. Towards A Theory of Spatial Database Queries. *Proc. 13h ACM Symp. on Principles of Database Systems*, 279–288, 1994.

110. J. Paredaens. Spatial Databases: The Final Frontier. *Proc. 5th Int. Conf. on Database Theory*, Springer-Verlag LNCS 893, 1995.

111. J. Paredaens, J.V.D. Bussche, D.V. Gucht. First-Order Queries on Finite Structures over the Reals. *Proc. LICS*, 1995.

112. F.P. Preparata, M.I. Shamos. *Computational Geometry: An Introduction*. Springer-Verlag, 1985.

113. M. Presburger. Über die Vollständigkeit eines gewissen Systems der Arithmetik ganzer Zahlen, in welchem die Addition als einzige Operation hervortritt. Comptes Rendus, I. Congrès des Math. des Pays Slaves, Warsaw, 192–201, 395, 1929.

114. R. Ramakrishnan. Magic Templates: A Spellbinding Approach to Logic Programs. *Proc. 5th International Conference on Logic Programming*, 141–159, 1988.

115. R. Ramakrishnan, D. Srivastava, S. Sudarshan. CORAL: Control, Relations and Logic. *Proc. VLDB*, 1992.

116. R. Ramaswamy. Efficient Indexing for Constraint and Temporal Databases. *Proc. 6th Int. Conf. on Database Theory*, 419–431, Springer-Verlag LNCS 1186, 1997.

117. R. Ramaswamy, S. Subramanian. Path Caching: A Technique for Optimal External Searching *Proc. 13h ACM Symp. on Principles of Database Systems*, 25–35, 1994.

118. C.R. Reddy, D.W. Loveland. Presburger Arithmetic with Bounded Quantifier Alternation. *Proc. ACM Symp. on Theory of Comp.*, 320-325, 1978.

119. J. Renegar. On the Computational Complexity and Geometry of the First-order Theory of the Reals: Parts I–III. *Journal of Symbolic Computation*, 13:255–352, 1992.

120. P. Z. Revesz. *Constraint Query Languages*. Ph.D. Thesis. Brown University, 1991.

121. P. Z. Revesz. A Closed Form Evaluation for Datalog Queries with Integer (Gap)-Order Constraints, *Theoretical Computer Science*, vol. 116, no. 1, 117-149, 1993. (Preliminary version in *Proc. Third International Conference on Database Theory*, Springer-Verlag LNCS 470, 187–201, 1990.)

122. P. Z. Revesz. Datalog Queries of Set Constraint Databases. *Proc. Fifth International Conference on Database Theory*, Springer-Verlag LNCS 893, 425–438, 1995.

123. P. Z. Revesz. Safe Stratified Datalog with Integer Order Programs. *Proc. First International Conference on Principles and Practice of Constraint Programming*, Springer-Verlag LNCS 976, 154-169, 1995.

124. P. Z. Revesz. Safe Query Languages for Constraint Databases. *ACM Transactions on Database Systems*, March, 1998, to appear.

125. P. Z. Revesz. The Evaluation and the Computational Complexity of Datalog Queries of Boolean Constraint Databases, *International Journal of Algebra and Computation*, to appear.

126. P. Z. Revesz. Model-Theoretic Minimal Change Operators for Constraint Databases. *Proc. 6th Int. Conf. on Database Theory*, 447–460, Springer-Verlag LNCS 1186, 1997.

127. P. Z. Revesz. Refining Restriction Enzyme Genome Maps. *Constraints*, vol. 2, no. 3-4, pp. 361-375, December 1997. (Preliminary version in [61].)

128. J. Robinson. Definability and Decision Problems in Arithmetic. *Journal of Symbolic Logic*, Vol. 14, pp. 98–114, 1949.

129. H. Samet. *Applications of Spatial Data Structures: Computer Graphics, Image Processing, and GIS*. Addison-Wesley, Reading MA, 1990.

130. H. Samet. *The Design and Analysis of Spatial Data Structures*. Addison-Wesley, Reading MA, 1990.

131. V.A. Saraswat. *Concurrent Constraint Programming Languages*. Ph.D. thesis, Carnegie Mellon University, 1989.

132. D. Srivastava. Subsumption and Indexing in Constraint Query Languages with Linear Arithmetic Constraints. *Proc. 2nd International Symposium on Artificial Intelligence and Mathematics*, 1992.

133. D. Srivastava, R. Ramakrishnan. Pushing Constraint Selections. *Proc. 11h ACM Symp. on Principles of Database Systems*, 301–315, 1992.

134. D. Srivastava, R. Ramakrishnan, P.Z. Revesz. Constraint Objects. *Proc. 2nd Workshop on Principles and Practice of Constraint Programming*, Springer-Verlag LNCS 874, 274–284, 1994.

135. G.L. Steele. *The Definition and Implementation of a Computer Programming Language Based on Constraints*. Ph.D. Thesis, MIT, AI-TR 595, 1980.

136. A. Stolboushkin and M.A. Taitslin. Finite Queries do not have Effective Syntax. *Proc. 14th ACM Symp. on Principles of Database Systems*, 277–285, 1995.

137. A. Stolboushkin and M.A. Taitslin. Linear vs. Order Constraint Queries over Rational Databases. *Proc. 15h ACM Symp. on Principles of Database Systems*, 17–27, 1996.

138. P.J. Stuckey, S. Sudarshan. Compiling Query Constraints. *Proc. 13h ACM Symp. on Principles of Database Systems*, 56–67, 1994.

139. I.E. Sutherland. *SKETCHPAD: A Man-Machine Graphical Communication System*. Spartan Books, 1963.

140. B.A. Trakhtenbrot. The Impossibility of an Algorithm for the Decision Problem on Finite Models. (In Russian) *Doklady Akademii Nauk SSR*, 70, 569–572, 1950.

141. A. Tarski. *A Decision Method for Elementary Algebra and Geometry*. University of California Press, Berkeley, California, 1951.

142. A. Tarski, F.B. Thompson. Some General Properties of Cylindrical Algebras. *Bulletin of the AMS*, 58:65, 1952.

143. B. Thalheim. *Dependencies in Relational Databases*. Teubner Verlagsgesellschaft, Stuttgart and Leipzig, 1991.

144. D. Toman. Top-Down Beats Bottom-Up for Constraint Based Extensions of Datalog. *Proc. ILPS*, 98–112, 1995.

145. D. Toman. *Foundations of Temporal Query Languages.*, Ph.D. Thesis. Kansas State University, 1995.

146. D. Toman. Point vs. Interval-Based Query Languages for Temporal Databases. *Proc. 15h ACM Symp. on Principles of Database Systems*, 58–67, 1996.

147. D. Toman, J. Chomicki, D.S. Rogers. Datalog with Integer Periodicity Constraints. *Proc. ILPS*, 1994.

148. S. Tsur and C. Zaniolo. LDL: A Logic-Based Data-Language. *Proc. VLDB*, pp 33-41, 1986.

149. J.D. Ullman. *Principles of Database and Knowledge-Base Systems.* Computer Science Press, vol. 1&2, 1989.

150. R. van den Dries. Remarks on Tarski's problem concerning $(\mathbf{R}, +, *, exp)$. In *Logic Colloquium*, North-Holland, 1982. Elsevier.

151. R. van der Meyden. The Complexity of Querying Indefinite Data about Linearly Ordered Domains. *Proc. 11th ACM Symp. on Principles of Database Systems*, 331–346, 1992.

152. A. Van Gelder. Deriving Constraints among Argument Sizes in Logic Programs. *Proc. 9th ACM Symp. on Principles of Database Systems*, 47–60, 1990.

153. P. Van Hentenryck. Constraint Logic Programming, *The Knowledge Engineering Review*, 6, 165–180,1989.

154. P. Van Hentenryck. *Constraint Satisfaction in Logic Programming.* MIT Press, 1989.

155. M.Y. Vardi. The Complexity of Relational Query Languages. *Proc. 14th ACM STOC*, 137–146, 1982.

156. P. Voda. Types of Trilogy. *Proc. 5th International Conference on Logic Programming*, 580–589, 1988.

157. H.P. Williams. Fourier-Motzkin Elimination Extension to Integer Programming Problems. In *Journal of Combinatorial Theory (A).* vol. 21, 118–123, 1976.

Redundancy Elimination and a New Normal Form for Relational Database Design

Millist W. Vincent

Advanced Computing Research Centre, School of Computer and Information
Science, University of South Australia, Adelaide, Australia 5095
Email: millist.vincent@unisa.edu.au

Abstract. The relationship between redundancy elimination and normal forms
in relational database design is investigated for the case where the constraints
contain functional dependencies (FDs) and arbitrary join dependencies (JDs).
Extending previous work on the relationship between fourth normal form (4NF)
and redundancy elimination, a general definition of redundancy is proposed
which is applicable to any type of relational dependency including arbitrary JDs.
It is then shown that redundancy is eliminated if and only if the set of
dependencies satisfies a new condition called key-complete normal form
(KCNF). KCNF requires that the left-hand side of every FD is a superkey and that
for every JD, every attribute in the relation scheme is contained in the union of
the components of the JD which are superkeys. It is also shown that KCNF is a
strictly weaker condition than projection-join normal form (PJ/NF), the original
normal form proposed for Jds.

1 Introduction

Although normalisation [11, 12] is perhaps the oldest topic in relational database
theory and many normal forms have been defined [11, 12, 14, 15, 18, 30], the issue of
understanding and justifying the use of normal forms from a semantic perspective is
one that, although mentioned as an unsolved problem in database theory [24], has not
been completely resolved. While some research has addressed the issue in the simplest
case where the only constraints are *functional dependencies* (FDs) [6, 7, 9, 10, 15-17,
27], little work has been done, apart from some recent work by the author [27-29] and
some older work by Fagin [15, 16], on the more general case where the set of
constraints contains *multivalued dependencies* (MVDs) or, more generally, arbitrary
join dependencies (JDs) [5]. The purpose of this paper is to further the investigation
of the semantic foundations of normal forms by examining the formal relationship
between redundancy elimination and normal forms in this more general case.

In an earlier paper [28], a formal definition of redundancy, which we refer to as
syntactic redundancy to avoid confusion with the other definition to be presented later,
was proposed and the relationship between normal forms and the elimination of
syntactic redundancy was investigated. In the definition of syntactic redundancy, the
set of attributes XY in an FD $X \to Y$ or MVD $X \to\to Y$ is interpreted as the
fundamental semantic unit of information (referred to as a *fact*) and a relation scheme
is defined to be syntactically redundant if there exists a *legal relation* (satisfies the set
of constraints) defined over the scheme that contains two or more tuples having the
same value for a fact. It was then shown that a relation scheme is in 4NF if and only
if it is not syntactically redundant. The problem with this approach to defining

redundancy is that it is dependent on the syntactic structure of FDs and MVDs and it is not clear how to generalise the definition to arbitrary JDs or to other types of dependencies [23]. In a more recent paper [26], this problem was resolved by showing that redundancy could be defined in a more general fashion, which we refer to as *semantic redundancy*, so that it is applicable to any type of relational constraint yet is equivalent to syntactic redundancy when only FDs and MVDs are present. We now briefly outline this new and more fundamental view of redundancy.

An occurrence of a data value in a relation is semantically redundant if it is implied by the other data values in the relation and the constraints which apply to the relation. So if a data value occurrence is redundant in this sense, then the occurrence is 'fixed' by the other data and the set of constraints and so any change to the occurrence must result in the violation of the constraints. We then use this observation to formally define a relation scheme as being semantically redundant if there exists a legal relation defined over the scheme which contains a data value occurrence such that any change to the occurrence results in the violation of the constraints. We now illustrate this definition by an example.

Consider the often used example where the relation scheme is {*SUPPLIER, PART, PROJECT*} with the meaning that a tuple $<s, p, j>$ over the scheme represents the information that supplier s supplies part p to project j. Assume also that the only constraint is the JD *[SUPPLIER PART, PART PROJECT, SUPPLIER PROJECT]*. In the relation shown in Figure 1, each of the values $s*$, $p*$ and $j*$ in the tuple $<s*, p*, j*>$ is semantically redundant since changing any of them to a different value results in the violation of the JD.

SUPPLIER	PART	PROJECT
s*	p*	j
s*	p	j*
s	p*	j*
s*	p*	j*

Figure 1. A relation containing redundancy

For the case where only FDs and MVDs are present, we have shown elsewhere that a relation scheme is in 4NF if and only if the relation scheme is not semantically redundant [26] and thus, from the results in [28], semantic redundancy is equivalent to syntactic redundancy for the case where the only constraints are FDs and MVDs. The main contribution of this paper is to extend these previous results and derive a necessary and sufficient condition for a relation scheme to be free of redundancy[1] when the set of constraints contains FDs and arbitrary JDs. We prove that the necessary and sufficient condition for the elimination of redundancy is a new normal form that we call *key-complete normal form* (KCNF). A relation scheme is in KCNF if the left-hand side of every FD is a superkey and every JD (any MVD is treated as a JD) has the property that the union of its components which are superkeys contains every attribute in the relation scheme. We also show that this normal form is a weaker condition than *projection-join normal form* (PJ/NF), the original normal form for JDs proposed by Fagin [16], and 5NFR, a recent corrected version of the normal form 5NF originally proposed in [19].

---

[1] For the rest of the paper, the term redundancy will implicitly refer to semantic redundancy.

The rest of this paper is organised as follows. Section 2 contains preliminary definitions and notation. A discussion and formal definition of redundancy is presented in Section 3. In Section 4 the normal form KCNF is formally defined and the main result of this paper, that KCNF is a necessary and sufficient condition to eliminate redundancy, is presented. KCNF is compared to PJ/NF in Section 5 and it is shown that KCNF is a strictly weaker condition than PJ/NF. Finally, Section 6 contains concluding comments.

2 Basic Definitions and Concepts

We assume that the reader is familiar with basic relational concepts and the definitions of FDs and MVDs as given in standard database texts [19]. We now outline some of the basic results and notation that will be used later in this paper.

Let R denote a relation scheme and Σ a set of dependencies defined over R. Σ^+ denotes the set of all dependencies implied by Σ. The closure of a set of attributes X, denoted by X^+, is the set of attributes such that an attribute $A \in X^+$ if $X \rightarrow A \in \Sigma^+$. The *dependency basis* for a set of attributes X, denoted by DEP(X), is a set of attributes sets which can be written as $\{X_1, \ldots, X_p, X_1^+, \ldots, X_j^+, W_1, \ldots, W_n\}$ with the following properties [4]:

(i) DEP(X) covers R, i.e. $R = \cup Z_i$ where $Z_i \in$ DEP(X);

(ii) The sets in DEP(X) are disjoint;

(iii) $X \rightarrow\rightarrow Y \in \Sigma^+$ if and only if $Y = \cup Z_i$ where $Z_i \in$ DEP(X);

(iv) $X_1, \ldots, X_p$ are single attribute sets such that $X = \bigcup_{i=1}^{i=p} X_i$;

(v) $X_1^+, \ldots, X_j^+$ are single attribute sets such that $X^+ - X = \bigcup_{i=1}^{i=j} X_i^+$.

Without loss of generality, we shall assume that the left and right hand sides of FDs and MVDs are disjoint [14]. Let $R_1, \ldots, R_p$ be nonempty subsets of a relation scheme R. If there are tuples $t_1, \ldots, t_p$ (not necessarily distinct) in a relation r such that $t_i[R_i \cap R_j] = t_j[R_i \cap R_j]$ for all i, j such that $1 \le i \le p, 1 \le j \le p$, then $t_1, \ldots, t_p$ are said to *join completely* on $\{R_1, R_2, \ldots, R_p\}$. In this case, there exists a unique tuple t such that $t[R_i] = t_i[R_i]$ for all $i, 1 \le i \le p$, which is called the *join* of $t_1, \ldots, t_p$ on $\{R_1, \ldots, R_p\}$. A *join dependency* (JD) is a constraint denoted by $*[R_1, \ldots, R_p]$. A relation r satisfies the join dependency $*[R_1, \ldots, R_p]$ if for every set of tuples $t_1, \ldots, t_p \in r$ which join completely on $\{R_1, R_2, \ldots, R_p\}$, r also contains the join of $t_1, \ldots, t_p$ on $\{R_1, \ldots, R_p\}$. $R_1, \ldots, R_p$ are referred to as the *components* of the JD. The result [14] that any MVD $X \rightarrow\rightarrow Y$ is equivalent to the JD $*[XY, XZ]$, where $Z = R - XY$, will be used often in this paper. A JD $*[R_1, \ldots, R_p]$ is *total* if $R = \bigcup_{i=1}^{i=p} R_i$. A JD is trivial if it is satisfied by every relation r. It can be shown that a JD $*[R_1, \ldots, R_p]$ is trivial iff there exists a component R_i such that $R_i = R$.

A JD $*[R_1, \ldots, R_p]$ is *total* if $R = R_1 \ldots R_p$. *In this paper all JDs in Σ will be assumed to be total.* We also note the following inference rule for determining when a total JD implies another total JD [5].

A1: Let $*[R_1, \ldots, R_p]$ and $*[S_1, \ldots, S_k]$ be total JDs defined over a scheme R. Then $*[R_1, \ldots, R_p]$ implies $*[S_1, \ldots, S_k]$ iff for every R_i there exists an S_j such that $R_i \subseteq S_j$.

The set of all relations which satisfy a set Σ of FD and JD constraints is denoted by SAT(Σ). Given a set Σ of FDs and JDs and a dependency σ, Σ *implies* σ if every relation that satisfies Σ also satisfies σ. The *closure* of a set Σ of FDs and JDs, denoted by Σ^+, is the set of FDs and JDs implied by Σ. Two sets of dependencies, Σ and Ψ, are *equivalent*, written as $\Sigma \equiv \Psi$, if $\Sigma^+ = \Psi^+$.

A set of attributes X is a *superkey* for a relation scheme R if the FD $X \rightarrow R \in \Sigma^+$. X is a *candidate key* if it is a superkey and it has no proper subset X' such that $X' \rightarrow R \in \Sigma^+$. The set of *key constraints*, denoted by Σ_k, is the set of all FDs in Σ^+ of the form $K \rightarrow R$ where K is a candidate key of R. Obviously, if a relation satisfies Σ then it also satisfies Σ_k but the converse is not true. The set of all relations satisfying Σ_k is denoted by SAT(Σ_k). Also, it is easily seen that a relation is in SAT(Σ_k) if and only if no two tuples in the relation have the same value for a candidate key.

Let R be a relation scheme and let Σ be a set of JDs and FDs that apply to R. Then (R, Σ) is in *Boyce-Codd normal form* (BCNF) [12] if for every nontrivial FD $X \rightarrow Y \in \Sigma^+$, X is a superkey. (R, Σ) is in *fourth normal form* (4NF)[14] if for every nontrivial MVD $X \rightarrow\rightarrow Y$ in Σ^+, X is a superkey.

2.1 Tableau

A *tableau* is a matrix consisting of sets of rows [2, 20]. Each column in the tableau corresponds to an attribute in U. Each row consists of variables from a set V, which is the disjoint union of two sets V_d and V_n. V_d is the set of *distinguished variables* (dv's) and V_n is the set of *nondistinguished variables* (ndv's). Any variable can appear in at most one column, a dv must appear in each column and at most one dv can appear in a column.

A *valuation* is a function ρ that maps each variable to an element in DOM(A) where A is the column in which the variable appears. This is extended to a function from a tableau T to a relation over R in the obvious manner. Let Σ be a set of FDs and JDs (any MVD is treated as a JD). The *chase* is the result of applying the following transformations to a tableau T until no further changes can be made:

F-Rule: If $X \rightarrow A \in \Sigma$ and T has rows ω_1 and ω_2 where $\omega_1[X] = \omega_2[X]$ and $v_1 = \omega_1[A]$ and $v_2 = \omega_2[A]$, then if either of v_1 or v_2 is a dv and the other is not, then the ndv is changed to the dv. If both are ndv's, then the one with the larger subscript is replaced by the one with the smaller subscript.

J-Rule: If $*[R_1, R_2, \ldots, R_p] \in \Sigma$ and there exists a row ω such that $\omega[R_1] \in T[R_1], \ldots, \omega[R_p] \in T[R_p]$, ω is added to T.

Let $chase_\Sigma(T)$ be the tableau that results from applying the F-rules and J-rules until no more changes can be made to the tableau. It can then be shown [19, 20] that the chase always terminates and the resulting tableau is unique, independent of the sequence in which the rules are applied, up to a renaming of the ndv's.

We will use the following results [19, 20] on the properties of the chase later in this paper:

Lemma 2.1. *Any valuation ρ of $chase_\Sigma(T)$ which is a one-to-one mapping satisfies Σ.*

Lemma 2.2. *Let T_X be the tableau constructed as follows. It contains two rows, one denoted by ω_d and the other, denoted by ω_X. Row ω_d contains only dv's and ω_X contains dv's in the X-columns and ndv's elsewhere. Let $T^* = chase_\Sigma(T_X)$ and let ω_d^* and ω_X^* be the rows in T^* that correspond to ω_d and ω_X in T (ω_d^* and ω_X^* may be the same row). Then $\omega_d^* = \omega_d$ and an FD $X \to Y \in \Sigma^+$ iff the Y-columns in T^* contain only dv's.*

Lemma 2.3. *Let T be a tableau, Σ a set of FDs and JDs and ρ a valuation for T such that $\rho(T) \subseteq r$ where $r \in SAT(\Sigma)$. If $T = T^0, T^1, \ldots, T^n$ is a sequence of tableau's generated in computing $chase_\Sigma(T)$, then for all i, $0 \le i \le n$, $\rho(\omega) = \rho(\omega_i)$ where ω is any row in T^0 and ω_i is the corresponding row in T^i.*

Lemma 2.4. *Let Σ be a set of FDs and JDs and let σ denote the JD $*[R_1, R_2, \ldots, R_p]$. The tableau T_σ is constructed as follows. It contains rows $\omega_1, \ldots, \omega_p$ where row ω_i contains dv's in the columns of R_i and distinct ndv's elsewhere. Then $\sigma \in \Sigma^+$ iff $chase_\Sigma(T_\sigma)$ contains a row of only dv's.*

Lemma 2.5. *If $\Sigma \equiv \Sigma'$ then, for any tableau T, $chase_\Sigma(T) = chase_{\Sigma'}(T)$.*

3 Defining Redundancy

As discussed in Section 1, the definition of redundancy that we propose is the following [26].

Definition 3.1. Let R be a relation scheme, A an attribute in R, Σ a set of FDs and JDs, $r(R)$ a relation in $SAT(\Sigma)$ and t a tuple in r. The data value occurrence $t[A]$ is *redundant* (RED) if for *every* replacement of $t[A]$ by a value a' such that $t[A] \ne a'$ and resulting in a new relation r', then $r' \notin SAT(\Sigma)$.

We then use this definition to define a normal form in which redundancy is absent.

Definition 3.2. A relation r is RED if there exists an occurrence $t[A]$ in r which is RED, and the pair (R, Σ) is in *redundancy free normal form* (RFNF) if there does not exist $r(R) \in \text{SAT}(\Sigma)$ that is RED.

Consistent with our other related work [27-29], RFNF is referred to as a *semantic normal form* in contrast to the classical normal forms, such as BCNF and 4NF, which we refer to as *syntactic normal forms*. The difference between the two types of normal forms is that semantic normal forms directly specify the set of relations with the desired design properties, whereas the syntactic normal forms only do this indirectly by being defined in terms of the syntactic properties of the set of dependencies. We believe that semantic normal forms, by making explicit the aims of database design, are the appropriate starting point for a proper understanding of the goals of database design. However, semantic normal forms are neither easy, nor efficient, to apply directly and so the role of syntactic normal forms are as computationally tractable equivalents for semantic normal forms. Hence the thrust of this, and other [7-9], work on the foundations of database design is centred on the formal derivation of equivalent syntactic normal forms for semantic normal forms.

Some comments on the definition of RFNF and some illustrative examples are appropriate at this point. Firstly, we emphasise that for a data value occurrence to be redundant every change to the value must result in a violation of the constraints. For example, consider the relation r in Figure 2 defined over the attributes $\{A, B, C\}$ and assume that the set of constraints is $\{A \rightarrow B, B \rightarrow C\}$.

r

A	B	C
a_1	b_1	c_1
a_2	b_2	c_2

Figure 2.

Although changing b_1 to b_2 (or b_2 to b_1) in r results in $B \rightarrow C$ being violated, neither occurrence is redundant according to our definition since all other changes to b_1 (or to b_2) do not result in a constraint violation. Intuitively, this makes sense since neither b_1 nor b_2 is derivable from the values in the relation and the set of constraints.

A second comment on the definition of redundancy is that it is a specific occurrence of a data value in a tuple, rather than the value itself, which is redundant. For example, in Figure 1 (see Section 1), the occurrence of $s*$ (similarly for $p*$ and $j*$) in the tuple $\langle s*, p*, j* \rangle$ is RED but not the occurrence of $s*$ in $\langle s*, p, j* \rangle$ or $\langle s*, p*, j \rangle$ since changing either of those occurrences does not result in the JD being violated.

The next comment on the definition of redundancy concerns the relationship between redundancy and the duplication of component values of a JD. If one considers the relation in Figure 3, then both occurrences of b_2 (and similarly all occurrences of b_1, c_2 and c_1) are RED if the only constraint is the MVD $A \rightarrow\rightarrow B$.

A	B	C
a_1	b_2	c_2
a_1	b_1	c_1
a_1	b_2	c_1
a_1	b_1	c_2

Figure 3.

In this example, the relation contains tuples with duplicate values for AB and AC which, when an MVD is equated with its corresponding JD $*[AB, AC]$, are components of a JD. As will be seen in the next section, the equivalence between a relation containing a RED occurrence and the presence of duplicate component values in the relation is always valid when only FDs and MVDs are present in the set of constraints. However, in the more general case where there are JDs which are not MVDs, a relation may contain duplicate component values of a JD but not be RED. For instance, if one uses the relation scheme of Figure 3 and assumes that the applicable constraint is the JD $*[AB, BC, AC]$, rather than $A \rightarrow\rightarrow B$, then the relation satisfies the JD yet is not RED since every value in the relation can be changed to a new value such that the JD remains satisfied. However, the relation contains tuples which have duplicate values for the components AB and AC.

Finally, we note that there is one other property that every normal form, semantic or syntactic, should possess and that is cover invariance [3]. A normal form is *cover invariant* if the property is invariant under replacement of the set of constraints by an equivalent set. It is easily seen that BCNF and 4NF are cover invariant since their definitions involve testing dependencies in the closure which is the same for equivalent sets of dependencies. From Definition 3.1, it is clear that if $t[A]$ is RED with respect to one set of dependencies then it is also RED with respect to any equivalent set of dependencies and so RFNF is cover invariant.

4 Redundancy And Normal Forms

In this section we will establish the main result of the paper that RFNF is equivalent to a new syntactic normal form called KCNF when the set of dependencies contains FDs and arbitrary JDs. Firstly, we demonstrate the utility of our new approach to defining redundancy by showing that RFNF is equivalent to 4NF when the only constraints are FDs and MVDs. A proof of this also appears in [26] but is presented again here for the sake of completeness.

Theorem 4.1. *If R is a relation scheme and Σ is a set of FDs and MVDs which apply to R, then (R, Σ) is in RFNF iff it is in 4NF.*

If : We shall show the contrapositive that if R is not in RFNF then it is not in 4NF. If R is not in RFNF then there exists $r \in SAT(\Sigma)$ and a value $t[A] \in r$ that is RED. Change $t[A]$ to a', where $a' \notin r[A]$, resulting in a new tuple t' and a new relation r' and suppose firstly that an FD $X \rightarrow Y$ is violated in r'. The violation must involve t' and some other tuple $t_1 \in r'$ where $t'[X] = t_1[X]$ and $t'[Y] \neq t_1[Y]$. Then $t_1 \in r$ since t is the only tuple changed in r. Also, $A \in XY$ since $X \rightarrow Y$ is satisfied in r but not in r', and since $a' \notin r[A]$ and $t'[X] = t_1[X]$ then $A \notin X$ and so

$t'[X] = t[X]$ and thus $t_1[X] = t[X]$. Hence X cannot be a superkey and the 4NF assumption is contradicted. Alternatively, assume that an MVD $X \rightarrow\rightarrow Y$ is violated and so there exists again t_1 where $t_1 \in r$ and $t_1 \in r'$ such that $t_1[X] = t'[X]$. So, since $a' \notin r[A]$, $A \in Y$ or $A \in Z$ where $Z = R - XY$. Again this implies $t_1[X] = t[X]$ and so contradicts the 4NF assumption.

Only If: The contrapositive that if R is not in 4NF then it is not in RFNF will be shown. Because R is not in 4NF there exists a nontrivial MVD $X \rightarrow\rightarrow Y \in \Sigma^+$ where X is not a superkey and so there exists $W_i \in DEP(X)$ such that $X^+ \cap W_i = \emptyset$. By a well known result (Theorem 8.3.5 in [1]) any relation r of two tuples which are identical on all attributes except those in W_i is in SAT(Σ). Firstly, if there exists an $X_j^+ \in DEP(X)$ then both values of X_j^+ are RED in r since changing either causes $X \rightarrow X_j^+$ to be violated. Alternatively, if $X = X^+$ then we claim that there are two sets W_i and W_j in $DEP(X)$ disjoint from X. If there is only W_i then, since $X \cap Y = \emptyset$, property (iii) of $DEP(X)$ implies $Y = W_i$ and so, by property (i), $XY = R$ contradicting the fact that $X \rightarrow\rightarrow Y$ is nontrivial. It then follows that every value of every attribute of W_j is RED in r. $\qquad\square$

We also note that since it is well known [19] that 4NF reduces to BCNF if only FDs are present, then this result also shows that BCNF is the exact condition required to avoid redundancy when only FDs are present. We now extend the analysis to the more general case where arbitrary JDs are permitted and introduce the notion of key-completeness for a JD.

Definition 4.1. Let Σ be a set of FDs and JDs. A JD $*[R_1, \ldots, R_p] \in \Sigma^+$ is *key-complete* (KC) if the union of its components which are superkeys is equal to R.

For example, if $R = \{A, B, C, D\}$ and $\Sigma = \{A \rightarrow BCD, B \rightarrow ACD, *[AB, BC, CD]\}$ then A and B are candidate keys. By inference rule A1, $*[AB, BC, ACD] \in \Sigma^+$ and is KC since every component is a superkey and their union is equal to R, but $*[AB, BC, CD]$ is not KC since CD is not a superkey. We now define a syntactic normal form based on this property.

Definition 4.2. Let R be a relation scheme and let Σ be a set of FDs and total JDs (MVDs are treated as JDs) which apply to R. Then (R, Σ) is in *key-complete normal form* (KCNF) if the left-hand side of every nontrivial FD in Σ is a superkey and every JD in Σ is KC.

We note that since the definition of KCNF only involves the dependencies in Σ, rather than Σ^+, it is not immediate that this definition satisfies the cover invariance requirement for normal forms discussed in the previous section. The fact that it does is a corollary of the main theorem of this section on the equivalence between KCNF and RFNF. We also note that testing whether a scheme is in KCNF can be done in polynomial time since testing if an FD is implied by a set of FDs and JDs can be done in polynomial time [21].

Before establishing the main result of the paper, some preliminary lemmas are first established. The first generalises a well known result on using the chase to determine if an FD is implied by a set of constraints. The proof follows that used in [20].

Lemma 4.1. *Let Σ be a set of FDs and JDs, let σ be a JD $*[R_1, \ldots, R_p]$ in Σ and let A be any attribute in R. Then for any component R_i of σ, $R_i \rightarrow A \in \Sigma^+$ iff $\omega_i^* [A]$ contains a dv, where ω_i^* is the row in $chase_\Sigma(T_\sigma)$ corresponding to ω_i in the tableau T_σ.*

Proof.
Only If
Let $T^* = chase_\Sigma(T_\sigma)$ and suppose to the contrary that $\omega_i^* [A]$ contains a ndv. By construction of T_σ, the J-rule can be applied to T_σ to create a row ω which contains only dv's. Since dv's are unchanged during the chase, ω must be in T^* and $\omega_i^* [R_i]$ must contain only dv's and so ω and ω_i^* agree on R_i in T^*. By Lemma 2.1, $\rho(T^*) \in SAT(\Sigma)$ for any one-one-one mapping ρ but $\rho(\omega_i^* [A]) \neq \rho(\omega[A])$ because $\omega_i^* [A]$ contains a ndv contradicting the assumption that $R_i \rightarrow A \in \Sigma^+$.

If
Suppose that $\omega_i^* [A]$ contains a dv, let r be any relation in $SAT(\Sigma)$ and let t_1 and t_2 be any two tuples in r such that $t_1[R_i] = t_2[R_i]$. Let T^1 be the tableau generated from T_σ by applying the JD $*[R_1, \ldots, R_p]$ to T_σ. This results in adding a row ω containing only dv's to T_σ. We firstly claim that there is a valuation ρ for T^1 such that $\rho(\omega_i) = t_1$ and $\rho(\omega) = \rho(\omega_2) \ldots = \rho(\omega_p) = t_2$. This valuation ρ is defined by mapping every dv in T^1 to the value in the corresponding column of t_2, every ndv in every row, except ω_i, to the value in the corresponding column of t_2 and every ndv in ω_i to the value in the corresponding column of t_1. This mapping is well defined because t_1 and t_2 agree on R_i. As a result, $\rho(T^1) \subseteq r$. Let $T^* = chase_\Sigma(T_\sigma)$ and consider the rows ω^* and ω_i^* in T^* corresponding to rows ω and ω_i in T^1. Since dv's are unchanged during the chase, $\omega^* = \omega$ and so $\omega_i^* [A] = \omega[A]$, since $\omega_i^* [A]$ contains a dv, and hence $\rho(\omega_i^* [A]) = \rho(\omega[A])$. Then applying Lemma 2.3 we obtain $\rho(\omega_i^* [A]) = \rho(\omega_i[A])$ and so $\rho(\omega[A]) = \rho(\omega_i[A])$ and thus $t_1[A] = t_2[A]$ by definition of ρ. Since r was arbitrary, it follows that $X \rightarrow A \in \Sigma^+$. $\qquad\square$

The next result is part of relational theory 'folklore', but for the sake of completeness we present a proof since we have been unable to locate a proof in the literature.

Lemma 4.2. *Let R be a relation scheme and let Σ be a set of FDs and JDs which apply to R. If X is a set of attributes that is not a superkey, then there exists a relation containing at least two tuples that satisfies Σ and in which all tuples are identical on X.*

Proof. Let T_X, ω_d, ω_X, T^*, ω_d^* and ω_X^* be as defined in Section 2. Also, let ρ be any one-to-one valuation of T^*. The claim is that $\rho(T^*)$ is the relation required.

Firstly, by Lemma 2.1, $\rho(T^*) \in SAT(\Sigma)$. Secondly, T^*, and hence $\rho(T^*)$, must consist of more than one row. This follows because from Lemma 2.2, if T^* consists of one row then it must be ω_d, but since ω_d contains only dv's, this would imply by Lemma 2.2 the contradiction that X is a superkey.

Secondly, we claim that for every attribute $A \in X$, the A-column of T^* contains a single dv and so all rows in T^*, and thus $\rho(T^*)$, are identical on X. This follows from an inductive argument. Let T^i represent the tableau at some stage of the chase and assume inductively that for all $A \in X$, $T^i[A]$ consists of a single dv. If a J-rule is applied to T^i to produce a new row ω', then by definition of the J-rule, for each attribute $B \in R$, there is a row ω in T^i such that $\omega'[B] = \omega[B]$. So, by the induction hypothesis, $\omega'[A]$ will contain the same dv as $T^i[A]$ and the inductive hypothesis is again true. Alternatively, if an F-rule is applied then the dv in each of the columns in X will remain unchanged since the F-rule does not change dv's. Initially, T_X satisfies the induction hypothesis and so the result is proven. □

We now present the main result of the paper which establishes the equivalence of KCNF and RFNF. Before doing this, an example is presented which illustrates the technique used in the proof to establish that RFNF implies KCNF.

Example 1. Let $R = \{A, B, C, D\}$ and $\Sigma = \{B \rightarrow ACD, *[AB, BC, ACD]\}$. (R, Σ) is not in KCNF because ACD is not a superkey. Consider the relation r, shown in Figure 4, which results from computing the chase for the tableau T_σ where σ is the JD $*[AB, BC, ACD]$. Denote the first tuple in r by t_1 and the second by t_2. Then $t_2[22]$ is RED since if it is changed to d_2, resulting in a new tuple t' and relation r', then $r' \notin SAT(\Sigma)$ because the tuples t', t', t_1 still join completely on $\{AB, BC, ACD\}$ to result in t_2 but $t_2 \notin r'$.

	A	B	C	D
t_1:	a_1	b_2	c_1	d_1
t_2:	a_1	b_1	c_1	d_1

	A	B	C	D
t_1:	a_1	b_2	c_1	d_1
t':	a_1	b_1	c_1	d_2

Figure 4.

Theorem 4.2. *If R is a relation scheme and Σ is a set of total JDs and FDs which apply to R, then (R, Σ) is in KCNF iff it is in RFNF.*

Proof.
KCNF $\Rightarrow$ RFNF
The proof is by contradiction. Assume that R is not in RFNF and so there exists a relation r and a value $t[A] \in r$ which is RED. Thus if $t[A]$ is changed to a new

value a' such that $a' \notin r[A]$ resulting in a new tuple t' and relation r' (so $t'[A] = a'$) then $r' \notin SAT(\Sigma)$. We consider separately the two cases of whether the dependency in Σ violated by the update is a FD or a JD (any MVD is treated as a JD).

(a) The FD case:

The same argument used in Theorem 4.1 shows that X is not a superkey and so (R, Σ) is not in KCNF.

(b) The JD case:

Assume firstly that r' violates a JD $*[R_1, \ldots, R_p]$ in Σ which we denote by σ. This implies there exist tuples $t'_1, \ldots, t'_p$ (not necessarily distinct) $\in r'$ which join completely on $\{R_1, \ldots, R_p\}$ to yield a tuple t'' such that $t'' \notin r'$. Without loss of generality, relabel the components of σ if necessary (and the tuples $t'_1, \ldots, t'_p$) so that the first k components of σ, $R_1, \ldots, R_k$, $0 \le k \le p$, are superkeys and $R_{k+1}, \ldots, R_p$ are not. Also, for any tuple $s \in r'$, denote by $P(s)$ the corresponding tuple in r. Since only tuple t in r was changed (to t'), it follows that $s = P(s)$ if $s \ne t'$. We shall firstly show that $P(t'_1), \ldots, P(t'_p)$ join completely on $\{R_1, \ldots, R_p\}$ in r by proving that $P(t'_i)[R_i \cap R_j] = P(t'_j)[R_i \cap R_j]$ for all i, j, $1 \le i \le p$ and $1 \le j \le p$.

Firstly, because $t'[A] \notin r$ and $t[A]$ is the only value in r which was modified, $t'[A]$ can appear in r' only in those t'_i which are equal to t'. So since $t'_1, \ldots, t'_p$ join completely, if $t'_i \ne t'$ and $t'_j = t'$ then $A \notin R_i \cap R_j$. Obviously if $t'_i = t'$ and $t'_j = t'$ then $P(t'_i)[R_i \cap R_j] = P(t'_j)[R_i \cap R_j]$ so suppose that $t'_i \ne t'$ and $t'_j \ne t'$. Then $P(t'_i)[R_i \cap R_j] = t'_i[R_i \cap R_j]$ because $P(t'_i) = t'_i$, and $P(t'_j)[R_i \cap R_j] = t'_j[R_i \cap R_j]$ since $P(t'_j) = t'_j$, and $t'_i[R_i \cap R_j] = t'_j[R_i \cap R_j]$ since $t'_1, \ldots, t'_p$ join completely and so $P(t'_i)[R_i \cap R_j] = P(t'_j)[R_i \cap R_j]$. Alternatively, suppose that $t'_i \ne t'$ and $t'_j = t'$ (by symmetry, the same argument applies if $t'_j \ne t'$ and $t'_i = t'$). Then, as noted previously, $A \notin R_i \cap R_j$ and so $P(t'_j)[R_i \cap R_j] = t'_j[R_i \cap R_j]$ because only $t[A]$ was changed. Also, $t'_j[R_i \cap R_j] = t'_i[R_i \cap R_j]$ since $t'_1, \ldots, t'_p$ join completely and $t'_i[R_i \cap R_j] = P(t'_i)[R_i \cap R_j]$ since $t'_i = P(t'_i)$ as $t'_i \ne t'$ and hence $P(t'_i)[R_i \cap R_j] = P(t'_j)[R_i \cap R_j]$. So $P(t'_1), \ldots, P(t'_p)$ join completely in r and the result of the join, denoted by $t*$, must be in r because $r \in SAT(\Sigma)$.

Next we claim that $P(t'_1) = \ldots = P(t'_k)$. This follows because $P(t'_1), \ldots, P(t'_p)$ join completely and so $t*[R_i] = P(t'_i)[R_i]$ for all i, $1 \le i \le p$, and hence $t* = P(t'_1) = \ldots = P(t'_k)$ since there cannot be two distinct tuples in r with the same value for a superkey. As a result, $t'_1 = \ldots = t'_k$ also. Then since $t'_1, \ldots, t'_p$ join completely to give t'', $t''[R_i] = t'_i [R_i]$ for all i, $1 \le i \le p$, and so since by the KCNF assumption $R = R_1 \ldots R_k$ and $t'_1 = \ldots = t'_k$, then $t'' = t'_1 = \ldots = t'_k$ contradicting the assumption that $t'' \notin r'$.

<u>RFNF $\Rightarrow$ KCNF</u>

We shall show that if (R, Σ) is not in KCNF then there exists $r(R)$ that is RED and so (R, Σ) is not in RFNF. Suppose firstly that there is a nontrivial FD $X \to Y \in \Sigma$ where X is not a superkey. A simple application of the inference rules shows that if X is not a superkey then XY is not a superkey and so by Lemma 4.2 there exists a relation r in SAT(Σ) of at least two tuples for which every tuple is identical on XY. Then r is RED since changing any value appearing in a Y-column to a different value results in $X \to Y$ being violated.

Alternatively, suppose that there is a JD $*[R_1, \ldots, R_p]$ in Σ, denoted by σ, which is not KC. By relabelling the components if necessary, let $R_1, \ldots, R_k$ be the components of σ which are superkeys and $R_{k+1}, \ldots, R_p$ be the components which are not superkeys. Because (R, Σ) is not in KCNF and the fact that all JDs in Σ are total, it follows that there is at least one component of σ which is not a superkey and so $0 \le k < p$.

As outlined in Section 2, the tableau T_σ is defined to consist of rows $\omega_1, \ldots, \omega_p$ where row ω_i contains dv's in the columns of R_i and distinct ndv's elsewhere. Let $T^* = chase_\Sigma(T_\sigma)$ and let $\omega_1^*, \ldots, \omega_p^*$ be the rows (not necessarily distinct) in T^* corresponding to the rows $\omega_1, \ldots, \omega_p$ in T_σ. By Lemma 2.4, T^* contains a row ω of only dv's and it is easily seen that ω is the result of joining $\omega_1^*, \ldots, \omega_p^*$ on $\{R_1, \ldots, R_p\}$ since dv's are unchanged during the chase. Then because $R_{k+1}, \ldots, R_p$ are not superkeys, it follows from Lemma 4.1 that each of the rows $\omega_{k+1}^*, \ldots, \omega_p^*$ must contain at least one ndv and so each of these rows is distinct from ω (but possibly not distinct from each other). If one replaces Σ by the set $\Sigma \cup \{R_1 \to R, \ldots, R_k \to R\}$ and uses Lemma 2.5, then it also follows that $\omega = \omega_1^* = \ldots = \omega_k^*$. Since (R, Σ) is not in KCNF, there exists at least one attribute A in $R - R_1 \ldots R_k$. Consider then, by Lemma 2.1, T^* as a relation in SAT(Σ) and change $\omega[A]$ to a new value a^* and denote the new relation by T'. This change leaves $\omega_1^* [R_1], \ldots, \omega_k^* [R_k]$ unchanged because $A \in R - R_1 \ldots R_k$ and $\omega_{k+1}^* [R_{k+1}], \ldots, \omega_p^* [R_p]$ unchanged because only row ω in T^* is changed and $\omega_{k+1}^*, \ldots, \omega_p^*$ are distinct from ω. So $\omega_1^*, \ldots, \omega_p^*$ still join completely on $\{R_1, \ldots, R_p\}$ and so σ is violated since $\omega \notin T'$ and, since T^* cannot contain duplicate tuples, no other tuple in T' can be equal to ω. $\square$

A simple corollary of this theorem is that KCNF is cover invariant since, as noted earlier, RFNF is cover invariant.

5. KCNF and Other Normal Forms for JDs

In this section we will discuss the relationship between KCNF and the two other normal forms for JDs. The first, called *projection-join normal form* (PJ/NF), was proposed by Fagin [16] and we recall its definition.

Definition 5.1. If R is a relation scheme and Σ a set of FDs and JDs, then (R, Σ) is in PJ/NF if for every JD $\sigma \in \Sigma^+$, σ is implied by the set of FDs in Σ^+ of the form $K \rightarrow R$; in other words, satisfaction of the key constraints implies satisfaction of all other constraints.

The second normal form, 5NF, was proposed in [19] and requires that every component of every nontrivial JD in Σ^+ is a superkey. However, in a companion paper [25], it was shown that this definition is inadequate because it does not coincide with 4NF when the allowable JDs are MVDs and a corrected definition of 5NF, called 5NFR, was proposed based on the following notion of a strong-reduced JD.

Definition 5.2. Let Σ be a set of FDs and JDs. A JD *[$R_1, \ldots, R_p$] in Σ^+ is *strong-reduced* if it is total and for every component R_i, $1 \le i \le p$, the JD obtained by removing R_i from *[$R_1, \ldots, R_p$] is either not in Σ^+ or it is not total.

For example, let $R = \{A, B, C\}$ and $\Sigma = \{A \rightarrow BC, *[AB, BC]\}$. Then *[$AB, BC$] is strong-reduced since removing either component results in a JD that is not total, whereas *[AB, BC, AC] $\in \Sigma^+$ by inference rule A1 but is not strong-reduced since *[AB, BC] $\in \Sigma$. It was also shown in [25] that every set of FDs and JDs has a cover in which every JD is strong-reduced.

This leads then to the following corrected definition of 5NF which was shown in [25] to coincide with 4NF when the allowable JDs are MVDs .

Definition 5.3. Let R be a relation scheme and Σ a set of FDs and strong-reduced JDs. (R, Σ) is in *reduced-5NF* (5NFR) if the lhs of every nontrivial FD in Σ is a superkey and, for every JD $\sigma \in \Sigma$, every component of σ is a superkey.

From a semantic perspective, the motivation for PJ/NF is the requirement to avoid key-based update anomalies [15]. A key-based update anomaly occurs when an update to a relation results in the satisfaction of Σ_k but the violation of Σ. Assuming that the candidate keys are known, satisfaction of Σ_k can be done more efficiently than testing for satisfaction of Σ and so the absence of key-based update anomalies allows for the efficient testing of constraint satisfaction after an update. It follows immediately from the PJ/NF definition that a scheme in PJ/NF can have no key-based update anomaly[2]. The motivation for 5NF (and 5NFR) is based on the requirement to minimise the storage cost of a relation. It is known that (R, Σ) is in 5NF if and only if the total number of values (including duplicates) appearing in any relation r defined over R is less than or equal to the total number of values in the relations

---

[2] A partial converse, that if a scheme has no key-based inserttion anomaly then it is in PJ/NF, has also been established [15].

formed by projection r on the components of any JD in Σ^+ [8]. In other words, 5NF guarantees that relations have minimal storage. More thorough discussions of these issues can be found in [8, 15, 25].

Addressing then the relationships between KCNF, PJ/NF and 5NFR, we now show that PJ/NF is a strictly stronger condition than 5NFR and 5NFR is strictly stronger than KCNF. Firstly, we recall the following algorithm, based on Lemma 2.3, for testing whether a relation scheme is in PJ/NF by determining whether a JD is implied by the set of key FDs [13, 16].

Algorithm 1

INPUT: A relation scheme R, a JD $*[R_1, \ldots, R_p]$ and
the set of key constraints $\{K_1 \rightarrow R, \ldots,$
$K_n \rightarrow R\}$ derived from a set of FDs and JDs

OUTPUT: True if $*[R_1, \ldots, R_p]$ is implied by $\{K_1 \rightarrow$
$R, \ldots, K_n \rightarrow R\}$ and false otherwise

VARIABLES: V: a set of attribute sets

METHOD:

Initialise V to $\{R_1, \ldots, R_p\}$;

DO UNTIL no more changes
IF there exist Y and Z in V and a candidate key K_i
such that $K_i \subseteq Y \cap Z$
THEN
Remove Y and Z from V;
Add the single set YZ to V;
ENDO;
IF there is a Y in V such that $Y = R$ THEN return True
ELSE return false;

For example, suppose that one starts with $R = \{A, B, C, D\}$ the JD $*[AB, AD, BC]$ and the key constraints $\{A \rightarrow R, B \rightarrow R\}$. Initially V is set to $\{AB, AD, BC\}$. The FD $A \rightarrow R$ can be applied to yield $V = \{ABD, BC\}$, then $B \rightarrow R$ can be applied to yield $V = \{ABCD\}$ and so the algorithm returns true.

We now use Algorithm 1 to show that PJ/NF is stronger than 5NFR.

Lemma 5.1. *If R is a relation scheme and Σ is a set of FDs and strong-reduced JDs which apply to R, then (R, Σ) is in 5NFR if it is in PJ/NF.*

Proof. Suppose that (R, Σ) is in PJ/NF and consider firstly any nontrivial FD $X \rightarrow Y$ in Σ. Suppose to the contrary that X is not a superkey. Construct a relation r of two tuples which are identical on X and distinct elsewhere. Since X is not a superkey, a simple application of the inference rules shows that $K - X \neq \emptyset$ for every candidate key K and hence r satisfies all FDs of the form $K \rightarrow R$ but violates $X \rightarrow Y$. This contradicts the PJ/NF property and so X must be a superkey.

Secondly, let $*[R_1, \ldots, R_p]$, denoted by σ, be any JD in Σ and consider the operation of Algorithm 1 applied to σ which, by the PJ/NF property, must terminate with a set $Y \in V$ such that $Y = R$. It can easily be seen that at every step of the algorithm, V contains only components of σ or unions of its components. Let $R_1, .$

. ., R_k denote the components of σ (by relabelling components if necessary) which are members of Y. Since $Y = R$, it follows that $R_1 \ldots R_k = R$. Next we claim that $k = p$ and thus every component of σ is in Y. To verify this, if there is some component R_i which is not in Y, then it follows that R can be generated by Algorithm 1 using only the set $\{R_1, \ldots, R_{i-1}, R_{i+1}, \ldots, R_p\}$ and so the JD $*[R_1, \ldots, R_{i-1}, R_{i+1}, \ldots, R_p]$ is also implied by Σ_k and thus is in Σ^+. It is total since $Y = R$ and so the strong-reduced property of is contradicted and hence every component of σ is in Y. Let R_i then be any component of σ. If $R_i = Y$ then $R_i = R$ since $Y = R$ and so the 5NFR property is satisfied. Alternatively, if $R_i \neq Y$ then R_i must be merged with another set $Z \in V$ at some stage of the algorithm to finally produce Y. For this to happen, there must be a candidate key K such that $K \subseteq R_i \cap Z$ and so $K \subseteq R_i$ and hence R_i is a superkey which completes the proof since R_i was arbitrary. $\square$

The next example then shows that PJ/NF is a strictly stronger condition than 5NFR.

Example 5.1. Let $R = \{A, B, C\}$ and let $\Sigma = \{AB \rightarrow C, AC \rightarrow B, BC \rightarrow A, *[AB, AC, BC]\}$. It can be verified that $*[AB, AC, BC]$ is strong-reduced and so R is in 5NFR. However, R is not in PJ/NF since Algorithm 1 does not generate a set equal to R.

We now show that 5NFR is a stronger condition than KC/NF.

Lemma 5.2. *If (R, Σ) is in 5NFR then it is in KCNF.*

Proof. Since KCNF is cover invariant from the corollary to Theorem 4.1 and since, from the results in [25], every set of FDs and JDs has a cover in which every JD is strong-reduced, then Σ can be assumed to contain only strong-reduced JDs. Because (R, Σ) is in 5NFR and every strong-reduced JD is by definition total, it follows that the union of the components of any JD in Σ equals R and thus (R, Σ) is in KCNF. $\square$

The next example demonstrates a case where KCNF does not imply 5NFR and so 5NFR is a strictly stronger condition than KCNF.

Example 2. Let $R = \{A, B, C\}$ and $\Sigma = \{AB \rightarrow C, BC \rightarrow A, *[AB, BC, AC]\}$. It can be verified (R, Σ) is in KCNF because AB and BC are superkeys and cover R, but is not in 5NFR since $*[AB, BC, AC]$ is strong-reduced but AC is not a superkey.

6. Conclusions

In this paper we have proposed a general definition of redundancy in relational databases and investigated its relationship to normal forms. The definition proposed is that an occurrence of a data value in a relation is redundant if every change to it results in the violation of the set of constraints. A relation scheme was then defined to be in redundancy-free normal form (RFNF) if there does not exist a relation defined over the scheme which contains a redundant value.

We then proved that when the set of constraints contains arbitrary JDs, a relation scheme is in RFNF if and only if it satisfies a new syntactic normal form called key-complete normal form (KCNF). The KCNF condition requires that the left-hand side of every FD in the set of dependencies is a superkey and every JD has the property that the union of its components which are superkeys contains every attribute in the scheme. We then compared KCNF to two other normal forms that have been proposed for JDs, PJ/NF and a recent corrected definition of 5NF, called 5NFR, and showed that KCNF is a strictly weaker condition than 5NFR and that 5NFR is a strictly weaker condition than PJ/NF. Thus the landscape of normal forms for JDs is quite subtle with there existing three syntactic normal forms, each corresponding to a different requirement of database design.

Another issue that needs investigation is to extend the approach used in this paper to understand database design in more general settings. The redundancy definition presented in this paper is applicable to any type of data model in which constraints can be formally defined, so an interesting avenue of research is to characterise the conditions on the set of constraints, both for the relational model when other types of dependencies such as inclusion dependencies are included, and also for other data models such as nested relational and object-oriented data models.

References

1. S. Abiteboul, R. Hull and V. Vianu. *Foundations of Databases*. Addison-Wesley, 1995.

2. A. V. Aho, Y. Sagiv and J. D. Ullman. Equivalences among Relational Expressions. *SIAM Journal of Computing*, Volume 8, Number 2, pages 218-246, 1979.

3. P. Atzeni and V. DeAntonellis. *Relational Database Theory*. Benjamin/Cummings, 1993.

4. C. Beeri. On the Membership Problem for Functional and Multivalued Dependencies in Relational Databases. *ACM Transactions on Database Systems*, Volume 5, Number 3, pages 241-259, 1980.

5. C. Beeri and M. Y. Vardi. On the Properties of Join Dependencies. In *Advances in Database Theory*, (H. Gallaire, J. Minker, andJ.M. Nicolas, ed.), pages 25-72, Plenum Press, New York, 1981.

6. P. A. Bernstein and N. Goodman. What Does Boyce-Codd Normal Form Do? In *6th International Conference on Very Large Databases*, Montreal, Canada, pages 245-259, 1980.

7. J. Biskup. Boyce-Codd Normal Form and Object Normal Form. *Information Processing Letters*, Volume 32, pages 29-33, 1989.

8. J. Biskup. Database Scheme Design Theory: Achievements and Challenges. In *6th International CISMOD Conference*, pages 1995.

9. J. Biskup and P. Dublish. Objects in Relational Database Schemes with Functional, Inclusion and Exclusion Dependencies. *Theoretical Informatics and Applications*, Volume 27, Number 3, pages 183-219, 1993.

10. E. P. F. Chan. A Design Theory for Solving the Anomalies Problem. *SIAM Journal of Computing*, Volume 18, Number 3, pages 429-448, 1989.

11. E. F. Codd. Further Normalization of the Database Relational Model. In *Courant Computer Science Symposia 6: Data Base Systems,* (R. Rustin, ed.), pages 33-64, Prentice-Hall, Englewood Cliffs, N.J., 1972.

12. E. F. Codd. Recent Investigations in Relational Database Systems. In *IFIP Conference*, Stockholm, Sweden, pages 1017-1021, 1974.

13. C. J. Date and R. Fagin. Simple Conditions for Guaranteeing Higher Normal Forms in Relational Databases. *ACM Transactions on Database Systems*, Volume 17, Number 3, pages 465-476, 1992.

14. R. Fagin. Multivalued Dependencies and a New Normal Form for Relational Databases. *ACM Transactions on Database Systems*, Volume 2, Number 3, pages 262-278, 1977.

15. R. Fagin. A Normal Form for Relational Databases that is based on Domains and Keys. *ACM Transactions on Database Systems*, Volume 6, Number 3, pages 387-415, 1981.

16. R. Fagin. Normal Forms and Relational Database Operators. In *ACM SIGMOD International Conference on Management of Data*, Boston, Mass., pages 153-160, 1979.

17. C. H. LeDoux and D. S. Parker. Reflections on Boyce-Codd Normal Form. In *8th International Conference on Very Large Databases*, pages 131-141, 1982.

18. T. Ling, F. W. Tompa and T. Kameda. An Improved Third Normal Form for Relational Databases. *ACM Transactions on Database Systems*, Volume 6, Number 2, pages 329-346, 1981.

19. D. Maier. *The Theory of Relational Databases.* Computer Science Press, 1983.

20. D. Maier, A. O. Mendelzon and Y. Sagiv. Testing Implications of Data Dependencies. *ACM Transactions on Database Systems*, Volume 4, Number 4, pages 455-469, 1979.

21. D. Maier, Y. Sagiv and M. Yannakis. On the Complexity of Testing Implications of Functional and Join Dependencies. *Journal of the ACM*, Volume 28, Number 4, pages 680-695, 1981.

22. J. M. Smith and C. P. D. Smith Database Abstraction: Aggregration and Generalization. Volume 2, Number 2, pages 105-133, 1977.

23. B. Thalheim. *Dependencies in Relational Databases.* B. G. Teubner, 1991.

24. B. Thalheim. Open Problems in Database Theory. In *Proceedings 1st Symposium on Mathematical Fundamentals of Database Systems, Lecture Notes in Computer Science no. 305*, pages 241-247, Springer Verlag, 1988.

25. M. W. Vincent, A Corected 5NF Definition For Relational Database Design. *Theoretical Computer Science*, in press.

26. M. W. Vincent. Semantic Foundations of 4NF in Relational Database Design. *Acta Informatica*, in press.

27. M. W. Vincent, *Semantic Justification of Normal Forms in Relational Database Design*. PhD Thesis, Department of Computer Science, Monash University, 1994.

28. M. W. Vincent and B. Srinivasan. Redundancy and the Justification for Fourth Normal Form in Relational Databases. *International Journal of Foundations of Computer Science*, Volume 4, Number 4, pages 355-365, 1993.

29. M. W. Vincent and B. Srinivasan. Update Anomalies and the Justification for 4NF in Relational Databases. *Information Sciences*, Volume 81, Number , pages 87-102, 1994.

30. C. Zaniolo. A New Normal Form for the Design of Relational Database Schemata. *ACM Transactions on Database Systems*, Volume 7, Number 3, pages 489-499, 1982.

Author Index

Lecture Notes in Computer Science

For information about Vols. 1–1296

please contact your bookseller or Springer-Verlag

Vol. 1333: F. Pichler. R.Moreno-Díaz (Eds.), Computer Aided Systems Theory – EUROCAST'97. Proceedings, 1997. XII, 626 pages. 1997.

Vol. 1334: Y. Han, T. Okamoto, S. Qing (Eds.), Information and Communications Security. Proceedings, 1997. X, 484 pages. 1997.

Vol. 1335: R.H. Möhring (Ed.), Graph-Theoretic Concepts in Computer Science. Proceedings, 1997. X, 376 pages. 1997.

Vol. 1336: C. Polychronopoulos, K. Joe, K. Araki, M. Amamiya (Eds.), High Performance Computing. Proceedings, 1997. XII, 416 pages. 1997.

Vol. 1337: C. Freksa, M. Jantzen, R. Valk (Eds.), Foundations of Computer Science. XII, 515 pages. 1997.

Vol. 1338: F. Plášil, K.G. Jeffery (Eds.), SOFSEM'97: Theory and Practice of Informatics. Proceedings, 1997. XIV, 571 pages. 1997.

Vol. 1339: N.A. Murshed, F. Bortolozzi (Eds.), Advances in Document Image Analysis. Proceedings, 1997. IX, 345 pages. 1997.

Vol. 1340: M. van Kreveld, J. Nievergelt, T. Roos, P. Widmayer (Eds.), Algorithmic Foundations of Geographic Information Systems. XIV, 287 pages. 1997.

Vol. 1341: F. Bry, R. Ramakrishnan, K. Ramamohanarao (Eds.), Deductive and Object-Oriented Databases. Proceedings, 1997. XIV, 430 pages. 1997.

Vol. 1342: A. Sattar (Ed.), Advanced Topics in Artificial Intelligence. Proceedings, 1997. XVII, 516 pages. 1997. (Subseries LNAI).

Vol. 1343: Y. Ishikawa, R.R. Oldehoeft, J.V.W. Reynders, M. Tholburn (Eds.), Scientific Computing in Object-Oriented Parallel Environments. Proceedings, 1997. XI, 295 pages. 1997.

Vol. 1344: C. Ausnit-Hood, K.A. Johnson, R.G. Pettit, IV, S.B. Opdahl (Eds.), Ada 95 – Quality and Style. XV, 292 pages. 1997.

Vol. 1345: R.K. Shyamasundar, K. Ueda (Eds.), Advances in Computing Science - ASIAN'97. Proceedings, 1997. XIII, 387 pages. 1997.

Vol. 1346: S. Ramesh, G. Sivakumar (Eds.), Foundations of Software Technology and Theoretical Computer Science. Proceedings, 1997. XI, 343 pages. 1997.

Vol. 1347: E. Ahronovitz, C. Fiorio (Eds.), Discrete Geometry for Computer Imagery. Proceedings, 1997. X, 255 pages. 1997.

Vol. 1348: S. Steel, R. Alami (Eds.), Recent Advances in AI Planning. Proceedings, 1997. IX, 454 pages. 1997. (Subseries LNAI).

Vol. 1349: M. Johnson (Ed.), Algebraic Methodology and Software Technology. Proceedings, 1997. X, 594 pages. 1997.

Vol. 1350: H.W. Leong, H. Imai, S. Jain (Eds.), Algorithms and Computation. Proceedings, 1997. XV, 426 pages. 1997.

Vol. 1351: R. Chin, T.-C. Pong (Eds.), Computer Vision – ACCV'98. Proceedings Vol. I, 1998. XXIV, 761 pages. 1997.

Vol. 1352: R. Chin, T.-C. Pong (Eds.), Computer Vision – ACCV'98. Proceedings Vol. II, 1998. XXIV, 757 pages. 1997.

Vol. 1353: G. BiBattista (Ed.), Graph Drawing. Proceedings, 1997. XII, 448 pages. 1997.

Vol. 1354: O. Burkart, Automatic Verification of Sequential Infinite-State Processes. X, 163 pages. 1997.

Vol. 1355: M. Darnell (Ed.), Cryptography and Coding. Proceedings, 1997. IX, 335 pages. 1997.

Vol. 1356: A. Danthine, Ch. Diot (Eds.), From Multimedia Services to Network Services. Proceedings, 1997. XII, 180 pages. 1997.

Vol. 1357: J. Bosch, S. Mitchell (Eds.), Object-Oriented Technology. Proceedings, 1997. XIV, 555 pages. 1998.

Vol. 1358: B. Thalheim, L. Libkin (Eds.), Semantics in Databases. XI, 265 pages. 1998.

Vol. 1361: B. Christianson, B. Crispo, M. Lomas, M. Roe (Eds.), Security Protocols. Proceedings, 1997. VIII, 217 pages. 1998.

Vol. 1362: D.K. Panda, C.B. Stunkel (Eds.), Network-Based Parallel Computing. Proceedings, 1998. X, 247 pages. 1998.

Vol. 1363: J.-K. Hao, E. Lutton, E. Ronald, M. Schoenauer, D. Snyers (Eds.), Artificial Evolution. XI, 349 pages. 1998.

Vol. 1364: W. Conen, G. Neumann (Eds.), Coordination Technology for Collaborative Applications. VIII, 282 pages. 1998.

Vol. 1365: M.P. Singh, A. Rao, M.J. Wooldridge (Eds.), Intelligent Agents IV. Proceedings, 1997. XII, 351 pages. 1998. (Subseries LNAI).

Vol. 1367: E.W. Mayr, H.J. Prömel, A. Steger (Eds.), Lectures on Proof Verification and Approximation Algorithms. XII, 344 pages. 1998.

Vol. 1368: Y. Masunaga, T. Katayama, M. Tsukamoto (Eds.), Worldwide Computing and Its Applications — WWCA'98. Proceedings, 1998. XIV, 473 pages. 1998.

Vol. 1370: N.A. Streitz, S. Konomi, H.-J. Burkhardt (Eds.), Cooperative Buildings. Proceedings, 1998. XI, 267 pages. 1998.

Vol. 1372: S. Vaudenay (Ed.), Fast Software Encryption. Proceedings, 1998. VIII, 297 pages. 1998.

Vol. 1373: M. Morvan, C. Meinel, D. Krob (Eds.), STACS 98. Proceedings, 1998. XV, 630 pages. 1998.

Vol. 1377: H.-J. Schek, F. Saltor, I. Ramos, G. Alonso (Eds.), Advances in Database Technology – EDBT'98. Proceedings, 1998. XII, 515 pages. 1998.

Vol. 1378: M. Nivat (Ed.), Foundations of System Specification and Computation Structures. Proceedings, 1998. X, 289 pages. 1998.

Vol. 1380: C.L. Lucchesi, A.V. Moura (Eds.), LATIN'98: Theoretical Informatics. Proceedings, 1998. XI, 391 pages. 1998.

Vol. 1381: C. Hankin (Ed.), Programming Languages and Systems. Proceedings, 1998. X, 283 pages. 1998.

Vol. 1382: E. Astesiano (Ed.), Fundamental Approaches to Software Engineering. Proceedings, 1998. XII, 331 pages. 1998.